ACCEPTING THE LANCE

ACCEPTING THE LANCE

A New
Liaden Universe®
Novel

SHARON LEE &
STEVE MILLER

ACCEPTING THE LANCE

This is a work of fiction. All the characters and events portrayed in this book are
fictional, and any resemblance to real people or incidents is purely coincidental.

A Baen Books Original

Baen Publishing Enterprises
P.O. Box 1403
Riverdale, NY 10471
www.baen.com

ISBN: 978-1-9821-2421-2

Cover art by David Mattingly

First Baen printing, December 2019

Distributed by Simon & Schuster
1230 Avenue of the Americas
New York, NY 10020

Library of Congress Cataloging-in-Publication Data

Names: Lee, Sharon, 1952– author. | Miller, Steve, 1950 July 31– author.
Title: Accepting the lance / Sharon Lee & Steve Miller.
Description: First edition. | Riverdale, NY : Baen Publishing Enterprises,
   [2019] | Series: Liaden universe
Identifiers: LCCN 2019034873 | ISBN 9781982124212 (hardcover)
Subjects: GSAFD: Science fiction.
Classification: LCC PS3562.E3629 A65 2019 | DDC 813/.54—dc23
LC record available at https://lccn.loc.gov/2019034873

Pages by Joy Freeman (www.pagesbyjoy.com)
Printed in the United States of America
10 9 8 7 6 5 4 3 2 1

To Sam, who drew all the bad cards.
See you in the World Beyond.

ACKNOWLEDGMENTS

Many thanks to the Mighty Tyop Hunters;
your efforts are appreciated!

Deb Boyken, Millie Calistri-Yeh, Andrew Donaldson,
Irene Harrison, James Kirby, Tee Lewison, Robert McKnight,
Evelyn Mellone, Abigail Miller, Rebecca Ouwehand,
Marni Rachmiel, Anne Reisser, Kate Reynolds,
Ken Shoemake, Linda Shoun, Anne Young

ACCEPTING THE LANCE

Prologue

. . . .

Runcible System
Daglyte Seam

COMMANDER OF AGENTS PRESIDED OVER A DESK AWASH IN FAIL-
ure and dismay.

The Scouts, the damned meddling Scouts, ever more temer-
arious, brazenly pursuing their agenda of eradication. Not satisfied with the destruction of Sinfreed Hub, the Department's last
intact communications and data center, the Scouts had pressed
on, capturing Engthrelt and Oonabrij. While neither facility had
ever been as vital to the Plan as Sinfreed, and each had taken
significant damage in the confusion immediately following Clan
Korval's terminal strike on Prime Headquarters, they had been
functional to a degree none of those remaining began to approach.

There was more.

She had ordered a force assembled from their stores of Old
Tech, the last and most potent of their strike forces. Specific
engines, known by name, which had served the Department well
in the past. Several had come forward to receive their orders.

Others had not.

Others, in fact, were—gone. Absent. Disappeared.

At first, it had seemed that the inventory systems, as all else,
were made unstable by the destruction of so much of the network.

A team had been sent to investigate; she had their report in
hand.

In fact, equipment was missing; a measurable—a significant—
number of specialized engines had vanished from the ranks, as
if they had been sent out on assignment. There had been no

1

protest from the devices; there had been no sign of sabotage or of forcible removal. It was as if their proper operators had simply relocated them according to orders.

Save that no such orders had been issued.

The fact that among the missing were the eldest and most destructive of the Department's accumulated machines, could only add to the general state of failure and alarm.

Teams—she could spare so few!—teams had been dispatched, to locate the missing and bring them back. If they proved recalcitrant, the order was to decommission. They could afford no rogues wandering the space lanes, acting on their own necessities.

There was more...

A few days ago had come a scattering of reports that Healers and others of the Department's *dramliz* had fallen into sudden faints, or woken from sound sleeps or trance, screaming and clutching their heads. There had been no new instances reported, and one might be tempted to assume a mere affliction of the nerves; those of the *dramliz* being oversupplied with nerves. However, Commander of Agents left nothing to chance. She passed the reports on to the Unit Head for follow-up, with a request to share her findings.

So, those, the smaller failures.

There remained one larger failure, overshadowing all other errors. Large enough, indeed, that it might well bring the Department to its knees, its purpose unfulfilled.

The team sent to acquire, or terminate, Shan yos'Galan Clan Korval had failed in its mission. Four senior field agents had been killed. The two surviving had been taken into custody by the local police, from whom they could have been expected to rapidly extricate themselves—save for the timely arrival of Scouts, bearing warrants of extradition and a long list of crimes for which the captured pair were wanted, on Liad...

Given repeated failures to bring Val Con yos'Phelium, rogue Agent of Change, back to Headquarters, in order to refresh his training and reaffirm his loyalty to the Department, the repurposing of yos'Galan into a weapon crafted to destroy Korval from within had become the centerpiece of the New Plan to destroy Korval. That failure was dire.

Alternatively, the actions to discredit Korval tradeships at key ports, and the blacklisting of Korval traders was going well.

Indeed, *Pale Wing*, a major Korval trader, second only to *Dutiful Passage* herself, had been compromised most effectively at Liltander.

Had they sufficient time, the Department *would* see Korval broken in the markets, the last choice remaining to the delm the dissolution of the clan. Lacking powerful allies, Korval would be absorbed by the barbaric Terran hordes, nameless, with neither *melant'i* nor wealth to shield them. Their blood would be polluted, the so-called Korval Luck diffused...

Eventually, oh, yes—*eventually*, the Department could see these things done.

Time, however, was in short supply; the Department in a disarray that hourly grew more profound. They were so disordered that the loss of even small systems became a significant difficulty.

They should, perhaps, Commander of Agents thought, have pulled back, regrouped, repaired systems...Korval would have believed the threat gone, themselves safe. The danger there had been that, while the Department healed and increased its strength, so, too, did Korval. A decisive strike while the enemy was weak... that had seemed the certain path to success.

Commander of Agents closed her eyes.

She was weary. Even that admission was a failure; Commander of Agents did not tire, did not become befuddled with lack of sleep; did not surrender to despair.

For a moment only, inside the privacy of her skull, Commander of Agents considered the unthinkable.

She considered disbanding the Department. It was within her power to do this thing; she knew it. The precise procedure eluded her at this present, but she was certain that she could retrieve it, if she merely concentrated...

Commander of Agents took a profoundly deep breath. She felt renewed, alert, and in control. There had been setbacks, yes, of course there had. Korval was a cunning and resourceful enemy; its delm had been one of the Department's best, before he had broken training and turned his hand and his considerable talents against them.

None of it mattered.

Were they vulnerable and in disarray? They were; and yet—not even the masters of the Accountants Guild had been able to find all of the Department's cash reserves.

Did they lack operatives?

No matter: Operatives could be bought, after all.

The Department would destroy Clan Korval. Utterly.

It would happen; and not only would it happen on her watch...
it would happen within the Standard.

One needed only to embrace the bold course—and stay on
target.

SIX AGAINST
THE UNIVERSE

THEY WERE SIX, AT THE START OF IT.

Immediately they put the plan into motion, they were five, having left one of their number in plain sight and vulnerable, fixed in the enemy's eye...

...And to avenge the five, should they fall.

This thing that they attempted—it was impossible. Anyone in possession of the barest facts of the matter—they were six against thousands—would have said so.

It was well, then, that the facts did not describe the whole.

One

· · · · ·

RED-HAIRED MIRI ROBERTSON SAT IN THE MIDDLE OF THE SO-
called "reading rug" in the ruckus room, watching her daughter
stalk her lifemate.

Lizzie wasn't doing too bad, she thought, given that she'd
only gotten the hang of standing relatively recently, and remained
deeply suspicious of two-legged locomotion. On all fours, though,
she was nothing more nor less'n greased lightning. Not that speed
was the name of this game.

Val Con, Lizzie's stalking horse, was keeping the action on
her level, crawling with a certain amount of low cunning, until
taking up a hiding place behind a large red-and-blue-striped ball.
He was currently on his belly behind this object, which meant
only the top of his head, one shoulder, and the entire length of
one arm was in plain sight.

He could, as Miri knew from experience, have completely
vanished behind that ball and possibly behind the stuffed monkey to the right of it, had this been the sort of game he was
most accustomed to playing, which was—thank the gods—above
Lizzie's pay grade.

For a couple more years, anyhow.

Lizzie'd been pointed the wrong way when Val Con took cover,
and now she was methodically moving back-and-forth, advancing
on the position of the ball, the monkey, and her father, a little
closer with every turn.

She made one more turn—and Miri saw her focus on the
ball. Deliberately, she straightened to her knees, the new height
giving her the perspective she needed.

With a squeal, she threw herself into a fast crawl, hurtling past the ball and onto Val Con, who rolled under the assault.

"Indeed, you did find me—and speedily, too!" he said, pulling her onto his chest. Lizzie shouted with laughter.

Miri shook her head.

Of all the things she'd never figured to have to care for in her life was a lifemate and a baby, never mind the whole rest of a small, but trouble-prone Liaden clan, which had been Val Con's marriage portion. Her own portion . . . well, she'd never had anything precious, really, though she had been a master sergeant of mercenary soldiers, so she did have some experience in taking care of her people.

And, given the particular sort of trouble the clan, the husband, and—depend on it, any day now—the daughter were prone to, her skills in that area were kept fresh.

Across the room, father and daughter were laughing uproariously as he rolled them across the floor, toward the reading rug. She grinned, despite her throat tightening—which happened whenever she thought about losing one of them, a thought that had paradoxically been occurring more frequently, now that they were peacefully settled.

'Course, when Val Con and her'd been returning live fire, running for their lives, and covering each other's backs, there hadn't been time to worry was she going to lose him. Now, there was time for all kinds of thoughts to move through a person's head, and not all of them welcome.

Plus, she thought, watching Val Con's rolling progress and hearing their daughter's laughter, there was the fact that they weren't, exactly, peacefully settled. They were still hunted by a dedicated and well-equipped enemy who knew exactly where they were, and who could, in theory, pick them off whenever they felt like it.

Well, that *was* a theory. Clan Korval wasn't without resources, or allies. Their enemy had taken losses.

And so had Clan Korval.

Val Con reached the edge of the rug, kicked and rolled—once, twice, thrice—coming to rest against her knees, right-side up and smiling into her face.

"*Cha'trez,*" he murmured under Lizzie's shouting.

"Couple of howling monkeys," she said. "Thought you was going to teach her how to be upright and polite."

"It is important to build from a position of strength," he told her solemnly.

Lizzie added to this, unintelligibly for the most part, though a couple bits of babble sounded Liaden-like, and a few more had a definite Terran flavor.

"What concerns you, Miri?" Val Con asked her, and she looked down at him with a sigh.

He'd know she was having a case of what on Surebleak was called the "chills." No big deal, really, everybody chilled now and then.

Except, looking at him just now, their daughter cradled in his arms, the lean, strong body, green eyes, and the brown hair that tumbled over his forehead nearly into those bright eyes—and that Lizzie was beginning to reach toward—

Miri leaned forward and caught the questing hand. "That's a foul."

Lizzie frowned, every bit as willful as her father. Not the only thing she'd caught from her father either—the green eyes were particularly nice with the burnished copper hair, as bright as Miri's own.

Their child.

Miri felt her throat tighten again, which was just—

"Jeeves," Val Con said. "Please ask Mrs. pel'Esla to come and take Talizea to the nursery."

"Yes, Master Val Con," said a mellifluous male voice from the ceiling. A moment later, it spoke again.

"Mrs. pel'Esla is on her way. She should arrive at the door to the rumpus room in a few minutes."

"Thank you, Jeeves," Val Con said, and looked to her.

"Talizea, bid your mother a proper and decorous good-night, please."

He opened his arms, and Miri leaned forward to lift the compact body into her lap.

"Good-night, Lizzie," she said, brushing the hair from her daughter's damp forehead. "Don't let the snowflakes bite."

It didn't make much sense, that good-night, but it had been what her mother had said to her when she'd been a kid here on Surebleak. Couldn't hurt, she guessed, to go with tradition.

Miri kissed Lizzie's cheek as Val Con rolled to his feet.

He bent down as the door chime sounded, and took the child from her arms.

"*Chiat'a bei kruzon*, Talizea," he said, settling her on his hip and kissing her forehead. "Here is your nurse now, come to take you to your bed."

He crossed the room, the door opened, there was a brief murmur from Mrs. pel'Esla, and the door closed again.

Miri looked up as he returned and dropped to the rug, stretching out to put his head on her lap.

"Comfortable?" she asked him.

"Extremely," he replied cordially. "Miri. What troubles you?"

"Well, I just watched my baby daughter set up a search grid to find a runaway. I'm thinking that should worry me."

"Should it? It was the most basic pattern, after all. I might be inclined to worry if she had quartered the room and called in allies."

She puffed a laugh.

"I didn't realize the bar was so high—no worries there, then."

"And yet," he said, "you *are* worried. May I know why?"

She sighed and brushed his hair off his forehead.

"It's been something of a while," she said slowly. "We haven't heard anything from Rys, or any of his team members. So . . . how will we know that they've done the job?"

"Possibly, when the Department of the Interior surrenders to the Scouts," Val Con murmured. "Possibly, when an army of Old Tech is found dismantling what remains of a planet, or a moon . . ."

He paused, and reached up to touch her cheek.

"There is else?"

"Else . . ." she rubbed her cheek against his fingertips. "Are we ever going to hear from them again?"

He sighed. "It seems unlikely."

Six agents had been recruited by Clan Korval to subvert, if not outright destroy, the Department of the Interior, Korval's great enemy. Each of the six was a former DOI agent, ranging from technician-grade, to the deadliest of all—Agent of Change. Four of the six had been reclaimed, and immediately dedicated themselves to the destruction of the DOI. Two had rebuilt their lives . . . somewhat before the call to service came to them.

One of those two was Rys Lin pen'Chala, who had found a place as a son of the Bedel, a wandering group living more or less hidden under the old warehouses in Surebleak City. Rys had become a trusted person in that community that trusted few outsiders, an acknowledged grandson of the group's wise woman; he had a lover, and a child on the way.

The second of the two was—

"Miri?"

"What about you?"

"Me?"

He lowered his hand, capturing hers, bringing it to his chest and pressing her palm over his heart.

"I am the decoy—the one who stands in the enemy's sight."

"Ain't likely to let that just go by, are they?" she said. "When do you expect they'll bring out the live weapons?"

"Ah. Well. One might argue that they have already engaged. After all, the four were captured attempting to do Korval real and lasting harm. Now that they have been removed from the board, the Department will become more bold. They *must* become more bold; they are at the end of their resources. If its last purpose is, as it seems to be, to destroy Korval entire, then it must strike—now—heavy and true. Everything they have left will be in that blow. There can be no more feints.

"My part is to oblige them with a visible target and take most of their attention to myself. Korval has set down new roots, accepted new obligations. We cannot simply flee before them."

No, Miri admitted to herself; they couldn't just run away. On the other hand, the DOI might be single-minded to the point of insanity, but that didn't stop them from being competent as mischief-makers and murderers.

Val Con had been an Agent of Change, trained by the DOI to be one of its elite and most deadly operatives. He had already beaten the odds—breaking training, and staying alive this long. Which was to say that he had a better chance than most of surviving a DOI attempt on his life.

Which didn't mean his odds were *good*.

"*Cha'trez*...they will not stop. They must *be* stopped."

"Right."

They'd talked about this, put plans in place, as much planning as could be done and put into place. Nothing was guaranteed in this life, safety least of all. She knew that as well as anybody—better'n most maybe, having lived to grow up on Surebleak.

"The longer I have you," she said now, looking down into Val Con's eyes, "the longer I *want* to have you."

He pressed her hand where he held it over his heart.

"I understand," he said. "To think that I might lose you... frightens me."

She took a hard breath against the tightness in her chest and managed to produce a smile.

"Guess I wish it would get done," she said. "Nerve-wracking, being the ones who have to wait."

"I agree."

He rolled up to sit beside her.

"How many are we for Prime?" he asked.

"Just you and me," she said. "Everybody else has meetings."

"Then I suggest we celebrate both our good fortune and each other, with a meal and wine, in our rooms."

"I like it."

"Good."

He came to his feet and bent down to offer her his hands.

She took them and let him help her to her feet, as if she wasn't just as light on her feet as he was, then slipped her arm around his waist, leaning into him as they walked slowly toward the door.

Two

· · · · ·

THEY WERE TWO, AT A SHIELDED LOCATION, THE COORDS OF which had been provided by the sixth member of the team.

They having established that their location was secure, Sye Mon opened the case which held his equipment, unfolded it carefully, and began to adjust the various tiles and wires.

Though he had seen it before, Bon Vit eyed the device with deep misgivings. It had no natural seeming, no form from which one might predict its function or utility. Merely a wire framework, and tiles slotted in, seemingly at random.

"Can you not simply call them on comm?" Bon Vit asked, only half meaning it as a joke.

Sye Mon glanced up, a smile glinting at the edge of his face.

"They reject our technology, deeming their own superior," he murmured, reaching again to the case and withdrawing a second folded wire frame.

"In truth, the Department could not retrofit all, so they are formed in groups of six and linked together by their native protocols. One is also fitted with a modern comm, by which orders are received. It then transmits those orders to the others in its pod."

Bon Vit moved his eyes from the confusion of tile and wire to Sye Mon's face.

"But you do not speak to the leader."

The other man met his eyes.

"You understand, it was the Department's decision, which of a pod of six was *leader*. A determination made for the convenience of the Department and its operatives. Orders are ... often obeyed, but not always. Pods tend to remain together, but they do not wholly tend to remain within the Department's care."

This was, so Sye Mon had told the others of the strike team, the reason why he believed he had a credible chance of recalling the Old Tech war machines the Department had gathered together, and denying the Commander use of them.

Something moved in the framework nearest to Bon Vit; perhaps a spark had jumped from one tile to another. A heartbeat later, there was a similar—exact?—reaction inside the other framework.

"Ah," breathed Sye Mon. "Now, let us see."

There had been much moving and resetting of tiles in the first framework, Sye Mon's fingers nimble amid the wires. The second framework, he touched not at all, but frowned as if the shifting patterns conveyed sense—bitter sense, at that.

At long last, he sat back, face a grim mask, and turned to Bon Vit. He made as if to speak, then merely closed his eyes, one hand rising, fingers forming the pilot-sign for *abort lift*.

"What's amiss?" Bon Vit demanded. "Will they not be recalled?"

Sye Mon opened his eyes.

"*Can*not be recalled," he said. "The Commander is before us, and has a mission locked in."

"You said that not all obey," Bon Vit said after a moment.

Sye Mon opened his eyes.

"That is true. Finding those who are not inclined will take time, but..."

"But?" Bon Vit repeated, when Sye Mon said nothing else.

"But the effort will have to be made. My correspondent—" He waved a hand in the direction of the two wire frames. "My correspondent did not feel able to share the coordinates of the target with me, but I believe we may make an educated guess."

"Indeed," Bon Vit said grimly. "Indeed."

· · · ✴ · · ·

Sye Mon sat back on his heels, shaking his head. He'd been in intense negotiation, via the tile racks, for close to two hours. His face was pale, lined and drawn, his hair stuck in sweat-soaked strands to his forehead.

Bon Vit, who had been watching over him this while, leaned forward and put a glass of cold water into his partner's hand.

"Drink this," he murmured. "I'll make you a mug of the yeast."

The yeast was a Terran concoction, called by them 'mite—and provided nutrition in a concentrated form. It was unparalleled as a restorative, and tasted the very devil, but Sye Mon made no protest, as he had on a previous occasion, nor asked instead for tea. Rather, Bon Vit received a worryingly subdued "Yes," as a reply, and nothing more.

He returned bare moments later to find Sye Mon still sitting on the floor, his back against the wall, legs stretched before him, the empty glass at his side. His color was somewhat improved, and his hair was sticking up in spikes where he had apparently run his fingers through it.

He received the mug with a careful inclination of the head, and a pale smile that grew somewhat wider when Bon Vit took a place on the floor facing him.

"No need for that, is there?" he asked.

Bon Vit looked up from considering his mug and its contents. "If we're to be on the same level, I prefer the floor than picking you up into a chair."

"That's fair," Sye Mon conceded, and raised his mug with a feeble flourish. "To saving the universe!"

Bon Vit raised his mug in answer. "I will drink to that, since drink we must, though I thought it was Korval we were saving."

They drank, draining the mugs in one go, which was the only sane way to consume the yeast.

"Gods, that's awful," Bon Vit said with a shudder.

Sye Mon drew a hard breath, and put the mug aside.

"I had thought it was ourselves we were saving," he said, "which is universe enough for me."

"I concede. Are we very likely to? Save the universe, that is."

"Well. There hangs a tale. My contact outright refuses the coordinates for Secondary Headquarters as a legitimate strike zone."

Bon Vit's stomach clenched.

"I thought it was eager for a fight of its own."

"Indeed, indeed. However, the new Commander of Agents has apparently learned somewhat from the mistakes of her predecessor. She took the precaution of setting safe zones, which the Department's devices may not attack. One of those is Secondary Headquarters."

"Can the programming not be overridden?"

"Possibly, with time, and patience, and the cooperation of the subject. None of which we have, alas. In the meanwhile, it is an article of faith with my contact that any of them who attempt to ignore the directive and move against a safe zone, will immediately be decommissioned. This would appear to be an internal preset."

"Then we have failed," Bon Vit said grimly. "What now, to save the universe?"

Sye Mon settled his shoulders against the wall, looking suddenly weary.

"We vary," he said. "There is an avenue we might pursue, to some good. My contact is, as the Terrans have it, *spoiling for a fight*. It feels its restrictions keenly, nor is it alone in this. I am promised a force to amaze, do I but provide a target outside of the safe zone."

"Old Tech promises you this," Bon Vit said. "Do we believe it?"

Sye Mon sighed.

"We had been prepared to believe it when we wished for them to go against Secondary Headquarters," he pointed out.

"If we vary," Bon Vit continued, "we will leave the strike at the Commander and Headquarters solely in the care of our teammates, who are expecting a two-pronged attack."

"And yet we have all known from the start that any one of us might fail. The essential parts of the plan are that one of us at least does *not* fail, and that the Department is rendered moot."

This, Bon Vit conceded, was true. It only mattered that the Department was destroyed; how or by whom were meaningless details. None of the Six had expected to survive this mission—no, not even the one of them seemingly safe on Surebleak.

"I agree," he said. "To deny the Commander a victory, to deprive her of her devices—that is a blow worth striking. When do we move?"

Sye Mon smiled wryly.

"As soon as my contact and I agree upon a rendezvous point, and the appropriate command lines."

Carefully, using the wall for support, he got to his feet. Bon Vit rose with less effort, and stood ready to catch him, should it be needful.

"My contact has been told to await my call, in four hours. Thus, I will shower, and nap, eat, and be as able as I may, when I make contact."

"It is well," Bon Vit said, with a side glance at the tiles and racks strewn around the floor.

"Leave them," said Sye Mon; "they will be needed soon enough. If I may, Comrade—rest you, also. I feel that when we do move, it will be suddenly, and at full speed."

Three

· · · · · · ·

"BEFORE WE EMBARK, YOU WILL PLEASE PROVIDE ME WITH A call-back phrase."

The request was spoken soft, in Comrade mode, which was proper between them, the inclusion of the word *please* oddly Terran—precisely the style of communication Claidyne had come to expect from Rys Lin pen'Chala, her partner in this mission.

The content of the communication however...

Claidyne inclined her head. "Your pardon? I fear that I do not understand."

He made a slight bow, wry, as his bows were often wry.

"No, *your* pardon, Comrade. We are much alike, we two—or, I should say, *we four.* Each of us is two of us, and I, at least, am not always mindful of my selves.

"So, to make myself clear: Among the company of which I am an adopted son, there is a tradition of deep meditation to facilitate learning. We call this state *Dreaming*, and it is of such intensity—such vividness—that it is possible for one to become lost in a Dream. Should that happen, the one who is sitting in watch speaks a phrase given them by the Dreamer before they entered the meditation. The phrase is one that will call them back, no matter how far they have journeyed away from themselves, on the wings of the Dream."

"You are a poet, I hear," said Claidyne, because he had paused and one must say something, even as one sorted this new information.

"Sadly not, but those who taught me surely were."

"And this...Dream you fear I may become locked within?"

18

"Your purpose is to Dream the Commander. I require a phrase that will recall the Claidyne ven'Orikle I am speaking with at this moment, even should the Dream be ascendant. It must be—you will pardon me; the poets speak again—it must be a charm that encloses your heart, and will let nothing between you and it."

She considered him, this Rys Lin pen'Chala. Wiry and tough, with one arm a work of very art in gleaming metals and enamels. The opposite leg was encased in an equally beautiful powered cast, which ensured that the weak limb did not betray him, so that he might walk and run, leap and fight, as if he were a whole man. The arm, as he had demonstrated, was lethal if he wished it so; he might crush a brick by merely closing his fingers. He knew how to govern himself, however, and he touched her now with warm, gleaming fingers, as gentle as a flutterbee's kiss.

"Humor me," he murmured. "I am set to guard you, after all."

That drove the dagger home. Claidyne looked at him now with understanding.

He *was* set to guard her, to stand as her backup—and to kill her, if necessary. It was his survival that he addressed with this strange request.

And her survival depended, absolutely, on his.

"A moment," she said to him, and he bowed his head.

"Indeed, take what time is needed. May I bring you tea?"

"That would be pleasant, thank you."

He crossed to the other side of the small galley, back turned, and very busy with kettle and cups. It was kind in him, to produce the illusion of privacy while she considered, but she already knew that there was only one phrase—one name—that would call her back from death, if not from madness.

She was ready when Rys Lin returned. She looked up, and perhaps he saw it in her face, for he did not retire again, but placed the teacups on the table and took the chair across from her.

"Thank you," she said again, and raised the cup to taste the beverage.

He did the same, and when they had both set their cups aside, she spoke: "You are two, you say?"

The question may have surprised him—he kept his own face, did Rys Lin pen'Chala—but he answered easily enough.

"Indeed. I am he who returned from the Department's care, and also the youngest of my grandmother's children."

"I understand," she said, and felt that to be true. "I am two-pinned by the yos'Galan witch's daggers into the seeming of one."

"Yes," he said.

"Once I take the download, I *will be* Commander of Agents. It is my belief that the work I have done in keeping my two selves simultaneously functional, yet unaware of each other, will allow me to reside side by side with the Commander. To direct the Commander, if you will."

"Yes," he said once more. "There is another possibility. I speak as one who has Dreamed widely and long. I carry the memories of many whose lives I Dreamed, and yet, I am none of them. It is possible that you will not so much become the Commander as you will *have access* to the Commander."

"Is that a preferable outcome?"

"More manageable, perhaps." He tipped his head, brows drawing together as he considered his next point. "Less dangerous," he added.

"So. The call-back phrase is *Isahra kez'Rofer.*"

He gave a small, seated bow.

"We were lovers," Claidyne continued, so that he would know the full power of what he held. "I killed her."

He gave her a sharp look. "Forgive me; I must ask who told you this."

She stared at him. "No one need tell me, sir; I did the deed with my own hand, to prove my training complete."

"Yes," he nodded, Terran-wise, "and I destroyed the ship of those who had taken me in and given me worth in my extremity, to prove *my* training complete." He held her eyes with his. "It was a lie, implanted by the trainers, as so much else was implanted by the trainers. The ship I *killed* still flies; the crew very much alive."

There was—pain. Sharp and bright and hot—no, cold. The room tipped, and she felt herself sliding—felt her hands caught and held.

"Claidyne."

"A moment," she gasped. "A moment, I am struck..."

"Struck with hope," he murmured. "I understand."

Hope? Well, perhaps so. It had been...so very long since she had felt hope, or any emotion save a grim determination, that she would, with her own hands, bring the Department of Interior down...

"Claidyne?"

"I am well," she told him, and withdrew her hands from his. "I am very well, indeed."

· · · ✺ · · ·

They left Vazineth with the ship: their last hope, Vazineth, aside being a pilot. Should the Commander overwhelm Claidyne and Rys Lin, despite all, then it fell to Vazineth to stop the threat—with prejudice.

They had discussed it among themselves, whether it might not serve them well, to have two Commanders pitched against each other. In the end, though, they had to admit that they did not know if there was a non-compete application built into the program. Far, far worse than the present situation, to have two Commanders collaborating on the subjugation of the universe.

The surrounding terrain was rocky; a path had been smoothed from the landing pad to the structures. Here and there the rock glittered coldly, like ice or crystal.

Claidyne approached the entrance first, Rys Lin walking behind, as befit a guard to the Commander's honor. This outpost was, as they were, also a last hope.

It was very old, a hall carved through oxidized rock into the very heart of a moon. Though it was tagged in the records as the fourth such transfer point, Claidyne had supposed it to be, in fact, the first, from which the others had been cloned. Those three points were outfitted with sophisticated identification methods; each held a list in memory of those who were cleared to rise to the rank of Commander should the present one fall.

This unit had no such modern blandishments. It required the mere inputting of preset codes into each of a series of doors. There was no list of qualified candidates for the download, no retinal photographs, no brain scans on file when the first Commander was recruited—how could there be? This *was* the first download point, arrived in mystery, discovered by who knew what arts or accident. The research she had done furtively offered no history for this unit, only the fact of its existence.

Claidyne input the next code, waiting with cool detachment for the door to open. The others had opened promptly, and it would not be well at all, she thought, as heartbeats passed and the second-to-last door remained closed, if she were thwarted *now*—

"Down!" Rys Lin shouted, augmenting this with a forcible shove, that sent her stumbling out of the doorway—

Out of range of the beam that leapt from the door, and the other, lancing down from the ceiling.

She came up onto her knees, weapon in hand.

"Rys Lin."

"Here," he answered, behind her and near at hand.

Claidyne took a breath and surveyed the situation. The gritty stone floor showed a bright patch where the first beam had struck it; the wall to the right, at about the height of her shoulder, showed a white scar among the several older, darker scars.

Behind her, she felt Rys Lin, poised and watchful. He did not ask her what she would do now. That was her question to ask, and in fact she asked it, within the privacy of her skull.

A booby trap. Well, of course, there would be at least one trap, to determine if whoever had come to propose herself was clever enough to survive.

And, she thought, rising and thrusting the gun back into its holster—if she was bold enough to try again.

She approached the door, set her fingers to the pad.

Behind her, she heard Rys Lin gather himself to his feet and take up his position. The skin between her shoulder blades itched; her eyes strained to look in every cranny—behavior unbecoming a candidate for Commander. She had her guard; more importantly, she had her own integrity and courage. She was worthy.

And she was not afraid.

She input the code once more.

The door before her opened, and she stepped through.

The last door had yielded. Lights came up—too bright, too yellow—revealing the walls lined with racks and tiles, and the chair with its restraints and connectors.

It was now. Now, her life came to fruition. Now, every terrible thing she had done by the will of the Department would be Balanced and put to rest.

She walked to the chair and sat down.

Restraints snapped 'round wrists and ankles. She welcomed them.

The last thing she saw before the hood slid down over her head, her face, was Rys Lin pen'Chala standing in the open doorway, gun in hand.

Perhaps she expected pain. Perhaps she had expected—

But, no. There were no expectations; there was only herself, and the voice praising her integrity, her courage, her determination.

Would she serve? came the question.

She would.

And would she accept perfection, until she was as perfect as it was possible for her to be?

She would.

There was a brief moment of disorientation, perhaps, in which she did not entirely know herself. It passed between one breath and the next, and she was herself, as she had never been herself before.

She had been a broken thing, imperfect, flawed, scarcely able to think. Now...

Now, she was worthy, she was strong, her thoughts flowed, and her intentions formed with clarity.

She was in command.

She knew—everything. She knew what must be done to implement the Plan, to bring it to a successful conclusion.

The upstarts would not prevail. Could not prevail. Not against *her*.

Commander of Agents opened her eyes.

Before her stood a soldier—one of her own; she knew him at once by the modifications he had accepted in order to make himself more perfectly able to serve.

"We must consolidate our strengths," she said to him.

"Indeed," he replied, perfectly civil but with a marked lack of respect for command.

She rose, and looked down upon him, with his gleaming arm and the articulated golden fingers.

"I can unmake you," she said clearly, "and bestow the knowledge woven into that arm on another, more worthy to serve me."

Dark eyes widened slightly. The salute he offered showed respect and not a little awe. She was pleased with his cleverness. Perhaps he was worthy to serve, after all.

"Report!" she snapped at him.

"Commander," he returned. "*Isahra kez'Rofer.*"

Pain sheeted through her; her brain burned, and for a moment it was as if she were standing in this very room, facing herself, weapons drawn, and a voice, a beloved voice, crying out, "Claidyne, close the door!"

Lurching, she grabbed the sharp metal edge and heaved the door across, shutting her second self away.

It troubled her briefly that she did not hear the lock engage—and then she forgot it as she opened her eyes to find Rys Lin pen'Chala standing before her, eyes intent, hand specifically away from his gun.

"That," she said, marking how her voice shook, "that is a strong program."

"Are you entirely yourself?" he asked her. "Can you remain outside of the Dream?"

"I believe so, on both counts," she answered, "but keep with me, Rys Lin."

"Yes," he told her, coming forward and extending his natural hand. "Every step of the way."

· · · ❉ · · ·

Vazineth ser'Trishan sat her board, awaiting the return of her comrades.

Awaiting, if the Plan sang according to scale, the arrival of Commander of Agents. *A* Commander of Agents.

This was the mission, and while Vazineth had her doubts regarding their likelihood of success, she'd not been able to offer a better plan, with a higher surety value.

In Vazineth's opinion, the best odds on the day's venture went to Claidyne being killed by the download. Second best was that both Claidyne and Rys Lin would be killed before they ever reached the download chamber, by booby trap or hidden guard.

Her third probability was that Claidyne would take the download, kill Rys Lin, and order in a battleship to escort her off-planet. There was a variation on this scenario: that Claidyne, lacking the means to call for escort and having murdered Rys Lin, would return to the ship, kill Vazineth and pilot herself to the nearest command safe-house.

There was also, Vazineth admitted, a vanishingly small chance that everything would go exactly as planned, but who, among the three of them, had ever believed *that* would be the case?

Well. Possibly Rys Lin, who seemed, improbably, to be an

optimist. But even Rys Lin had made provision should he not survive Claidyne's attempt.

He had given Vazineth a name to research while she sat with the scans, largely idle, awaiting whatever came out of the tunnels. *Isahra kez'Rofer.*

Had she access to proper equipment, and been under no constraints to be invisible, she might have done more. As it was, she flattered herself that she had done rather well. Research was her specialty, after all; she could wring data from dead husks, and often proved it.

This... was not so good as her best, but she was inclined to be pleased with her work. Whether it might save her life, as Rys Lin had hinted, should the worst occur and the Commander come back to the ship without him—*that* she doubted.

Still, she made plans for that eventuality. If the information she had found would produce even a moment's distraction, she might make a push to survive.

A chime sounded, and she spun to the board, scanning the screens.

The tone—that was the beacon Rys Lin had carried with him. He would activate it, so the agreement went, when he approached the first door, to alert the ship of an egress from the tunnel.

So, the alert had been activated, Vazineth thought grimly, which in no way guaranteed that Rys Lin had pressed the button.

The tunnel was center on her number one screen. She gave it the attention it deserved, even as her fingers toyed with the cover on the atmospheric weapons. The plan was, if Claidyne returned alone, to open to her, for, said Rys Lin, there was no way to know if she were herself or the Commander ascendant, by looking at her.

Vazineth, recently returned to life and her own self, was... somewhat conflicted regarding this part of the plan, especially should there be no Rys Lin present to enforce it.

She had not been so avid as the rest of her comrades in this venture, and might simply have withdrawn had there been any opportunity to do so. True, there was some part of her which did clamor for Balance, but Balance at what cost? That was the question that vexed one. And as had lately been proven, some costs were far too high to pay.

The egress door opened. Vazineth stilled in the pilot's chair, her hand yet on the weapons lock.

Claidyne came into view, walking firm and proud, which was her way, and no proof for the Commander or against her.

Rys Lin came after, walking two steps behind on her offside, precisely as he had gone in. The alert was in his hand.

Neither appeared greatly changed from when they had entered the tunnel by that very door, several hours ago, and it occurred to Vazineth that there was another possible scenario available to this situation: that Claidyne would survive the download, the Commander ascendant and able to place Rys Lin into her service.

Vazineth's fingers tightened on the weapons lock.

In the screen, Rys Lin increased his pace slightly and came alongside Claidyne, his metal hand touching her shoulder.

Vazineth waited as he spoke to her, then continued alone toward the ship, both hands up, one showing the alert, the other gleaming metal, palm open, fingers wide.

She sighed then and released her hold on the weapons lock in favor of flipping the toggle that opened the hatch.

"Have you had," Rys Lin asked, when they were all on the bridge and Claidyne had declared herself in possession of, yet not possessed by, the download. "Have you had any success in that line of research we spoke of?"

"I—yes." Vazineth threw a glance toward Claidyne, who raised her eyebrows.

"Show her," he said.

Yes, of course, Vazineth thought. Anything that they might give Claidyne, so that she remained possessor, rather than possessed.

"Rys Lin had given me a name," she said to Claidyne now, "and asked me to find what had come of her. Here..."

She brought the research screen up with a touch, and rose, ceding the pilot's chair.

Claidyne stepped forward, her eyes on the screen—and sagged. She might have fallen, Vazineth thought, save that Rys Lin caught her by the elbow and spun the chair so that she sat, abruptly and without grace, her whole attention still on the screen.

"We will make a meal," Rys Lin said then, and pointed toward the galley with his chin.

Vazineth needed no more hint than that. She left the bridge and had just started the kettle heating when he joined her.

"We move to stage two."

SUREBLEAK

Jelaza Kazone

. . . .

"CAPTAIN."

The voice was quietly urgent, utterly familiar.

"Joyita?"

Theo opened her eyes, blinking in confusion. This was not her cabin aboard *Bechimo*. This was—was...

...her personal suite in her brother's house on Surebleak. Right. She remembered now.

She remembered *all* of it, now.

"What's amiss?" murmured Kara, who was sharing Theo's pillow.

"Hold," Theo said to her; and, "Joyita, what news?"

"Captain," Joyita's voice carried an unaccustomed edge of irritation. "Surebleak Portmaster requests your presence in her office immediately, regarding the drones we set in Surebleak orbit." There was a short pause. "She did not sound happy."

Kara raised herself on an elbow and looked at Theo. Theo looked at Kara. Kara sighed.

Well, they'd known it was possible that someone would figure it out—and would care. They hadn't, to be fair, thought that anybody at *Surebleak*, which wasn't precisely the tightest-run port in the universe, would have cared.

"What time is it?" Theo asked. They'd landed opposite Surebleak time, and yesterday had been—well. And then there'd been the crew meet, which went late for celebrating *Bechimo*'s newly legal status as a Complex Logic, and they *had* landed off-time, so the party went on 'til pretty near local morning, and she'd *still* been dancing when she left for her rooms, and she'd asked

29

Kara if she'd like to share pleasure, and she had—all of which meant that by the time they'd gotten to sleep the sky was showing dawn, and—

"It is midmorning," *Bechimo* said inside her head. "I did not think it necessary to wake you, but Joyita would have it."

Theo sighed. *Not* late then, and she was short on sleep. Not *dangerously* short on sleep, but...

"Joyita's right," Theo said aloud. "The portmaster shouldn't be kept waiting."

"Especially," Kara added wryly, "when she is already unhappy with us."

"There's that," Theo agreed and tossed back the covers, swinging her legs over the edge of the bed.

"Joyita, please tell Surebleak Portmaster that I have received her message and will come to her with all possible speed."

"Yes, Captain," said Joyita, followed by a subtle click, as if he had closed a connection.

"Jeeves?" Theo asked, grabbing the robe she'd flung onto the bottom of the bed only a couple hours before.

A different voice—also male, very mellow, speaking Standard Terran, which nobody did, really, but it suited him.

"Yes, Captain Waitley?"

"Jeeves, please ask Tommy Lee if he's available to drive me to the port, more or less immediately. I'll need time to shower and dress."

"Certainly, Captain. He will be waiting for you at the front door in half an hour."

And, Theo thought, it was nice to know, definitively, how long *immediately* was, with regard to Surebleak's portmaster.

There was a rustle behind her; Theo turned to find Kara had pushed back her blankets and was on her feet.

"Shall I come with you, as crew representative?" she asked. "The entire ship had agreed on—"

Theo shook her head.

"The portmaster will take it as given that the captain speaks for the ship," she said. "You might as well go back to bed." She produced a lopsided grin. "*One* of us ought to get some sleep."

"Hah," said Kara, tipping her head. "Perhaps I will update the executive officer."

Theo looked at her with interest.

"Do you have a particular reason to want Clarence mad at you?"

"Not *particularly*, no," Kara said. "I will wait for you here, if it pleases?"

"It pleases," Theo told her. "I should be back soon. How long can it take to pay a fine, after all?"

· · · ✳ · · ·

"Good morning, Tommy," Theo said, sliding into the back seat of the town car.

"Morning, Captain," he answered easily. He looked perfectly cheerful and wide awake, lucky man.

"I'll have you to the port in no time at all. You just take a quick zip-nap back here and leave the piloting to me."

Which wasn't, Theo admitted, a bad idea at all.

"Thanks," she said.

"No worries," he answered, shutting the door and going around to the driver's seat.

Theo dropped her head back against the cushion and closed her eyes. Breathing deeply, she accessed a pilot's board drill—meant to impart the benefits of a good solid two hours of sleep in one intense fifteen-minute exercise—and was deep into the trance before the car had passed through the front gate.

Theo woke on a deep breath and did a quick scan. She felt rested and relaxed, alert and ready to talk with the portmaster. There'd be a fine, naturally enough. It was the least that the port could do—well, it was really the *only* thing the port could do. Littering the lanes was a definite violation, even though the little surprises they'd dropped strategically at probable entry points for *Chandra Marudas* had been too small to damage a ship, and rigged to disintegrate within twenty-four hours of release. They'd been meant to embarrass Captain yos'Thadi, and that they had done—loudly.

No less than what he'd deserved, Theo had thought, her ship and crew in agreement. Not only had the good Scout captain been maliciously pursuing her ship and a crewman, he'd taken leave to insult *Bechimo*'s abilities.

Yeah, he'd deserved to be publicly embarrassed.

Worse than that, he'd come to Surebleak confident that the field judgment requested of Scout Commander Val Con yos'Phelium, coincidentally Theo's brother Val Con, would put *Bechimo* into his hands for deprogramming and destruction.

Well, Captain yos'Thadi had gone away unsatisfied, while Val Con's field judgment had the potential to change...nearly everything, and the drones they'd dropped had disintegrated hours ago, having done no more harm than they were intended to do.

Or maybe not.

Theo opened her eyes, frowning.

Had they somehow unwittingly damaged a ship? The drones were so small, so fragile that, had a ship encountered one, it would have seemed like nothing more worrisome than a patch of dust. Joyita had said that the portmaster sounded peeved, and come to think of it, if it was only a matter of paying a fine, the port should've billed the ship. There wasn't any need for the portmaster to get involved.

"Theo."

Bechimo spoke to her in bond-space, sounding perfectly calm.

"Your blood pressure is rising," he continued. "I can assure you that the drones each disintegrated according to the presets. There were no collisions; no ships were harmed. Of course, I monitored them."

Of course he had. *Bechimo* wouldn't leave such a thing to chance. Theo took a breath.

"Sorry," she said in bond-space. "Just borrowing trouble."

"Indeed," *Bechimo* said. "Not that there isn't some cause for concern. You are correct that, if it were only a fine, you would not be called to speak with the portmaster in person. Portmasters, even on such a port as Surebleak, are busy with higher matters. The collection of fines is best left to flunkies—or to automatics."

"So, she wants to read me a lecture," Theo said. "Or—wait! Maybe she got Val Con's judgment, and she wants to talk to the captain of a Complex Logic—*the* Complex Logic, the one who triggered the need for a field judgment."

Bechimo was silent for a long moment.

Theo stirred.

"Do you think she's working with Captain yos'Thadi?" she asked, her hand already moving toward the intercom, to tell Tommy to turn the car around.

"No," *Bechimo* said, and she paused. "I do not think so. Joyita has been doing research."

Of course Joyita had been doing research, Theo thought. There was nothing Joyita liked better than to pry into other people's secrets. He routinely violated privacy codes and security gates, and unfortunately, the information he mined was almost always useful.

"What did he find out?" she asked.

"That Portmaster Liu has been an exemplary master of an unruly and unprofitable port. Joyita expresses some curiosity about why she was assigned here. He is undertaking further research on that line."

Theo considered that.

"As long as he doesn't open anything he shouldn't," she said.

"I am certain he will be discreet," *Bechimo* answered, which wasn't exactly what she had in mind.

She bit her lip.

"Unless it's the field judgment, there's no reason for her to see me. And Joyita said she sounded irritated. If she's—"

"Time to wake up, Captain," Tommy's voice came over the intercom. "Arrival at the portmaster's office in three minutes."

Surebleak Port

Portmaster's Office

. . . .

CAPTAIN WAITLEY WASN'T QUITE WHAT PORTMASTER LIU HAD been expecting.

No, scratch that. In a lot of ways, Captain Waitley was *exactly* what Portmaster Liu had been expecting: short for a Terran, tall for a Liaden, lean for the height she did have; shoulders showing attitude under a Jump jacket older and bigger than she was. Whatever else she was—and recklessly negligent wasn't off the table, in Portmaster Liu's not exactly objective opinion—Theo Waitley was definitely a member of Boss Conrad's extended family, Clan Korval. Portmaster Liu had been spending a lot of time lately with the Boss and the Boss's little brother, the Road Boss; she knew the family look when she saw it.

What did surprise her was the wild scramble of wispy fair hair, the pale skin, and the obvious frown. Captain Waitley was ticked off, which was fair enough. What was interesting, though, was how plain she let that bad temper show.

On several occasions over the course of their profitable, if not entirely placid, relationship, Boss Conrad had reason to be annoyed with Portmaster Liu, which she'd never known from his face. Crisp overpoliteness was the first clue, followed by frozen good manners and a toxic increase in irony levels, if whatever was making him peevish didn't subside straight off.

Well, and maybe Captain Waitley had found that a frank and open display of temper got her the results she wanted. It probably took a fair amount of practice to perfect Boss Conrad's style . . .

"Portmaster Liu, I'm sorry to have kept you waiting," the captain said—well, snapped. "You wanted to talk with me about the drones we dropped off?"

Liu blinked.

Got right down to the business at hand, did Captain Waitley, without even so much as an inquiry into the portmaster's general health and the state of the port. Nothing rude about it—a classic Terran approach really. Some of the kids attached to Conrad's family were taking up the Terran mode, from what she'd seen and heard, so—fair enough, again.

"I appreciate you coming so quick," she answered. "Good timing, as it happens. There's a survey team on-port, and they'll be wanting my attention pretty soon. So we'll need to settle our business fairly smart."

Captain Waitley nodded briskly. "I won't waste your time. I've come to pay my fine."

Well, now—the fine. On the one hand, it was good that she knew she'd be having to pay a fine and wasn't making the smallest suggestion that it could be lost, friendly-like, in the paperwork.

You'd think, though, given a captain with a reputation of a certain kind, attached to a family that valued their ships more than the lives of their children ... you'd think that captain'd consider the fine—hefty as it was—the least of her problems.

Which maybe meant that Captain Waitley hadn't quite reasoned her way into a full set of understandings.

Well, Portmaster Liu thought, consciously bringing herself taller in the chair; this'll be fun.

"Have a seat, Captain," she said, nodding at the smaller chair by the side of her desk.

Captain Waitley's frown got frownier, but she sat down, civilized enough, and as a seeming afterthought, folded her hands on her knee.

"The fine, now," the portmaster said, forcing herself to talk easy in the face of that visible increase in bad temper. "You'll take care of that with the bursar. I'll point you in his direction after we get done talking about the citation."

Space-black eyes blinked.

"Citation?" she repeated, real quiet.

Right, thought the portmaster. *This* was the street Captain Waitley was willing to die on. Money was only money. Well,

Portmaster Liu could agree on that point, most times, but a citation, now—that was an assault against *honor* and, the little gods of nuts 'n bolts save her, she *might've* just let it go with a stern talking-to, rather than fight that fight with one of Conrad's own, but . . .

"Citation?" Captain Waitley said again, even quieter.

"That's right," Portmaster Liu said, giving the thing weight with a brisk nod. "We're laying a *grava citajo*—a major citation—for violation of spaceway protocol against your personal license for one Standard Year, and a six-monther against your ship."

"That's . . . steep," Captain Waitley observed, which as a response was a lot milder than the portmaster had braced herself for, considering that it was going to be *damned* 'spensive in terms of hazard fees and dangerous-docking levies. Smalltrader was gonna *feel* that.

"It is," she agreed. "And I'm sorry to say that I can't let either one slide off the table."

Another blink, the frown fading into thoughtfulness.

"Aren't you the portmaster?"

Quick on the pickup—well, that was the family, too, grandpa to babe in arms.

"That's right," she said equitably. "I'm the portmaster."

"Well, then, what prevents you, if you *can't*?" the captain asked, which was a reasonable enough question. "I admit that we—theoretically—imperiled traffic. I have no quarrel with being fined. The drone didn't cause an accident; it's gone by now, and even if it had collided with a ship, the most they would have thought was they'd caught a patch of dust. Still—you're the port-master and I was out of line. We agree."

She took a deep breath, visibly settling into being calm, and Portmaster Liu took a similar breath in solidarity.

"Typical offenses that merit a *grava citajo* are: law-breaking, port-breaking, child-stealing, illegal dealings, piloting to endanger—"

Girl knew her regs, plain enough. Portmaster Liu held up a hand, palm out.

"You're right. I'm calling down a blizzard where a squall would do, like they say out in the city. Between us, if you'd dropped your little party favor in my shipping lanes on any other day, I'd've fined you, dressed you down like you'd never worn clothes before, and we'd've parted on good terms.

"But you happened to pull this stupid stunt at the exact same time we got a TerraTrade survey team on-port, trying their best to figure out how to hold back that upgrade you might've heard Boss Conrad is so set on us getting."

That got her another frown, and a speculative look.

"You're saying that you not only have to go by the book, you've got to go by the strictest reading possible, or the survey team will find cause to withhold," Captain Waitley said with a slight nod. "I see that; I don't have a problem with the fine. I won't like it, but knowing the reasons, I'll even swallow the six-monther against the ship, but—"

Portmaster Liu held up her hand again and glanced at the clock on the wall.

"There's another factor you're not taking into account, Captain. This is gonna sound brusque, but take it for the truth. The reason the survey team is looking *so hard* for reasons to deny this port its upgrade is because of what happened at Solcintra. At least one member of the team has it as his stated opinion that Clan Korval is outright pirates and all Surebleak Port deserves is a Do Not Stop until such time as you and yours leaves the planet."

She paused, and tipped her head slightly. "Pardon?" she asked politely.

Captain Waitley shook her head. "Nothing; sorry. Why are they even bothering to survey if that's their opinion?"

"It's only *one* opinion out of a possible three. The other members of the team state that they've brought no preconceptions to the survey. Which might be so, but even if it *is* so, it doesn't necessarily mean that TerraTrade thinks the same. In which case, they've got the team doing the survey so's to have the record full and proper and no questions this time. Nor any appeals."

Captain Waitley's frown was back; she fluttered her fingers, pilot-sign for *go on*.

"Right. So, what I have to make plain as the snow in front of your nose is that the portmaster's office doesn't put up with any kind or size of shenanigans, and that we're particularly keeping a *very* close eye on the members of Clan Korval. Any of 'em step outta line, and they get slapped, fast and hard."

She took a hard breath, aware that she'd been getting a little emphatic, and finished it off quiet. "On account of this is *Surebleak Port*, not Port Korval—nowhere even close."

There was a little bit of silence, which she didn't interrupt, despite the time.

"I'm not a member of Clan Korval," Captain Waitley said eventually. "I'm a citizen of Delgado."

Right or wrong, Portmaster Liu couldn't help but feel some sympathy. The captain was doing a good enough job of holding on to her temper and working through the possibles, as clean and crisp as if the whole of it was a problem out of Ethics Class. Unfortunately...

"That might work as a dodge on some other day, Captain," she said kindly, "but I'm betting the survey team's not ignorant of the fact that you're the Road Boss's sister. You being a Terran and a citizen of Delgado—all that's aside. You're family, even if you aren't clan."

There was a longish silence.

"I pulled an extra heavy fine and two *grava citajos because* I'm Val Con's sister," Captain Waitley repeated, seeming like she just wanted to be sure she had the info right.

"That's right, Captain. I'm real sorry about it, but we got a lot riding on getting this upgraded certification. Ain't just your family wants it. All Surebleak *needs* it."

Deep breath then; muscles visibly loosened. Captain Waitley rose, inclined her head—and froze.

"Wait," she said.

Portmaster Liu sighed quietly. Might've known it wouldn't be that simple.

"Portmaster, have you had a chance to read the Scout Commander's field judgment on Complex Logics yet? It was just made yesterday, but I understood the local Scouts were to be sending it right out..."

Portmaster Liu nodded toward her screen. "It's in my inbox."

"I know it's an imposition, but could I ask you to read that? Right now? It's pertinent."

Portmaster Liu looked at her closely, but she seemed sincere. A glance at the clock showed half an hour before the survey team was due.

"All right," she said, and touched the screen.

Captain Waitley resumed her chair.

· · · ✳ · · ·

"Theo," *Bechimo* said. "You are—excited. What are you planning? I do not recommend aggression against the portmaster. She has been reasonable, within the constraints she believes have been set upon her. The penalty is harsh, but there may be some mitigating—"

"There is!" she interrupted. "On Delgado, people who have done something antisocial, they repay the community for their lapse by doing a service, for free, until their debt to society has been paid."

Theo took a breath, watching the side of Portmaster Liu's face as she frowned at her screen.

"I think," she said to *Bechimo*, "that we might be able to get the *grava citajos* against you downgraded, or forgiven, if you're willing to do some service for the port. Crew and ship, that'll be. I don't know what we could offer, but—"

"I do," *Bechimo* said abruptly. "Yes, I'm willing. Very willing. We will redeem ourselves to the community of Surebleak Port, and to the community of pilots and ships. At the same time, we will establish a precedent in support of the Scout Commander's field judgment."

Theo blinked.

"I hadn't thought of that," she admitted. "You're right. The judgment gives the Complex Logics room to establish themselves. Us, here, starts that. But we need to get the word out—"

To a community that was deliberately hidden, and too aware of their danger from humankind.

"I'm not sure how to get the word out," she said.

"I believe that we are not without resources. Jeeves has an extensive network of acquaintances. And I know you do not discount Joyita's research abilities."

Theo hiccuped a laugh, then nodded when Portmaster Liu glanced up.

"Pardon me," she said. "I just thought of something."

The portmaster nodded and returned her attention to her screen.

· · · ❈ · · ·

Portmaster Liu read the field judgment once, then read it again.

So, in addition to being an attitude case, like the rest of her family, Captain Waitley's ship was—*of course*—a Complex Logic, which just yesterday had been a crime, punishable by, well—death. The actual word used in the actual law was "reprogrammed," but that didn't change the finality of the thing...in Portmaster Liu's opinion.

Today, though, courtesy of a field judgment rendered by Scout Commander Val Con yos'Phelium—coincidentally the Road Boss or, as they had it, half of the Road Boss—being a Complex Logic in possession of a good job meant that Captain Waitley's ship was every bit as much a legal entity as Captain Waitley.

And wasn't *that* just going to stand the universe on its ear. Not that she'd, personally, thought the Complex Logic Laws were the best work humankind had ever produced, but she'd comforted herself with the belief that it was unlikely she would, herself, meet such a person and be required to invoke the law. After all, part of the point was that AIs weren't *stupid*. They'd scarcely call attention to themselves by coming into a well-regulated port, such as Claren Liu administered.

Had administered.

On Surebleak Port, now, anything could happen—and often did; a tendency that had only gotten more pronounced with the arrival of Clan Korval.

The portmaster ran her hand through her hair. Honest to space, if they weren't doing so much that was right, for the planet and the port, she'd throw the lot of them off-world.

She sighed and closed her eyes, her basic honesty forcing her to admit the truth.

No, she wouldn't.

Well, then. Best get on with it.

She opened her eyes and considered Captain Waitley wearily.

"So," she said. "Your ship wants a word, is that it?"

"Yes. We'd appreciate it—we'd *both* appreciate—if you could find time to listen to what he has to say on his own behalf."

"Well," said Portmaster Liu, nodding toward the screen that still displayed Scout Commander yos'Phelium's field judgment.

"Since Surebleak Port has apparently been chosen to participate in a test case, I can't very well beg off, can I? The ship's here, the judgment's been made and is going out through channels, and none of us really has a choice, now do we?" She sighed and shook her head, wryly acknowledging the truth of what she was about to say.

"I would've had to make a call as soon as I'd gotten around to reading this anyway. All you did was jump ahead in line."

It wasn't like she'd never been a test case before, she thought. With hardly any luck at all, this one would go better than her first one.

"We realize that this is awkward," Captain Waitley said, sounding genuinely apologetic. "You're going to be hearing a voice on the comm, and you're going to have to trust that the ship is speaking with you."

Portmaster Liu considered her suspiciously, but, no, it seemed the captain was serious. Well. Viewpoint was a wonderful thing, after all.

She jerked her head at the screen again.

"I don't see a Scout Commander risking his reputation and his career on a practical joke. Says right in this doc that this judgment came about because of a Scout challenge brought against the starship *Bechimo*, Complex Logic. That suggests to me that, when we get the starship *Bechimo* on comm, it will be the starship *Bechimo* I'll be talking with."

She turned the comm pad around.

"Call your ship, why not? Let's get this thing done."

"So, you're offering free labor against a major citation?" Portmaster Liu asked, having listened to the courteous voice on the comm while it told down its proposal. She'd liked it, that voice; she'd also liked that there hadn't been any attempt to claim he was innocent of littering the lanes.

Her question, now, that was a test, and she waited for maybe a little temper, or for a backup to the beginning and a complete repeat of what it—*he*—had just said, or—

"That equation of course would not balance," *Bechimo* said calmly. "No, what I ask for is an opportunity to redeem my reputation, and the reputations of my crew and captain; to demonstrate to you, to Surebleak Port, and to the TerraTrade survey team, that we are not mere mischief-makers with no regard for life and law."

"And what do you suggest as a fitting...Balance?"

"In order to bring both sides of the equation into Balance, I would suggest that the port allow us to clean the most energetic rubbish out of Surebleak's nearspace. There are several resonant orbits at work which we can trawl for the densest groups; we can also create a stereo map of the larger out-orbit potential problems. We understand that the Gilmour Agency had such a map, which we can update and provide to your organization as well as to the Scouts, who will surely be pleased to extend it as they come and go. Also, we can assist in placing weather satellites, if they are ready to be deployed. All of this increases the safety of the lanes, improves the landing experience for those arriving at the surface, and improves the lives of the citizens of Surebleak."

Portmaster Liu closed her eyes briefly. The punishment fits the crime, now doesn't it? she asked herself.

"You can work that tight?" she asked, because previous unsuccessful attempts to do this exact sort of cleanup had foundered on human error.

"Portmaster, we are highly qualified for close-in work of just this type. We excel in retrievals."

Well. It was tempting, so it was. She could okay it right now, but that might look too eager. Better to give them all a chance to cool down and look at the thing from all sides. Talk it over. Take advice.

And besides all that, she'd eaten up all her margin and was running close to the survey team's appointed time of arrival. Instinctively, she knew that she didn't want the survey team and Theo Waitley in the same space.

"I'll need to run it past my advisory board," she said, "in case we've missed something. I'll get back to you this afternoon, if that suits."

"Portmaster," *Bechimo* said, "it suits very well. Thank you for your consideration and your time."

"You're welcome. Thank you for bringing this to me. I'll be in touch."

She closed the connection and looked to Captain Waitley, sitting quiet and calm in her chair, and took a deep breath.

"He's...really a person," she said, which hadn't been what she'd meant to say.

Theo Waitley grinned. "He really is," she said, and rose into a gentle bow. "We'll look forward to your call, ma'am. Thank you for your time."

Jelaza Kazone

. . . .

TOMMY LEE DROPPED HER AT THE FRONT DOOR, WHICH MR. pel'Kana had open by the time she reached it.

"Good morning, Captain Waitley," he said in Terran. "Your brother asks that you go to him in his office upon your return."

"Thank you." Theo took a breath, thinking of her priorities, such as breakfast and bringing her crew up to date, and—gods, Kara! who'd been waiting for her all this time...

Val Con wanted to see her. He wasn't her delm, she didn't owe him unquestioning obedience—which Kara *still* took as given—but he was her brother; he had recently done her the not insignificant favor of saving *Bechimo*'s life, and his request, through the filter of Mr. pel'Kana, was polite and—

Her brother might be able to suggest a strategy for getting the *grava citajos* against *her* license reduced or removed.

And that was definitely ship business.

"*Bechimo*," she said in bond-space, "please ask Joyita to give Kara my apologies. The meeting with the portmaster got complicated, and my brother wants to speak with me. Also, please ask everyone to meet me in the Southern Suite common room in two hours."

"Yes, Theo. May I suggest that you may want to eat a meal? Your blood sugar is low."

Right.

She glanced at Mr. pel'Kana standing by patiently, apparently waiting to guide her to Val Con.

"Would you please tell my brother that I'll join him very soon? I just need to stop by the kitchen and get something to eat."

"Captain, there is not the slightest need," Mr. pel'Kana said reproachfully. "I will bring a tray. Follow me, please. We will see you comfortable in very short order."

Theo opened her mouth—and closed it.

This was not an argument she could win. As far as Mr. pel'Kana was concerned, it wasn't even an argument they ought *to have.* Val Con wanted her; it was Mr. pel'Kana's job to take her to him. She wanted breakfast; Mr. pel'Kana would bring it to her because, by doing so, he accomplished his first task more quickly. It all worked together, and no need for argument from an upstart star captain.

"Thank you," Theo said with a small inclination of the head, meant to indicate that his service had been noticed. "I will go to my brother at once."

"Captain Waitley, sir."

Mr. pel'Kana stepped aside to allow her to enter the room.

Val Con turned from his place in front of the window and came forward, hands extended.

"Theo, I hardly expected you so soon. Have you eaten?"

She heard the door close quietly behind her as she gave her hands to Val Con.

"Mr. pel'Kana's bringing a tray."

"Excellent." He drew her down the room, back toward the window, where four chairs were grouped around a small table.

"Please, sit," he murmured.

She took the chair that put her back to the bookshelf and gave her a view of the garden, if she turned her head a fraction, and of the door, if she turned her head a fraction in the other direction.

Val Con sat facing the window, his back to the door. It was his house, after all; the likelihood of an armed enemy making it through that door was vanishingly small.

"You're up and about early," he said. "Business at the port, I believe Jeeves said?"

Theo sighed lightly. Val Con was worried about the port and the survey team, just the same as Portmaster Liu, and he wanted to make sure she hadn't run over the portmaster with her boots on.

"Portmaster wanted to talk to me about the drones we'd left in Surebleak space," she said.

"Was she displeased?" Val Con asked, too innocently, in Theo's opinion.

"You could say so. *Bechimo*'s fined a cantra and there's a *grava citajo* against him for six Standard Months."

She met his eyes.

"My personal license has a *grava citajo* laid against it for a Standard Year."

"That seems...steep," Val Con murmured, holding her gaze easily.

Theo drew a hard breath and looked away, feeling a flicker of anger.

"It *is* steep," she began...and stopped because Mr. pel'Kana had arrived with the tray.

"I understand that the port's expanding," Theo said, finishing the first of several muffins Mr. pel'Kana had provided—"and that's why they needed to lay a cantra fine against us. But to hit us with those citations—survey team or no survey team! That's not just reading the regs with a heavy eye; it's inventing whole new paragraphs!"

Val Con was slouched at ease in his chair, ankle on opposite knee, teacup cradled in his hands.

It was, Theo thought, not very good tea. Surprisingly bad, really, with 'way too much caffeine and an oily texture—more like coffee than a proper tea. Despite which, she had a swallow, hoping to loosen her throat.

"The regs," Val Con said, apparently having decided that she'd finished saying her piece, which she guessed she had. "The regs do give portmasters discretion. Necessary, as I think you would agree, as all ports are not one port, and conditions even at sister ports may vary...significantly."

Theo slumped back in the chair and *fuffed* her hair out of her eyes.

"But this portmaster—"

"Portmaster Liu, as all of us, very much wishes for TerraTrade to find Surebleak Port worthy of an upgraded rating. The survey team has many reasons to find for us—there are not so many full-service ports in this sector."

"There isn't any *trade* in this sector," Theo pointed out.

"No; you are harsh. There is some small amount of trade and

traffic in the sector, and the presence of a certified port can do nothing but *increase* both. Which is an attractive proposition to TerraTrade."

He sipped his tea—carefully, Theo thought.

"However, it does not benefit TerraTrade, which is to say, it does not benefit *trade* to certify an unworthy port. Above all, the process by which ratings and upgrades are determined must be beyond reproach. If the portmaster on a given port is known to read the regs with a heavy eye, as you have it, that is acceptable. A lax portmaster on a port which will, appropriately rated, become the primary draw to trade in the sector—that endangers the process, and TerraTrade's *melant'i*, as well as Surebleak's chances for an upgrade. So Portmaster Liu has reasoned . . . and I think she is correct."

Theo shook her head.

"She said she came down *particularly* hard on *Bechimo* because I'm your sister. That's not running a tight port, that's reading the regs out of one eye for me and the other for everybody else."

"Ah. Do you have evidence that she has imposed lesser sanctions on other ships which have compromised the shipping lanes?" Val Con asked interestedly.

Theo frowned at him.

"Where would I find evidence?"

"The portmaster's log, naturally," he said mildly. "We might easily find if you are the first, and a warning to others—or if you have been shamefully mistreated solely because you are my sister. The log for the last six months is on the public net."

She blinked, and after a moment, Val Con murmured.

"Will you like more tea?"

Well, yes, she would like more *tea*. This particular beverage however—

"No, thank you," she managed, and added, "What is the blend? So I know to avoid it."

It was honest, but it wasn't polite, and Theo bit the inside of her cheek.

Inner calm, she told herself, biting hard, and raised her eyes to Val Con's face, expecting at the least a cool glance and an upraised brow.

But Val Con was laughing.

"I shall make you a gift of the tin, so that you may always have it before you as an example."

"No, I—"

She took a deep breath.

"I'm sorry," she said.

"Sorry? For being Father's daughter and a member of this family?" He shook his head, grin lingering. "Allow me to compliment you, Theo. That was *perfectly* done."

She glared at him.

"Why're you drinking it, if you don't like it?"

"The tin was sent to us *gratis*, possibly in the hope that we will become a customer of the house."

He raised his voice slightly.

"Jeeves, please ask Mr. pel'Kana to bring today's tin, and also a fresh pot of Morning Sunrise."

"Yes, Master Val Con."

"*Bechimo*," Theo said in bond-space. "Can you access the Surebleak Portmaster's log back...two years? Before Clan Korval arrived on-planet?"

"Of course, Theo." He sounded surprised.

Theo didn't sigh. Between *Bechimo* and Joyita, no encryption in the universe was safe. She was raising a couple of AIs with no respect for personal boundaries, was what. On the other hand, the information would be...useful.

"Look for legitimate channels for requesting the information before you...get creative," she said.

There was a soft knock at the door. Val Con rose from his chair, picked up the teapot and went to open.

"Of course," *Bechimo* said, like he'd never unlocked a private file in his life.

"I know it'll take longer that way," she said. "We're not on a tight deadline. And while I know you probably won't get caught, let's not take the chance, with the portmaster already jumpy over the survey team."

"Will you undertake the search of the portmaster's log?" Val Con asked from too near at hand.

He bent and put a small tray holding a fresh teapot and two clean cups in the center of the breakfast tray, and placed a tea tin by her hand.

"I've asked *Bechimo* to take the search back two years, assuming the records are available, so we can compare."

"Thorough," Val Con said, reaching for the pot. "I will be interested to learn if there is anything irregular. May I ask *Bechimo* to keep me informed?"

"*Bechimo*?" she murmured aloud for Val Con's benefit, and heard the answer in bond-space.

"It will be my pleasure to send your brother a copy of our analysis."

"Thank you," she said, and looked to Val Con, whose whole attention appeared to be on pouring tea.

"*Bechimo* will be happy to share his findings with you."

"I am grateful." He handed her a cup and she took it, happy to catch the aroma of real tea.

She sipped, sighed, and set the cup aside before picking up the tea tin.

"Bitter Truth?" she asked, feeling her eyebrows rise. "Who names a tea Bitter Truth?"

"Plainly, the White Wing Beverage Company does, though in earnest or in jest, I dare not speculate."

He settled back into his chair again, and considered her seriously.

Theo put the tea tin aside and picked up the last bit of pastry on her plate.

Val Con waited, sipping, until she finished and leaned back into her own chair, cup in hand.

"I wonder, Theo, if you wish to . . . emancipate yourself, so that you might establish your own family or corporation. As you point out, being known as Korval kin is not necessarily advantageous and, in fact, has been dangerous for you and for your ship."

She stared at him. *Emancipate* herself? Repudiate Father, and Luken, Miri, and, well—Val Con? Even Lady Kareen was—

"Um, no," she said carefully, to her brother's speculative green gaze. "I don't want to divorce myself from the—*our*—family." She sighed. "I just wish you were a little less prone to trouble!"

He grinned.

"One might return the compliment, were it not well known *in the family* that we are, as individuals and as a unit, *prone to trouble*."

She felt her mouth soften, and gave him a nod.

"Point. But, even if I did start my own family, and formally . . . divorce myself from Clan Korval, I don't think the people who've been hunting *Bechimo* are going to see—or care about—that level of detail."

"They do seem to find the fine print a challenge," Val Con agreed. "And here we approach my topic. As you are yourself kin without being clan, it may have escaped your attention that Clan Korval is a very small... family, indeed. Dangerously small, one might say. For our own security, we need to improve our situation. The choices before us are to disband and allow each member to form their own alliances with other families or clans—or we might merge with another small clan and thus form a larger, to the benefit of both."

He gave her a wise look.

"However, as we have just discussed, Clan Korval's marriage portion will inevitably include trouble, and there are not many clans—of any size—who seek to add to their stores of that particular commodity. As we are now placed on Surebleak, and as Surebleak will, sooner rather than later, so I believe, evolve a hybrid culture, Miri has proposed a third solution, which looks toward the future, rather than seeking to accommodate the past."

He paused, head tipped to one side.

"Mind, you will receive scarcely any benefit, save what is already yours: as safe a docking as may be managed, a home port, and a home base. Kin to draw upon. A share in all the business of the family.

"You would also be asked to contribute—to give support and provide backup to other family members. At present, the clan is given a share in all personal business of its members, which strikes me as more equitable than assaying dues, because the clan not only shares in profits, it bears a percentage of any loss. Internally... a clan structure seems most workable to me, which is perhaps not surprising—but that may well be modified as we move forward."

He inclined his head with, Theo thought, a certain amount of irony.

"I believe I may promise that you will not be bored. We would, of course, still be prone to trouble—which does make mutual aid and support somewhat risky. On the other hand, where else would you find backup who perfectly comprehends that sometimes things just—happen?"

Theo laughed.

"It *was* convenient to know a Scout Commander who could render a field judgment on the status of Complex Logics," she said. "Having *Bechimo* declared a solid citizen who works for his living and benefits the community—in fact, that's how we . . . might get *Bechimo*'s six-month citation reduced."

"You intrigue me. May I know the details?"

Briefly, she outlined it, and saw with some amount of foreboding that both of his eyebrows were raised.

"So, we figured that it would be reasonable and . . . forward-looking for *Bechimo* to contact the portmaster on his own behalf, make that case, and offer to perform a service for the community. That would demonstrate that he's an asset to society, which is directly in line with your judgment."

"So, you have created a test case, here—immediately?" asked Val Con.

"It was going to have to be tested, sooner or later. The Scouts will eventually get around to reviewing your judgment. Wouldn't it be helpful to them if there were real-life examples already on the record of AIs actually being social and responsible?"

Val Con sighed. "I note that there is a TerraTrade survey team on port at this moment."

"But that's great!" Theo said excitedly. "They'll be able to report that Surebleak is ahead of the curve in accommodating Complex Logics."

He grinned suddenly.

"Reasoned, if I may say it, like a yos'Phelium. You will be an asset to the family, Theo, if you decide that way. Do you?"

Theo took a breath and bowed her head.

"Yes. I do."

He had offered her another cup of tea, and she had accepted. For a little time, they merely sat, wordless and relaxed, honoring the tea together.

Theo stirred.

"Last night," she said slowly, "I talked with . . . Father, and with—your mother."

He inclined his head politely.

"I trust you found them well?"

"Astonishingly well," Theo said. "And . . . and *youthened*, too.

Father looks like your younger brother, and your mother looks to be about Padi's age."

"Yes," Val Con said calmly. "We will need to exert ourselves to educate the youth, I fear."

Theo glared at him. "They said they were under the Delm's Order to establish new identities. Do you think that's going to ... stick?"

"In-clan?" He shook his head. "I expect it to be a very open secret. However, we do not wish to strain the credulity of those who are not familiar with us. Better that a guildsman, or a portmaster, or a prospective client be presented with a license that matches the face. They will also each need to pass a piloting test. The tickets must be valid."

"Yes, they said that, too." Theo sighed and finished her tea. "It's going to take some getting used to," she said, meeting his eyes.

Val Con grinned.

"It will, indeed. I did promise that you would not be bored."

She laughed, and stood up. "Yes, you did. I'm sorry to cut this short, but I've got a crew meeting."

"Of course." He rose as well, leaned over and picked up the tea tin. "You won't want to forget this."

"I could *never* forget this," Theo said fervently and walked with him to the door.

Jelaza Kazone

. . . .

"LAST I HEARD, IT WAS BETTER TO BE DOIN' SOMETHING THAN doin' nothin'," Clarence said into the silence that followed Theo's account of her meeting with the portmaster.

He glanced around the circle of present crew, including Joyita, on the big screen at the bottom of the room.

"Speaking only for myself, o'course. I'm the last to deny the fleshpots o'Surebleak to any who wants 'em."

"*Fleshpots?*" Kara repeated, wrinkling her nose. "A kind of stew? It does not sound at all appetizing."

"Fleshpots," Joyita said, "is an archaic usage referring to a place of bold or lascivious entertainment."

"One readily comprehends how it came to fall out of use," said Kara, and glanced to Theo. "Are there...*fleshpots*...on Surebleak, I wonder, or is this Clarence's fancy?"

"Listen to the woman! Isn't there Ms. Audrey's House o'Joy right downtown? Best of its kind on the planet, is what I hear—though Mack had some rare words to speak on the topic of Angel's Place out in Boss Feenan's turf, what was." He shrugged. "Not visited myself, and I don't doubt it's fine, but that's Mack's growing-up territory there, and memories o'home are always sweetest."

"So it is said, by some," Win Ton commented, not being one of those so afflicted, as Theo knew. "We assume that the portmaster will accept *Bechimo*'s proposal," he continued, "but what if she does not?"

"Borrowing trouble?" Theo asked him.

"Planning for all contingencies," he told her, with a little too much dignity.

"Of course," she said politely, and leaned back, her eyes straying to the ceiling.

"My feeling is that Portmaster Liu knows an opportunity when it comes into port. She'd *rather* everything was smooth and, and, *unexceptionable* while the survey team's working, but at the same time, it's hard to show yourself and your port to advantage when it's all running glitch-free.

"*Bechimo*'s proposal gives her a chance to show she's flexible and versatile, and not afraid of change. It makes sense that Surebleak will be the test zone—the judgment was made here and the ship named in the appeal for a judgment is here, too. No better place to test it, really."

She sighed.

"I want to say the survey team will be favorably impressed, but the only thing I know about this particular survey team is that at least one team member thinks that Clan Korval's home port isn't fit for anything but a Do Not Stop."

"Survey teams are theoretically objective," Win Ton said.

"If there's a team bias, it's supposed to be included in the final report," Clarence added. "Still, that's a long hill to climb, even grantin' it's one o' three. Might be Portmaster Liu is feelin' a little extra pressure to excel, which'll do well for *Bechimo* and his crew, assuming he'll have us along."

"Of course, I will have you along, Clarence," *Bechimo* said, his voice originating from Joyita's screen. "I would scarcely undertake such a project without my crew; we are a team. This is aside the fact that it will increase the value of the test case, to demonstrate that Complex Logics do, indeed, work well with humankind, and that such teamwork is beneficial to both sides of the equation."

"Never did agree with the premise o'the Complex Logic Law—that the AI population is set on wiping out humankind. If disgust hasn't driven 'em to it by now, I'd say we're safe from that quarter."

He paused, eyes on Hevelin as the norbear bumbled over to Win Ton and arranged himself against the former Scout's knee.

"As to what we'll be doin' with ourselves if Portmaster Liu decides she can't afford to be bold—"

"Your pardon, Clarence," Joyita said, looking up from the row of screens in his supposed tower workroom. "Portmaster Liu has just called and asked to speak to *Bechimo*."

Theo grinned and leaned forward, watching Joyita's face. There was a general feeling in the room as if the crew was holding its collective breath. Hevelin, against Win Ton's knee, murbled and turned to face the screen.

"Captain." *Bechimo*'s voice sounded a little...rushed. Theo felt a jolt of elation; inside her head, bond-space was glowing.

"Captain, Portmaster Liu has given me leave to pursue my service to the community. I have provided her with a map of those areas identified as most in need, and a tentative timetable. I will need to coordinate closely with her office, so that we do not disrupt traffic or cause a hazardous situation."

"Excellent," Theo said, feeling the grin get wider.

"I have been cleared to lift in three hours local."

There was a small pause.

"Will my crew accompany me?"

Theo looked around the circle of them, seeing her own eagerness reflected in their faces.

"We'll be boarding within the hour," she said.

"Yes, Captain," came the answer four times over.

"That," said *Bechimo*, "will be satisfactory. The ship is ready."

· · · ❄ · · ·

The schedule here in the stronghold of the captain's kinsman was much like the schedule Chernak and Stost had followed aboard *Bechimo*. In addition to language, history, social studies, and maths, they were fortunate to have gained two new sparring partners with novel and challenging methods—a real gift, as they had been too often of late sparring with each other.

There had also arrived in their quarters a so-called *field judgment* which they read with puzzlement, awe, horror and, at the very last—applause. Joyita need no longer hide his nature! Captain Waitley need no longer expend energy better used in command defending her ship *Bechimo*—a Work, yet not of the Great Enemy's making—from brigands and cowards such as Captain yos'Thadi. It meant—it meant that this new universe in which they found themselves had been changed in amazing new ways.

So great was their hilarity that they drew the attention of Nelirikk, Captain Robertson's aide, who, upon understanding the root of their joy, introduced them formally to Jeeves, not a mere security 'bot—no! Named also in the judgment, the foundation

on which this new document of liberation had been raised, it was a heady few hours of discussion with like minds, and learning to know Jeeves a little.

Truly, this was a brave new universe in which they found themselves, that such things might happen.

There were also interviews. This was a benefit provided to them by the captain's kinsman, so that they might be assigned where they would be of the most use.

They had only yesterday been interviewed by Commander Relgen of Relgen's Raiders, a mercenary force, which their studies gave them to understand was an honorable path for soldiers in this time and place.

Commander Relgen and her second had been soldierly, displaying and expecting proper discipline. She put her questions with a commander's sternness, giving attention not only to their answers, but how they presented themselves.

Near the end of the interview, she took time to speak directly to their former service, and to praise their dedication to duty.

After she and her second had departed, Stost had attempted to find from Diglon if he thought she might offer them a place in her troop, but Diglon, wisely, did not claim insight into the mind of command. They would need to wait, which was the lot of soldiers in all places and all times.

Wait, then, they did, filling their time with study and with exercise.

They missed, which they admitted only to each other, the company of Joyita and of Grakow, whom they had met on the grounds during a march around the perimeter. He had saluted them as a comrade, while introducing another of his persuasion, with orange and white fur, identified by Diglon as "Paizel."

They missed also Clarence, and Kara, and Win Ton, Hevelin, Captain Waitley...well, all of *Bechimo*, which had been their first posting in this strange new universe.

It was only, said Chernak, that they wanted the familiar, after all the change they had endured. Likely, this odd emotion would leave them once they had found a new duty station.

They were in the study room, working through advanced equation sets. Both were pilots and very good at math, so they returned to the maths program as a reward for having successfully completed modules in more difficult subjects.

"We ought," said Stost, "petition the house to allow us to train on dummy boards."

Chernak gave him a stern look.

"*Dummy* boards, my Stost? Have we not left the creche?"

"Assuredly, Elder. Do you think that the generosity of the captain's kinsman will extend to ceding us a ship so that we might practice live?"

Chernak sighed. "In truth, neither he nor Captain Robertson are fools."

"A request for practice boards will show our enthusiasm and—"

The door to their study room opened. A slight figure in an overlarge leather jacket strode in, pale hair rippling in the breeze of her passage.

Chernak and Stost scrambled to their feet, chairs squeaking across the stone floor as they came to full attention and each brought a fist smartly to the opposite shoulder.

"Captain!" they said in unison.

She paused in her purposeful stride and looked up at them, brows drawn.

"At ease," she said in Terran.

They relaxed into parade rest.

She looked well, Stost thought, taut and full of energy—the look, in fact, of a soldier with a mission before her. Could it be possible...?

"I came to let you know," Captain Waitley said, continuing in Terran, "that *Bechimo* has been assigned a task by the port. We're lifting within the next few hours. Is there anything you require from the ship, anything you're missing here that we can provide? Do you have any messages that I can deliver for you?"

"Captain," Chernak said. "We want for nothing."

She hesitated, but Stost did not.

"Respectfully, we remind the captain that we are not without skills and may be useful to her and to the ship in this new assignment."

The captain sighed, thin face showing what might have been regret.

"I'm aware. I've written a letter of recommendation for both of you, outlining all of your skills. If I was selfish, I'd bring you on board for this, but that would be short term. You need to

settle yourselves, long term, and I respect you too much to rob you of that opportunity.

"My brother and his lifemate are committed to seeing you honorably situated. You can depend on them as you would... myself. Am I understood?"

Stost felt rather than heard Chernak's sigh.

"Captain, you are understood," she said. "We would," she added, "wish the crew to know that we recall them as comrades. It was an honor to serve with them."

"Yes," Stost said, hollowly. "An honor."

Bechimo

. . . .

"THEO."

Bechimo's voice in bond-space sounded...tentative, which—*Bechimo* had mostly given up tentativeness as a mode.

Theo rapidly reviewed the projects under way. Absent this *particular project*—prepping to lift and start cleaning up the garbage—she couldn't think of anything that might produce tentativeness.

"Yes?" she answered lightly. "Have you realized that the crew will be in your way on this?"

There was a short, sharp silence as if *Bechimo* had *blinked*.

"My crew will never be in my way. *Never*."

This time, Theo blinked, breath-caught at the intensity—the *passion*—in his voice. Deliberately, she breathed in, nice and deep, and sighed the breath out.

"Was that," *Bechimo* asked, voice cool now, "meant to be a *joke*?"

"Not entirely," she said. "Partly, I was acknowledging that this is the beginning of a new phase for you—in your life. Always before, you've had to hide who—and what—you are. Val Con's field judgment means—ought to mean—that you'll never have to hide your true nature again."

There was another palpable pause, somehow softer, as if *Bechimo* was thinking in a new direction.

"I had not considered," he said eventually. "This bargain we have made with the portmaster will, possibly, hasten awareness of the field judgment and the new status of Complex Logics with regard to the law. Still, change will require time—quite a lot of time."

Especially for those who told time like *Bechimo*, Theo thought.

"You're right," she said. "It's going to take a whole lot of small steps forward—and some steps back, too. There's a lot of changes that'll have to be made, because that judgment has the potential to make a whole new future—"

This wasn't a new thought, but it wasn't any more comfortable on a second thinking. Almost, she wondered if Val Con knew what he'd done—but *of course* he'd known. He hadn't crafted his judgment *only* to save *Bechimo*'s life or *just* to spit in Captain yos'Thadi's eye. Val Con had *wanted* a future where AIs were fully integrated, and when the chance had come past him, he'd grabbed it.

Which led to wondering…*why* did Val Con want that future?

And *that* wasn't comfortable thinking at all.

"Theo," *Bechimo* said again. "I have a question."

"All right," she said, sitting back in her chair and closing her eyes, so she could concentrate on him totally. "What's your question?"

"When you accepted your brother's invitation to formally join the new extended family, did you consider what that might mean to us?"

Eyes closed, Theo frowned.

"I didn't," she admitted. "And now that you've raised the question, I'm afraid I don't know why it should mean anything other than I—"

She stopped.

"This isn't about Korval being on your disallowed list again, is it? I thought that was settled a long time ago."

"It is not, and it was," *Bechimo* snapped.

"Then I don't understand the question," Theo said. "Can you please rephrase or elaborate?"

"We are a bonded pair: captain and ship. We are *we*. Together, ship and captain are stronger, faster, more versatile, *more able*.

"By accepting the invitation to formally join a family, you have placed something—you have placed *another allegiance*—between captain and ship. We are no longer *we* when you are *them*."

Theo took a deep breath.

"I've always been Val Con's sister, my father's child."

"Yes…"

"We're not the same; we're different. We've always been different, starting with the fact that I'm human and you're a starship.

We each bring something to the bonding. We each bring *different strengths* to the bonding. That's why your Builders decided that a bonded pair was the optimum model.

"My...induction into Val Con's family doesn't change *any-thing* between us. It's surely not a threat to our bond. *Nothing* can threaten the bond, can it? The *fact* is that we *are* a bonded pair. Can you decide to leave our relationship and take up with another captain?"

"No!"

"Well, there's your answer," she said reasonably. "I have no plans, and no desire, to bond with another ship. We're exactly the same as we were."

This was greeted by a profoundly unhappy silence, interrupted by an announcement so brisk it sounded like a recording.

"We are cleared for lift, Captain. You are needed on the bridge."

"In a minute," Theo said. "I can feel that you're not satisfied. Bring this to us again, when we're not pressed for time."

"Yes, Captain," said *Bechimo*, still in that impersonal tone.

Theo sighed, and opened her eyes.

The Bedel

. . . .

THE SOUND BELLOWED ACROSS THE CAMP, ECHOING IN THE GAR-
den, rattling the steam pipes inside their confining metal belts,
intruding, even, into the din and thunder of Rafin's forge.

The *kompani* leapt to their feet as one, hearts pounding,
breath caught. Not one among them had ever heard that alarm,
yet all knew it for what it was.

Droi had been sitting beside her hearth, having just finished
her first cup of tea. Kezzi, who had been sharing her tent in
accordance with the *luthia*'s wisdom, had just gotten to her feet
and Malda with her. Kezzi was to go up into the City Above,
and the *gadje* school, while the dog stayed with Droi and Maysl,
Droi's child within.

She froze, looking down at Droi, dark eyes wide.

"The ship!" she said.

"No," Droi said, forcibly calm, and as if the distinction made
this event less significant, "only *news* of the ship."

She put the mug on the hearthstone, and struggled to get
her feet fairly under her. Her belly defeated this effort, as had
become its habit. Droi sighed and held up her hands.

"Help me rise," she said moderately, though it was hard for
her to ask for aid.

Kezzi obeyed with alacrity and, in addition, made certain
to stand so that a steadying shoulder was within reach should
Droi's feet become foolish.

On this rising, she was steady enough, though her blood
remained chilled by the klaxon's blare. It was quiet now, having
destroyed the *kompani*'s peace, and already there were those of

61

her brothers and sisters moving past her hearth on the way to the common fire.

To hear news of the ship.

"I'll be late for school," Kezzi said, keeping pace as Droi turned her face, as well, toward the gather-place.

School had become important to Kezzi, as had her brother in the City Above. It had come to Droi just lately, as she dozed and dreamed by her hearth communing with Maysl—it had come to her that the *kompani* had developed many ties with the *gadje* here, on this world. There was Kezzi and her brother; Silain the *luthia* with the Lady and the Professor; Udari, Memit, Syaera, and Isart with the madman at the end of the road; Rys and his Brother Undertree, not to mention his mad oath to the headwoman there...

Indeed, thought Droi, it had come to her a few nights ago that the common thread running through all these now-woven relationships—was Rys. Rys, who had himself been an outsider, until he had understood his true soul, and came before the fire, there to accept his nature, and the *kompani* to bind a new brother to them. Rys had also bound himself in brotherhood to Val Con yos'Phelium, headman of the People of the Tree; Kezzi's brother Syl Vor was of that folk, as were Lady Kareen and Professor Waitley.

The madman, farmer Yulie Shaper, might as well be undertree, as near as his holding stood, and it had been Rys's brother, the headman, who had brought news of the work to Memit, who had brought it to Silain the *luthia*, who had dreamed long upon it...

...and now there were four of the *kompani* at the far end of the Port Road, to help Yulie Shaper take in his crops.

"Droi?" Kezzi said again. "I'll be late for school. Syl Vor will worry if I don't send a message."

The brother, yes. Yes, he *would* worry, being, by everything Droi had heard, a tender boy who would, she made no doubt, grow into a man of heart.

"We must to the fire," Droi said. "Your brother's mother is a *luthia*, is she not?"

Kezzi nodded.

"So. She will advise him. This thing—is of the *kompani*..."

She shivered suddenly, black showing ragged at the edge of her vision.

"This," she said, feeling the burn in her blood, "will *alter the fate* of the *kompani*. We must all of us be present, to witness."

Her foot caught on an uneven stone, and she staggered. Kezzi thrust a shoulder beneath her questing hand and, so steadied, they went on, in silence.

After all, Droi thought, Kezzi was Silain the *luthia*'s 'prentice. She knew a foretelling when she heard one.

The common fire was lit, the Bedel grouped in a half circle facing it. A hand rose in the air, which was Luma, Maysl's hearth-mother, beckoning them.

They joined her, Kezzi and Luma helping Droi to the blanket before sitting, one to a side, and Malda curled on Kezzi's lap. They gave their attention to the fire, before which stood Alosha the headman, Silain the *luthia*, and Pulka, who listened along the byways of the stars.

The Bedel, so say the Bedel of themselves, speak with many voices, as heedless of their song as the birds. Yet it was not so, this day. Those assembled sat quiet, tension roiling above their silence.

Up before the gather-fire, Droi saw Silain the *luthia* make a small gesture, and the air lightened somewhat. She drew an easier breath, sighed it out, and put her hand on her belly.

Maysl, she said inside her head, *attend this well.*

She felt her daughter's attention sharpen, even as Alosha the headman took one step forward and raised his hands.

"All of you heard the klaxon," Alosha said. "We have received a message from the ship. Pulka will explain the nature of that message, and what is required of the *kompani*."

He stepped back to Silain's side; Pulka took one step forward.

He looked, Droi thought, tired and very nearly grim. Pulka was not, by nature, a happy man, nor was he a stern one. A placid man, who liked his comforts; who could, occasionally, be nagged into brilliance. Very little of life was sharp enough to cut Pulka. The ship's message, though, which he would have been the first to read, had burned a tiny scar on his heart. Looking with *luthia*'s eyes, Droi could see it, still hot and hurtful.

"Sisters and brothers," Pulka said, "we have this morning received a message from the ship. It is not a direct message, meant for this *kompani* alone, but an automated dispatch which has been wide-cast to several *kompanis* such as ours, which have missed their pickup date by a certain number of years."

He paused, in anticipation, Droi knew, of the flood of questions which would normally engulf him at this point.

There was silence; not one voice was raised, no single one of the *kompani* rose to their feet to speak.

Pulka cleared his throat, glancing at Alosha the headman, who gave him a grave nod, and turned again to face those waiting, silent, and finished what he had to say.

"The ship requires an answer. If we fail to answer, it will assume that we have not heard; that we are, in fact, Lost, and the logs will reflect this as our *kompani*'s fate. The ship will not query again."

Another pause, but the exclamations of horror, of outrage did not arise.

"A proper answer to the ship requires codes which I have Dreamed. When that answer is returned, the ship will flag it for the captain, who will review it, and who will eventually send pickup instructions and an estimated time of the ship's arrival."

At long last, one of the *kompani* raised herself to her feet: Jin, the *luthia*'s good right hand.

"How long," she asked, "will it be, after a message is sent, for the ship to arrive here for us?"

Pulka showed empty palms.

"That, we cannot know. Such information will doubtless be given us, when the captain responds to our ack."

"Thank you, Brother."

Jin sat down. Pulka waited for more questions.

Droi, sitting beside Kezzi and Luma, had many questions, though none that she would willingly shout out before all the *kompani*. She...the ship was so late, she had thought it would never come, that it had forgotten them. And yet, here was news: the ship had *not* forgotten; it remembered. And that—that altered *everything*.

From the far edge of the circle rose a tall, powerful figure—Rafin.

"Why did the ship not come," he asked, "at the appointed time?"

Again, Pulka showed empty hands.

"That, too, we will doubtless be told later. This automatic sending—it only seeks acknowledgment; it does not give reasons."

"We are certain, then, that this is from the ship. *Our* ship?" Rafin pursued, which was, Droi thought, a good question, and one which had not been among the dozen others clamoring inside her head.

"I have confirmed that it is from the ship. It is on the correct band; it utilizes the correct codes; it matches all the necessary protocols. If you want to do so, come to me and I will show you the message itself."

"I will do that, Brother," said Rafin, and sat down again.

Pulka looked 'round.

"If any others are interested, come to me and I will show you the protocols, the bands, the codes, the match-ups. I have, also, the original Dream from the communications technician who was set down with the *kompani*, if any wish to Dream it."

There was a small murmur 'round the circle at that, and here came another of the *kompani* to his feet. Apparently, thought Droi, her brothers and sisters were beginning to waken from their shock.

"How long," asked that brother, and Pulka blinked.

"I—" he began.

"No, I'll ask it proper," said the brother. "How long do we have to Dream on this? Before the ship needs its answer?"

And that, thought Droi, was the most interesting question at all. In story, in Dreams, every *kompani* is eager to be taken up again into the bosom of the ship. It would seem that her brothers and sisters had not embraced these stories with all of their hearts.

Alosha the headman stepped forward; Pulka dropped back one step, to stand next to the *luthia*.

"The ship needs its reply at once," said Alosha. "There are technical reasons for this that Pulka is also able to explain. But there is no call for a decision on this matter. The decision was made when this *kompani* was formed. We guaranteed to return to the ship with those things we had learned, and those things which we had found. That the ship is late makes no difference to our guarantee."

He paused and looked around the circle, his gaze seeming to rest on each one of them in turn.

"We have heard the ship," said Alosha the headman, "and we will answer the ship. We are here; we are ready for pickup."

Surebleak Port

Scout Headquarters

· ·

IN POINT OF FACT, THEY WERE LATE. AND NOT ONLY LATE, BUT over a day late, which revealed them for the sad wastrels they were.

Happily, the deadlines involved were entirely between the two of them, dictated by nothing more than their mutual desire to achieve licenses and be free to fly once more. That they had put off the accomplishing of this desire for an entire day spoke entirely to the worth of she with whom they had tarried. Daav wondered if Kamele would be flattered to know that she rated higher than a pilot's license with Aelliana.

"It might mean something to her now," said his lifemate, having heard his thought. "And you, of course, would have left on the hour, having accomplished a mannerly and by-the-Code morning visit with an old friend, and proceeded with important business."

"You know me too well," he answered, and smiled when she laughed.

In the way of things, they were seeking another old friend— older even than the mother of Daav's daughter, Theo, whose side they had just quit. He had been concerned, before the visit with Kamele, that she might find him too strange to her in his present state, or that she might slight Aelliana, whom she had never—overtly—met.

He ought to have known better—he who had been Kamele Waitley's *onagrata* for more than twenty Standards. But, no, he had been a fool, and it had fallen to Kamele to demonstrate his error.

This other old friend...he had sought another path to their licenses, as had the delm. Aelliana had acknowledged that their arrival might surprise Clonak, and even dismay him, but that he was a practical man, who had long been a Scout, thereby having long ago achieved an easy way with regulations. He might possibly refuse to assist them, but he would be unlikely to report them as unnatural, which was their biggest fear, until their records had been firmly established.

Daav sighed as they gained the entrance of the so-called Surebleak Scout Headquarters. Despite his new, youthful appearance, he was feeling old and behind change. He remembered, for instance, a time when the Scouts—the Liaden Scouts—had been a single organization. There had been differences of opinion naturally, but not an outright break, as now. Liaden Scouts. Surebleak Scouts. And the Surebleak Scouts open, so they said, to training *all who qualified*.

There had been other changes, too, since he'd left Surebleak at the Delm's Word, an old man, his lifemate a ghost tenanting what he must suppose to be the abundant empty parts of his brain. Not only had he returned as a young man, his lifemate walking at his side, but the port—Surebleak Port—had bestirred itself toward improvements.

Improvements meant construction, and construction meant detours; in the present case, an unanticipated and lengthy detour around construction of a recruitment center for the mercenaries, a temp agency, and a multiuse building, which had leapt into being between the old port and the civic mainstream.

The Surebleak Scouts were headquartered, for the moment, in a slightly renovated hangar in a part of the port that had long been abandoned for lack of need. The hangar was easily adaptable to Scout necessities, and by reason of its unfashionable location, they had their own yard and their own traffic manager. The slight distance from the heart of the port had likely been seen as a feature, Daav thought, but the emergence of the work zone had rendered the Scouts very nearly isolated.

Still, here they were, at last, through the doors and into the warmth. They paused for a moment just to appreciate that warmth, to put their hoods back, and pocket their gloves.

They approached the reception station, the Scout sitting there considering them with bright-eyed interest. It was the tradition that any Scout who was wounded or bored might sit reception. This one, with his bright, roving eye might have been of the latter class.

"Service, Pilots?" he asked.

"If you please," Aelliana said, stepping forward. "We seek a meeting with Commander ter'Meulen, if he should have time for us."

"ter'Meulen? I daresay you'll find him in the cafeteria, drinking tea and reading a novel. He'll want to hear names. I can make up a pair, if you'd like, but I think it might go less well than if you only gave me yours."

"Daaneka tey'Doshi and Kor Vid yos'Phelium," she answered serenely, those being the names they had chosen for themselves at the delm's direction. They stood ready to produce a homeworld every bit as rooted in fantasy, should it be required, but the receptionist was satisfied with the names. He tapped a series of keys on his board, waking a soft buzzing. When it interrupted itself, he spoke with such high good humor that Daav was certain he had roused Clonak in the middle of his sleep shift.

"Master Clonak? Two young pilots here to see you, sir. One Daaneka tey'Doshi, and one Kor Vid yos'Phelium. Are you—Sir? Yes, sir: yos'Phelium. Indeed, sir: Kor Vid. The small meeting room? I will, yes. Is there—"

He frowned, for which Daav hardly blamed him, the snap as the connection was cut had seemed rather too loud to *him* from his position across the desk.

"Master ter'Meulen will see you in the High Commander's own meeting room, Pilots. Have you been?"

The gleam in his eye betrayed him; clearly he wished to receive a negative, so he might try out some new riddle masquerading as directions.

"Never, I thank you," Daav said severely, which ought to have brought the scamp to a lowering sense of his own worth. He was a hardened lad, however, and only grinned the merrier.

Aelliana turned slightly and, spotting a Scout with a tool belt 'round her waist, stepped forward.

"Your pardon, Scout. My partner and I are to meet Master ter'Meulen in the Commander's small parlor, only we do not know the way. Could you advise us?"

The Scout paused and glanced over her shoulder to the reception desk, her gaze thoughtful. He on the desk did not, precisely, cringe, but it was clear he felt that a rebuke had been delivered.

The tool-belted Scout looked again to Aelliana.

"As it happens, the small parlor is on my way to debriefing. Please, Pilot, I would welcome your company—and your partner's, too."

The small parlor was locked when they arrived; Scout sig'Attaj was kind enough to unlock it for them and point out the teapot on the side table.

With that, she left them, and they stood at a loss for a moment, neither wanting tea, nor to sit down, and both brought sharply to mind of the difference between the *best* course and the *only* course.

The door snapped open and, yes, Daav thought, Clonak *had* been roused from his bed for this, damn the boy on the desk for a mischief-maker.

Besides the look of weary ire on his face, Clonak looked much the same as he had when Daav had last seen him, some months ago. They—

Clonak stopped between them and the closed door, hands on hips, looking from one face to the other, and back again.

His gaze finally settled on Aelliana.

"They didn't get you quite right, Goddess."

"No, he didn't, Clonak, and you never saw anyone so apologetic. But you know, there was nothing to work with, after all these years, even had he been forewarned. He did the best he was able, working from what records were available and such material as he had put by. The gene map is a comedy, so I'm told—I can scarcely be counted Liaden at all. But, you know, I can't be angry, when we imposed on him so dreadfully."

Mouth tight, Clonak turned his attention to Daav. "You agreed to this."

"In fact, I did not. I lay one breath from death at the time the decision was made. When I woke...I will tell you frankly, old friend, I had no heart to die again."

"You woke. You were well, you were strong, you were young—and he had given you Aelliana Caylon back, or near enough. What was that worth, Daav?"

"Oh!" said Aelliana and moved one step closer to Clonak.

Daav bit down hard on his impulse to grab her arm and pull her back. Clonak was his oldest friend. Clonak loved Aelliana. He would die rather than see her harmed. And yet...

"No further," said his oldest friend coldly, and with that look in his eye.

Aelliana stopped and folded her hands before her.

"You might at least be interested in knowing that I am not a doll created for Daav's amusement. In fact, it was the very circumstance of my being resident in Daav's mind for so very many years after my murder that imposed the necessity of improvisation upon our benefactor. He had been prepared to generously give one of his own—blanks, as they are called—in order to preserve Daav's life and his peace with Korval. Then, what should he discover but there were *two* requiring resurrection—and he did not stint us."

She moved her shoulders.

"I can see that you are out of sorts, Clonak. We would have told the boy on the desk not to disturb your rest, had we known. But, indeed, you must think! We have been to the delm, and we have not only our lives, but a place in the clan. Would Korval accept monsters?"

"Korval is thin," Clonak said, and Daav laughed.

"Not so thin as that."

Clonak's mouth twitched.

"Your point," he conceded, and raised a hand to smooth his mustache. "You want licenses, I suppose."

"We want testing," Daav said, "and proper licenses." He reached to his jacket and withdrew the packet that had been waiting for them on their wakening yesterday morning.

Clonak looked at it sourly. "Jeeves's work?"

"Yes."

"Put it away then; no question those papers will pass."

Daav tucked the packet back into its pocket and waited while Clonak took consultation of the floor.

"I'll put you both on sim," he said at last. "We can do that now, if you have time."

"We have time," said Aelliana.

Clonak nodded. "Sim, then. While you work, I will take a look about. You'll want Jump pilot tickets, at least. Master if we can manage it."

"Korval," Aelliana said, "insists that the tickets be accurate. If we test at third class, then that is how we will fly."

Clonak nodded again.

"Understood, and the sim will help us determine if we are looking in that direction. If so, we can test you live right here. If it comes about that you will go for first class though—arrangements will need to be made."

He sighed. "Come with me," he said, and paused in his turn toward the door, head tipped.

"Daav?"

"Yes."

"It pleases me, that you are not dead."

"Thank you, Clonak."

"Goddess?"

"Yes, Clonak."

"You gave me quite a fright, you know."

"Yes," she said softly. "I will try not to do so again."

The Consolidated School

. . . .

"ARE YOU ALL RIGHT?" SYL VOR ASKED, AS SHE SLIPPED ONTO the bench next to him at the long table. He had his lunch tray before him. Kezzi, uncharacteristically, had walked past the food lines, neglecting to fetch a tray entirely. Her stomach was, maybe, a little upset, and she was cold. Syl Vor would be warm: that was her thought, when she saw him across the room.

Which was . . . actually true. Syl Vor had a warm nature and a bright soul. That he would warm her was a fact of the universe, very simple, as all such facts tended to be. That she sought him particularly for this special warmth meant it wasn't just her hands that were cold, but her spirit, too.

"Why are you late?" Syl Vor asked, breaking his roll and putting half by her hand.

Had he been any of the others seated at the table with them—*gadje* all—she would not have answered that question . . . or she would have answered with a lie. Syl Vor was her brother, and a brother's part was the truth, but there were all those others seated near them, some with very sharp ears indeed.

"There was a meeting called," she said. "I needed to help my sister."

Those statements were both true, she congratulated herself, and neither one put Bedel truth in *gadje* ears.

Syl Vor frowned, sensing that she had not quite given him a brother's full portion of the truth, but he only pointed at the half roll she had crushed in her hand.

"Eat your bread," he said, and returned to the tray, cutting the meat in half.

"Anna is a little under the weather," he said to those nearby, using the local idiom which meant either that someone had a queasy stomach, had had too little sleep, or ached from a discipline delivered with too much enthusiasm. "Can someone give her a spoon or a fork?"

"Here, Anna," said Benet, from across the table and two seats down. She slid a spoon down the table toward Kezzi. "I picked up two by accident."

"Thank you," said Kezzi, which was easy and even... correct. Benet was no sister of hers, who would be insulted by the phrase; and she had, after all, been kind, and useful to Kezzi. *Gadje* supposed that those things *earned* them a thank you. It was not a position that Kezzi cared to debate.

"Here," said Syl Vor, cutting her half of the meat into pieces with his knife. He also pushed half of the stewed carrots toward her side of the plate.

Kezzi sighed. She was not an admirer of stewed carrots in general. But today, cold and just barely not shivering as she was, she made no protest.

"Anna?" he said.

"It is well," she said, bringing her spoon into play with the carrots. "Did I miss anything important in history class?"

"I'll repeat it for you, when we get home," he said, which she knew very well he could do, since he had a very good memory indeed. "Also, there's reading."

She sighed. Of course, there was reading. Mr. Beerdriki, the history teacher, was mad for reading.

She extended her spoon again, again for the carrots.

Around them, the *gadje* children grew loud again, so that she dared to lean close and murmur, in Bedel, for his ear alone.

"I will tell you, when we are home together."

Jelaza Kazone

. . . .

IT WAS THE SECOND MORNING AFTER REN ZEL HAD DONE BATTLE for the continued existence of the universe, died of it, and been resurrected.

Yesterday, Ren Zel, and also Anthora, his lifemate, who had taken—possibly—less severe wounds in the great invisible battle that had preserved all as it had been . . . those two children of the clan had been transported to the Healer Hall in the city, there to be examined and, insofar as it was possible, Healed.

Escorting the wounded to the hall had been two . . . newly youthened, not to say entirely problematical, members of the clan. After, they had intended to visit an old friend to restore Balance between them; thence to the port, where there were two ships awaiting their inspection. While at the port, they were to propose themselves for pilot testing at Scout Headquarters, a notion that was not quite entirely harebrained, while being at the same time the most nearly viable plan available.

Today, Val Con stood as Delm Korval, Miri having chosen to be Road Boss. He therefore entered the delm's office, after having seen the Boss and her 'hand off, his thoughts on the delm's business.

"Good morning, Jeeves," he said. "Is there anything I should know?"

"*Bechimo* reports himself in orbit and in the first stages of cleanup, *Spiral Dance* has landed in the back field, Lady Nova and Mike Golden have returned to her city house. Lady Nova bids you a good-day."

Val Con winced.

"That was Lady Nova herself?" he asked, moving over to the sideboard and pouring himself a cup of tea.

"So she stated. She did not wish there to be any confusion."

"She has achieved her goal. I am not confused in the least. Is there else?"

"The Pathfinders continue to study and to exercise. They put themselves at the service of the House, should there be any task that they might usefully take up.

"Daaneka tey'Doshi and Kor Vid yos'Phelium overnighted at Lady Kareen's city house. Pilot tey'Doshi called this morning to say that they were bound for the port and Scout Headquarters, where they hope to speak with Scout ter'Meulen."

That would be the scheme that had satisfied none of them, which had been put into play only because nothing more satisfying had arisen. Val Con sighed. Well, and who better for the thing than Clonak ter'Meulen, a veritable connoisseur of harebrained schemes?

"Also, today is my scheduled verbal quarterly report, which follows.

"My workshop and storage area in the sub-basement are currently safe to enter with your keycode. While we can quickly build or rebuild a Tocohl-style chassis if required, I am currently assembling and testing other household security devices in the area as suggested by recent interactions with *Bechimo*, as time allows. I will report noteworthy progress when there is some."

At last, a normal note on the day! Val Con actually sighed.

"Thank you," he said, moving to the desk.

There were no cats on the chair. Fondi was curled around and snoring in a basket meant to hold hardcopy. Val Con sat down, put his teacup on the desk well away from Fondi, and tapped the screen up.

Unsurprisingly, there was mail in the delm's inbox.

What *did* surprise was the letter from Lady yo'Lanna, directed to himself, personally.

He considered it for a moment, as it sat unopened, there in the queue.

To: Val Con yos'Phelium Clan Korval
From: Ilthiria yo'Lanna Clan Justus

He shivered slightly—apprehension, perhaps, as he recalled her ladyship's last correspondence with his sister Nova. It would seem that Lady yo'Lanna was suffering from the chiefest infirmity of advanced age: She had outlived her lifemate and nearly all of her contemporaries.

Worse, she who had been always at the center of society, privy to the ambitions and intrigues of each of the fifty High Houses, the most brilliant host of two generations, was now relegated to a chair at the edge of the dance floor, watching the children gracelessly cavort.

In that last letter, she had confessed to Nova that she might like to visit such a frontier world as Surebleak—she who had lived her entire life in the most privileged segment of the most privileged world in the known universe.

On the face of it, Lady yo'Lanna and Surebleak would not suit. She was a canny woman; surely she would know this, Val Con thought.

Wouldn't she?

He drew a breath, gathered his courage, and opened the letter.

Val Con, I offer greeting from one who was your grand-mother's truest friend and closest confidante, and a good friend to your father, your mother, and your maternal aunt.

I flatter myself that you and I have been friends, though I have not been able to know you as well as I have known previous generations of your Line.

Were Chi still with us, I would naturally appeal to her. Alas, she has gone ahead of me into the peace that has no ending, as have her son and his lady.

Necessity therefore places me in your hands.

I will be brief.

I have applied to my delm, who agrees to my reloca-tion, with my household, to Surebleak.

Justus has neither agents nor properties on Surebleak, a wretched condition that I shall improve once I am arrived. However, I must have a fitting residence available for my use when I do arrive, which will be in approximately two months, Standard.

It is here that I solicit your assistance.

If you will be so good as to locate an appropriate house

for us, I would consider myself in your debt. It need not be furnished; we will be bringing much of what will be required for our comfort and to host modest entertainments.

You will of course recall how we were fixed on Liad—a house slightly removed from the city, yet convenient to both city and port would be preferred. If there could be gardens, that would please me, but gardens are not of the first necessity.

My delm has advised me that he does not wish my household to be mixed with Korval's, as he wants no unpleasant surmises made by those fixed upon the home-world.

I will therefore require a suitable residence for myself, two children and their tutor; three adults of the Line; butler, cook, and understaff. One is informed of Surebleak custom, which requires that persons of melant'i *will be accompanied by security personnel. I have hired several competent persons to accompany us and to remain with us temporarily. It is in my mind that we will do better to hire locally, once we are fixed.*

We will expect to remove from the port directly to our residence, and will set ourselves to call upon the neighbor-hood, and host perhaps a small gather, within twelve days of our arrival.

You would lighten this duty considerably by providing a list of persons who it will be advantageous to know.

I may now turn my full attention to those matters which must be accomplished here on the homeworld before I depart. I do so with a great gladness in my heart, know-ing that my necessities for journey's end are in the most capable hands possible.

Pray convey my very great affection to your lifemate, and my promise to your heir that I will soon indulge myself by making my bow to her.

Until soon,
Ilthiria yo'Lanna Clan Justus

Val Con closed his eyes.

A house. In fact, a Liaden clanhouse, suitable for immediate residency by an elderly lady of fixed understanding...

No, he had made an error.

He scrolled up. Yes, here it was: *One is informed of Surebleak custom, which requires that persons of* melant'i *will be accompanied by security personnel . . .*

Lady yo'Lanna had been studying. She was both informed and flexible. Indeed, she knew Surebleak for a frontier world—had she not phrased it thus to Nova? That she might wish for a house the equal of Glavda Empri, where she had lived for most of her life, after she had lifemated young Lord yo'Lanna, who had been elevated to Justus Himself with unfortunate promptness . . . that was precisely a wish—not a demand. She had, he thought, traveled modestly to Liaden worlds, but there was variation, even among Liaden worlds.

She was also, he recalled suddenly, a great reader and a patron of Scouts. Indeed, she was known for hosting small *exploratory soirees* every *relumma* or so, where Scouts were invited to speak on the topic of worlds that they had visited, and what strange customs they had encountered.

He remembered hearing some complaint here and there regarding those gatherings—*Ilthiria's follies*, according to those who were properly world-bound and assured of Liaden superiority. Her follies had been tolerated because of the brilliance of her other, more convenable entertainments.

Yes! And she had learned Terran. When she came to tea with his foster-mother, which she had done regularly, she would insist that they speak Terran, so that she might perfect her command.

No. No, not a fixed understanding at all.

This notion of where the house ought to be situated—a little way out of the city, but not by any means so far out as the Road Boss was fixed . . .

He almost recalled something—something he had heard, only recently, at one of the gatherings of Bosses. He couldn't quite bring it to mind . . .

Well. It would come. In the meanwhile, he was reminded that he had a letter to write, as well.

He reached for his tea, found it tepid, and rose to warm it from the pot.

Sipping warm tea, he returned to the desk, sat down and called up a blank screen.

"Jeeves," he said conversationally.

"Yes, Master Val Con?"

"Pray prepare a pinbeam packet for Master Trader yos'Galan. He will want the field judgment, all current information on Tinsori Light and an introduction to Tocohl. I will include a letter to my brother Shan. Also, the delm will be sending instructions."

"Yes, sir," said Jeeves.

Val Con nodded, sighed slightly, and began to write.

Brother of my heart, I greet you with all joy...

Surebleak Port

Scout Headquarters

. . . .

SHIVERING WITH ADRENALINE AS SHE WAS, AELLIANA MADE A slow and careful business of walking down the long hall to the cafeteria where she had been directed to await Master Clonak's pleasure. It had been too long since she had sat a board, she thought, even a sim board. It had been . . . exhilarating, terrifying, absolutely correct, and horrifyingly wrong . . . and if she had not scored at least first class, her heart would surely break.

She considered that last thought as she entered the cafeteria and placed herself at the end of the modest queue.

No, she decided. Oddly enough, her heart would not be broken should she prove to be less than first class in this new body the Uncle had provided her. She was no Daav yos'Phelium, who had been born with wings, and flying its own reward.

It had taken a threat to her very life to induce her to embrace her pilot nature. Once she had done so, she had seen it as a tool to gain her freedom. It had taken others—pilots and comrades—to teach her the joy of flight. And once she had tasted the life of a courier, she had embraced her wings willingly.

Still, she had been a mathematician before she had been a pilot, and one does not simply stop being a mathematician because one has found a second vocation. She had written several scholarly papers while she had been discorporate. Now, she would be able to see them published, assuming Jeeves was able to produce a compelling narrative which made Daaneka tey'Doshi Aelliana Caylon's prime student, best suited to carry on her work.

The line moved, and she with it, automatically gathering a cup of tea and a muffin as she passed along.

At the finish, she stood for a moment, tray in hand, looking about her.

Daav was not in the cafeteria.

Well.

She carried her tray to an empty table, sipped her tea, and sighed, her thoughts returning to their previous round.

All of their plans had been built on the supposition that they would take up again as courier pilots. That plan died stillborn should only one of them test as first class, though it might be managed if the other tested second. There was also history in play. Despite the many years they had spent together, Daav had met her as a beginning pilot, and it had been his very great pleasure to introduce to her the joys of her new estate. Should she be found to be nothing more than a scholar...

"If you wish to eschew courier work for scholarship," he said, his voice sounding perfectly good-humored inside her head, "then we may make a plan that will see you pursuing your study. Recall that I have been a scholar these last twenty Standards as well. Courier pilot is a young person's game."

"We *are* young people," Aelliana said.

"I submit that we are *hybrid* people, but we may have that argument at our leisure. I am in the sim room with Clonak, reviewing the results of our testing. Would you care to join us?"

"Yes." She stood, pocketing the muffin and taking the cup in hand.

"I am coming."

"Clearly, you are both in need of more board time," Clonak said, moving aside so that she might see the screen from her perch on the arm of Daav's chair. "That, however, is easy to remedy—in fact, the scheme I have in mind for you to prove your tickets will provide ample opportunity for practice at live boards in real space."

Aelliana ran her eye down the screen, seeing a pattern of hesitation in her scores.

"I have forgotten much," she said.

"No, Goddess; you *remember* much. Merely, you are no longer at the level where you might choose correct action without thought. This can be remedied. Note that your times are well within tolerances. Jump is easily within your reach. You simply need practice.

"Here"—the screen now displayed Daav's scores—"here, you see such sluggard times as I am astonished to learn were produced by one of Korval, though they are entirely acceptable for mere mortals. Again, what we learn is that the pilot has lately been concerned with matters other than piloting, and must needs refresh his skills.

"Live boards, live flight, and the uncertainty of real-time will mend"—he leaned back in his chair and swept a hand up and out, as if freeing the scores into flight—"all of it."

"And you have a scheme for providing us with these benefits," Aelliana said, sipping her tea. "What is it?"

"Odd that you should ask. I propose to foist the pair of you off onto my good friend, Scout Strategist yo'Vremil, who is tasked with overseeing a rather delicate decommissioning. He professes himself delighted to have two such bright new pilots profit from the journey, while he hides in his quarters with his paperwork."

Aelliana considered him.

"Are we called upon to do anything other than pilot?"

"You will be pilots. yo'Vremil has agreed to having the recording module activated on his ship, so that your performances may be evaluated by your sponsoring master pilot—that would be me."

He paused. "There is, however," he said, looking to her and then to Daav, "*a catch*."

"There always is," Daav said resignedly. "What is it this time?"

"yo'Vremil leaves in two hours, Surebleak time."

"I see you mean this to be a test indeed," Daav said. "We will have just enough time to inspect our ship..."

"And to contact Korval with our plans," Aelliana added.

"Yes," Daav agreed. "That would be mannerly."

Clonak leaned toward the board and toggled a switch.

"Do I have an official agreement from Pilots tey'Doshi and yos'Phelium that they accept, as part of their certification process, sitting as pilots to Scout Strategist yo'Vremil, bearing him to his assigned destination in the manner set forth by him. As this is a test flight, there will be no remuneration for the pilots' labor; they will be fed and kept as crew. Scout yo'Vremil stands as their immediate supervisor, and may declare the testing done at any time."

"I, Daaneka tey'Doshi, agree to these terms," said Aelliana.

"I, Kor Vid yos'Phelium, agree to these terms," said Daav.

Clonak thumbed off the recorder and rose.

"Well, Pilots! Allow me to conduct you to your ship!"

Blair Road

Boss Nova's House

· · · · · · · · · · · · · · · · · · · ·

"BUT THAT'S *GOOD* NEWS," SYL VOR SAID BRIGHTLY, WHEN THEY were finally alone in his room at the top of Boss Nova's house. He paused and considered her, eyes narrowed.

"Isn't it?"

"Yes," Kezzi said miserably, and then, "No."

"Both?"

"Yes," Kezzi said.

They were sitting on the floor, on the soft rug next to Syl Vor's tall bed. Kezzi sat cross-legged and straight-backed, because she was the *luthia*'s apprentice and one day would be *luthia* in her own right, and a *luthia* did not curl into a ball upon the rug and wail.

At least not where she could be seen, even by a brother. Kezzi swallowed suddenly, as a Truth woke in her.

A *luthia* has no brothers, she thought, or sisters, too. All the *kompani* are the grandchildren of the *luthia*.

Syl Vor, who had been stretched on his side along the rug, his head propped in one hand, suddenly rolled to his feet and went over to the desk.

He returned in a bare moment, holding a pad of paper and his pen of three colors, and sat facing her, cross-legged.

"Here," he said, drawing a line down the middle of the sheet. He wrote "GOOD" at the top of the left space, and "BAD" at the top of the right.

Kezzi frowned. They had been learning about decision-making

84

models in Life Skills. This thing that Syl Vor offered was a variation of the pro/con method.

"What decision will I make?"

He frowned slightly.

"Mike Golden says that sometimes a problem isn't really a problem once you change the way you think about it. If you think about the problem as an opportunity, then that helps you to think of ways to use it, instead of having to fix or solve it. If we can look at what's bad about the ship coming, then maybe we can think about it differently, and make it into something good."

Kezzi frowned in her turn, thinking.

"Mike Golden should have been a headman," she said slowly, and did not say the other thing that her Sight had shown her: that Syl Vor, too, should one day lead.

"So!" said he, clicking his pen. "What is good about the ship coming?"

Kezzi took a breath.

"We no longer need to worry that it was lost, along with our brothers and sisters," she said.

Syl Vor wrote: "ship not lost" and "kin alive" under "GOOD."

"What else?"

Kezzi thought, and turned her hands palm up, fingers curled.

Syl Vor waited as long as it might take him to count, slowly, to twelve, and said. "Let us go to the other side. What is bad about the ship coming?"

"We will need to leave Surebleak," Kezzi said, the words spilling out. "I will—I will no longer be Silain's apprentice, but will be required to take tests. If I pass the tests, I will be admitted to a class. If I do well in the class, then I will be seated as one of many *luthia* who advise the captain and the crew of the ship.

"I will never see you again," she said, and then, despite all of her intentions elsewise, she cried out in real pain, tears starting...

"I won't be able to bring Malda with me!"

Jelaza Kazone

. . . .

MIRI WATCHED THE CAR OUT OF SIGHT BEFORE TURNING BACK toward the house. She'd argued for the delm's office today, and Val Con hadn't fielded anything more than token resistance. Which meant they'd been on the same page, and it really didn't matter if that was courtesy of the lifemate link, or just a case of great minds thinking alike.

What mattered was getting him another set and order of problems to chew on, so he could come back fresh to the mess that was Clan Korval's ongoing personal business. And, truth told, they had to open the Road Boss's office today—most especially with the survey team from TerraTrade on-port, asking questions, counting heads, reviewing systems, and in general making everybody irritable and nervous.

There was, Miri acknowledged, as she walked down the hall to the delm's office, some risk in having Val Con at the same port as the survey team, but after the little dust-up at the reception, she counted on Team Leader Kasveini to make sure it was herself who conducted the interview with the Road Boss.

And, if it turned out that the team leader wasn't sensible or wanted to push an issue, then she'd just have to depend on Val Con wanting Surebleak Port upgraded and certified more than he wanted to visit mayhem on idiots who questioned Korval's honor.

In the meantime, all they really had to do was to keep their heads down and not do anything outlandish that skewed more attention in their direction. How hard could that be?

She opened the door to the delm's office and went directly to the buffet to pour herself a cup of coffee. The scanner was on, which was Val Con's habit. The names and home ports of ships incoming, and the filed destinations of ships outgoing imparted actual meaningful information to him. To her, not having been raised to have a familiarity of ships and ports and politics, the scanner was at best an occasional amusement and at worst... just noise.

Still, she didn't detour on the way to the desk to turn the thing off. Today, the calm voices talking over the details of her homeworld's traffic were... comforting.

She pulled the chair out, checked to be sure a cat hadn't taken possession before her, and sat down, tapping the screen on.

There was mail in the delm's inbox. Not exactly a surprise.

She pulled up the first, which was from Ms. dea'Gauss acknowledging receipt of the delm's direction to discover funding for the clan's newly acquired space station. She assured them that the project was a priority, and that she expected to have preliminary figures within the week. In the meanwhile, she allowed that a schematic of the station, systems inventory, a list of needed upgrades in order of urgency, as well as a detailed report on the damaged portion of the ring would assist her greatly in her work. Also, if the station keepers would send their estimate of expected traffic and a ranked list of services and amenities required by said traffic, that, too, would be of assistance.

Miri sipped coffee while she wondered whether the keepers had any notion how much traffic they were likely to see, and what services the Free Ships she understood were expected to be Tinsori Light's main clientele would want most. Well, they had Tolly Jones to consult there... She shook her head.

"Gonna be a job of work," she commented to no one in particular. And that was *before* anybody figured out how Free Ships paid their bills.

"Jeeves."

"Yes, Miri?"

"I need to send a pinbeam to Chief Light Keeper Jen Sin yos'Phelium. Text as follows..."

• • • ❈ • • •

Val Con yos'Phelium was Road Boss for the day. The duty carried some peril, as he well knew, but he really felt that it was the outside of too much to be obliged to host the senior officer of the TerraTrade survey team a mere five minutes after he had opened his office.

Still, if he wished Surebleak Port to be upgraded—and he did most earnestly wish for that happy outcome—then it was prudent to display his manners to their best advantage and answer her questions, no matter how impertinent, calmly and completely.

So, then, they were addressing the question of what the Road Boss precisely *did* here on Surebleak.

"Because the idea of an open supply system from the port throughout the city and to the settlements beyond the city is a relatively new one, the Road Boss does, as you see, hold open office hours," he told Soreya Kasveini. "Our object is not only to answer questions regarding the rules of the road and to share information, but also to learn from the native population. We have had valuable input regarding the history of the main supply routes—of which the Port Road is merely the longest—how the costs of maintenance and patrol were apportioned before the colony was abandoned by the Gilmour Agency, and the local culture devolved.

"The Road Boss and others of the Council of Bosses are working in committee to identify the secondary routes, assess their value, and to produce a timeline for the establishment—I should say *re*establishment—of those routes, in cases where it is warranted."

"Then the Road Boss's office primarily benefits the city?" asked Soreya Kasveini.

"Supply flows in both directions," Val Con said patiently. "Goods move from the port to the city. Likewise, workers move from the city to the port. It is a symbiosis; the success of each depends upon the vitality of both."

"The file on this office which was provided by the portmaster indicates that there are protocols in place for ensuring that the Port Road remains open. One of those protocols involves armed enforcement. Does your office employ soldiers? Mercenaries, perhaps?"

Val Con took a careful breath, and produced a Terran smile for the benefit of the interviewer.

"Surebleak has been enjoying a period of population growth. Among those who have chosen to establish a base here are a number of active mercenary units. In addition, Surebleak has in its native population a significant number of retired military. This is to say that, should it become necessary to keep the Port Road open by force of arms, then the means to implement that protocol is close to hand."

He moved his shoulders and looked wry.

"Speaking as Road Boss, I do not think we will find any necessity to use such means to secure the road. We are fortunate, that those who live in the city largely see the Port Road as a benefit. There is some complaint with regard to the usage fees, but it is traditional, after all, to be aggrieved by the fees."

Team Leader Kasveini actually put forth a smile of her own.

"It is, isn't it?" she said, and sighed, looking up to meet his eyes.

"What is your estimation," she said, "of the possibility of an attempt to close the road from the port side?"

He lifted an eyebrow. "An invasion, do you mean?"

"Something along those lines. Clan Korval is not, I think, without enemies. It must have occurred to you that your presence endangers not only the port but this entire planet."

Anger flared, though she spoke nothing but the truth. Jeeves had done what he could, given the meager infrastructure that had been in place. Certainly, there was nothing like a planetary defense net in place around Surebleak... one might, without exercising undue optimism, say *yet*. They had plans, and a design, but that was *well* outside of TerraTrade's need to know.

He took another careful breath and met Soreya Kasveini's eyes as calmly as he was able.

"Clan Korval has never been without enemies. It had long been our practice to extend such protections as were available to us to the port and the planet on which we were based. That is, after all, both good business and good husbandry."

Her gaze remained firm and for a moment he thought she might ask further.

Self-preservation, or a simple realization that this line of questioning was... somewhat aside her mandate, brought a sigh to her lips, even as she glanced down and touched the button of her recorder.

"Thank you. I believe that those are all of my questions. If a need for clarity or expansion arises, I or another member of the team will stop by to speak with you again."

"I understand."

He stood when she did, and bowed.

"I appreciate your efforts," he said, "on behalf of Surebleak Port."

She returned the bow, but not the sentiment, which he supposed was fair enough. He touched the plate on his desk and the door to the anteroom opened to reveal the largeness that was Nelirikk.

"Team Leader Kasveini is leaving," Val Con told him. "Pray see her out."

Well, Val Con thought carefully, it wasn't as if the survey team leader had stated in so many words that Korval's mere presence on-world was being weighted as an ongoing and active threat to the welfare of the port.

On the other hand, it hadn't been necessary to be explicit.

His temper was badly frayed. A glance at the screen showed Nelirikk alone in the anteroom, the portside door decently closed, and no one waiting on the bench for a moment of the Road Boss's time.

Good. That was good.

He considered closing the office and going over to the Emerald for a cup of tea—or a glass of wine—but the thought of perhaps meeting Pat Rin there and being required to relate the details of his recent interview while he was thus unsteady...no.

Best simply to sit and collect himself. A cup of tea would not be amiss, and that he could provide for himself.

Closing his eyes, he worked through a mental exercise that imparted calm and clear thought. After the exercise was done, he sat for several more minutes, eyes closed, just...breathing.

Somewhat calmer, he rose and moved to the back of the little office, stepping 'round the partition into the private area. The door to the utilitarian facilities was at the far left; quick oven, tea-maker, and cold box, grouped as a small galley, center; and the back door, or as Miri had it, the bolt-hole, at the right.

He touched the kettle to turn it on, and opened the cabinet, considering the small store of teas. Tucked among the more invigorating blends was a small tin of Shamolei—an herbal blend well known to soothe raw nerves. Neither he nor Miri particularly cared for the sweet, green flavor; as he recalled it, they had brought the tin into the larder in case they should be required to calm a visitor to the office.

The kettle whistled; he dropped the sachet into the bottom of a local-made mug, and poured boiling water over it.

Returning to the office, he put the mug carefully on the desk, and—another glance at the screen showing the outer office yet empty of visitors—reached to the shelf and turned on the scanner.

He settled into his chair and, the business of the port a comforting background, closed his eyes and considered the song of Miri, which he heard, always, inside of his head, and which never failed of soothing him.

· · · ❀ · · ·

Miri leaned back in the chair and stretched.

She'd gotten the pinbeam off to Jen Sin, reviewed the agenda for the next meeting of the Council of Bosses, and read Commander Relgen's letter concerning the recruits proposed to her by Captain Robertson—that being Miri herself, in unlikely fact.

Commander Relgen was complimentary—a bad sign. The proposed recruits—Pathfinder Chernak and Pathfinder Stost—had shown well; their skills were unquestionably superior. They had been respectful to command and displayed a seemly modesty when questioned about their part in past actions.

But, Relgen continued, it was the very superiority of the recruits' skills that posed the most insurmountable difficulties.

A mercenary unit, as Captain Robertson of course knew, was a delicately balanced machine. A *unit*. While excellent skills were desirable in each soldier, what was more desirable was balance, coordination, and control. Recruits who were markedly superior to every other soldier in the unit would throw the machine off balance.

And so it was, with regret, that Commander Relgen declined the opportunity to sign Pathfinders Chernak and Stost to Relgen's Raiders. She wished them the best of luck with another unit.

Miri sighed, and closed her eyes.

She'd *hoped* that the merc would be the answer to the riddle that was Chernak and Stost. They *were* military, after all, and after everything they'd been through—including escaping the universe where they comprised the desperate rear guard in a flight from an overwhelming enemy—and landing in this very,

very different universe . . . and behind time, too . . . after all of that, military order could only be a comfort.

O'course, they weren't exactly—or only—soldiers. They were Pathfinders, the old military's version of Scouts.

So, it might be that Val Con's notion of having the happy tots looked over by the Surebleak Scouts had some real merit. In fact, there was a Scout recruiter coming to talk with them tomorrow. If their skills were so superior, maybe the recruiter would overlook their need for training in certain core subjects including—

"Space weather alert. This is a space weather alert from Surebleak Control."

Her ears perked up. As little as she cared about the names and destinations of ships, space weather amused her, although it was often nothing more than a report of sunspots or a sighting of some distant comet.

"Anomalous object approaching Surebleak major operations area—"

"Sleet and snow!" the scanner shouted. "Didja see that! It come right outta the sun, I'm tellin' you! No signature, no glare—"

"This is Surebleak Local. Corona-skimming object snuck through in-system scans, first approximation is a near-Surebleak skim. Keep to assigned orbits. If you are on approach, stay on course as long as your scans say you're good."

Miri spun to stare at the scanner. Object. *Meteor?* she thought. Came right out of the sun, was it? She felt a slight chill in the warm office.

"Jeeves, can you see that rock?"

"Yes, Miri. The approach route is . . . unconventional, but I believe that it is a *route*, not stellar detritus—"

"A ship," she interrupted, realizing that she had come to her feet.

"Yes," Jeeves said again. "I have a broad match with the Clutch vessel that transported Korval's holdings to Surebleak. However, the vessel incoming is . . . much smaller and . . . ah.

"I am coordinating with *Bechimo* now. They've backtracked it to an entry point. We have very good reason to believe that it is using the electron substitution drive. I have extrapolated its course . . . on a heading for . . ."

"Our back field?"

"No, Miri," Jeeves told her solemnly. "It is on course for our driveway."

She blinked.

"Odds of survival?"

"One hundred percent," Jeeves said promptly. "It is already slowing its descent. I estimate arrival in—"

"I retrieved an earlier communication on house frequencies from the approaching vessel," came a pleasant, unfamiliar voice. Comm Officer Joyita that must be, Miri thought, patching in on the shielded house line. She decided to be pissed about that later.

"Proceed, please, Mister Joyita," she said.

"Yes, ma'am. Pilot identifies herself as Emissary Twelve and states that she is on the business of the Elders. An immediate in-person meeting with the Delm of Korval is requested." There was a small pause.

"She apologizes for this unseemly haste, and pleads...necessity, ma'am."

"Thank you, Mister Joyita." Miri sighed, and turned toward the door.

"Jeeves, with me, please."

"Yes, Miri."

Keep our heads down, she thought. Sure.

"Readiness report," she said, walking quickly, but not running, toward the front door.

"The nursery has been sealed and shielded. House shields are engaged. I am recording and sending live to the office of the Road Boss."

"Does Mr. Joyita have permission to access in-house communications?"

"Miri, he does, retroactively, and also *Bechimo*. Among other things we have been discussing are comm security protocols, as Joyita was kind enough to point out an error in my configurations. This present event overtook us before I could effect a repair. We are using a relay from *Bechimo* now, so communications may bypass local repeaters."

"I see."

She felt a slight niggle at the back of her mind, and glimpsed the glitter of an intense and tightly woven pattern. Val Con had the feed now and was focused on it, all his training to the fore. He wasn't worried so far as she could tell, and that soothed her in a way Jeeves's assurances hadn't.

Still, she thought, coming to a branching of the hall; big rocks that were only small in comparison to out-of-reason enormous rocks, coming down 'way too close to a good subsection of the people she cared about most... Even the Clutch made mistakes—at least, she assumed so.

And, if the house shields were up, there wasn't one damn bit of good in her going to the door.

She turned right and followed the hall to the morning parlor, where there was a screen. For that matter, there was a screen in the delm's office, but she hadn't been thinking, had she?

It was then that she felt it, a warm pressure, as if Val Con had kissed her cheek.

Smiling, she stepped into the parlor.

"Show me, please," she said.

The screen came live, one half displaying the projected course, with deceleration rates, approach path, and approximate time of arrival on their doorstep.

The other half of the screen showed a distant view of the object itself, rocklike as it was. As she watched, a ghost overlaid and dwarfed the approaching vessel: the image of the ship that had brought Jelaza Kazone, house and Tree, all of yos'Galan's household goods, with room left over for a few atmosphere flyers to get tucked 'round the edges, to Surebleak.

"Courier ship," she said. Jeeves must've figured she was talking to herself, because he didn't answer.

She felt the sense of Val Con's interested attention intensify, and then fade, as if he was satisfied with both the ship and its proposed docking, and had stepped back into being Road Boss.

Frowning, she scrutinized the screens again. Seventeen and a half minutes, more or less, before Emissary Twelve was with them. Time for a cup of coffee.

Surebleak Port

Portmaster's Office

. . . .

PORTMASTER LIU HAD A HEADACHE.

In fact, she had *earned* her headache. Angry star captains, suddenly legal Complex Logics offering to do orbital cleanup as a way to redeem their good name, a not-quite hostile survey team bent on tripping her up, and now—the dubious pleasure of having a Clutch ship approach the planet in her care for the second time in her tenure as portmaster.

It had been... tense, when the Big Rock had come into Surebleak space for the purpose of off-loading the Road Boss's house and effects. It *had* been tense, despite she'd had plenty of warning, and a plan, and an approach that the Big Rock had scrupulously followed.

Still... the Big Rock had been—*big*. If something had gone wrong... but nothing had gone wrong, and it turned out that she had wasted a lot of perfectly good anxiety on that mission.

It had taken the arrival of the Little Rock coming in, so far as the instruments were concerned, straight from Galaxy Nowhere, blazing a trail across all lanes of traffic and by some fool's luck managing not to collide with anything or punch a hole in the planet, but settling down, light and sweet as you please, in the Road Boss's driveway.

It was a truth among the Guild that the Clutch were a law unto themselves. Clutch ships rarely put into Terran ports; that was the good news. Of those very, very few that did, some actually made an attempt to obey port direction. Witness the Big Rock.

The limitations of their drive made this a nontrivial exercise however, and most just followed their own inclinations and the port worked around them.

Still, it would've been . . . better if the Clutch had put off any visits to their ally, the Road Boss, until after the survey team had finished up their business and left planet.

In fact, it would've been . . . neighborly of the Road Boss to give Port Admin a tiny hint that such a visitation was about to occur.

That brought her up. Say what you would about the Road Boss and most of Conrad's people, in matters of port safety, they were stringent. If the Road Boss had known they had company coming, they'd've called. That would've been most like them. Still, it had to be checked.

She was reaching for the comm to put the question directly to the Road Boss, but it beeped first, interoffice, and Carla, on reception, was saying that Survey Team Leader Kasveini would like a word.

Of course she would. The survey team would need to know if Clutch traffic was a usual thing and, if so, what protocols the port was putting into place to deal with the disruption in normal traffic flow.

The survey team would probably also want to know why this particular Clutch ship wasn't landing at the port at all, but making straight for a landing at the Road Boss's house. Which they'd be *obliged* to see as suspicious, in keeping with their theme of Tree-and-Dragon was bad for Surebleak and the rest of the universe, too.

The portmaster ran her hand through her hair.

"Portmaster?" asked Carla, sounding worried.

Right.

Portmaster Liu sat up straight behind her desk, smoothed her hair, and settled her face in lines of calm authority.

"Thank you, Carla," she said calmly. "Please show Team Leader Kasveini in."

Surebleak Orbital Influence Zone

· ·

THEO WASN'T EXACTLY LAZING AT THE BOARD, BUT HER CON-centration *was* elsewhere when Clarence repeated his question, louder.

"Would the Captain, currently lazing at her boards, be inter-ested in turning her chair over to her second and visiting the mess for the duration of her break?"

The message having reached her, she raised a hand, fingers shaping *hold*, her head filled with the intricate dance of gravity, rock, flotsam, jetsam, and scrap. It was a complicated dance, and even with *Bechimo*'s assistance, demanded very nearly all of her attention—until, it began to fade, the bridge overlaying the gyrations of junk.

"Theo," *Bechimo* said quietly, "I've stored the data and am updating real-time. You can come back to it very easily later. At the moment, the crew needs your attention."

Bond-space and its fascinations faded away. She blinked at the well-lighted bridge, her returning sense of the here-and-now sorting sounds into words, her eyes catching movement, her nose—

"Maize buttons? You've got *maize buttons*?"

Clarence laid a small tray before her, keeping himself between an interested norbear and the treat.

"That'll be for you to tell me. These're just samples—I've got four different batches testing for time and technique. For some-thing that oughta be simple, there're enough secrets, tricks, and must-do preferences in the recipes to make my head spin. And since you're the expert, you'll have to let me know which ones the crew can be roused to duty to cull for you..."

Kara appeared then, smiling and nodding Terran-style, remains of some delicacy held daintily in an upraised hand.

"This is a duty I will suffer to do for you, O my Captain."

From her chair, Theo lightly bowed acknowledgment of one acting out of the interest of others, which brought an outright laugh. Theo hoped it wasn't because she'd done it badly. *Bechimo*'d been coaching her on her bows.

She took the tray from Clarence and rose, waving him to her chair.

"Sit, by all means! My expertise is required elsewhere."

The sorting of Kara and Clarence into stations had caught Hevelin's interest, so Theo and *Bechimo* had the galley to themselves.

There'd been a recent discussion among crew, regarding what favorite foods and treats they particularly missed. Kara had lamented the lack of a certain cheese tart; Win Ton a seed cake.

Theo had remembered her father's preferred snack, with a sigh as much for his absence as the tasty treat.

"*Bechimo*, what are you doing?"

Even as she took the first delightful bite of a lightly browned and slightly crunchy maize button, Theo was in bond-space again, feeling *Bechimo*'s watchful presence over her shoulder, as it were, before she was distracted again by the button—the slightly moist yellow interior, and butter—ah, butter! And the dainty texture of the properly ground meal, far more present and piquant than a simple powdered maize flour . . . and the butter smoothly at odds with the grittiness, textures to tease her tongue and please her mouth . . .

"I have watched the process of this baking," *Bechimo* said. "I am attempting to determine exactly how the . . . individual parts of the recipe trigger your enjoyment. I—I am not able to taste in exactly the way you do, but I can use my sensors to . . ."

His voice faded off, as if he was embarrassed.

"To what?" Theo asked.

More hesitation, which was even more intriguing than the maize button. *Bechimo* had mostly gotten past his . . . reticent phase; this return to uncertainty was . . . puzzling. Especially since maize buttons, in Theo's experience, weren't particularly frightening.

The pause grew longer.

She put the rest of the maize button into her mouth and sighed. Butter!

And, as if the act of eating the last half of the button had released him from some moment of intense observation, he spoke.

"Through our bond I have access to sensors—extra sensors, which are providing me with data that I am...not equipped to analyze. Taste is a complex sequence of events. Through you, I am experiencing a...unique delight. I would, with your permission, like to share this sequence with Joyita. As comm officer he may need to be able to discuss similar experiences with those with whom he comes into contact."

Theo chose a maize button from the tray in the far upper corner of the table and considered it for a moment. It felt... right...in her hand; it was the proper weight for its size, it had the proper density, and was properly toned from pale yellow to tan on its surface.

"So," she said carefully, "you're learning to taste?"

"And to anticipate taste, as you are doing now, which is a different level of enjoyment. The shading of flavor appears to be an act of art rather than science. I am attempting to analyze in what—!"

Space blazed around Theo; her mind naked to the stars, as distant Chuck-Honey, along with a thousand known moving objects within Surebleak System, cycled into acceleration curves. Shielding increased, the blaze dimming, threat assessments blending over each tracked object. There was a new brilliant energy as powerful as Jump glare, dulling even as they sought the new energy source, the blare of its energies dissipating, becoming a point, an object, a—

Rock.

Bechimo's automatic subsystems were already working with spectrum analysis, timing the actual entry real-space, understanding vectors, attentive to everything at once.

"What?" Theo managed, immersed in the whole of it, almost understanding, if she could only—

"Anomaly," *Bechimo* said, isolating the pertinent data into a single line that unrolled before her mind's eye, suddenly comprehensible. "That was not a Jump; it was energy displaced by drive function."

"Drive function!" she exclaimed, seeing it as the data continued to unroll. "This close to a planet, that's—"

"A Clutch-style approach," *Bechimo* said, and there was more data now, in a second line. "Without more information we cannot be certain that it is a Clutch vessel, but evidence strongly indicates that—"

An image of the thing flickered into Theo's consciousness, a subsystem showing it in multispectra display, too far away for active radar, but closing into that range fast.

It came to her then that it was *not* just a rock. If not a traditional hull, it had still been shaped, it was visibly elongated, and—energy flowed as the object's vectors changed.

Theo felt the flutter of systems working; focusing on one allowed the others to fade somewhat into the background. She blinked predictive tracking closer, finding no ambiguity there.

"It's headed directly for Surebleak," she muttered, to herself or to *Bechimo*; it was all the same. "This isn't an accidental entry."

"Agreed. There is no indication of hostile intent, no indication of Old Tech influence, no active scan emissions. Joyita..."

He paused, as if verifying something on the main board, and in that instant Theo saw it herself—comm lines open.

"Joyita is in communication with the incoming vessel, and with Jeeves," *Bechimo* said.

The crew, Theo thought, then. The crew was enjoying Clarence's latest culinary experiment, with no idea what was happening outside the galley, much less the ship.

"Comm," she said or thought, and it was hers.

"Object incoming," she said, her voice dragging across her ears almost too slow to hear, while the data flowed through her, bright and crisp.

"Joyita, live feed to main screens! All crew to bridge!"

Joyita was abruptly at the edge of bond-space, and the feed was enriched with information gained from his analyses, weaving seamlessly into the loop of what was known and extrapolated.

"Show me that entry," Theo demanded, "which sensors reacted first!"

The feed blurred; re-formed into a list of sensors in order of their reaction, by nanoseconds, found the trace of an event occurring, which next, when the sensor checked again against random noise and determined that *this* was a signal, then when the individual sensor triggered the array that notified a higher system to attend this happening, when the...

"Butter?" Theo asked in wonder.

The sudden taste of butter in her bond-space mouth fled.

"Calculating," *Bechimo* said, which he never did, and finally in an almost sheepish sharing *sotto voce*, "Yes, butter, Theo. You were sharing the sensation of butter overwhelming the tongue's first taste buds, and it became...connected to the event of the sensor report by happening simultaneously."

"That happens," Theo told him. "These...associations...happen. But I didn't think it would happen to you."

"I am," *Bechimo* reported austerely, "in contact with Jeeves. He has asked for our assistance in coordinating what is reported to be a visit to Delm Korval. Joyita is in contact with the pilot, confirms Clutch."

Theo blinked back to the feeds, located the projected course.

"That's close to the house."

"Yes. All projections agree: the Clutch ship will land in the driveway."

"Miri's going to like that."

"It will be very convenient for her," *Bechimo* said, and Theo laughed.

"The port has issued a space weather alert," he said. "Clarence has called all hands to stations. I believe this includes Captain Waitley."

"It probably does," she said, and sighed as bond-space melted away around her.

Win Ton, hair tousled with sleep, swung into the galley as Theo was rising from the table.

He grinned, snatched a handful of maize buttons, and bowed lightly.

"Captain, please. Precede me."

Jelaza Kazone

· · · · · · · · · · · · · · · ·

THE SCANNER WAS A CONSTANT, COMRADELY PRESENCE AS CHER-
nak and Stost pursued their studies in the Troop common room.
This morning, they had an additional comrade in Diglon Rifle,
who was also at study, which they understood to be a part of
his assigned duty for the house.

So, three soldiers at duty, the scanner a cheerful babble in
the background, naming ships, issuing lane changes, chastising
the laggards, assigning berths, and lift-out times...

"Sleet and snow!" the scanner shouted.

Three soldiers spun in their chairs. Stost went so far as to come
to his feet, head at an angle as the port issued its instructions.

"We need a screen!" he said. "If someone is throwing rocks
at the planet, we need to see!"

"Agreed," Diglon said, and raised his voice somewhat. "Jeeves,
we would profit from a feed in the common room."

The screen hanging on the wall over the scanner flickered
and, indeed, there was an image, a large rock, cutting across the
orderly lanes of Surebleak traffic as if it were navigating plain
space. An overlay appeared.

"The larger, that is the rock-ship which brought this house
and all its goods from the world of Liad to this location," Diglon
said. "There are similarities, but this one incoming is smaller.
More rapid, I think."

In the background, elsewhere in the house, Captain Robertson asked a question, and Jeeves answered, "On course for our
driveway."

"Divert it!" Chernak snapped.

"Descent is already slowing," Jeeves stated. "House shielding is up. I anticipate a soft landing."

Stost turned to look at Chernak. Chernak turned to look at Diglon.

"A soft landing," she repeated. "Rifle, you have some experience of these?"

"Only one other—the larger rock I spoke of. It came in soft and set the house down with precision. Mr. pel'Kana said it was so gently done, not a wine glass was broken."

"Who pilots such a craft—in such a manner?" demanded Stost.

"The Clutch," said Diglon, and paused, as if awaiting some moment of recognition.

Chernak showed open, empty hands. "We are not familiar."

"No? This, more than anything else you have said, convinces me that you hail from another universe," Diglon said, his eyes on the screen.

"You see? It slows again."

"It does," Stost agreed. "But these—Clutch. What manner of pilot? How are they allowed to land with such disregard of the lanes and order of approach?"

"A function of the drive," Diglon said. "You know that I am not a pilot, but there are papers written, some of which I have read. So far as I understand, the drive demands that the craft work close, using surrounding mass to navigate."

Stost reclaimed his abandoned chair.

"They are warlike, these Clutch?" asked Chernak. "You are surprised that fellow soldiers do not know them."

"I think...not warlike," said Diglon. "They prefer to give fair warning. Many, many years ago, they gave fair warning to the Troop: Cease what you are about in this area of space, or we, the Clutch, will lay waste to your ships and yourselves."

He paused, frowning somewhat. "The Clutch, they do not *appear* warlike. They are large, it is true, but impeded by their own bodies. They do not move rapidly. They seem, so my wife assures me, comical...not beings that soldiers, even such as I, might consider to be a threat."

"Nor did the soldiers who confronted the Clutch so many years ago?" Stost guessed. "They ignored the *fair warning*?"

"They did," Diglon said somberly. "And so the Clutch made good their threat. Two Conquest Corps were lost, and outlying ships. And, to this day, should a ship of the Troop find itself in the vicinity of a ship of the Clutch, it is the Troop who run away."

"And these . . . warriors are going to land in the driveway. Where will we run to, Friend Diglon?"

"We will stay where we are, unless the Captain calls us," Diglon said with dignity. "If we are wanted, we will go. We are soldiers of the house, under the Captain's command. *I* will shame neither."

"Well said," Stost said solemnly. "Have you an idea of how many might be in the rock incoming?"

Diglon frowned at the screen.

"It seems . . . very small," he said. "Maybe a Clutch, or two, new from the creche might comfortably fit in such a vessel. The Scout's Clutch-brother, Edger, whom I have seen and been made known to—he could not fit."

"Is he so large then?"

"Large, yes, but also, he cannot bend. When this one is down and away from the ship, you will understand why that is."

In the screen, the rock-ship had slowed again.

The three of them gave up any pretense of study, and watched the ship's progress, until it landed, very lightly indeed, on the drive at the front of the house.

"Will the Captain want us?" Chernak asked then.

Diglon shook his head.

"She has not called us. And look—she brings Jeeves."

In fact, the screen showed Captain Robertson approaching the vessel through eddies of steam, Jeeves beside her.

"We will watch," Stost said.

"Oh, yes," said Diglon. "We will watch."

· · · ❈ · · ·

It sat, steaming gently, on the driveway. Not much bigger, Miri thought, than the forty-eight-seat touring bus mothballed in the garage, darker than hull plate and vaguely cigar-shaped. There was no visible hatch, no visible instrumentation or lights. No obvious identification.

Just a rock, that was all.

It'd made a good landing, too, Miri noted; hadn't even dimpled the tarmac. She allowed that to be a point in the pilot's favor, but not enough to off-set her growing irritation.

She turned her head to address the man-high canister topped by a ball that was, at the moment, glowing palely orange.

"Jeeves, please ask Mr. Joyita to find out when our visitor intends to emerge. The delm of Korval awaits. Impatiently."

"Transmitting the delm's request," Jeeves said agreeably.

There was a brief pause.

"Joyita reports that the pilot thanks the delm of Korval for the gift of her time. She will emerge with all haste."

A crack appeared in the rock's pitted surface, and another. Soundlessly a hatch opened, and a figure, stooped, yet still taller than either Miri or Jeeves, emerged, moving awkwardly.

It achieved the surface of the drive and straightened, a young— no, Miri corrected herself—a *small* Clutch.

Among the Clutch the tell for age was shell size, not height. A youngster, like He Who Watches, would have a very small shell, nestled between the shoulders, like a daypack.

This person's shell covered them from shoulder to shoulder in the back, like proper armor, tapering down to where their waist might be, if they'd had one. Over the shoulders at the front, there was more armor, lighter in color and maybe, Miri thought, in weight.

Compared to Edger's bulk, this person was short, slim—almost streamlined. But they were, she was sure, an adult.

Suddenly, the person—"she" according to Joyita, from whatever store of knowledge he was working from—stretched as suddenly and as sinuously as a cat. Somewhere halfway through, the stretch morphed into a bow, full of grace and meaning.

Miri had seen Edger turn graceful like this, and was searching her memory for appropriate response, but their visitor spoke even as she finished her bow.

Hasty, thought Miri, and felt a distant agreement from her lifemate.

"I am called, for the purpose of this mission, Emissary Twelve."

The voice was light; nowhere near Edger's occasionally head-rattling boom.

"I am charged by the Elders to deliver a message directly to Delm Korval, on the matter of the short-term security and well-being of planet Surebleak."

She felt Val Con's presence rise, until it seemed like he was standing there on the drive next to her. Barely behind and scarcely less physical, the vast green intelligence of Korval's Tree swelled out of the depths of a self-imposed restorative slumber and into her awareness, curiosity roused, eager to be included in this new diversion.

That's all we need, she thought, and felt Val Con laugh.

Surebleak Orbital Influence Zone

· ·

THE CLUTCH SHIP WAS DOWN.

Bechimo had not given the port the first report of the anomaly, nor done anything more than confirm other reports on the sighting. They *did* share the information that the rock was piloted by Emissary Twelve, bound for an urgent meeting with the Delm of Korval. The setdown in the Road Boss's drive—that by itself would be gossip for a week; no sense adding to the river of chatter.

"Now that we're all at stations and awake," Theo said, offering Win Ton a wry grin, "let's take a couple minutes to go over the form and substance of this first report we're supposed to be submitting to Portmaster Liu in a few hours."

"Portmaster Liu," Clarence commented, "has had an unusually hard day, I'm thinking, even for the master of Surebleak Port."

"She has," Theo agreed, "which is why we should take some time to make sure our report is clean and professional."

"And perhaps soothing," Kara murmured, "to a pain in the head."

"Right," Theo said. "Kara, you were working on the libration point scans, we'll want to deal with them first in the body of the report since those are effectively Surebleak orbital situations. I know *Bechimo*'s given you a lot of current information there…"

Kara nodded, began to move toward her screen controls—

Theo fingered *not yet* in pilot-sign, and Kara settled again into her chair.

"Win Ton's writing the intro since he's got so much experience writing reports—" Theo continued.

107

The former Scout snorted. Theo ignored him.

"There's vocabulary. You and Win Ton will want to make sure we're using consistent terminology. The old reports he's using as background were made by a mix of first-in Terran contractors, then ongoing piloting reports for the seventy years or so of heavy traffic. What we use to pull these together will probably set the standard for long-term report formats."

"No doubt there," Clarence said agreeably.

"On Surebleak," Kara amended. "Perhaps."

"Surebleak could use some consistency," Theo said.

"Now, that's so, Kara," Win Ton said. "We serve the port."

"Very well. Joyita ought to also be in the vocabulary loop."

"Good idea. Joyita?"

"I am eager to assist," the comm officer assured her from his screen.

"Good. Now, Clarence has been reviewing the incident reports from the early days; he and *Bechimo* have compiled a grid of incident types by distance from the sun and orbital plane as well as the Jump run problems. They've discovered evidence of two unreported meteor streams so far. So Clarence will write a pilot-side on that and *Bechimo* will put together the technicals.

"*Bechimo* and I will be lead co-authors, since we were called on the portmaster's carpet and fined; that'll just keep it simple. If anybody else wants their name on the report as co-author, speak up."

No one spoke up. Kara went so far as to shake her head.

"I think simplicity serves us all best," she said and sighed, apparently struck by a thought.

"I do wish that we had time to do a rush test on one of the libration points so that we may be certain of the density of the dust..."

Theo signed *understood*.

"While we can visit the libration zones, it would be good to be able to get more hands-on at four and five, so that's for later.

"Joyita, please put together a common work area where we can grow this."

"Yes, Captain."

A flutter of fingers in peripheral vision. Theo spun her chair.

"Win Ton?"

"I wonder if we may properly invite TerraTrade to search

their archives for old trip reports and incidents—crew reports from outgoing Jumps often do not come back to the planet of origin, you know. It would be interesting and perhaps informative to all parties."

Theo eyed him.

"And it would let the TerraTrade survey team know that Surebleak Port is working to clean up its situation."

Win Ton opened his eyes too wide, feigning innocence. "Surely they could not object to such a laudable project?"

"Port Surebleak has lifted the space weather alert." Joyita waved a casual hand at a screen in his comm center. "All ships are advised to proceed in an orderly manner."

"Good advice wherever you find it," Clarence said, and spun his chair to face Theo.

"Now, lassie, tell me what you think o'them maize buttons."

Surebleak Port

Office of the Road Boss

. . . .

HAVING GOTTEN THEIR ATTENTION, EMISSARY TWELVE WAS NOT, Val Con noted, in any great hurry to follow up her opening statement. Being Clutch, she might not think the pause overlong. Miri, however, was of a different mind.

"The delm of Korval is before you," she said, not *very* impatiently, "and eager to receive the message from the Elders."

"It is known among us," Emissary Twelve replied in very nearly the same tone, "that the delm of Korval is two linked in partnership. I will await the arrival of the second partner, so that what I say will be fully known to both."

There was a very brief pause in which the crackle of Miri's temper was loud inside his head.

"I mean," Emissary Twelve added, perhaps out of a fine instinct for survival, "no disrespect."

He felt Miri swallow her anger, and leaned back in the Road Boss's chair, wondering how she was going to—

The portside door was opened with enough force that the bell jangled and clanged. Miri, Emissary Twelve, and the boulder in the driveway vanished. He blinked, fully back in the Road Boss's office, spinning the chair so that he could see the screen and Survey Team Leader Kasveini's arrival, her shoulders set at a belligerent angle, her face tight.

Nelirikk rose and stepped out from behind his desk, placing his considerable self between the angry woman and the inner door to the Road Boss's office.

"State your business," he said, not gently.

"I demand to speak to Val Con yos'Phelium," she said, her voice absolutely flat, "on the business of his clan."

Nelirikk hesitated, of half a mind, as Val Con saw from his stance, to throw her out onto the port. Or perhaps merely to call the Watch.

Neither of which was possible, given her *melant'i*, and Surebleak's necessity.

Val Con leaned forward and touched the switch set into the desktop.

"Nelirikk, please let Survey Team Leader Kasveini through to me," he said calmly, so very calmly. "Also, put the CLOSED FOR LUNCH sign up."

He offered her tea, which she refused, as well as a chair. She would remain standing, she said icily. Her questions were brief.

Taken on whole, Val Con thought, it was well that there was the desk between them. He rose, not so much as a bow to Balance, nor even because he didn't care to get a kink in his neck from staring up at her. Rather, he wished to be able to move quickly should she decide to leap at him over the desk.

For a woman who professed to have questions, and of a kind to infuriate, the team leader did not immediately speak.

In fact, she took a moment, now that she was in his presence, to breathe, deeply and carefully, visibly calming herself.

He approved of this and therefore said nothing, allowing her to gather what resources remained to her.

At last, she looked directly at him and said harshly, "*Am* I speaking to Korval Himself?"

He would rather have denied it. Direct petitions to Korval Himself had an unfortunate tendency to go sideways of expectations. However, she *had* asked and, while he might be able to deny the delm to a Liaden, who would grasp the subtleties, Team Leader Kasveini was Terran. She was sophisticated, in that she knew Korval Himself to be separate and distinct from the Road Boss, but that was surely all she knew, and this was not, so he judged, the best time for a lesson in Liaden social structures.

So, then.

"You are speaking to Korval Himself," he assured her, as if it were a perfect commonplace to declare himself so in Terran.

"As the leader of the survey team assigned to do a thorough and objective review of Surebleak Port for the purposes of determining a proper rating, I require information regarding Korval's plans."

He waited.

She drew in a noisy breath.

"I need to know how many Clutch landings Korval expects to receive on average across the next ten Standards, as well as the number of courier ships and smalltraders it expects to land at the clanhouse, rather than on the accredited port."

Well. Nova had brought *Spiral Dance* down last night into Korval's back field, from whence it had lifted, having been brought there as cargo by smalltrader *Bechimo*. Irregular, yes, but necessary.

"I also need to know if Clan Korval intends to build an auxiliary or private spaceport on its property at the end of the road, and, if so—have plans been filed with Surebleak Portmaster?"

That was merely sarcasm. Or possibly frustration.

The delm of Korval waited. When nothing more was forthcoming, he deigned to speak.

"Is this the sum of your inquiries?" he asked her, his voice icy, and, despite he spoke Terran, very nearly in the mode of the-delm-speaks.

"It is."

They *hardly* needed the delm for this, Val Con thought crankily, but he supposed Team Leader Kasveini would have reasoned that these were not questions that fell within the Road Boss's honor, and she did, indeed, have a certain need to know. Well, best to finish the play as they'd begun.

"Korval speaks," he told her, and paused. She looked momentarily wild-eyed, then produced a very credible bow in no particular mode, certainly not honor to the delm. The intent was plain, however, and the delm was able to overlook the violence done to protocol.

"In the matter of the Clutch, the Pilots Guild, TerraTrade, the Liaden Port Standards, and the Scouts all agree that they will do as they will and, as they rarely do harm, or even mischief, no penalties accrue to any port or property where they may arrive. As a representative of TerraTrade, you are surely aware of this." He paused in case she might wish to speak. Wisely, she made no answer.

"It is true that Korval contracted with the Clutch for transport of the clan's personal goods from Liad to Surebleak. The delivery and the manner of it was cleared with Surebleak Portmaster before the event, and it was performed within the parameters agreed to by all parties."

He inclined his head. "Today's visitation is as much a surprise to Korval as it is to Surebleak Portmaster, the Scouts, and the TerraTrade survey team. Attempts are being made, as we speak, to determine the reasons behind this abrupt arrival. Had Korval been aware that such a visit was imminent, we would of course have alerted the portmaster.

"As to any future visitations, perhaps the information gained from today's arriving Clutch will clarify this further. At the moment, Korval may say that they expect none, across the next ten, twenty, or more Standards."

He paused, then asked, as gently as the mode allowed. "Have you any further questions regarding the Clutch?"

Her anger had cooled under the chilliness of the Delm's Mode; her face was still stern, but her shoulders had softened. He thought that, indeed, she was beginning to realize what she had done, and what it might mean to her, personally.

"No, sir. I do not," she said quietly.

"Very well. We move to your second set of inquiry.

"The smalltrader which arrived at Korval's field was urged to land at port; the captain would have none of it and, as she is kin, and represented her case as desperate, she was given permission to land in Korval's back field, after the portmaster had been properly notified.

"The courier ship which landed also in Korval's back field, lifted from that location. Again, the portmaster was apprised of both lift and landing."

He paused and considered her gravely. She looked, he thought, a little pale. She might even benefit from a cup of tea. Sadly, Korval Himself did not offer cups of tea to upstart Terrans who demanded that he justify clan business to them.

"In the case of the smalltrader and the courier, had Korval's yards at Surebleak Port been up to spec, the factors that made back-field lift and landings necessary to the clan's purpose would not have existed.

"Clan Korval is working with the port to bring its yards to full capacity, a circumstance that will benefit both the clan and the port."

He paused once more.

"Surely, you were able to find the contacts between Korval and Surebleak Port in the portmaster's logbook."

Team Leader Kasveini was looking markedly unwell. Korval Himself naturally had no sympathy, though the Road Boss might have expressed concern.

"They were," she said, her voice admirably steady, "recorded in the portmaster's log, yes. It had seemed to me, in my capacity as team leader, that Surebleak Portmaster was too willing to allow irregularities when they involved Clan Korval. I sought to be certain that this was not the case."

Therefore, the delm judged coldly, these inquiries did fall within her honor. Though they might have been brought forward more gently.

He inclined his head.

"I ask, as Korval, if you are satisfied that there is no collusion between Korval and Surebleak Portmaster, and that Korval is held accountable for its transgressions against the port."

"I am, yes." She cleared her throat. "Portmaster Liu shared with us the parole she has given the ship *Bechimo* and its crew for littering the lanes."

He said nothing, and after a moment, she produced another well-intentioned, if somewhat shaky, bow.

"Thank you for your time and for your patience," she said. "I will leave you now."

She did so.

Korval Himself glanced at the screen, seeing that she was properly escorted to the portside door.

The Road Boss leaned forward and pressed the intercom button.

"Nelirikk, please lock the door," he said. "We are going to the Emerald."

· · · ✺ · · ·

Credit where it was due, Emissary Twelve knew how to create a moment, Miri thought. Unfortunately, her timing on the punch line needed work.

She counted to one hundred forty-four, twice, aware of Val Con's interested presence, and then spoke, patient as she could, which wasn't very. "The delm of Korval is before you and eager to receive the message from the Elders."

Large yellow eyes, slitted like a cat's, regarded her solemnly.

"It is known among us," Emissary Twelve said, sounding a little testy herself, "that the delm of Korval is two linked in partnership. I will await the arrival of the second partner, so that what I say will be fully known to both."

Miri's temper sparked. Both? When he was right here with her?

"I mean," Emissary Twelve added, "no disrespect."

Miri took a deep breath. Well, no, 'course she didn't. Val Con was at the port, fair enough, and only in her head because they were lifemated—not an advantage Emissary Twelve shared. Still, she supposed she could make a push to explain that he could hear what she heard, right now, in the interests of getting news of this oncoming disast—

There was a noise inside her head, and Val Con was—gone. Oh, she could still see his pattern and feel him—astonished, was it?—but he was no longer absolutely present in her head, looking out from her eyes, hearing exactly what she heard.

He had, in short, another problem.

Miri sighed.

"Very well," she said to Emissary Twelve, "the point is yours. It will be some few hours before the delm may complete themselves. I ask—will the well-being of the planet suffer by this delay?"

Emissary Twelve blinked her yellow eyes. "Not at all," she said composedly. "I had anticipated a time of waiting."

Miri nodded, and waved a hand toward the house. "Will you come inside and take your ease," she asked, "while waiting is?"

"If it is not a breach of courtesy," said Emissary Twelve, "I am charged with a message for the Elder Tree from he who is known to the delm of Korval as Edger."

That, thought Miri, actually solved a problem. Svelte as she was, there weren't so many rooms in Korval's clanhouse that would accommodate Emissary Twelve without rearranging the furniture.

"I will be happy to conduct you to the Tree," she said, which was actually true. "If you will walk with me, we can do that now."

· · · ❖ · · ·

Pat Rin will have to be told the whole of it, Val Con thought, as he and Nelirikk entered the Emerald Casino. Not only the survey team, but about Emissary Twelve's arrival and provocative assertion, Theo's bargain with the portmaster...

"Pray find your nuncheon," he said over his shoulder to Nelirikk. "I will be speaking with my cousin." He paused, and added, "I may well be some time. Please amuse yourself until I return."

"Scout." Nelirikk didn't quite salute, but he gave the impression of having done so, and moved off toward the kitchens where he was a general favorite among the staff.

Val Con continued toward the restaurant where he could see Herb, the daytime 'tender, behind the bar. He approached and put his boot on the rail.

"Afternoon, Boss!" Herb said cheerily. "What can I get for you this fine, warm day?"

It wasn't, to Val Con's sensibilities, a particularly warm day, though it was less cold than the day before, which he supposed could be made to support "warm" for a native Surebleakean.

"Is Boss Conrad's door open?"

"Alla time for you, ain't it?" said Herb easily. He nodded at the screen set on the work surface. "Says on the schedule, he's got no appointments."

"Thank you," Val Con said. "I'll show myself up."

Pat Rin rose, smiling, as Val Con crossed the threshold.

"Val Con! I was just wanting you! What..." He paused, smile contracting into a frown.

"I see," he said, and pointed. "Sit. You want a glass of wine. Have you eaten?"

"It's early to eat, surely?"

"Surely," his cousin answered from the wine table at the back of the room. He approached, a glass in each hand. He gave one to Val Con and put the other on his desk while he punched a button.

"Maynif, good-day to you. Please send a light nuncheon for two to my office. Thank you."

He settled into his chair and raised the glass in half salute. Val Con matched it. They drank.

"Now," said Pat Rin, putting his glass aside. "Tell me."

· · · ⁕ · · ·

They left Jeeves's chassis in the driveway with Emissary Twelve's runabout, which was nothing like leaving Jeeves behind, though

Emissary Twelve didn't necessarily know that. And even if she did, Miri thought, it wasn't like the Clutch was here to kidnap or kill her.

...It would be refreshing, though, to know exactly why she *was* here.

"The path is overgrown," she said, as they rounded the second bend where the plants had really taken over. "I will go ahead and open the way."

Emissary Twelve didn't answer; she seemed to be...humming.

Fine, then, thought Miri, and didn't bother talking anymore until the path ended and she led the way across the root-stitched grass to the base of Korval's enormous, meddling, sentient Tree.

Though the sky was cloudless, the Tree Court was what might be called comfortably dim, the air calm and slightly damp. A picture of peace and decorum.

That was because all the action was going on inside Miri's head, where the Tree was jumping up and down like Lizzie when she saw one of the cats in the garden outside the window.

"Behave yourself," she said, which only got her a private little breeze of her own, playfully tugging on her braid.

Brat.

She paused about six paces out from the Tree's mammoth trunk. Emissary Twelve joined her, and she made the introductions.

"Jelaza Kazone, here is Emissary Twelve, who bears a message for you from Edger. Emissary Twelve, Jelaza Kazone, Clan Korval's ancient ally and friend."

That was the formal thing to say on those rare occasions when somebody was introduced to the Tree. She'd once asked Val Con how they *knew*, and he'd admitted that they didn't, but that one must say *some*thing.

"And, after all," he'd added, "it hasn't tried to kill us—yet."

"No, it's still having too much fun," she'd answered.

"Exactly. I believe we are safe, so long as we remain amusing."

Right now, in the dim garden, Emissary Twelve accepted the formula and made one of her swift, sweeping bows.

"I am honored to stand before such age," she said, and looked to Miri. "If you would leave us? The message is of a...personal nature."

Miri blinked, torn between laughter and outrage. Thrown out of her own garden, was it?

Another breeze tugged her braid; the Tree offered an image of the apartment she shared with Val Con, and she reluctantly decided on the side of laughter.

Right, this was the *Tree* Court, wasn't it?

She gave Emissary Twelve a nod.

"I will leave the two of you together," she said. "When you wish to return to the house or to your ship, only speak. Jeeves will hear and guide you back."

"Thank you; your care warms my heart."

And that was a stock formal phrase right out of Liaden. She was dismissed, Miri thought, and there being nothing else to say, she turned and left the Tree Court.

· · · ⁘ · · ·

The telling was done, and the nuncheon, too. The two of them sat in thoughtful silence, nursing a second glass of wine.

It was Pat Rin who stirred first, putting his glass aside with a sigh.

"I believe that we must divide the most pressing tasks. Theo having negotiated her own fortune, it would seem that sorting out our honored emissary of the Clutch must fall to you and to Miri."

"She calls upon the delm in fullness," Val Con said with a sigh and a nod. "Duty is seldom more plain."

"Which leaves the survey team for me," Pat Rin continued, with a sour look. "One might almost be brought to believe that the survey team arrived with the intention of denying an upgraded rating to this port."

"Appearances are often difficult to unravel," Val Con said seriously, "most especially across cultures. They may only be maladroit."

"As you say," Pat Rin said politely and sighed. "It may be that this sudden Clutch is a trump to our hand. I had judged it best not to intrude myself into the survey, but if their quarrel is with Korval Entire, then I may, with the delm's permission, step closer to them while the Road Boss is granted leave in order to pursue the preservation of the planet."

"The delm's permission is in your pocket, Cousin. You have my condolences."

"Yes, well. What shall you do now?"

"I believe that I will go home and open negotiations with

Emissary Twelve. I will, I think, have Nelirikk at his post while the Road Boss is away, in order to take messages and also to call us, if there should be an emergency."

"A good plan. Please assure your lady of my continued good regard."

Val Con smiled.

"I will indeed, and you will please carry my admiration to Natesa."

"Admiration, is it?" Pat Rin said, with mock severity. "Mind how you go."

"That is, I believe, my cue," Val Con answered—and left him.

Jelaza Kazone

. . . .

"GREETINGS FROM THE ELDERS TO THE DELM OF KORVAL IN FULL-ness. I, Emissary Twelve, am empowered to speak with the voice of the Elders and to act in their behalf. We offer aid."

Val Con considered her.

"The delm is interested to learn what the Elders would aid us in accomplishing."

"Yes. The planet Surebleak, which the delm of Korval has chosen for the residence of the Elder Tree, as well as the many humans affiliated with the delm of Korval, is not stable, and will soon fail, catastrophically, if repairs are not taken up. It is in the matter of repairs to the planet that the Elders offer aid."

Miri felt a thrill of dread. The Clutch, though. The Clutch lived staggeringly long lives, like the Tree. They simply didn't look at time the way "short-lived" humans did, and "soon" depended on outlook. It wasn't likely that the world would come to an end next week. But in a century? Or two? That would be "soon" enough to get a young and mobile Clutch in a lather, never mind an impossibly ancient Elder. So...

"How ... soon," she asked carefully, "will the planet ... fail?"

"If no intervention is attempted, the Elders see that Surebleak will succumb to the insults done to its core in approximately twelve thousand Standard Years."

Miri bit her lip harder and didn't laugh.

"Ah," said Val Con seriously. "And if the Elders produce their aid in our behalf?"

"In that case, we see a gratifying extension of the planet's life to approximately one hundred twenty million Standard Years."

This time Val Con didn't laugh, loudly. Miri said nothing, since she still didn't trust her own voice. Emissary Twelve may have taken their silence for dismay.

"It is very possible that, with the Elders' aid and careful planning, the life and usefulness of the planet may be extended beyond one hundred twenty million Standards. Until repairs are under way and the extent of the trauma is known, we cannot predict with accuracy."

"Of course," Val Con murmured. "One wonders if the Elders will be coming to us themselves."

Emissary Twelve tipped her head.

"In one sense, yes, and in another, equal sense, no. The Elders travel far in their minds. Several lately journeyed in the manner of Elders to the planet Surebleak, the better to know this new arrangement that has been taken up by the delm of Korval, for the benefit of the Elder Tree.

"During this journey of exploration, they discovered faults in the planet's core which, left uncorrected, would bring the world to an early end. They brought this information back to the council entire, where it was decided to extend the assistance of the Elders to the delm of Korval on behalf of the Elder Tree."

She paused, then summed up: "The Elders will not be physically present on Surebleak, but they will be very much involved in the healing process."

"I understand," Val Con said, which as far as Miri could tell was the unpainted truth.

"As the voice of the Elders, empowered to speak and act on their behalf, I will require certain things," Emissary Twelve continued.

Miri closed her eyes.

"We are of course eager to assist the Elders and the representative of the Elders," Val Con said properly. "You will understand that the delm of Korval cannot promise all and everything, as our resources have contracted since our removal to Surebleak. However, we honor the Elders, and even more so our brother Edger, and will give what we may with a glad heart."

Emissary Twelve bowed very slightly.

"I require very little at present," she said. "Merely a comfortable cavern, where I might set up an office and communication center.

"Also, I will require local transportation. One might adapt

the vessel one arrived in, but it is in my mind that this might disconcert the local population as they go about their lives. The Elders do not wish to disrupt the delm of Korval, nor any of the people of Surebleak."

"Local transport can be provided. Also, Korval can house your vessel until such time as you require it."

"It would be a kindness," Emissary Twelve said, "if you may provide space in the grassy area beyond the Elder Tree."

Miri felt a flutter of resigned humor from Val Con, who inclined his head.

"We will be pleased to provide a suitable location for your ship in the back field," he said. "The matter of an appropriate cavern—I believe that we may provide something that will serve you well. However, we must negotiate with an ally, and it is come late while we sat and reasoned here together. May we offer you guesting this night in the house, or perhaps in the Tree Court? Tomorrow, the two of us will call upon our ally together."

"You are gracious. It is not yet my time to sleep. I will be pleased to sit in company with the Elder Tree during your hours of rest, and watch the stars at their dancing."

"That is well then," Val Con said and stood, Miri with him. They bowed, and Emissary Twelve did the same.

"Have you any other needs or desires that the House might fulfill?" Miri asked, which was only polite.

Emissary Twelve raised her three-fingered hands.

"I have all that I require. Please, seek your rest. I anticipate tomorrow's negotiation with your ally."

"You think Yulie's got a spare growing room?" Miri asked Val Con when they reached their apartment.

"He may, though there were plans to put everything into production. What I recall is that the location was thought to be promising for the establishment of the growing rooms because there was an extensive cave system already extant. The installation took advantage of that feature."

"So, there may actually be an empty cave?"

"Perhaps. Mr. Shaper will know—or there will be a section in one of his binders to guide us. Would you like a glass of wine?"

"You know, I would."

She curled into the corner of the couch and closed her eyes while he continued across the room to the compact kitchen.

"Jeeves?" she said, without opening her eyes.

"Yes, Miri."

"Would you please ask Mr. pel'Kana to bring up a tray of cold dinner?"

"Mr. pel'Kana has retired for the night," Jeeves said. "I will bring a tray, if that is acceptable."

"Thank you," she said. "Absolutely acceptable."

The couch moved. She opened her eyes as Val Con settled next to her. He offered her a glass of deep red wine.

"Thanks."

"You are very welcome." He raised his glass. "To saving the world."

Miri choked with the wine glass halfway to her lips. "It's good they take an interest."

"Indeed it is."

Miri sipped her wine, sighed, and leaned her head against the back of the couch. "How do you think Yulie's going to take Emissary Twelve?"

"Tomorrow will tell. Myself, I'm interested in what Emissary Twelve will make of Yulie."

He sipped. "And also, what Nathan will make of Emissary Twelve."

"Rys's brother, that is."

"Yes. An interesting man. Well, we shall—"

The door chime sounded. Val Con put his glass on the table before them, and rose to fetch their dinner.

Surebleak Port

Office of the Road Boss

. . . .

THERE WAS A LINE IN FRONT OF THE OFFICE DOOR WHEN MIRI and Nelirikk arrived.

Not much of a line, granted, but six 'bleakers in their mild winter day clothes, standing not in a clump or a crowd, but an actual and orderly queue.

Miri was stunned.

"These people are excited," Nelirikk said, in a rumble that was for her ears only.

"They are," agreed Miri, having seen the tells. "But I'm not seeing *over*excited, if you understand me."

"Captain, I do. As your aide, I will go forward to unlock and hold the door clear until you have entered."

That was common sense; Nelirikk was good at common sense.

"Sure," she said, and stopped, letting him get ahead of her.

"Make way," he said just loud enough to give somebody a bad start. In fact, the second person in line *did* jump, his hand going to his chest, as if his heart had missed a beat.

"The Road Boss comes," Nelirikk said, not any less loud, but they knew he was there now. "Make way."

They shuffled back away from the door and to the side, looking sheepish and shy, like any batch of new recruits who hadn't quite been in step with their formation.

Nelirikk applied himself to the lock, and Miri strolled forward, giving each of her customers an easy nod as she passed.

"Boss," they said, nodding back.

"'Mornin', Boss," said the one nearest the door, who didn't exactly look familiar.

"'Mornin'," she answered.

Nelirikk was holding the door open for her, so she stepped inside, giving him a nod, too, and passed through the entry room to her own office at the back. She closed the door, shucked off her coat, and hung it on the peg.

In the interoffice screen, Beautiful was admitting the streeters one by one, taking their names and what they wanted to talk to the Road Boss about...

...which it turned out was—Clutch Turtles.

All of them wanted to talk about Clutch Turtles.

Miri frowned.

They weren't ready to talk about Clutch Turtles yet. Pat Rin, and therefore the Council of Bosses, knew there was a Clutch Turtle on Surebleak. But they hadn't been told the nature of the imminent disaster—or even that there was an imminent disaster. At least from the viewpoint of the Clutch Elders.

The sixth petitioner gave her name as Mitsee Runion and stated that she wanted to speak to the Road Boss about Clutch Turtles.

Miri sighed—and made a Boss decision.

They weren't ready to talk about Clutch Turtles, but people—at least some people—were ready to worry about Clutch Turtles. The Council of Bosses had made it a part of their operating policies to tell the truth and, if all of the truth couldn't be told straight out, to tell as much of the truth as possible and say that more information would be forthcoming, as the Bosses studied the situation.

Miri nodded to herself.

She could work with that. Her hand moved to the switch.

"Nelirikk, please open the door between the offices and set chairs so everybody can see and hear. When we're set up here, please put yourself outside, in case any more people're coming in. Explain that the Road Boss is giving a group talk, and as soon as the first group is over, you'll be admitting the second."

He didn't like the notion of leaving her alone with six strangers, a significant portion of whom were armed just as part of being dressed. On the other hand, they couldn't have the place much more crowded than it was. Surprised people with worry on their minds might draw first and think later.

It wasn't as if she didn't have some minor ability to take care of herself, so... "Yes, Captain," said Nelirikk.

In the screen, she saw him turn to the group cluttering up his waiting room, and explain that the Road Boss would speak to all at once as, between them, they had one topic in hand.

"We will open the doors between the rooms and place chairs," he said.

"Right you are," said the guy who had given his name as Torje Gullard, and each of them turned to find a chair to pick up and move.

Nelirikk opened the door and came into her office, looking an inquiry.

"Set up in a double semicircle," she said, "with your desk in the center. I'll stand behind—crowd ain't big enough to have to stand on top—and give out the no-frills edition of what we know about Clutch Turtles to date. You take the portcomm with you, and keep an ear on me. You hear anything worrisome, come on back in, fast."

"Yes, Captain," Nelirikk said, picking up a chair in each hand. He waded into the crowd, growling orders about placement.

Miri closed her eyes, reviewed her facts, nodded, and went out into the waiting room.

"'Mornin'," she said, leaning against Nelirikk's desk. "Since you all have Clutch Turtles on your minds, I thought I'd save some o'everybody's time and talk about Clutch Turtles all together. Anybody here not good with that?"

She waited for the count of twenty-four; then, having gotten no objection, she nodded.

"So how I think this'll go best is that I'll tell you what I know, and then take specific questions. Understand, we don't know a lot yet. Clutch Turtles like to be thorough, and it takes some time to get to the central point. This one—Emissary Twelve she calls herself—is more on point than some other Clutch Turtles that I've known, so I'm hopeful we'll have a full and complete answer within a week."

She paused to consider the six hopeful faces before her.

"Now, what I just told you is that I've got previous experience of Clutch Turtles. You all know that before me and my partner landed here to help keep the road in order, that we roamed around a bit. Before even I met him, my partner'd fetched up against some

Clutch Turtles and, in the way of things, he'd become brothers with one of 'em. Some of you remember the Big Rock that brought the Road Boss's house down to the planet surface. That rock was on loan from that particular Clutch Turtle—Edger, his name is.

"Now, being as we're family, we do from time to time get family visits. We weren't expecting Emissary Twelve, but she's not *un*expected either, if you get my drift. She's got a message and a proposition. When we're sure we've got the whole story—and like I say, it could be a week or two coming—we'll turn it over to the Council of Bosses, and they'll put the news out on the street."

She paused, reviewed what she'd said, and nodded at the six rapt faces.

"Who has a question?"

Well, it turned out that there'd been questions, none of them having to do with alien invasions, which she was inclined to think her preemptive speech had put to bed. The remaining questions had to do with the likelihood of finding Emissary Twelve on the street and how to deal with her, if so.

"Be polite, bow. Answer whatever questions she might ask. She talks Terran—not streeter, unnerstand, so talk slow. You don't know the answer—say that. Clutch Turtles value truth, and they can smell a lie like you can smell a blizzard."

Miri looked 'round the room again. "More questions?"

There weren't any.

"All right then. If you think of something else, you come by again. The office is back to the reg'lar schedule now."

She paused, but nobody even asked why the office'd been closed, and she let that just slide away.

The comm on the desk buzzed. Miri leaned forward and touched the switch. "Yes?"

"Captain, there are eight people here, who wish to talk about Clutch Turtles." Nelirikk's voice was admirably clear. Her little crowd of half a dozen got themselves onto their feet and were buttoning their coats.

"Let your bunch know that there will be people exiting the front door," Miri told Nelirikk, "and to step back until the room's clear. When everybody from the last session is gone, the new folks can file in. We've only got the chairs we have, but if some can lean against the wall in the back, we can get this done."

"Yes, Captain," said Nelirikk.

She thumbed the switch off and straightened to see her first Clutch seminar packed up and ready to go.

"Thanks, Boss," more than one of them said as they filed out.

The door closed behind the last one, and Miri had time to take a deep breath and review a mental relaxation exercise before the door opened and the second class filed in.

Jelaza Kazone

. . . .

"I FORESEE THAT THE TECHNICAL TEAM WILL REQUIRE INSULAT-
ing robes as they go about their work on the planet surface,"
Emissary Twelve said, as she and Val Con crossed the brittle
field toward Yulie Shaper's land.

Val Con threw her a quick glance. "Are you cold? Please do
not stand upon pride. Cold kills on Surebleak."

"I am somewhat chilly, but not, I judge, in a dangerous situation. I am able to regulate my own body temperature somewhat."

"Pray keep me informed of your physical state," Val Con
insisted. "And, please, when we return, allow the House to provide you with a cold-resistant garment."

"You are gracious, which is nothing less than he whom you
know as Edger had said to me. Tell me now, this ally, Yulie
Shaper, has he experience with Clutch?"

"Mr. Shaper has lived his life on Surebleak. He devotes himself
to growing food and tending plants. He is very knowledgeable in
his field, but he has been known to be timid. I cannot predict
how he might react to yourself. Allow me to precede you, to
lessen the impact of any dismay he might feel."

"Of course."

They walked on in a not-quite-companionable silence. As he
had not yet been persuaded to accept a comm unit in his house, the
only way to gain Yulie Shaper's attention was to walk over to his
house. This approach held its own dangers, as he had, in the past,
had a tendency to view anyone arriving on his land as a threat to
the cats and, as such, likely to be shot at. This immediate escalation
to armed warfare had been decreasing due, so Val Con feared, to

the influence of the small Tree given to him by Jelaza Kazone, and also very possibly to the influence of his recent Bedel assistants. Four had come away from the *kompani* to assist him in the harvest, and had stayed after, beguiled by the promises enclosed within the three-ring binders, which told of the intended use and capacities of the facilities, in addition to outlining maintenance schedules, optimum crop rotations, and plans for expansion.

It was heady stuff, and Val Con understood its attraction for the Bedel. He had feared, at first, that the four helpers had been part of a scheme to relieve Yulie of his farm, but here he had been proven a poor judge of character.

Far from robbing Yulie of his birthright, the Bedel who had come to assist him *wanted* to assist him. He was treated as a brother, for his own sake, as Val Con understood it, as well as for the sake of Rys, who had survived the Department of the Interior only to fall among the Bedel and become a son of the *kompani*—and for the sake of Rys's *gadje* brother, who had been surprisingly accepted as such.

Yes, the Bedel were a good influence on Yulie Shaper, Val Con thought, as he and Emissary Twelve reached the crack that was the shared boundary of their land. In fact, he allowed himself some optimism, that Rys's brother Udari—Nathan, by another name— would soon prevail upon the farmer to accept a comm unit.

In the meanwhile . . .

Across the healing crack in the land, something moved among the dark shadows of the trees. Val Con froze, and moved his arm out, fingers signing *stop*, before he realized that Emissary Twelve probably did not read pilot's hand-talk.

The shadow moved easily out from among its fellow shadows, and became . . . Yulie Shaper, wearing a good warm jacket, and a peaked cap.

"There y'are, Boss," he said cordially, as he approached. "Was wonderin' if I'd got it wrong."

"Not at all," Val Con answered. "I hope we haven't kept you waiting long."

"Not in the scheme o'things. Woke up with the notion in my head you was bringing a young lady over to see me, and I should go meet you at the boundary. Got up and grabbed a cup o'coffee, thinking it was the tail of a dream, but it had a hard hold on me, so I come on out to see was you here—and here you are."

He grinned. "Ever hear anything like it?"

"From time to time," Val Con said. "In fact, I have had similar wakings. One must blame the Tree and its love of meddling."

"Well, I don't mind that, s'long as it's useful," said Yulie, and looked over Val Con's shoulder.

"This the young lady?"

"Exactly so."

He motioned Emissary Twelve to step forward, which she did do, until she was at his side. She stopped then, and stood calmly, three-fingered hands in plain sight, and her yellow eyes with their vertical slits opened wide and guileless.

"Emissary Twelve, I give you our good neighbor and ally, Yulie Shaper. Mr. Shaper, here is Emissary Twelve, who will be setting up a field office in advance of the arrival of repair technicians."

"Sounds busy," said Yulie, with great good nature. "Come on across, the two of you. Too cold to be standing out in the wind, when we can talk inside. Miss Emissary don't hurt cats, right?"

"I had not had much experience of cats until last night," Emissary Twelve said composedly, following Val Con across the boundary line. "I sat the night watch, and two came to share the duty."

"That's cats," said Yulie wisely. "Always eager to share the work. You'll do fine, just be gentle with 'em. If it looks like they're upset or unhappy with you, you freeze and give them a couple cat smiles—like this"—he squinted his eyes together deliberately—"and they'll know you mean to be friends."

"I am obliged," said Emissary Twelve. "I will do my utmost to be gentle with the cats."

"That's good then. Right down this way."

"Now, that's better," Yulie Shaper said, as they all three sat around a small table in a far corner of the kitchen, each with a mug of hot...beverage before them. If the room was not as warm as Val Con preferred, it was certainly warmer than outside, and the lack of breeze was a boon.

"Thank you," he said. "It is very much better."

Yulie grinned at him. "You'll get used to the cold, Boss. Give it a couple winters."

"It may be," Val Con said, foregoing any mention of the project to gradually increase Surebleak's temperatures to something more temperate year round.

Yulie took a drink of his beverage.

"So, you need an office, Miss Emissary?"

"Yulie Shaper, I do. I need a very specific sort of office. When I mentioned this requirement to our mutual ally, the delm of Korval, he immediately thought that you might assist me."

"I'd be happy to help, but what I got here's a working farm. Surebleak being what it is, and the need for food being what it is, most of the growing's done underground in environmental units. That way, we can guarantee our crops. Which—Surebleak being what it is—is important. Office space—well, you see what I got here—" He waved an arm, showing them the kitchen table obscured by binders and stacks of paper.

"Yes. I would not intrude upon your work, Yulie Shaper. I have unique necessities. My people—on our homeworld, we live, some of us, on the planet surface. Others of us do not. But all of us have access to the deep places—caverns, tunnels and the like—where we may renew ourselves, and sleep safe."

Yulie paused with his mug nearly to his mouth.

"Caverns, is it! Well, then, the Boss here brought you to the right place! I got deep places—told you about underground rooms, right? So happens I got a—well, call it a spare room. What it is, see—it was the first room built. It was the field office an' staging area for the rest of the construction. Wasn't ever really used for anything after construction was done. Me an' Nathan'd been talking about what it could do for us best, but the trouble for us is it's backwards to the rest of the rooms. There's a skinny little connector hall, but nobody used it. Truth is, it wasn't really needed. Be pleased to see you use it, if you think it'll do you."

"We will," Val Con murmured, because Yulie Shaper tended to forget his own advantage in discussions like this one. "We will pay you a reasonable rent should the space prove adequate to Emissary Twelve's needs."

Yulie looked at him, somewhat owlish, and it came to Val Con how *much* he was altered from the timid, inarticulate, and nearly savage person he had first met. The small Tree that had been granted to Yulie Shaper was meddling at a rate that was truly astounding. One wondered what it might portend, besides an inclination toward tidiness...

"Well, Boss, if you gotta, I guess you will, but what I'm thinking is, if the young lady is coordinating repairs and like that—" He turned to Emissary Twelve.

"What sorts o'repairs were those, Miss? 'Cause if you come to need local help, we got a crew on-world I'm told can fix anything." He held up a hand. "Ain't saying that's factually true, but I got four of 'em working for me, and I'll say they can fix *a lot*."

"I thank you, Yulie Shaper, for your offer. It may be that I will require the assistance of the local population. I must perform a detailed survey and analysis. The case is..." She put a three-fingered hand flat on the table next to her mug of beverage. "The case is that the planet has undergone trauma. There is a flaw in the structure of your world, Yulie Shaper. If it is not repaired, the world will die."

"Well, that ain't good," Yulie said solemnly. "Ain't zackly a surprise, though, the way the Agency did bidness. They was mining, but according to what my grampa heard 'bout it, they wasn't using best practice so much as they was using what would get 'em the fastest profit. Wouldn't much cared, if they'd known, which I ain't saying they did or didn't, if they cracked the planet—they'd bought an' paid for it. If they wanted to break it, too, that was their lookout."

There was a sharp silence. Val Con thought he heard Emissary Twelve gasp.

"This... Agency seems to have been remarkably shortsighted, even for—your pardon. Such a policy seems very shortsighted."

"Not the best company in bidness, but there—they left us here, an' 'bandoned their claim, so it's ours to tend now, like you said."

He looked to Val Con.

"I reckon I can let her use a room I ain't using anyways, so she can get it set up to save the world."

Val Con inclined his head.

"B'fore you make any decision, though, you'll be wantin' to see the place."

Yulie Shaper stood with rare energy, and looked down at them, grinning.

"Show it to you right now, you got the time—b'fore things get busy here."

"Yes," said Emissary Twelve, rising in her turn. "That would be most useful, Yulie Shaper. Thank you."

It was an unexpectedly large space, in need of cleaning and perhaps some furniture. The temperature was cool, but not nearly so cold as the outside air. At the touch of a switch, light glowed gently from panels on the walls and ceiling.

"Door to that inside hallway I was telling you about, that's right here," said Yulie Shaper, crossing the room and touching a blue switch on the opposite wall. A door slid silently away into a pocket, and lights came up in a thin corridor beyond. There was the sound of distant voices echoing off the walls.

"Just leave this shut and you won't be bothered by any of our noise," Yulie said, sealing the door again.

He turned to Emissary Twelve. "Whatcha think?"

"I think this will do well for me, Yulie Shaper."

She walked to the far wall and placed her hand, palm flat against the ceramic. Drawing a breath, she sang, two inquisitive notes in the midrange that made the walls shiver around them.

For the first time that morning, Yulie Shaper looked spooked; eyes wide.

Val Con slid two steps nearer to him.

"It is a measuring protocol," he said softly, which it was, among other things. "There are species on other worlds that are essentially blind. They navigate by casting their voice ahead of themselves and following the echoes. This is a similar tool."

"Right."

Emissary Twelve turned from the wall.

"There is another small, pocket cavern behind this wall. If it becomes necessary, may I install an access door?"

"You talk to me before you do that," Yulie said, surprisingly firm. "I'll be needing to take tolerances and load and best practice equations, so we don't disrupt the working rooms. Can't have that."

"I understand. If I find it necessary to have access to the room behind, I will contact you so that you may do proper analysis."

"That's all right then. You'll be moving in?"

"Yes."

"The House is able to clean the space for you and to provide furniture from stores, if that will assist you," Val Con said.

"Yes," she said again. "I will come with you to stores, if I may. We must solve the problem of the insulated garments."

"You can come and go as you want," Yulie said. "Let's just get your palm print for the door..."

✳   ✳   ✳

It had taken some persuasion to convince the door to accept the palm of Emissary Twelve, but the thing was finally done, and the three of them entered Yulie Shaper's kitchen again, worn but victorious—

—to find Nathan, Rys's brother Udari, standing at the kitchen table, his hands flat on the pile of binders and his head bent.

"What's wrong?" Yulie Shaper asked sharply.

Nathan raised his head, showing a swarthy face gone pale, and tears glittering in his eyes. He glanced at Yulie, nodded, and turned his eyes to Val Con.

"The ship," he said huskily. "It is coming."

Surebleak Port

Office of the Road Boss

. . . .

"ANYBODY ELSE?" MIRI ASKED, HER VOICE A TRIFLE RASPY.

"Captain, no. We have come to an end."

"Good. Put the OUT TO LUNCH sign up on the door, and let's—"

The scanner, running at low volume on Nelirikk's desk, *screamed.*

"This is the portmaster. Lock down! All port personnel, get inside, and lock down! Flash mob in the port! Port Security has been alerted. Get inside, lock down, wait for the all-clear!

"Message repeats..."

Nelirikk was already at the door, the sound of the locks snapping into place punctuating the portmaster's announcement. Under the racket, Miri heard a chime and spun, dodging chairs to get into her office, and hit the comm.

"Robertson," she snapped.

"McFarland," came an answering snap. "You in and locked?"

"And I've got an Yxtrang between me and a 'splosion-proof door. Val Con's at the house. We're fine. What's going on?"

"Riots," he said shortly. "Funny kind o'riots, you want my opinion. All over the city, and on the port, too, which is funny enough, given there ain't been any hints we was cookin' unrest on the street. But the really funny thing—you being a native 'bleaker, you'll 'preciate this."

"What?"

"They all started at the same time, just like somebody rang the start-shift bell."

Miri blinked at Cheever McFarland's big square face in the comm. "Pull the other one," she said.

He grinned. "Knew you'd like it. Stay put 'til the all-clear."

"Got that. Cheever!"

"Yeah?"

"Can you get me a feed?"

"Patching through now. Stay safe, Boss."

"You, too."

The screen blanked, then bloomed with action: a sidewalk crowded—too crowded—with people pushing, shoving, punching; here and there a Watch uniform among the heaving mass of 'bleaker motley.

There was sound, too: voices shouting, screaming, and crying; glass breaking; horns honking; the pop of a pellet pistol so sharp and clear that Miri involuntarily ducked to the left of the screen, her hand dropping to—

The scene changed. The general theme was the same—too many bodies tangled together, the clear sounds of mischief being done—but on a different street. The first had been Blair Road; Miri thought, Pat Rin's territory. This was Hamilton—Penn Kalhoon's territory, and if there was anything Penn Kalhoon didn't allow on his streets, it was mayhem.

The scene switched again—Vine's street this time, same song and dance. Vine didn't mind a little excitement now and then, but he'd been leading the way in cleaning up his streets, mostly because his territory abutted the port and he stood to profit from presenting a clean, safe Surebleak experience to anybody who ventured outside the gates.

The scene changed again—different street, more of the same—and it was Andy Mack's garage, right here in the port that she was looking at, and a flicker of what might've been live flame, before the scene changed and it was the Portmaster's Office, and a crowd yelling so loud you couldn't hear the words... and there came Port Security, sticks out and peacemakers on stun...

"They are not soldiers," Nelirikk commented from behind her.

"No, just streeters," Miri said, frowning.

"Why do they...riot now?" Nelirikk asked.

Miri sighed.

"That's a good question. Let's hope the Watch gets hold of somebody who has the answer."

Jelaza Kazone

. . . .

"WILL YOU GO TO STORES AT ONCE?" VAL CON ASKED EMISSARY Twelve, as they crossed the brown lawns to the main drive.

"I think," she replied slowly, with a certain note of surprise in her voice, "that I will visit the Elder Tree. That seems...necessary. For an hour."

Ah, indeed?

Val Con sought the Tree's presence, and found it, lurking with some amusement.

Do not, he thought at it sternly, *break the guest.*

Laughter greeted this, and the impression of having his cheek kissed roguishly. He sighed.

"Certainly, if the Tree requires you, there is nothing I may say," he said, aware again of the Tree's laughter. "Ask Mr. pel'Kana, the butler, to find me for you, when you are returned and ready to explore stores."

"You are generous with your time. I am in your debt."

"Not at all," he said politely.

He received Emissary Twelve's bow with an inclination of the head, and watched her walk away toward the garden before he entered the house.

Mr. pel'Kana met him at the door, rather pale of countenance.

"Sir," he said breathlessly. "There is, perhaps, an—emergency."

Val Con paused. Mr. pel'Kana was not prone to overstatement.

"Very well. May one know the nature of the emergency?"

"It is...Jeeves, sir. He is—he is on the drive, and I believe—I believe you ought to attend him. Sir."

"I will do so at once," Val Con said, which did not seem to

138

soothe the butler noticeably. "Please, take a few minutes to calm yourself. I've found that Mrs. ana'Tak's raisin cakes have great restorative powers."

That sally produced a half-smile.

"They do, indeed, sir. They do, indeed."

Had he continued with Emissary Twelve down the driveway, he would have seen Jeeves at once, poised as it were, very near the Clutch vessel. His attitude was...unusual. If one might say that a man-high metal cylinder with a glowing ball situated at the apex was standing too still, then Jeeves was standing too still—preternaturally still.

There was also the matter of the headball itself, which most usually glowed orange, occasionally blue, or pale red. At the present it was a dull and grubby white, barely aglow at all.

Val Con took a breath. He had seen something like this, many years ago. The low energy display indicated that all nonessential functions had been assigned to a particularly large task.

That Jeeves stood here, now, in this state, was—unsettling.

Jeeves was house security: he controlled the gate, the shielding, and life support. As Val Con was well aware, there were backup systems, even unto tertiary backup systems, woven into Jelaza Kazone. Even if—unthinkable!—Jeeves should become incapacitated, the house would be protected.

However, one would, naturally, very much like to *know* if Jeeves were incapacitated.

Val Con approached the too-still cylinder with its grubby headball.

"Jeeves," he said quietly.

Silence. There was a single dull flicker...and Jeeves spoke.

"Working," he said in a flat, mechanical voice.

"Working," Val Con repeated, walking forward. "Working on what, I wonder?"

Jeeves's headball flared orange.

"Master Val Con, please return to the house. The shields are going up."

Val Con blinked—and bowed.

"I will be in the delm's office and will receive your report when it is ready."

*   *   *

The amber light was lit.

Val Con paused. The amber light was the dedicated channel for the Bosses of Surebleak, and it was seldom used. The Bosses of Surebleak preferred to meet face-to-face every ten days local, as a demonstration that peaceful meetings could not only be maintained, but produced useful results.

Between meetings, the preferred method of communication between Bosses was comm call and, rarely, letter.

For the channel to be put into use...something must be wrong, Val Con thought, and recalled Jeeves, standing on the drive...

Shields are going up.

Val Con sat down and touched the channel button.

Violence exploded onto the screen—rioting, he saw, not military action; the few uniforms were Watch jackets, and it was notable that the crowd melted away from those jackets, rather than attacked.

The scene changed, showing him in quick succession Hamilton Street, Blair Road, Joppa...

...and the port.

There was a noisy crowd at the portmaster's door, armed with rocks, which were ineffective against the blastcrete walls. Port Security was moving in there, and the one face Val Con saw clearly before the feed moved on was decidedly not amused.

The Emerald was next—there were flashbangs in play there—and just down the street, the office of the Road Boss, and a particular optimist throwing himself against the door.

Val Con drew a breath, his hand moving toward the comm just as it chimed.

"Miri," he said, as the inner office unfolded before his mind's eye. "There is a man trying to break into the front door."

"Wish him luck with that," she said calmly. "We're locked in all right an' tight. McFarland says to stay put, which don't seem a bad notion."

"Not a bad notion at all," Val Con said, blinking away the office at the port in favor of the feed on his screen.

"There are several blocks in the city engaged," he said, "though it seems as if the Watch is making its will known."

"Good," Miri said. "Funny thing about all those different parties—Cheever thought so anyway, and so did I. They all started at the same time—like somebody hit the start-shift bell, he said."

Val Con frowned. "One would have supposed we would have heard of something so... uncharacteristically organized."

"You would, wouldn't you?" She took a breath. "So, we got a pro organizing."

"It may be so. There are, after all, pros on-planet."

"That's so. But you gotta ask, *why now?*"

"Yes," Val Con said softly. "That is the question. Answer it, and we will know which pro, and the ultimate goal. If it is local, then the Bosses have more work to do."

"And if it's the DOI..."

"This seems rather... small for an operation planned by the Department," he murmured, eyes on the feed.

Definitely, the various actions were breaking up. The Watch was mopping up. Port Security, with the assistance of Scouts on duocycles, were clearing the crowds.

"The entrance to the Emerald has been cleared," he murmured, "and also the door to the Road Boss's office. Those who targeted Andy Mack's garage are inclined, it seems, to hold—no. A duocycle has made a compelling argument, and there is nowhere to run. Hands are extended for binders."

"Hope some of those people know something useful," Miri said.

"In—" He drew in a sharp breath at the new screen.

"What's wrong?"

"Shan's building site has been bombed," he said. "I—"

He had seen devastation among the equipment and stockpiled supplies, nothing that seemed to be a body—

Opening a subscreen, he slapped up the schedule and breathed a sigh of relief.

"There was no one scheduled on site today," he told Miri. "We have something more—Melina..."

Melina was Boss Sherton, who held the territory behind their own land—and even as his fingers moved over the keyboard, seeking more information, he remembered that it was Melina who had control of a property that might solve Lady yo'Lanna—

"Melina's been bombed?" Miri asked worriedly.

"No, your pardon. Some abandoned mining and farming rigs spontaneously woke and are moving toward the village."

"*Were* moving toward the village." Jeeves's voice came from the ceiling, sounding a little thin still. "Master Val Con, I regret that my concentration on that solving caused you concern. I am quite well and in no danger; merely, I had reallocated my resources in order to halt the machines before they reached the village. This has been done."

"How?" Val Con asked, feeling Miri's concentration sharpen.

"A simple matter of finding and transmitting the correct command codes. Unfortunately, in this case, simple did not mean easy. There were many sets of command codes for the particular machines that had waked. I needed to establish the exact machine identification, locate the proper command codes and, ah, *insist* that I was a key-holder empowered to transmit those codes."

"What influenced them to wake, I wonder?" Val Con murmured.

"I am investigating that now and will report when I have information."

"Thank you. Are you aware that Shan's property has been attacked?"

"Yes. I am reviewing the feed and querying the port for ID."

"Thank you," Val Con said again. "And the shielding?"

"I believe that I may drop full shielding, though I will remain on alert."

"Thank you, Jeeves," Miri said. "How's Emissary Twelve?"

"She and the Tree are in rapport. Emissary Twelve has her hands against the Tree's trunk in the classic stance. I believe that she may—yes, I see on the grass the remains of a seed pod she has been given to eat."

Miri groaned. Val Con laughed.

"It's funny?" she asked him.

"Possibly."

"Okay, then. How about I'll come home, so we can figure out just how funny it is."

"McFarland told you to stay where you are."

"Well, he did, but all I'm seeing on the feeds is cleanup, like you said. And, yanno, there's something streeters say sometimes that's pertinent here."

"And that is?"

"Cheever McFarland ain't the boss of me."

Val Con laughed.

"A useful phrase. I shall remember it. May I ask that you and Nelirikk undertake not to get killed on your way home?"

"We'll be careful," she told him, and said, gently, in Liaden, "Until soon, Val Con–husband."

"Until soon, *cha'trez*."

The comm light went out.

He glanced at the screen; the feed showed calm streets with Watch uniforms here and there. People were boarding up broken windows, sweeping up glass, righting overturned carts, and testing kicked-in doors for hinge damage.

There was some residual smoke on Blair Road, and a cluster of volunteer firefighters taking care of it. That seemed the worst problem still ongoing.

The riots had stopped as they had begun, at very nearly the same moment.

And, thinking of that...

"Jeeves, how many territories were involved in today's action?"

"Five confirmed small riots in the territories of Boss Conrad, Boss Kalhoon, Boss Vine, Boss Threadle, and Boss Wentworth. Targets at the port were the Portmaster's Office, Emerald Casino, the office of the Road Boss, Andy Mack's garage, Tantara Floor Coverings.

"It remains uncertain if the action against the village under Melina Sherton's protection was part of that larger action."

"The machines—what roused them?"

"A remote command; much the same as that which put them back to sleep," Jeeves said. "I had hoped to discover an operator signature in the logs, but whoever transmitted the codes left nothing behind."

So, Miri had not been wrong, Val Con thought. They were dealing with a pro.

He shivered.

Surebleak Orbital Influence Zone

Northern L5 Limits

. . . .

"THE STINK OF SPACE," SOME CALLED IT, AND IN THIS SYSTEM IT was more of a stink than in others, according to Win Ton, who had handled the recovery of the first two derelict spacecraft and had far more prior experience than Kara.

To her, the odor was of hot metal and ozone, surprisingly sweet. The scent permeated the deck as Kara opened the face-plate of the light-duty suit, pleased to see that the venerable ion propulsion units on this relay unit weren't dust-crusted or pitted. The failure that had put it out of service was elsewhere—perhaps something as simple as a suspend-service order from a frugal, departing, mission control agent.

For all that it was potentially functional, the thing was, to Kara's eyes, ugly. The columnar-framed bus was similar to one of the other units they'd brought in, the brain stage wrapped in a very basic honeycomb micrometeor shield while the modular propulsion systems were wrapped in foil, pulse magnets hanging— or protruding, anyway. In space, they wouldn't look so odd, but here the craft was cradled so she could get at it without hazard.

"Model? Serial Number? Builder?" asked Joyita, which was the data required for each craft they took on board, with identifica-tion and the condition of each.

Though they had not yet received the portmaster's acceptance of their written proposal, Theo said that they should proceed as if it *had* been accepted, which was only reasonable in Kara's opinion.

Kara climbed around the cradle, nose, and sensor units, seeking signs of chemical leakage while her eye, trained by ghosting after Win Ton's exploration of the other units, was quick.

"The bus says it is a Remco-Carresens Mark II, Margate Zone Works. This is engraved on a plate, with a number: four zeroes leading and... perhaps it is one-kay-zero-one-seven. Do you think that Margate Zone Works truly built a thousand of these units?"

Joyita stifled a laugh.

"The engineer does not approve of the equipment?"

"Not entirely..."

"Regarding your question," Joyita said. "The unit we found at Libration Point Four was one-kay-zero-zero-six, behind four zeros. I think, if there were thousands of them, these are not proof! I suspect that the Gilmour Agency bought buses and used them to drop in whatever they needed."

"This bus is more than adequate for its purpose," Kara said. "A good shop might well have turned these out between larger jobs. I am made unhappy with the tie-ons and mixed equipment—such as we have here—which have not been duplicated in any of the other units. It is as if each one was cobbled together from the spares bin! Clearly, the parts were not expected to serve long, but the bus will outlive its tie-ons, as it is quality-built."

"I'm relieved you consider the bus adequate," Joyita said, with a half-smile. "You'll find Margate Zone Works plates in several locations on this ship, which was plainly built for the ages."

"My point," Kara said, picking up the hand-scanner. "Margate Works undertook smaller projects when there was nothing larger to hand, but they did not stint on quality."

Joyita suddenly frowned down at one of the screens on his desk.

"Do a quick sweep," he said. "*Bechimo* has located a dense ball of dust, which is giving off—peculiar signals. Theo is taking us in close, to investigate. All hands are called to the bridge."

Kara settled into her station, watching the screens. The dust-ball *was* odd; the signals it was emitting even odder. *Bechimo*'s approach was, of course, cautious. Theo was first board, utterly concentrated on her screens and, so Kara feared, also on an internal dialogue with her ship.

"How do you find our newest capture?" Win Ton asked from third screen. It was not idle curiosity, nor boredom which prompted the question, Kara thought. Win Ton had trained her, and he therefore held a teacher's interest in her work.

Kara turned her chair slightly to face him.

"The newest is much the same as the first," she said, "a sturdy and well-made bus burdened with makeshift monitors."

She sighed.

"I believe that what we are discovering is that each of the libration points was...*somewhat* properly monitored at the beginning of the Gilmour Agency's residency on Surebleak. At first, they simply launched what was required from Surebleak orbit since—as the records indicate—they were doing a significant amount of prep work. Later, they used company ships to pop things off near where they were wanted and allowed the survey work to stand as status quo."

Win Ton moved his hand, inviting her to go on.

"Yes, well, here we have the rest of the repeating story. The monitors were left hanging in orbit, abandoned, though they might have been retrieved and repurposed. However, the Gilmour Agency, from the records provided by the port, seems to have cared little for economy.

"Today's capture is dirty, of course, but like the others, it can certainly be cleaned. I wish for more hands aboard, if you will have it, so that we might refurbish the buses. Surebleak can surely find a use for them."

She shook her head.

"There it is: if we are to survey properly, we cannot undertake rebuilds, and if we begin to rebuild, we may inadvertently stint the survey."

"Now, that is a very Scout-like conundrum," Win Ton said. "We must, of course, do the survey properly. Meantime, there is perfectly good equipment that requires only the most modest attention and care to make it functional again—but that work, too, must be done properly. Also—gods forfend!—there is paperwork."

Kara stared at him, then slapped her hand on the chair arm as his meaning took root. "Salvage claims! How *could* I forget?"

"Indeed. Tell me, though, what ought these devices monitor once we have rebuilt them to better than spec?"

Perhaps he meant to trip her up but, in fact, Kara had given a good deal of thought to just that question.

"We will build in self-pairing and pair-crossing, then we will reseed the libration points, using the monitors in tandem for synced stereo searches along multiple wave lengths. Also, we might—"

"There!" Theo's voice was sharp with excitement.

Kara spun back to her station. The dustball was displayed on three screens now, two of them showing multiple overlays of chemical notation, colors, temperatures—spectra overlays on top of density.

"Timonium in that for sure!" Clarence said, like he'd just been given a Name Day gift.

Kara frowned, misliking the way the dust rippled around its indistinct core.

"The center—" she began, but the sensors were already adjusting, seeking out that extra-dense core.

"We will maneuver around the object," *Bechimo* stated. "We will remain outside of the cloud fringe. Shielding on low."

The dust cloud grew larger on the screens—known metals and a strange isotopic agglomeration of ice, dust, grit, chunks of rock. The core grew more distinct, as the sensors relentlessly sought it out, revealing—

Yet another probe. By Kara's estimation, this one was larger than those they had previously captured, the rolling shadows giving her to guess that it consisted perhaps of four of the Mark II Remco-Carresens, each with an ion drive packed on the near-invisible outer edge cloaked beneath the debris.

Four?

Kara brought up her work screen, fingers flying over the pad, accessing the records they had from port and the records from the Gilmour Agency—incomplete, as the Scout librarian in Sure-bleak City had admitted, but becoming more complete every day.

"Is there a record of a probe going missing in this zone?" she asked the bridge at large. "That—I think we are seeing one device, rather than a cluster of devices which lost their way."

"Confirm one large device," *Bechimo* said.

"Opening comm," Joyita said.

"No mention of a probe lost in this zone in the records we have been given," Win Ton said from his station. "We have been advised to look for an update shortly."

"Shortly's not here!" Kara snapped.

Seated, Win Ton bowed, ironically granting her point.

"Shortly'll be here sooner'n you're ready for it, lassie," Clarence added, but Kara's attention was back on her screens.

The dust cloud—and wasn't it a very *busy* dust cloud, with energy levels spiking, swirling patterns outlining shifting magnetic flows, static across several frequencies, and that other signal, buried deep—was, she thought, what had prompted Joyita to open comm. But, surely, there was nothing rational in all of—

She felt a tug on her sleeve, bent absently, and brought Hevelin to her lap.

"Affinity reaction," Kara said, her eyes still on the screens. "But there's nothing else here! Just us and—that."

The tendency of timonium to attract timonium was a well-known challenge in dealing with it in bulk. The dust cloud was, according to the shifting analyses on the screens, far denser than she would have assumed; the energy levels higher than mere dust would account for, even granting high concentrations of timonium . . .

Kara extended a hand to her pad, fingers tapping in equations.

"That isn't just . . . some . . . timonium," she said. "It must be nearly pure timonium. How—"

"Surebleak," *Bechimo* said in what Kara privately thought of as his *lecture voice*, "has numerous major veins of timonium. That is what attracted the Gilmour Agency, whose intention was to mine it out. As Theo knows, I also carry certain amounts of timonium; the new Struven unit alone . . ."

He paused and, after a moment, Theo spoke, perhaps to explain the breach—

"There's directionality to the energy flow, Kara. We're concentrating."

On the screens, energy levels spiked, static growing . . . light flared, and the levels fell to nothing.

Kara frowned.

"That looked like a brown dwarf that fell short of the ignition limit."

"Too small by a trillion," Win Ton answered, "but, yes, a definite similarity."

"Anomaly!" Theo said sharply.

"We have apparent energetic neutrino emissions but no obvious source," *Bechimo* said, as a fourth screen blossomed with energy states and flow patterns.

"These readings are not from the object we have under observation. There are several possible explanations, including an aftereffect of the Clutch ship's drive, the remnants of a star cluster explosion, or..."

"Or a cause for a new search pattern," Theo said, nearly toneless, as if she were voicing a comment from an inner dialogue. "We're receiving a cluster of signals, faint, but *Bechimo* believes he's heard something like them..."

Kara shivered, sensing a subtle interplay between *Bechimo* and Theo in the pause that followed.

"We're not transmitting images of our little dust storm live, are we, Joyita?" Clarence asked suddenly.

"No, Clarence, we're not transmitting to the public, or to the port. We are sending to Jeeves, in deep encryption. We have some flexibility in what we report, and when, and there's no apparent urgency in reporting this event. Why do you ask?"

"Because we don't want every loose-end treasure hunter with an empty hold and cantra in their eyes trying to come in here and scoop this stuff up, claiming salvage. On the other hand, if the dust somehow works as a detector...we oughta know that. Soon, I'm guessing."

"Excellent consideration," Joyita said. "I've made a note, which I am certain that the captain will take up, after we Jump."

"Everyone to stations, strap in," Theo said then, sounding quite herself. "That includes Hevelin."

"Where're we going, Captain? If it can be told."

"We have an urgent communication from Jeeves," Joyita said. "We are urged to move as rapidly as possible to confront the source of ghost signals. Jeeves expresses—alarm."

"That's urgent, alright," muttered Clarence, watching the boards go from static to live.

"Up shields," Theo said, "targeting going live, please. Now!"

Kara checked her straps, made certain of Hevelin, and looked again to the screens.

On the bridge, the smell of butter wafted.

"Jumping *now*," said Theo.

The screens went dark.

The Bedel

. . . .

"YOU DREAM LONG." THE VOICE WAS SOFT, FOR ALL IT WAS MALE, and serious.

Droi stirred out of the thinning trance and looked up into the gentle eyes of her brother Udari.

"I dream long," she agreed. "I dream late and I dream early. What else have I to fill my time, after Maysl is bored with hearing of her father?"

"You might teach her the *fleez*," Udari said, "and keep your fingers limber."

"She refuses the *fleez*," Droi said wryly, "though I keep my pact with the cards, Brother."

She paused, chest squeezing, for there was no need of the *fleez* aboard the ship. So did the old dreams tell her, and so did she try to forget when she was waking.

"What brings you, Brother?" she asked quickly. "I thought you were in the world above until the madman's harvest was in."

"The harvest is nearly done," Udari said, "and I will not be missed for one day. Or two."

He tipped his head and asked courteously.

"May I share your hearth, Sister?"

She might have told him no; she remembered a time when she *would* have told him no. But she was weary from dreaming, filled with dread, and feeling the absence of Rys Dragonwing... very much.

So... "Sit," she said, brusque.

Udari settled on the rug across from her, and reached inside his vest for pipe and pouch.

150

"If she wishes it, I will gladly tell Maysl how her father came to the *kompani* and how he found his hand and leg."

Droi felt the stir of her daughter's interest.

"She would be happy to hear these stories from Udari the brother of Rys."

"Then I will tell them—but later. Now, Sister, I wish to speak with you."

Maysl, denied her story, withdrew to sulk or sleep.

Udari filled his pipe from the pouch and pulled the string with his teeth.

"Before he left us, Rys would Dream," he said slowly. "Sometimes— no, often—the Dreams would trouble him. When that was so, we would rise and seek the hearth together, to smoke and talk."

He reached out to pick up a bit of firestone, used it to light his pipe.

"What did he Dream," Droi asked, "that troubled him so?"

Udari drew on the pipe, making the bowl glow, and sighed, releasing a fragrant cloud of smoke. He paused, the pipe held a little away from his mouth, his eyes contemplating something in the World Unseen, or some past hearth shared late at night with a beloved brother.

Droi waited. Neither Seeings nor memories ought to be disturbed; at last Udari sighed again and gave her a faint smile.

"Silain the *luthia* had given him to Dream the Dreams of past headmen," he said, meeting her eyes.

Only those who were to become headmen Dreamed the lives of those who had walked before them. The *kompani* would be reduced to children, Rys the last adult, before he would stand as headman. And, yet, Silain did nothing without a reason; she had been *luthia* for many years and knew the *kompani*'s heart. It might be said that she *was* the *kompani*'s heart, as Alosha the headman was the *kompani*'s head.

"Why did the *luthia* set Rys to this study?" Droi asked Udari.

He shrugged.

"Who can know the *luthia*'s reasons, save herself and the wind between the stars?"

So said the Bedel, with a certain amount of pride in the inscrutable ways of the *kompani*'s heart. Droi folded her hands.

"Who indeed?" she said, which was the given answer.

Udari drew on his pipe, sighed out a small storm cloud of smoke.

"When Rys understood what he had been given to Dream, he went angry to the *luthia* and demanded to know her reasons."

Went *angry* to the *luthia*, Droi thought. That was both like and unlike him. On the one hand, Rys was as calm as Rafin was stormy. While the blacksmith existed in a constant state of ill temper, she, Black Droi, shivered, only to wonder what might move Rys to *anger*.

On the other hand—how like Rys to demand an accounting from the *luthia*. He must be deep in Silain's heart, son returned or wander-soul found, that she had not rendered him mute, or impotent, for such temerity.

"What," she asked Udari, "did the *luthia* answer?"

"She told him that these Dreams were to prepare him for his brother-task."

His brother-task. Droi nearly spat. His brother-task, which no true brother would have put upon him. Truly she wished for bad luck to tangle the feet of Rys's Brother Undertree, though, for love of Rys, she stopped short of ill-wishing him in truth.

Instead, she said to Udari, "That may be so. We do not send our brothers and sisters forth unarmed." She drew a breath. "Even those who will never return to us."

Udari was dismayed; she saw it in his face before he leaned forward and, very gently, put the tips of his fingers against the back of her hand.

"Rys is gone from us," he said gently, "but he is not gone *beyond* us."

And that...was the truth, as the Bedel knew truth. Rys had given himself, heart and soul, before the fire, to the *kompani*. Whatever he had been before that rebirth, *now* he was Bedel, and while he might go elsewhere, he would never again be apart from them. In time, he would return in what manner he might. If he were held away against the yearning of his heart, his will over-powered, his soul beset—then would his brothers and his sisters fulfill their promise never to leave him alone among strangers.

That was the truth that Udari knew.

But Udari did not know *all* of the truth.

"Rys himself did not expect to survive this task his Brother Undertree set upon him," Droi said carefully. "The *luthia* therefore had him Dream his Soul-Dream."

She raised a hand, fingering one of the several silver chains around her neck. From her bodice rose a creamy rectangle of tiles, joined and bordered with silver.

Udari's eyes widened to see it, and he bent his head, as one might to a *luthia*.

"It does my heart good," he said gravely, "to see my brother's soul so well protected."

Tears stung her eyes, which in turn made her angry. Udari was a gentle brother: kind and, with her, only as wary as a wise man should be. She was fond of Udari in her own heart—and fond again, because Rys loved him.

Still, she did not bear the burden of Rys's soul to forge Udari's peace, nor to gain his approval.

She looked away, tucking the tiles back into her bodice.

"Why are you here, Udari of the Bedel?"

"Well." Udari leaned forward and knocked the dottle out of his pipe before placing it on the edge of the hearth.

When he straightened, he looked her fully in the face, his own showing weariness and excitement. And fear.

"I am troubled in my mind, Sister, and I am troubled in my heart. I would speak of these matters to you, if you will hear me."

Droi blinked, and made a show of scrutinizing him. Udari was a dreamer, a devout man who loved quickly, and deeply. "A man of heart," so said the Bedel, without any suggestion that the heart was weak. Men of heart persevered, though they felt each wound and loss keenly.

"I will listen," she said to Udari, whose smile reached all the way to his tired eyes.

"I will make tea," he said.

"So," Udari said, when he had poured the tea and settled once more to the rug. "I have heard that the ship is coming."

"Eventually," Droi said. "Pulka received an automated message, questing along the correct channels. An answer from us would bring the ship's headman into it, and Alosha had Pulka reply. We now await the captain's notice."

Udari nodded.

"I wonder," he said slowly, "if it will be a good thing for our *kompani*—the coming of the ship."

Udari wondered this? Droi lowered her mug and stared at him. He met her eyes and waited.

Droi cleared her throat and considered carefully.

Udari was devout; Udari was a man of heart.

Udari came to *her*, Black Droi, with this thing lying upon him, rather than to Silain the *luthia*.

Why?

Because, she reminded herself, Black Droi had been trained as a *luthia*—by Silain herself—and because Black Droi also loved Rys Dragonwing.

"Why would it be otherwise?" she asked. "Surely the *kompani* was set down here, the numbers fixed and a return agreed upon. This *kompani* has always meant to return to the ship. That does not change because the ship is late."

"No."

Udari leaned forward, tea mug held tight between his palms.

"*That kompani*, who had been born to the ship, *they* had meant to return. But *this kompani*—is not that one. The numbers are the same, but the individuals are not. *This kompani*—*we* form a different soul."

He paused and sent a hard glance into the glowing hearth, then met her eyes once more.

"For myself...I do not think that I would like to be confined by the ship. I was born on this world; I like the way the snow kisses my face, as if we are old and comfortable lovers. I like the single star in the day sky, and the two moons in the night sky. I *like* the madman at the end of the road, and I like working among the growing things."

He seemed to recall his tea then, lifted the mug and swallowed.

"If Pulka were this moment to receive a message from the ship naming the day and hour of its return, I would go to the *luthia*, and I would Dream myself into the tiles, so that I will not be lost to future *kompanis*. I would help my brothers and my sisters to make ready. But when it came time to board—I would not be among *that kompani*."

At the fire, she had seen her brothers and sisters...dismayed by the sudden intrusion of the ship into their lives. She had seen them distressed that their right, to argue among themselves until a consensus, was denied them, by the actions of that...*first kompani*.

But this! And from Udari. She had thought herself alone...

She drew a breath and looked again to the gentlest of her brothers, seeing the determination in his heart.

"You would be left alone among those who are not Bedel," she said, which was a prospect that had frightened even her.

But Udari was not frightened. Udari smiled, bright and wide.

"Would I? Rafin's father was a man from the City Above, and Rafin was born here. What use, inside the belly of the ship, for a blacksmith or an artificer? He has more than once said to me that, should the ship at last find us—which he doubted it would do—he would not board, but rather go into the City Above and make himself a place there."

Well for Rafin, thought Droi, wild and fierce as he was. He would make a place with his fists at first, then with his skill, and at last with his heart, as men of action always did.

"Memit," Udari continued. "Memit used to speak of a garden out under the sun, in the free air. We know that the ship has gardens, and she might have been pleased enough with them—but now she has found the extent of what Mad Yulie tends. I spoke with her before I left last night, and she said to me that she was content there for life, and if the ship *had* called, she was of no mind to answer."

Droi drew a breath; said nothing.

Udari lifted his mug and drained it in one long swallow.

"Luma," he said, placing the mug on the rug at his side.

Droi raised her chin, feeling the prick of her daughter's interest. "Luma is to take Maysl to her hearth. It has long been arranged."

Udari nodded. "So Rys said. I spoke to Luma before I came to you. She has doubts. She does not like walls, and most nights sleeps beside the hearth, rather than withdraw to her tent."

"I knew that, but this other—she did not say so, to me."

"There was no need—the ship had not yet spoken when she agreed to take Maysl to her hearth. Now, it becomes something to consider, and Luma's heart...is unsure."

Droi finished her tea and put the mug down.

"There are others," Udari said. "When the time comes to board ship and become, each of us, one of *that kompani*...I think there will be others who cannot—or will not—give up the sky, and the snow, and the free air. I think that we might have numbers sufficient to a *kompani*."

"A *kompani* with no hope of a ship in the future," Droi pointed out. "Soon or late, you must take *gadje* to you. Your children will not be Bedel."

"It is in my mind," Udari said softly, "that there is more to being Bedel than blood, and that a *kompani* of souls who are bound together goes beyond blood. Is Rys not Bedel?"

"Yes!" she said fiercely, and looked down at her hands, twisted together so tightly that she was in danger of breaking a finger.

"What do *you* think, Sister?" Udari asked, his voice yet soft.

Droi sighed and looked up to meet his eyes.

"The Dreams teach me that ship rules do not accommodate those like Black Droi, whose Sight is dark, and who may strike out even at those she loves. The Dreams provide...protocols... which are applied to *disruptive* persons who might damage or endanger the ship. These make the ship safe—and the person a stranger to her soul."

Udari extended a hand to touch her knee. He did not speak.

"I Dream," she said, staring into the glowing hearth. "Early, and late, old Dreams and older yet—searching for a way to cure me of myself, Brother, but in truth..."

Udari's eyes were wet. A man of the heart, indeed.

"In truth," she said, her voice roughened by her own unshed tears, "if the ship were to come for us this night, I would take myself and Maysl to the house of Silain's sisters in the City Above and...wait for Rys to return."

She raised a hand, and touched a particular chain about her neck.

"I have his soul after all."

Blair Road

Boss Conrad's House

. . . .

BREAKFAST HAD BEEN SERVED IN THE HOUSE'S COMMON DINING room; it was only they two, which was unusual. The rest of the house, Pat Rin thought ironically, had doubtless been up for hours.

"What may be your plans for the day?" he asked his lifemate, though really, there was no doubt what Natesa the Assassin would be doing today.

"I intend to accompany you to the Emerald," she said serenely. "Mr. McFarland is already gone to the Watch House, to find what there may be to know."

"Such ambition."

Natesa sipped her tea.

"I believe he considers this . . . event to be a personal insult," she said. "We ought to be beyond these 'shines,' as he has it."

"It is possible that we are—beyond 'shines,'" Pat Rin said, considering the so-called cheese scramble before him with some doubt. "The native population does not incline to coordinated action across territories: it runs against the cultural wisdom of generations. It may be that what we saw yesterday was—an opening move to a longer game. Something, as it were, to focus our attention."

"That is possible," Natesa conceded. "How will we know if we are in the long game?"

"When we see the next move," he replied, picking up his fork and addressing the sticky mass on his plate. "Unfortunately."

In another part of the house, a bell rang. Pat Rin heard Mr. pel'Tolian's deliberate tread on the plastic floor.

"Is your breakfast not edible?" Natesa asked.

Pat Rin sighed and looked at his plate.

"It is very nearly edible. In fact, I am persuaded that I have eaten something like with pleasure, only recently. This morning, however, it . . . bemuses."

"Perhaps you would like something else to eat?"

"Perhaps I would," he said cordially. "If only I could think what."

He reached for his cup, realized that Mr. pel'Tolian's footsteps were growing louder, and turned toward the door just as the butler crossed the threshold, looking—if one could imagine such a thing—irritated.

He carried an envelope in one hand and, when he reached table side, he bowed, offering it across his two palms to Pat Rin, as if it were a dagger.

"Your pardon, sir. I would most usually of course put this in your office, but the young person who delivered it was adamant: You must see it at once."

"Thank you, Mr. pel'Tolian. I daresay it is a very important letter."

"As you say, sir." He bowed again, and left them.

Pat Rin considered the envelope—local make, rough against the fingers; *Boss Conrad* spelled out in thick, handwritten, black letters across the face. Sealed, of all things, with a wafer.

Pat Rin broke the seal, shook out the single rough sheet, and read the few lines therein, twice, before he met Natesa's eyes.

"We have a demand letter," he said.

She sighed and put her fork down.

"From?" she asked.

He looked back to the page.

"*Take back Surebleak*, over the signature of *Boss Surebleak*." Pat Rin lifted his eyes. "A touch, you must admit."

"But I do not," she said. "Though I will admit that it is wonderful, how having an alias to hide behind emboldens the weak of character."

"You are severe," he said, and glanced again at the letter.

"Boss Surebleak demands that the Council of Bosses immediately retire Conrad and the Road Bosses. Children and those adults of Clan Korval who were not involved in the invasion and hostile takeover of Surebleak will be allowed to leave the planet.

All real property of Conrad, the Road Bosses, Clan Korval, and all of their holdings, on-world and off, will be confiscated to partially offset the damage deliberately and maliciously done to a sovereign world."

He sighed and refolded the letter.

"All of this to be accomplished within the next two weeks, local."

Natesa leaned back in her chair, frowning.

"Are we to assume that *retiring* is used in the local sense?"

"Given that our correspondent styles herself *Boss Surebleak*, it could scarcely be otherwise."

"Hmm." She reached for her cup.

Pat Rin slid the letter back into its envelope and put it next to his plate. The eggs...the eggs had not improved themselves. He reached to the warming basket in the center of the table and chose a piece of cinnamon toast.

It was quite good.

"Someone," Natesa said eventually, "has been tutoring *Boss Surebleak*."

"It seems so, does it not?"

"I propose that we have this next move you were so eager to see, Master. What shall you do?"

Pat Rin finished his toast and brushed the crumbs off his fingers.

"Boss?" The door to the kitchen slammed open and Jennetta rushed in, a copy of the morning paper clutched in her hand, her face white. Behind her, other white faces, and Mr. pel'Tolian, frowning.

"Boss, the paper just came," said Jennetta and thrust it under his nose.

On the front page, above the fold, bordered in thick black, which lent it a certain gravitas, was the text of the letter he had just received, signed, yes, by Boss Surebleak.

"Boss," said Jennetta—the child was shivering, Pat Rin saw. "Boss, what're you gonna do?"

It was an excellent question, and his answer was no different than the one he had been about to give Natesa, but as it happened, he was not allowed to speak on his own behalf...for Mr. pel'Tolian arrived at the table just then, teapot in hand. He slipped between Jennetta and Pat Rin, refreshed the cups as if nothing untoward were about, and put the pot by Natesa's hand.

"Will you like anything else, sir?" he asked while the kitchen door remained open, and his household held its collective breath.

"Thank you, Mr. pel'Tolian. I believe we are quite well."

"Yes, sir."

The butler turned and moved toward the kitchen, the waiting multitudes melting before him, snow to his sun.

"Boss Conrad will, of course, do everything that is proper." Pat Rin heard him say, before the door swung closed again.

Natesa looked up from the paper.

"Boss Surebleak plays a bold game," she commented. "How will you answer, Master?"

"It is not mine to answer," he said, sipping from his warmed cup. "As to what I *will do,* as Jennetta asked it so neatly, I will send a copy of the letter to every member of the Council of Bosses, so that even those who have not yet read the paper are informed. I will include a complete list of yesterday's targets, and I will invite the Bosses to attend a remote conference in two hours, so that *we* may plan our answer."

He inclined his head. "Have you other suggestions?"

"No—yes." She smiled at him, picked the basket up, and offered it to him.

"I suggest that you have another piece of toast."

Jelaza Kazone

. . . .

THE COMM PINGED.

Miri detoured to the unit and touched the button.

Val Con paused, spun on a heel—and felt the flash of her anger in the same instant that he heard her hiss.

"What's to do?" he asked, crossing the room.

He looked at the screen over her shoulder, reading the letter in a blink.

"I see," he murmured. "That does clarify a few matters."

Miri took a hard breath, and straightened, her back against his chest. He put his arms around her waist.

"Leaves just as many murky, too," she said. "It'd be nice to know for sure if this is street-grown."

"I agree. Pat Rin sends this, does he? Is there anything more?"

"A list of the streets and other locations targeted in yesterday's fun, and an invitation to a virtual meeting of all Bosses in—just under two hours."

"Nothing from the Watch?"

"Not here. Prolly have that at the meeting."

"Shall I—"

"No," she interrupted. "I'll do the All Boss, you take the Road Boss."

"Are you certain?"

She turned in his arms, slipping her hands around his waist and leaning her forehead against his shoulder.

"I'm certain. I gave enough speeches yesterday. If anybody still cares about Emissary Twelve after yesterday, *you* can speechify."

"It is very proper in you to share these small pleasures," he murmured.

161

She sighed and stood with her head against him, thinking about the letter.

So. *Boss Surebleak*, was it? And *Boss Surebleak* wanted to retire the Road Boss—that being her and him—and Conrad, too? One missed stitch right there, if *Boss Surebleak* thought he could retire Pat Rin and leave Natesa standing...

Retired. In street slang, retired meant murdered and was Boss-specific. Pretty usually, a Boss was retired by the next person who wanted to be Boss. And pretty often, the Boss in question *needed* retiring. The sad truth of Surebleak being that the new Boss was hardly ever an improvement on the old Boss.

No mistakes, the Road Boss in particular hadn't made a lot of friends 'mong the streeters, and there were definitely people who might want them out of the way, so that a Road Boss could be set up who accepted bribes, skimmed off the top, sold their own brand of insurance, and just acted like a Boss from the time before Pat Rin yos'Phelium hit Surebleak and changed everything.

And then, just like always, there was the Department of the Interior, who wanted Korval erased from the universe and who hadn't been shy, in the past, about pushing the local politics 'round to their view of things.

"Miri?" Val Con murmured.

She sighed again and stepped back, looking up into his face.

"So!" she said brightly. "Let's get some breakfast. Then you can open the port office, and I can be present and accounted for at the meeting. We'll debrief when you get back. Deal?"

Val Con bent and kissed her forehead. "Deal," he said.

Five Light-Hours out from

Surebleak Libration Point Five

. . . .

IF THEY HAD A PECULIARLY POWERFUL TELESCOPE OR A VERY
sensitive Jump detector and the leisure to look, the crew of
Bechimo could have seen where they'd been five hours earlier.
As it was, there were a few seconds of quiet in between as the
Struven units split and merged the space around them.

The aftermath of that transit was immediate: alarms, warnings,
and noise. The bells sounded hoarse, and Theo sat dangerously
calm, as she considered the roiling cloud of timonium dust centered on the targeting screen, the Gilmour Agency space probe
perfectly visible at its heart.

"It came with us!"

Dismayed, Kara stared at the cloud. It *was* the same cloud—the
proof was in the scan analyses sharing the targeting screen—
though the visibility of the probe had changed, as if the transit
through Jump had thinned its dusty cloak.

"Not good," Theo muttered. "We don't want it here."

"Communications intercept," Joyita announced. "I'm receiving
five clear bands, all of them . . . unusual."

"Ship signals, device signals," Clarence said from his board.
"I've got gibberish: no voice, all data. Somebody lost a load of
toasters and they're talking to themselves? No, wait, what's this?
Joyita, can you bring this up—"

"Yes, Clarence, I have it!"

"Let's all hear it," said Theo.

There was a faint crackle, then a mild, well-modulated voice
filled the bridge with clear and unhurried Terran.

"...resuming active service. Probe Stone Ronin asserts rights of unfettered passage, navigation, and exploration within this system as a unit of Surebleak Power Minerals, under duly-filed exploration patents recognized by TerraTrade Intergalactic. Interfering with my operations without permission of the Gilmour Agency or related contractors is against civil space law and custom. Only properly authorized tenders may interact with this unit. Service status update follows. Service status update follows.

"Probe Stone Ronin is resuming service. Beware potential rotation or orientation adjustments. Full status checks available via usual links." There was a pause before "Message repeats."

...which indeed it did do, this time in Trade.

Joyita dropped the volume, so the voice was merely a pleasant-sounding whisper.

"Why is it *here*?" Clarence muttered under his breath. "We're none of its kith nor kin."

"I have an image of its maker's plate," *Bechimo* said suddenly. "Screen five."

Kara drew a hard breath.

Remco-Carresens Mark II Margate Zone Works.

ID 00001K001.

"Kin," *Bechimo* said then. "I was built in that yard many years before Stone Ronin, but there will be similarities."

"You've got the clan face," Theo said, and then, "Subether's wild. Shields up."

"Shields up," *Bechimo* agreed, and Kara saw the confirmation on her board.

"All weapons live," Theo continued. "Win Ton, you're fire officer. Joyita, can you talk to Stone Ronin?"

"I do not believe a dialogue is possible," Joyita said. "I believe I have the command set, however."

"Quick," muttered Clarence, half-admiring.

"Do you?" Theo sounded interested. "That *was* quick. Tell Stone Ronin that we're the boss, and to be perfectly quiet. We don't need her insulting whatever's out there and making them any madder than they already sound.

"Clarence, keep paying attention to those transmissions. Kara, work with Joyita to get Stone Ronin's specs—and a schematic if you can convince her to release it."

✻　　✻　　✻

"Who are you? Are you from Headquarters? Do you dare declare lead? What are your energies? How much destruction do you carry?"

The subether was full of color and sound, *Bechimo* by necessity sharing all of it with Theo, as there had not been time to shield her. The flow was mixed—no. It was chaotic. Information and demands for information, hints of information, hints of threats, threats of hints, hints of most primal desire, hints of death barely averted, beseechings of mad beings and absolutely insane data-driven plans to shred Surebleak and all life in-system.

Having given her orders, Theo immersed herself again. Somewhere within a light-minute, dozens of devices demanded attention, obedience, or called out in languages Theo knew—ranging from ancient Yxtrang to fine Liaden and poor-docker Terran to voices that may have been nonhuman...Who knew what a Clutch in a hurry sounded like?

"What are you? We know your scars! What are you *now*?"

"Are these all ghost ships?" Theo demanded inside of bond-space.

Bechimo hesitated, reluctant to tell her...but she was his captain, and she deserved only the truth.

"Not ghost ships," he said quietly. "These are...old ships and devices of mayhem. They are here to kill Surebleak, if no one convinces them otherwise."

Blair Road

. . . .

IT WAS UNDOUBTEDLY AN HISTORIC MOMENT, BOSS CONRAD thought, as he looked upon the mosaic of faces before him. For the first time in modern Surebleak history, the entire Council of Bosses were met together, not in one room, but on one screen.

That was a measure of the seriousness of the situation. Never before had all of the Bosses of Surebleak met together remotely. Even Boss Marriott, who was very nearly a technophobe, was sitting in his place, hands folded before him, eyes grim. Conrad allowed himself to be gratified: Marriott *hadn't* broken the unit the Boss of Bosses had sent him, as he had suspected. The other Boss had simply never turned it on.

He ran his eye over those assembled one more time. The mood of the meeting ranged from Marriott's grim-faced stoicism to Penn Kalhoon's cool pragmatism. Miri, representing the Road Boss, sat soldier-faced, which he had the privilege to see only twice previously, and very glad he was that it had been no oftener. She gave him a nod when their eyes met, but she did not smile.

The countdown at the bottom of his screen flicked to zero and vanished. The tally box showed twenty in attendance.

Boss Conrad inclined his head.

"As we are all timely and present, I declare this meeting in order. A recording is being made of what we say today; a copy will be sent to each of you, after we have completed our business."

He paused.

"I trust that you have all read Boss Surebleak's letter of demand. Has anyone something to say?"

"*Boss Surebleak*," Boss Schroeder snorted from midscreen. "S'posed to take this serious, are we?"

"Oh, I think we gotta take it serious," said Penn Kalhoon. "These riots the Boss is taking credit for did a bit o'damage to my streets, and the fact we didn't get anything more fatal than a broken arm from it wasn't necessarily in the Boss's plan."

"I don't think there was any killin' in the plan," Ira Gabriel said in his matter-of-fact way. "This was just a demo, See how many turfs I got to sing for me at the same time? I'm the Boss of Surebleak—can you beat that?"

"I agree," said Conrad. "Yesterday's riots were to ensure that Boss Surebleak captured our attention, while validating her claim. She was able to mobilize action across five turfs, and specific targets on the port. Clearly, we are meant to take her seriously."

"Not only the turfs and the port," Melina Sherton said, shaking a sheet of printout at her screen. The paper snapped and crackled.

"There was more?" asked Boss Engles.

Melina nodded.

"There's a bunch o' old machines out by the pit sideways o'my land. Been there since the Agency left an' before. Yesterday, all of a sudden, after sitting there peaceful for a generation or three, they woke up."

She glared at them, one by one.

"Woke up," she repeated. "An', being awake, they started walking away from the Tapout. If they'd kept on course, they'd've crushed Gapton Village, 'cept we got some friendly help from the Road Boss's head o'security."

"Doin' what?" asked Boss Wentworth.

"Got into the command line, long distance, and issued a stop order," said Melina.

"Somebody's brighter'n new snow," said Engles. "How'd the machines get started up?"

Melina shrugged.

"Remote signal, I'm figurin', just like what stopped 'em. There's a set o'manual override keys. I know where they are, and I ain't tellin' you, just like I ain't told nobody else. Not been touched since I come Boss, and they were right where they belonged yesterday."

"Remote signal," Marriott repeated. "We got so many remote

signals flyin' around late days, there's no sayin' but that one of *them* triggered the machines, accidental."

"Maybe." Melina shrugged. "I'll hold it as a consideration. Might be the Road Boss's security guy can do a trace as to what zackly did set 'em off. But 'til we hear it was an accident, I'm going with deliberate mischief."

"Somebody hit the land we bought from Yulie Shaper, yesterday, too," Miri said quietly. "Air strike. In and out and no IDs. It looks like Boss Surebleak's got more than streeters and stones in her hand."

There was silence.

Marriott shifted. "You lose people?"

"No. We thought, yesterday, that it was luck nobody was hurt, but now I'm thinking it was planned. Which not only tells us that Boss Surebleak knows some inneresting things, but makes her threat explicit."

"Well?" snapped Vine. "Tell an ol' Boss what the wannabe's sayin', why not?"

Miri inclined her head.

"The way I read it, she's saying that she could've killed people this time, and if we don't meet her demands, that'll be her follow-up. Yesterday's rocks will be guns; armed drones will take out a work crew—Gapton Village, too, why not? It's not that hard, flying."

Silence.

"This list of targets portside," said Boss Wentworth. "I get why they hit Conrad's casino, the Road Boss's office, and the old uncle's rug store. Mack's garage—well, he's pro-Conrad, sure. But—the portmaster? Where's that make sense?"

"Portmaster's gotta know who's boss sooner 'r later," said Ira. "Might as well sort that, too, while she's putting everything out in rows."

"Looking that way, if Boss Miri's right about the threat—why's she waitin'? Boss Surebleak, that bein'. If she can kill us all easy as that, why's she botherin' with threats? Why not just go in and get it done? Surprise retirements hardly ever go wrong. Just askin' fer trouble, tellin' the retiree 'bout the party ahead o'time."

Vine knew his subject, as did most of the Bosses gathered; there was no disagreement with his observation. The silence grew...long.

Miri cleared her throat.

"What Boss Surebleak wants," she said, "is to be Boss of all Surebleak. You don't get that with a couple retirement parties. She needs the streeters doing the heavy lifting. The streeters have got to rise up against the—what's she got here?—*hostile invaders*? Demand they pay retribution, and give the planet back. Leastways, it's gotta look like that."

She looked at Vine.

"That's a vary on the old ways," she said, and he nodded.

"That it is, Boss. So, she's playing a game. Who for?"

"The survey team," said Penn Kalhoon, looking to Conrad. "That's the other threat. That's the real threat."

Conrad inclined his head.

"I believe so. TerraTrade will not grant an upgrade to a world under dispute. Boss Surebleak therefore offers a method by which the world is . . . no longer under dispute, so that the survey and potential upgrade may proceed."

"And if the world continues to be *under dispute*?" asked Melina.

Conrad sighed. "It is in TerraTrade's power to close the port."

There was another pause as the assembled company thought about this.

"That'd be bad," said Marriott, breaking the silence.

Conrad nodded at him. "It would be very bad, yes."

"While we're all thinking," Penn Kalhoon said. "I got a prelim report from the Watch. They got three actors who claim to've been paid to make a little fun, at a specific place and time. They was all paid in Surebleak cash—handsome pile o'Surebleak cash, which is where they all agree. Two say the hirin' was done by known jobbers. One says her jobber wasn't no 'bleaker, might've been one of the newbies, and she thought a minute before taking the nice, warm cash, on account she didn't want to get mixed up in any newbie Balancin', which she figured might be harmful to her continued good health."

"They find the jobbers then?" asked Josh Cruthers.

Penn Kalhoon's normally calm expression turned grim.

"They found one of 'em. She's in no condition to answer questions, and it's come to a matter o'Watch ethics, do they go looking for the second, or hope he found a snug hole in the snow, and stays low—and alive."

"Who was she?" asked Engles. "The one they found."

"Norene Jimba."

"She's one a'mine," Boss Torin said harshly. "Always dancin' on thin ice, that woman. I'll need to tell 'er ma." He rubbed a hand over his face and shook his head. "Morly Aze, too, dammit. Sweet on 'er since they was kids, is what I been tole."

He shook his head again.

"I'll pass you the Watch report," Penn said quietly. "Might not be what you wanna tell her ma, though."

"Still gotta know it," Torin said heavily. "I'm Boss, right? One a'mine gets killed that bad, I gotta take notice."

"Right you are," Penn agreed.

There was another silence, as if they all had paused to take a breath and bear honor to the dead woman.

"Boss Surebleak," Conrad said, when he had judged the moment had passed, "has generously given the planetary population a deadline by which her . . . orders must be obeyed. This gives us time."

"Time for what?" asked Vine.

"It gives us time to place a notice in the newspaper."

"Saying what?" Penn Kalhoon asked, fair brows drawn together.

"Why, that the body duly constituted to speak for the people of Surebleak—which is to say, the Council of Bosses—is in receipt of Boss Surebleak's letter and have perused her list of suggestions, some of which may have merit. We therefore invite her to come to the Bosses in council, share a light meal, and discuss our best path forward."

Penn blinked.

"They'll come in shootin'," said Vine. "If they come at all."

"Perhaps. Or perhaps not. We can but make the effort."

More silence, as each Boss turned the idea over and examined it.

"It's what we gotta do," said Ira abruptly. "That's what people do, they have differences; they try to work 'em out. Give a little, get a little; nobody's happy, but everybody's still standing. If we don't want Surebleak took back to the way it was—if we want Surebleak to be better than it ever was—then we gotta do different from the old Bosses."

There was a general murmur of agreement. Conrad inclined his head.

"I will draft a notice for the paper, and send it to each of you no later than midafternoon. Comments and suggestions may come back to me before sundown. I will place the approved notice in the paper tonight, and it will run beginning in the morning edition."

He looked at each face on his screen.

"Does that meet with the approval of the Council?"

Ayes were given, and Conrad stood.

"In that case, I bid you all good-day. Let us be watchful, and stay in touch. If it comes about that there is more mischief, please contact Penn Kalhoon with a detailed report. He will keep a list and share it with council members."

That, too, gained approval, and one by one the screens went dark as the Bosses signed out of the conference.

Pat Rin sat down again with a long sigh, and met Natesa's eyes.

"Do you intend to retire Boss Surebleak?" she asked.

He gave her a wry smile.

"No. But before you paint me with virtue, it is only because a retirement will not solve the problem. Retire one Boss Surebleak, and a second will arise, stronger than the first. We must find another way. And also"—he gave her a light, seated, bow—"we need to discover who is giving Boss Surebleak her lessons."

Surebleak Port

Portmaster's Office

. . . .

PORTMASTER LIU SAT IN HER OFFICE NURSING A CUP OF COFFEE. It was not her first cup of coffee on the day nor, she suspected, would it be her last. Port Security Chief Lizardi had just left, having stopped by to deliver her report, which consisted mostly of negatives, and which might've been disheartening if that hadn't pretty much been what the portmaster had been expecting.

Surebleak had a history. A history of violence and betrayal, though that started sounding like something right out of your *Thrilling Stories of Adventure and Romance*.

Regardless, it was true.

Back just a couple generations ago, all the employees of the Gilmour Agency under a certain grade had been left behind when the Agency vacated their Surebleak operations for cheaper-to-mine timonium elsewhere.

The Boss system had evolved naturally, given what those left behind had known in terms of culture. It might even have worked—it might *even still* work, dammit!

Portmaster Liu drained her coffee.

Conrad and his Council of Bosses were trying to make the system work. A system that was just like the old one, except the New Bosses were, mostly, competent, and understood that it was their job to help everybody get by, not just the Fat Cats; not just the ones who were strong enough to take what they wanted.

The *truth* was, if the most-down-and-out streeter started doing better in everyday life, then *everybody* was doing better.

The secret was, that kind of improvement only worked from the bottom up. Conrad knew the secret, whoever'd taught it to him, and he'd taught it to the other Bosses and, dammit, it was working!

Except...

Except there were some who'd *liked* the old ways. They couldn't make it on their own merit maybe, or they were afraid they couldn't.

Or... they just preferred to take what they wanted and got a thrill outta taking it from people who couldn't fight back.

And those—the local term was *slush-for-brains* and in Portmaster Liu's own private opinion, that was a fair description. In her public opinion, though, they were "disaffected citizens" who had been outplaced by the new order.

She was going to need to remember that phrase, she thought, because by her calculation, she ought to be receiving another interested visitor real soon now, and she had to be objective, informative, and professional.

Why now? she thought, which—well, it was obvious, wasn't it? Somebody who wanted the Bad Ol' Days back had decided that having an upgraded port wasn't in their best interest. That was prime Old Boss thinking right there, proving one more time, in case she hadn't been paying attention all those long years before Conrad took it into his head to rescue Surebleak from itself.

If any of the Old Bosses had an ounce o'sense, they'd've known that having a full-service port would be good for them. All they'd had to do was get creative with fees and accesses and what have you—but that would've taken cooperation, and the Old Bosses didn't trust anybody, especially not another Boss.

With a sigh, she closed her eyes and thought herself through a couple of focusing exercises. She'd just finished when the intercom beeped.

Portmaster Liu opened her eyes, knowing what was coming next.

"Portmaster," Carla said, "Survey Team Leader Kasveini is asking to see you. Are you able to accommodate her request?"

Portmaster Liu actually smiled. She'd bet her last snowball that Survey Team Leader Kasveini hadn't done anything like requesting and had managed to piss off Carla, too. Briefly, she toyed with the notion of allowing as how she was right out straight and could the team leader come back tomorrow.

It was a warming thought, but not practical. If Portmaster Liu knew her woman, and she thought she did by now, Team Leader Kasveini only heated up more when her ... requests weren't met in a prompt fashion.

Well.

Portmaster Liu smoothed her hair, straightened her jacket, and tried to set her face in neutral lines.

"Please send the survey team leader in, Carla," she said composedly.

If Team Leader Kasveini was in a towering fury, she was doing a damned good job of hiding it, Portmaster Liu thought a few minutes later. She looked ground down, rumpled, and just plain exhausted. Portmaster Liu felt a flicker of—not pity, exactly, but fellow feeling.

She rose and nodded the other woman toward the chair.

"Coffee?" she asked, moving toward the machine.

"I'm awash with coffee," said Kasveini, and then—"Yes. Thank you."

"I'm sloshing myself," Portmaster Liu said, filling a mug. "Sweetener? Milk?"

"Just black," Kasveini said. "Why go half measures?"

"My thoughts."

She came back to the desk, put the guest's mug by her hand, and settled into her own chair.

For a few minutes, there was only companionable silence in the office as they each sipped coffee.

Then Kasveini put her mug down, reached into her carry bag and pulled out a folded newspaper.

"Have you seen this morning's city paper?" she asked.

"Not yet."

"Please," said Kasveini, handing it across the desk. "There is an ... item on page one that we need to talk about."

Portmaster Liu took the paper, unfolded it and stared at the block of text prominently displayed at the top of the front page, bordered in funereal black.

She read the letter.

She read it again.

Then she put the paper down and picked up her coffee mug.

"Boss Surebleak, is it? And we're supposed to take that serious?"

"I am from off-world and am not privy to private cultural

jokes," Kasveini said, staring down into her mug. "I'm required to take—ah, *Boss Surebleak* seriously, especially when their actions reach into the port. A city prone to riot and unrest, we can work with, in the reports. There are, as I am sure you're aware, any number of well-regarded ports the entries for which read 'do not leave the port; city unsafe.'"

Portmaster Liu sighed.

"And here's Boss Surebleak with the bad manners to bring his tantrum inside the port."

"That is one thing." Kasveini looked up and met the portmaster's eyes.

"The second thing is that Boss Surebleak alleges that Clan Korval, in the persons of Pat Rin yos'Phelium, Val Con yos'Phelium, and Miri Robertson Tiazan—Boss Conrad and the Road Boss—engineered an invasion and hostile takeover of a sovereign world."

She sighed and looked down again into her coffee mug.

"I can assure you that TerraTrade will not upgrade a port on a world under dispute. Indeed, the best possible outcome will be that TerraTrade will do nothing."

She looked up again, her face drawn.

"The most probable outcome is that TerraTrade will issue a Do Not Stop."

"That'll kill us," said the portmaster quietly.

Kasveini shrugged.

"Even in the bad old days, we didn't rate a DNS."

Kasveini sighed.

"In the bad old days, an ongoing criminal enterprise had not demanded that TerraTrade certify their pirate holding as a legitimate port."

Portmaster Liu took a deep, careful breath. "Is that TerraTrade's official stance?"

"TerraTrade has no official position until the survey team concludes its study and files its report. The survey team has been diligent, and we have been objective, despite the presence of . . . opinions within our ranks. However"—she pointed at the paper spread atop the portmaster's desk—"the survey team cannot ignore that."

"Even if it's a joke?"

"Do you have evidence that it is a joke? If so, we will include both data points in our report."

Portmaster Liu shook her head.

"I don't have evidence that it's a joke. What I do have evidence of is that this planet is head and shoulders better now, after the event Boss Surebleak's styling a hostile invasion, than it's been—well, if the stories the streeters tell are even half true—ever in its history. The Gilmour Agency didn't care about its employees under a certain pay grade. The reason there's any Surebleak at all is that the Agency left *nonessential* personnel behind when it closed its operations here. Corporate culture being what was known, everybody who had any ambition shot for to be Boss, and being Boss meant you had everything you wanted, and if what you wanted belonged to somebody else, you took it.

"Conrad turned all that around. Not only made a council of equal bosses to level up the lives of regular citizens, but got in the road boss, to make sure that the Port Road stayed open, so material can get to the port for trade, and that the benefits of trade can get out to every territory along the road."

She leaned over.

"We're *better* now, invasion or no invasion. Boss Surebleak wants to go back in time, only he's taking an ace from Conrad's deck and playing like one o' the Old Bosses. All the benefit will come to Boss Surebleak and those who can pay Boss Surebleak."

Kasveini looked at her bleakly.

"Can you prove any of that?"

Portmaster Liu took a breath, blew it out, and said slowly, "No, I can't...but I know who can."

· · · ✳ · · ·

There had been a modest group awaiting the arrival of the Road Boss this morning. The chosen topic of all had, indeed, been the newly arrived Emissary Twelve, and her intentions for Surebleak.

Val Con had stuck to the broad outlines of Miri's speech, though he did think it prudent to drop in a hint that there might, in future, be a team of Clutch specialists on-world, pending the Clutch and the Council of Bosses coming to a mutually advantageous agreement. There was, he emphasized, no cause for concern in regard to Emissary Twelve in particular or the Clutch in general.

Which was, he reflected, very true. If the Clutch wished

to dispose of Surebleak, they might do so with a thoughtfully crafted song, and no one of those living on-planet aware of their own demise.

"Are there any questions?" he asked, having come to the end of what he considered prudent to share.

A woman in a pink sweater with a raveling sleeve stood up.

"Boss, what's gonna happen 'bout Boss Surebleak? You and Conrad gonna retire 'im?"

Yes, of course; he should have anticipated this. The succession of Bosses was a matter of great popular concern.

"The Council of Bosses is meeting this morning to discuss their answer to Boss Surebleak's requirements. Boss Miri is attending that meeting while I am here to answer you."

"We're behind you, Boss," said a man in a bulky grey jacket, the hood pushed back to show a beaked nose and a quantity of blond curls. "Boss Surebleak's fulla sleet."

"Who got the streets bust up yestiday?" demanded another man. "Man's fulla something 'sides sleet, is what I'm thinking."

"'Slong as he can pay for it, there's them willing to take 'is money," said the woman in the pink sweater. "Don't mean he's got real backing. *I* got Conrad's back—" she looked up abruptly and gave Val Con a broad smile that exposed gaps in her teeth. "You, an' Boss Miri, too, Boss. I ain't forgetting what you done for us—just so far! Tollbooths gone—who'd even thought it could happen?"

"Thank you," said Val Con holding his hands up, palms out. "I thank you for your support, but I must ask if there are any more questions about the Clutch?"

There were none.

"In that wise, I must ask you to leave. If you have other questions, I will be pleased to see you individually in my office, only let Nelirikk have your name. On the question of Boss Surebleak's proposal—none of us can know anything until the Bosses have met and reasoned with each other."

They gathered themselves up and left, good-naturedly enough, with another few assurances of personal support before the door shut behind the last one.

Val Con closed his eyes briefly.

"It is good to have allies," Nelirikk commented. "Can they be depended upon, in battle?"

"That is an answer I hope never to learn," Val Con said. "The city is not, after all, a battlefield, nor should it be. The Council of Bosses will need to craft a new answer to an old question."

He sighed.

"I believe I shall have a cup of tea. Will you join me?"

"No tea for me," said Nelirikk, who preferred water. "I am pleased that none of them stayed."

"As I am," Val Con said, turning to his door. "As I am."

He drank his tea while he read the Road Boss's scant correspondence. Having finished both, he considered calling Miri to learn the outcome of the Meeting of All Bosses, when he heard the bell on the portside door jangle.

He looked to the screen in time to see Survey Leader Kasveini step over the threshold.

His thought skipped to the bolt-hole, as Miri had it, the back door that opened onto a not especially fresh-smelling alley, which eventually wound its way to the back door of the Emerald, where one with the appropriate key or palm print might enter at will.

In the screen, Team Leader Kasveini gave her name to Nelirikk calmly, seeming very nearly a rational woman. Her shoulders were drooping somewhat and her TerraTrade survey jacket was rumpled. Val Con wondered if she were well.

"I would like to speak with Val Con yos'Phelium, on the business of his clan," she said, very calmly indeed.

Nelirikk hesitated.

Val Con leaned over and touched the intercom's switch.

"Please send Team Leader Kasveini in, Nelirikk," he said.

It would be his very great pleasure to send her to Pat Rin, he thought, and so vivid was his anticipation that he was smiling when she entered his office and bowed.

"I ask," she said, "to speak to the delm of Korval."

Val Con exhaled.

"Do please let us not play at that again," he said irritably. "It takes a quantity of energy to bear the delm and I do not feel at all strong this morning."

She blinked and, to her credit, inclined her head. "As you wish."

"Thank you. Will you take a seat? May I give you some tea?"

"No tea, thank you," she said and slipped into the chair next to his desk.

"Very well. What may I do for you, Team Leader?"

She sighed. "You have seen today's newspaper?"

"I have, yes."

"I have been speaking with Portmaster Liu. She is of the strong opinion that, despite Boss Surebleak's claims of a hostile takeover, conditions on this planet have improved considerably since Clan Korval has been resident. That is social and economic improvement, in the city and on the port."

She paused.

He waited.

After a moment, she inclined her head.

"I asked if she could prove this, and she said that the delm of Korval had tasked one of his clan to collect any existing papers and correspondence from the Gilmour Agency, and also letters, from the time of the subsequent Boss culture. Portmaster Liu feels that these documents will prove Korval's benign effect."

Val Con frowned. "There is such a project ongoing. An archive is being built, but as you may know, the challenge in collecting old documents is not the collection, but the collation. The team has made the decision to create broad categories of topics, each topic occupying its own volume, as it were. The last index I saw was merely a list of documents deemed to belong under the topic of Gilmour Agency employment policies. There has been no attempt, not even a rudimentary attempt, at cross-referencing."

"Yet documents dealing with the history of Surebleak and its people, life under the Gilmour Agency and under the Boss system—the Old Boss system, as Portmaster Liu has it—are in the possession of the archivists?"

"By no means all, but yes, documents detailing daily life, policy manuals and the like, are in the possession of the archive."

"I would like to have copies of those documents, for inclusion in the survey team's final report."

Val Con frowned. "Why?"

"In order to demonstrate that the arrival of Clan Korval on this planet has been no disaster for the citizens of the world, nor is there evidence of criminal behavior, though there are—irregularities."

"That is laudable," Val Con said softly, "but—forgive me for speaking plainly. It had seemed to me that your purpose was to deny an upgrade to this port. One wonders at this new effort."

"It was not the *purpose* of the survey to deny an upgrade," she snapped. "The survey team is charged with identifying areas of potential danger for traders and impediments to trade. However, a new concern has arisen with the publication of Boss Surebleak's assertions that Surebleak was the victim of a hostile invasion.

"If we find that to be true, TerraTrade may issue a DNS notice."

Val Con froze.

Team Leader Kasveini nodded.

"I don't want to be responsible for killing a world," she said softly, "or for pushing a world into piracy in order to survive."

"Thus the need for documents. I believe that I may be able to accommodate you. Will you wish to see the indexes and choose documents for yourself, or will you accept what an archivist chooses for you?"

"Is there someone . . . official on this project?"

"There are at least three Scout Archivists on the team."

"It will serve my purpose well if one of the Scouts would choose representative documents, sign off on them, and hold herself available for follow-up questions from TerraTrade."

"I believe that will be possible," Val Con said. "Is there anything else I may do for you at this present?"

"No," she said, rising slowly. "I think that will prevent—the worst case scenario."

"Very well."

He touched the intercom switch.

"Nelirikk, Team Leader Kasveini is leaving now. Team Leader—"

She turned.

"Yes?"

"Thank you for your care."

Jelaza Kazone

. . . .

PAT RIN DISMISSED THE MEETING AND THE SCREEN WENT DARK.

Miri closed her eyes and sagged in the chair, concentrating on breathing. After six breaths, she felt something drop into her lap and raised her eyelids halfway. Fondi was turning in a careful circle—once, twice—then settled down, back against her belly, chin on paws.

Miri sighed, put a hand on that furry warmth, felt the beginning of a purr, deep down, and closed her eyes again.

So...Boss Surebleak. Two would get you ten that Boss Surebleak wasn't anywhere near local. The set-up—it was too complex; there were too many threads. Your average 'bleaker: they weren't happy with Boss Conrad or the Road Boss, they'd set it up to throw a couple retirement parties. Nice, linear, almost...well, childlike, she thought, half-smiling as she remembered Lizzie's single-minded pursuit of anything she happened to want *right now*.

This thing here though...

She opened her eyes and tapped up Boss Surebleak's demand letter.

Right.

Retire Conrad and the Road Boss. That was your 'bleaker beginning and ending, right there. But Boss Surebleak moved on from there, knife out: Strip the retired Bosses' kin of all their property and cash, and throw 'em off-world.

Well, that wasn't Surebleak thinking at all. What 'bleaker cared about somebody else's kin? Sure, the retired Boss might've had a sister, but until she moved to make trouble for the new Boss, she wasn't worth a pellet.

Liadens, though. Liadens *cared* about kin. Liadens ate, drank, slept, and breathed kin. Liadens stood together in clans; a sizable portion of their own personal *melant'i* was tied up in the honor of their clan and their kin.

Retiring annoying people—in a way, that was Just Business, not *exactly* like it was with 'bleakers, but close enough to look the same from a distance.

Busting open the clan and scattering the surviving kin, broke, their *melant'i* irreparably tarnished—that was straight-up Liaden Balance.

She paused, thinking it over. Balance was another thing Liadens set store by. The idea was that, left to itself, the universe was perfectly balanced. Human beings, with their pesky tendency to action and their love of change, kept the universe in a constant state of flux. It was held to be the duty of honorable persons to be balanced in their dealings. If you did somebody a wrong turn, you were morally bound to balance it out with a good turn.

Boss Surebleak's business proposition, now, it was—it was dressed up like Balance, but at core it wasn't more'n plain and fancy revenge.

. . . which fit right in with the Department of the Interior's policy manual. Miri sighed. The DOI might've started out being an ultra-secret group to ensure that Liad and Liadens were always at the top of the heap, but they'd strayed off that path long ago and into the bog of ensuring that the Department of the Interior was the greatest power in the universe with a clandestine army of enforcers, the elite members—like Val Con'd been—brainwashed to carry out the Department's goals without question or complaint.

The Department's goals having lately shrunk to the annihilation of Clan Korval, the various deaths of prominent clan members was an understandable goal.

The ruination of Surebleak, though—that didn't fit their mandate.

Or did it?

"They don't need TerraTrade to certify the port here," she said to Fondi, or to the empty air. "They take over, use known methods to recruit the population, and they've got a new base, and a new mission."

Without Korval—with its resources, its uncanny allies and its unsettling relationship with luck—to stand against them.

A vision rose before her inner eye: fire; a tower of orange and blue flame roaring into the nighttime sky. The Tree—burning.

Smoke stung her eyes and she coughed, gasping for air...

In her mind's eye, pods began to fall—to explode—from the burning Tree, and wherever they struck, green shoots burst forth.

"Not optimum," she rasped, and took a deep breath as a cool, sweet breeze eddied around her.

"Not optimum," she repeated, and had the sense that the Tree agreed with her, even as the vision left her, with a last flash of what might have been black wings against a soot-dark sky.

"Miri," Jeeves said from near the ceiling. "Emissary Twelve wonders if you might come to the east patio. She has several topics to discuss with you."

She took another breath of cool air and opened her eyes. Fondi was still curled on her lap, but his head was up, ears pricked and alert.

"I saw it, too, kid," she said. "We're gonna do our best not to let it get that way."

Carefully, she urged the cat from her lap to the desktop and stood. Her muscles were quivering like she'd just done a hard march, which was—well, how did she know how much energy visions used?

"Jeeves, please tell Emissary Twelve that I'm on my way to see her. I apologize for the delay."

"She can scarcely notice so small a delay," Jeeves said. "But I will tell her that you will be with her very soon."

The outside day was cloudy, and not exactly warm. Miri had stopped in the hall to snatch a jacket off a peg before she stepped through the tall window and onto the patio.

Emissary Twelve was sitting on the stone ledge that bordered the stone-floored space, and she was wearing a...garment.

It was, thought Miri, stopping short and considering it, more like a tent than any real garment, cut out right off the bolt of all-weather cloth down in the basement. It enveloped the Clutch Turtle from shoulder to foot, and there was, she saw as she came closer, a hood, presently folded back.

Val Con had told her that the House would be providing their visitor with a custom garment to keep out the cold, but she'd only managed to imagine something sort of jacketlike, built out, maybe, to accommodate the shell. This...

Well, who but Jeeves, who had apparently volunteered to design and create the thing, could have imagined this?

"Good morning," she said in Liaden, moving to Emissary Twelve's side. "I hope your cloak is adequate to your needs."

"It serves my needs admirably," the Clutch said, turning luminous eyes on her. "It is, you understand, the prototype, but I am encouraged that it will be possible, once we have studied its performance at length, to be usefully adapted for the technicians. I feel, for instance, that it might be less voluminous, as the technicians will be required in the course of their duties to enter smaller rooms and corridors.

"But that is for later. For today, I will be removing to the base given for my use on the land of Yulie Shaper. I have requests to make of you before I go."

Miri blinked. Emissary Twelve was much hastier even than Edger, who was counted downright speedy by most Clutch. And she was growing hastier still, as if she were taking on the mode of madcap humans. Miri hoped she didn't hurt herself, remembering that she and Val Con had pushed so many exertions onto Edger that he had grown his next shell years before it was time.

"We are, of course, delighted to assist the guest," Miri said. "May I know your requests?"

"Yes. First, I would like maps of Surebleak. Especially of the more sparsely populated areas. This will assist me in choosing sites to visit in anticipation of the arrival of the technicians. Their work will be delicate in the extreme, and they will wish to have a base that is not subject to the bustle and busyness of the cluster-dwellings."

Miri frowned.

"The Scouts have been exploring and cataloging the outback land, as it has been called," she said. "I will make a call and find if the survey maps can be shared with you. Given the nature of your mission, I am certain that there will not be a problem. What else may I be pleased to do for you?"

"I will require a vehicle. It will be necessary for me to visit those areas which I identify on the map, to take measurements and assure myself of the suitability of each."

A vehicle.

Miri considered the picture in her head of a smallish, but still hefty Clutch Turtle driving a battered all-terrain across Surebleak's outback, and winced.

"While I am speaking with the Scouts, I will inquire for one who may serve as your escort, perhaps conveying you to the areas you have identified in one of the survey craft."

Emissary Twelve blinked slowly.

"That would be an acceptable arrangement," she said, after a longish pause. "If such a one could be found, I would be grateful."

"Do you have a comm at Yulie's?"

"The House has been generous. I have everything that is required for my work."

"Excellent. I will call you after I have spoken with the Scouts. Is there anything else the House may provide at the moment?"

"I believe I am well provisioned. Also, I am informed that there is a Tree—young, yet worthy of conversation—at Yulie Shaper's farm. It has been given some education from the Elder Tree, so that it might more quickly begin to shape its nature as this world requires. I will be most interested to make this Tree's acquaintance, and to hear what thoughts it has."

The affinity between Clutch and Tree was, Miri thought, unsettling, but not as unsettling as the thought that just occurred to her.

"Before you go," she said, "I will make you aware of a developing situation. It may be that the delm of Korval will...live less long than we had anticipated. Will you, and your technicians, be able to continue with your work in the event that there is a different delm of Korval? Or none at all?"

Another slow blink of yellow eyes.

"It is understood that the scope of the project necessitates that the technical team will interface with several delms of Korval," she said, and Miri had the impression that Emissary Twelve was trying to phrase her answer as gently as possible. "It is well known that those of the Clans of Men are not long-lived. While we regret this fact of nature, still we cannot allow it to impede us in this critical work. It may be, as event moves forward, that it will become, from the perspective of continuity, more efficient for all to interface with the Elder Tree or its offspring.

"But that," she said, standing up, her weather tent rustling about her, "is also for later. We will do one thing, then another thing, in order, until the task is done. We have found this to be the best way to proceed."

Miri smiled slightly.

"So have we."

Blair Road

Boss Conrad's House

. . . .

The Bosses of Surebleak greet Boss Surebleak. We are in receipt of your message, and we invite you to meet with us in order that we may discuss our various plans for Surebleak's prosperity. We will be meeting on Graupelday at the fourteenth hour, in the Council Meeting Room inside the Mercantile Building. We wish very much to find you seated with us there at that time.

Pat Rin considered this notice with some amount of satisfaction as he drank his tea. This morning's breakfast was a nut-butter sandwich with poizinberry jam, which despite the infelicitous name, was apparently not a poison at all. It was, in fact, quite delicious.

Natesa, who was watching him over her bowl of hot grains, asked softly, "Is it well, the letter to the void?"

"I flatter myself that it is extremely handsome," he answered, placing the paper on the table before her.

She glanced at it and spooned up more cereal.

"Do you think Boss Surebleak is likely to attend?" she asked.

"More likely to just hire a gun to sit on the roof across from the doorway and pick off Bosses when they go in," said Cheever McFarland, who had just come into the room. He stood at the end of the table and glared down at Pat Rin. "You really think all the Bosses of Surebleak'll even make a dent in this guy's plan?"

"Good morning, Mr. McFarland," Pat Rin said softly. "You

appear to be somewhat out of sorts. I suggest that your mood will improve after you have had some breakfast."

The big man turned to Natesa. "Does he think Boss Surebleak is any kind of innerested in a meetin' of the minds?"

Natesa reached for her teacup.

"I believe not," she said thoughtfully. "However, the consensus of the Bosses of Surebleak was that they are, as the ruling body, committed to improving the lot of the planet entire. They are therefore constrained to produce a new way to deal with such persons as Boss Surebleak, since we are able to see what long-term success the old way produced."

Cheever stared at her.

"The coffee was brought out only a few minutes ago," she said, returning her attention to her bowl.

"The jam tarts are also just out," Pat Rin said. "Do serve yourself and join us."

"The pair of you . . ." Cheever muttered, but he did cross the room to the buffet, poured coffee, and put a pair of jam tarts on a small plate.

Pat Rin had finished his sandwich and put the plate aside. He sipped tea and waited until the big man had eaten one whole tart and drunk half of his coffee.

"We are not quite idiots," he said. "We are making arrangements for increased security at the Mercantile Building, the approaches to the building, and the room itself. Joey Valish has been talking to the Watch regarding appropriate coverage. It would please me if you would approach the Mercenary Hall with the logistics and see what they might do for us.

"We will, of course, wish to be discreet. It is no part of this to frighten our invited guest or to make her anxious for her safety."

"I will be speaking to the Scouts this morning," Natesa said, putting her bowl to one side and reaching for her cup.

Cheever sighed, drained his mug, crossed the room, refilled it, and resumed his chair.

"Do you actually *expect* Boss Surebleak to attend this meet-ing . . . in good faith, is what I'm askin' now, not just to shoot the place up."

Pat Rin frowned slightly.

"Do you know? I can quite easily convince myself that she will do no such thing, and then five minutes later become just as convinced that she will attend," he said. "In truth, we cannot know what she will do. If she were a . . . traditional Surebleak Boss, we might be able to predict her probable answer with some accuracy. However, she has already shown more . . . shall we say, creativity than a traditional Boss, though she has taken on some of the trappings in order, so I feel, to appeal to that percentage of the population which is disaffected and wishes for a return to the old ways."

Cheever looked thoughtful.

"So, she's something new, is she? Or she's got a sophisticated advisor."

"I lean toward the second theory myself. In which case, it is imperative that we find who that advisor is and neutralize them, unless we wish to entertain a limitless parade of Boss Surebleaks."

"I think," said Natesa, "that Boss Surebleak has time constraints."

Pat Rin looked to her. "More levels?"

"Why stint herself?"

"And, here's the question that's gotta be asked: what's an outworlder—are we thinking Liaden?—want with Surebleak?"

"There is timonium here," said Pat Rin mildly. "The Gilmour Agency found it too much effort for too little return, but that may not apply to—a pirate operation, let us say."

"Pirates wouldn't need a port upgrade," Cheever said slowly. "Might be cozy to have one, but not at the cost of being free to operate openly."

"Miri's theory," Natesa said, "is that the Department of the Interior is behind this—which possibility also cannot be ignored."

"In which case, you gotta wonder about that time constraint you mentioned," Cheever said, "and what's standing as Boss Surebleak's backup."

"Speaking of Miri and Val Con," Pat Rin said, changing the subject ruthlessly, "you will wish to know that they have spoken with Emissary Twelve, our Clutch visitor. She brings news that the planet is flawed at core—perhaps as a result of the Gilmour Agency's approach to mining. There is a strong probability that Surebleak will break apart in twelve thousand Standard Years."

Cheever started to laugh—and changed his mind.

"So, are we evacuating?"

"Not at all. Emissary Twelve is in search of a reasonable place to establish a team of Clutch technicians who will be working to repair the flaw."

"We're going to have a team of Clutch Turtles on Surebleak?"

"That would seem to be the case. Surebleak will set the precedent. Can you think of another mixed human and Clutch world?"

"I can't. And my gut says it's a bad idea."

"Perhaps it won't be so much of a tragedy. I should have added that Korval's Tree quite likes Clutch Turtles."

Cheever drained his mug. "Terrific."

Blair Road

Boss Conrad's House

. . . .

PAT RIN HAD SPOKEN TO HIS MOTHER, LADY KAREEN, WHO HAD received a request from the TerraTrade survey team for documentation illustrating Surebleak's social and economic situations during the Gilmour Agency years, under the Old Bosses, and under the care of Conrad and the so-called New Bosses.

Scout Historian vey'Loffit, so Pat Rin's mother assured him, was competent and willing to review and certify the requested documentation. She, herself, was as excited and pleased as he ever remembered hearing her, in all his life.

"For I tell you, we have treasure to place into the survey team's hands," she said crisply. "The very manual from the Gilmour Agency's employee management department, in which each of the rules that was amended by the Board of Directors was notated, the new rule affixed on the page next to the one it supplanted.

"It is clear from this account of the proceedings that the directors deliberately created a structure that would allow them to abandon those listed as lower grade. The money they saved on transportation and relocation costs ensured that they would retain a place in the larger company, rather than being shut down as unprofitable."

She'd paused and glanced down at her desk.

"We also have letters from the grandmothers, as the Boss system began to take shape, and personal accounts from people who had been living on the turfs of each Boss who was in power immediately before Boss Conrad began his project of consolidation."

Glancing up, she smiled. "I think you need have no fear that the survey team will rule against your agenda."

"We may hope that is the outcome, but the survey team only recommends. It is TerraTrade that must be convinced."

"Very true; I merely wish you to know that the history of Surebleak testifies to the benevolence of Boss Conrad's subjugation of a sovereign world."

"I am grateful for the reassurance," he told her, which was true.

She inclined her head and broke the connection.

Pat Rin leaned back in his chair with a sigh. He ought to call Penn Kalhoon, though the lack of contact from his second would indicate that—

"Master Pat Rin."

Mr. pel'Tolian stood at the door to his study.

"Yes?"

"Security requests that you come to them. There is something on their screens which they feel will interest you."

"Of course; I'll go at once."

He rose, trying not to think what might interest him on Security's screens. Anything from a corpse on the front sidewalk—recognizable as one of his own residents—or several such. Swallowing hard, he moved more quickly along the hallway to the front of the house.

Gwince was on the screens, as Quin was off-world, gaining flight time.

"Boss," she said, shifting to make room for him at the console. "Take a look at this."

Bodies crowded the street in front of his house: live bodies, people—his people. He recognized many faces, but not all—

People were holding signs—large, crude, hand-lettered signs. Gwince had muted the feed, but he could still hear a faint roar of voices.

"Conrad! Conrad! Conrad!"

The signs—the signs bore several messages: NO MORE RETIRE-MENTS; NO MORE INSURANCE; BOSS SUREBLEAK AIN'T THE BOSS OF ME.

There were also, Pat Rin saw, other signs here and there, perhaps not being held as high, but visible nonetheless.

TAKE BACK SUREBLEAK!

"What is this?" he asked Gwince softly, as if they might hear him out on the noisy, crowded street.

"Dif'rence of opinions, I'm guessing," she said. "So far, nobody's swung at anybody else's nose. Got a call from Valish a little o'er minute ago; they got the same thing out front o'Boss Kalhoon's place. We split the rest o'the Bosses between us to call and find did they have anything like, but I thought you should know first."

"Thank you, Gwince. Has the Watch been alerted?"

"Figured it was house security, sir. Valish is treatin' it the same way."

"Very well. Please send that feed to my desk sc— Wait. What is this?"

This was an odd couple indeed. Walking side by side, with identical purposeful strides, he adapting his to hers: a lanky male in Surebleak motley, his hair a grey fog around his head, and a Liaden woman in sober business dress, sleek dark hair liberally striped with grey. She was carrying a briefcase.

The crowd—sign-bearers of both opinions—gave way before them as they continued, looking neither to the left nor the right, directly up the front steps to the door.

The male extended a hand and pressed the call button. A bell rang in the hallway, closely followed by Mr. pel'Tolian's brisk footsteps.

Pat Rin stepped out into the hallway, arriving at the vestibule in time to hear the woman speak in clipped, accented Terran.

"I am kaz'Ineo. I come with my apprentice to speak with Boss Conrad on the matter of Boss Surebleak."

"Mrs. kaz'Ineo," Pat Rin said, walking forward before Mr. pel'Tolian could speak, "and Mr. Hufstead. Be welcome in my house."

The two of them were the first successful pairing to come out of Miri's "storefront *qe'andra*" project. Mrs. kaz'Ineo was of a respected Line of Liaden *qe'andra*; Jorish Hufstead had for many years been a so-called cornerman—a dispenser of rough Balance—on Penn Kalhoon's turf. They had previously assisted the Road Boss in untangling a knotty Liaden-Surebleakean ethical issue, and had been tireless in tutoring other nascent teams.

"Boss Conrad." Mrs. kaz'Ineo inclined her head, not quite a bow, which was proper Surebleak manners.

"Boss." Jorish Hufstead also nodded, being Surebleakean.

"I would be pleased to hear your insights regarding Boss Surebleak. If you will just step down to my office, we may be comfortable. Mr. pel'Tolian, please bring a tray."

"Certainly, sir."

✳   ✳   ✳

"A vote," Pat Rin repeated, looking at his mismatched callers. "I am afraid I do not understand."

"In theory, it is a simple procedure," said Mrs. kaz'Ineo. "Its charm is that it partakes of both Liaden and Surebleakean custom. Its... drawback is that honor alone enforces the outcome."

Pat Rin picked up his cup and leaned back in his chair, feigning a relaxed patience he did not quite feel.

"Tell me," he said.

"Of course. Apprentice Jorish, please give Boss Conrad the Surebleak history."

"Yes, ma'am." He turned his long, clever face toward Pat Rin.

"This goes 'way back to the Gilmour Agency, Boss. I did use it, once er twict, when I was cornerman, but most of what I was solving for weren't so complicated as to need it.

"Now, what it was, is if one of the Board of Directors wanted to do a particular thing, and another one wanted to do another thing, and neither one could be talked to the other one's side, the whole board—all the directors, y'see—would have a vote. One director, one vote, and whichever idea got the most votes, that's what got done."

The Council of Bosses worked by consensus, which took time but produced workable compromise. This all-or-nothing approach was... slightly mad, Pat Rin thought. In his experience, which was increasing daily, it was the compromise—the melding of the two or three original ideas—that was the best answer.

He turned toward Mrs. kaz'Ineo. "And there is something like, in Liaden culture?"

She inclined her head. "There is, and you are, I trust, familiar with its use at Festival. How is the Most Artful Mask chosen?"

Pat Rin frowned.

"They are displayed side by side with a bowl on a table in front of each. One leaves a coin in the bowl before the object of one's preference."

"Yes," said Mrs. kaz'Ineo, "and the mask which receives the most number of coins is declared the Most Artful."

"Yes," Pat Rin agreed. "You are correct; I see the similarity with Mr. Hufstead's procedure. How will this assist us in the matter of Boss Surebleak, I wonder?"

Mrs. kaz'Ineo raised one slim hand and gestured toward the front of the house.

"There appear to be two ideas tugging at the ascendant," she said. "Boss Conrad, representing the New Order, and Boss Surebleak, representing the Old. Rather than go to bloodshed, which partakes firmly of the Old, and solves nothing for the New, how if we require every person on every turf to place her coin firmly on one square: Boss Conrad or Boss Surebleak."

Pat Rin stared at her.

"An' whoever gets the most votes, that's who'll head the Council o'Bosses," Jorish finished.

"I feel constrained to point out that this... method does not address Boss Surebleak's demands."

"There is," said Mrs. kaz'Ineo austerely, "no need to address Boss Surebleak's demands in any way. We must work within the system as it exists; to go backward is not an option. In today's vernacular, Boss Surebleak wishes to be Boss of Bosses, and Boss Conrad—does not wish to relinquish his position."

Pat Rin was struck dumb.

"What I'm really likin' about this particular solving, ma'am," Jorish Hufstead said to his master, "is how there's no blood in it. And there ain't any confusion. Boss Surebleak wins, she just starts goin' to work in Boss Conrad's shoes, and Boss Conrad, he gets to take some time off and relax. All the ongoing Council projects like get reported in the papers keep going on like they're s'posed to, an' nobody has to miss anybody else."

"Boss Surebleak also wishes the Road Boss to be... retired," Pat Rin pointed out, rather feebly, to his own mind.

Mrs. kaz'Ineo sniffed.

"The Road Boss is under contract to the Council of Bosses. Should Boss Surebleak succeed in her bid to become Boss of Bosses, she may release the Road Boss from their duties, in accordance with the appropriate clauses in the contract, and contract with another to be Road Boss."

This was, Pat Rin thought, lunacy, truly. Who would enforce the win? Ah, yes, that had been covered at the very first.

Honor.

He took a deep breath and leaned forward to put his cup on the table, taking the moment to scan both serious faces before him. Neither looked a lunatic.

"Well." He sat back into his chair. "Tell me, then. How would you design this... vote?"

Jelaza Kazone

. . . .

THE HOUSE WAS TOO QUIET, VAL CON THOUGHT, AS HE WALKED toward the delm's office, having seen Miri on her way down to the port and the office of the Road Boss.

A clanhouse wasn't meant to be empty. A *proper* clanhouse never was empty.

Jelaza Kazone had, of course, never been a proper clanhouse, yet it had not been built with the intention of enclosing empty rooms and dead air. It had been built, at least, as a refuge for those of Korval, their allies and their friends. Perhaps Grandmother Cantra had not thought in terms of a full nursery, and the voices of kin in the hallways...

Or perhaps she had. Grandmother Cantra had passed her early years in what had amounted to a clanhouse, and if all of one's near-kin had been specially designed to certain specifications, surely that made them kindred?

Korval had never been a large clan, even in the days of relative peace, when their luck had deemed it fitting that Korval pilots lived to a respectable old age. It had over time become smaller still. Two generations back, Jelaza Kazone had been home to his grandmother Chi, and her sons, Er Thom and Daav. Chi had died, Er Thom had taken up his duties as master trader and thodelm of yos'Galan, removing from the clanhouse to Trealla Fantrol, yos'Galan's line house, leaving Daav, after he had been recalled from the Scouts to take up Korval's Ring, to live in the clanhouse alone.

Eventually, Daav had been joyously joined by his lifemate, and they produced a child, had eager plans, so his father had written in the diaries, for a second...

195

Save that his lifemate had been murdered, leaving Daav in fear for his own reason, targeted by an implacable enemy...

His father had left the clan, hoping to pull the enemy with him. He placed his small son, the heir and hope of Clan Korval, into the care of Er Thom, his *cha'leket*, and—vanished.

Jelaza Kazone had been swept, sheeted, and shuttered. Grounds and maintenance were seen to by staff; the public rooms and the gardens were open on the appropriate days, as every other Great House; and Uncle Er Thom had of course visited the Tree in its court... as often as necessary.

But Jelaza Kazone had ceased to be a clanhouse; it was a resource, of course, and there *was* the Tree, but as for kin—even Korval's heir stayed in his rooms at Trealla Fantrol when he was on break from school or the Scouts.

Truly, it was only since the relocation to Surebleak that Jelaza Kazone had come into use once more as a *clan*house, even a *proper* clanhouse; the seat of the delm; a safe harbor for kin, allies, friends; full-staffed and, sometimes, just a little noisy.

He had, Val Con realized with some surprise, become very quickly used to a—say, a *fuller* house.

Perhaps, he thought, the delm ought to make a protocol: Every twelve days, every clan member on Surebleak would return for two days to the clanhouse, there to refresh themselves with each other, talk over the business not only of clan, but of kin...

That might, indeed, be a reasonable notion; he would remember to mention it to Miri. Certainly, if they were to go down the path of recruiting non-kin—no... *fellow travelers*... into Korval, such group meetings would be necessary...

As he had been concerned with kin, it was perhaps not surprising that his first act upon entering the delm's office, before he even poured a cup of tea or removed Fondi from the desk chair, was to call the Healer Hall to inquire after the health and necessities of Anthora yos'Galan and Ren Zel dea'Judan, wounded children of Clan Korval.

· · · ※ · · ·

They had been alone at study in the early hours. Nelirikk Explorer was, as most days, escort and bodyguard to the Road Boss. Diglon Rifle, so he had informed them yesterday, would early be out with his wife, in her *melant'i* as Scout botanist, assisting her in the gathering of those plants which thrived in the pale, frigid dawnlight. He had assured them, earnestly, that there were such, which the Pathfinders doubted not, they having seen a great many odder things than cold-loving plants along their various tours.

The early study completed, Chernak and Stost repaired to the mess, where there were such foodstuffs and drink that might be found suitable for a midmorning snack. They each drew a cup of coffee, which they found curiously pleasing in taste despite its acrid odor, with a few of the chewy fruited bars, and took up station at the table near the door—a soldier habit that they could no more have broken than they could have stopped breathing.

"Our schedule remains remarkably free of duty," Chernak observed, after she had sipped her coffee. "It would seem that we have exhausted the curiosity of the commanders of mercenaries, nor have we seen a follow-up from the exploratory corps. Have we alternate plan for our future, now that we have seen the last duty placed upon us by our former command resolved?"

"This place, it is acceptable as a post if matters fall that way," Stost said carefully. "If Nelirikk Explorer becomes our superior, I believe we all might work with that; he is fair and has the trust of command. Diglon is a boon companion of complexity, which I approve of for all that my approval leads to no benefits for myself. And truly, Senior, a house like this, where great events have taken place, that draws both unexpected action and unexpected persons—there would be honor here, I think."

Chernak sipped her coffee.

"I agree," she said. "The post would not be without honor, nor would it be beyond our abilities. I see that we would need to be stern with ourselves, to preserve our skills in service of the house, but we might easily make that case to Nelirikk's captain."

She paused.

"Making the case that we ought join the house Troop—that may be more difficult, my Stost. Note, I do not say insurmountable because I know your powers of persuasion. It seems that the house is not eager to increase the strength of its force."

"We might put our reasoning before Nelirikk and ask for the benefit of his experience. After all, this is not our universe. We are as soldiers newcome from the creche."

Chernak choked slightly on her coffee.

"Certainly," she said, when she had her breath back. "We are babes."

"Will we not, then, ask for the aid of a more knowledgeable comrade?" asked Stost. "For myself, I would like to have a range on when the house will grow tired of feeding the dutiless, and what is likely to occur when it has done so."

Chernak sighed.

"That is knowledge that I would welcome, myself," she said gravely. "As you say, it would be no dishonor to serve this house." She paused, and added, "One might prefer Captain Theo, if *that* choice were made available."

"And who," said Stost wisely, "would not prefer Captain Theo?"

He picked up his cup and drank off what was left of his coffee.

It had been a short conversation with Healer Hall. Anthora and Ren Zel were still under evaluation. Because of the... unusual nature of their separate gifts, the Healers in the Hall were proceeding cautiously. Lady Anthora had asked several times to see her lifemate. As Lord Ren Zel was not in what the attending Healers considered to be a stable condition, it had not been deemed wise to bow to these requests. To her credit, Lady Anthora had acquiesced to the prohibition placed upon her, stating that she understood the concern of the attending Healers, and was most grateful to them for their care.

Of Lady Anthora—the child she carried had taken no damage. The lady herself... was depleted. There was no sign of wounding or scarring, merely a low—which was to say *lower*—energy state, as if she had overextended herself.

The task of the Healers attending her was twofold: to be certain that there was no continued loss of energy; and to ascertain if the new state were permanent or whether, with rest and time, she might recover her full abilities.

Was there anything else that Lord yos'Phelium wished to know?

"Might one speak to Lady Anthora?"

The administrator offered regrets. Lady Anthora was engaged with the attending Healers. If he wished, a note might be left for her.

"If you might ask her to call her brother Val Con when she feels able, I would be grateful."

He was to consider it done. Was there anything else?

"No, I thank you."

Val Con sat in his chair for a moment, eyes closed, stroking Fondi, who had appropriated his lap during the time he had been speaking with Healer Hall.

Anthora...had been, by the estimation of those whose concern it was to estimate such things, one of the two strongest—possibly *the* strongest—*dramliza* of the current generation. Her gifts had made it easy for her to do things—in a wide range. For instance, one could not be certain, even yet, if she actually was a master pilot...or only flew like one.

Well, Val Con thought, putting Fondi aside and rising to fetch himself a cup of tea...

They would all need to learn to cope with new realities. A brother could hope for a sister that she had not lost too much of what had been hers; he imagined that losing a limb would cause her far less pain and despair.

For Ren Zel...a brother might hope that he survived, and returned very soon to joyous good health, though not necessarily to his talents. The ability to see and interact with the forces that bound the universe—that had been a cruel gift; no one should have had to bear such a burden, least of all Ren Zel, who was a kind man, who constantly strove to do what was right.

He had also had what Val Con had been informed was a very minor gift of Sight, which allowed him infrequent glimpses elsewhere. Both of his gifts had come upon him later in life than was usual; therefore, he had not learned to lean upon them.

No, Ren Zel's biggest challenge going forward might well be coming to terms with being alive, after he had chosen to sacrifice himself for the continuation of their universe.

Val Con carried his cup to the window and stood sipping, gazing out into the inner garden. Snow dusted walkways, bare branches, and leaves. The Tree kept the inner garden somewhat more temperate than the Surebleak surrounding the house, but not even the Tree could vanquish winter entirely.

On the topic of sacrifice, he found himself wishing that the Department would make its move. He had no wish to die, certainly; in truth, he had so much engaged upon him that he did not wish even to be inconvenienced. He did, however, very much wish the striving against the Department to be over.

Bad enough when it was only himself in the Department's sights. But they had widened the field to Korval entire and now, apparently, once more, to Surebleak. One hesitated to wonder to what dizzy heights the stakes would rise next—the galaxy? The universe?

No. It would stop here—with him. Talizea would not be forced to endure the Department; Miri would be free to live a full life, even if he fell.

It would be a hard trade, if he did fall. For he would die for nothing less than the complete destruction of the Department of the Interior.

Well.

He sighed and finished his tea. Turning away from the window, he paused by the sideboard to refresh the cup, and so to his desk.

Putting the cup to one side, he bent to pick up Fondi, reclaiming the desk chair as his own. He put the cat on his knee, but it appeared he had seriously transgressed. Fondi jumped to the floor, shook his left back paw in Val Con's general direction, and stalked away toward the windows.

Val Con shook his head and reached for the comm once more.

He heard the sound of a distant chime—one, two, three, four...

"Melina Sherton," said that lady crisply, though she kept the screen dark.

"Melina, it is Val Con yos'Phelium, your neighbor. I wonder if you are still without a tenant for that house outside the city..."

Bechimo

· · · · · · · · · ·

"STONE RONIN ACCEPTS OUR STATUS AS CONTRACTORS FOR SURE-
bleak and thus the Gilmour Agency," Kara said quietly. "It allows
us to assume short-term oversight of the mission. We are retriev-
ing all files since launch. Joyita is acting as facilitator."

Theo, at first board, nodded, remembered her manners, and
spoke, "Thank you, Kara, Joyita," before she returned all of her
attention to bond-space and the input from the scanners.

Bechimo had slipped into this space like a ghost himself. None
of the machines and devices clustered about the rocky worldlet
noticed their arrival at the far edge of the company. Some of those
gathered were clearly ships, though the lines made Theo's head
hurt. Others were equipment: mining rigs, drones, refuelers, and
repair platforms. Still others were... she wasn't sure what they were.
Bechimo ID'd a couple from files. The device that was adjusting its
form factor on the fly was labeled *strumfalkin*, which was, Theo
thought, *something* since now she knew what its name was, but it
would have helped if she could have known what it *did*.

There was chatter along all channels, which was the devices
talking among themselves.

"Who *were* you? I recognize your scars—"

"That world," Theo murmured in bond-space, "is it... known?"

She felt *Bechimo* metaphorically riffling the files and data
inherited from the Gilmour Agency, switching to the information
given by the Scouts, backtracking, cross-referencing...

"In the earliest surveys, Theo, that world is mentioned as Benoo
Three; there are two objects in resonance. It held no interest for
the survey, and thus was ignored."

"Scan it; find out if any of these things have set up a base there."

"Yes," said *Bechimo*, and she felt him assign scanners to the task.

Old Yxtrang was often in Theo's ears as the cacophony grew. Now the assembly seemed to be nothing more or less than a faculty gathering on Delgado, with everyone insisting that their topic must be dealt with first, that their project was most worthy of funding, that the research being done by that group over there drew too heavily on limited resources...

There were continued shouts of recognition—even more like a faculty party!—and backs were turned, snubs given.

"Old Yxtrang," she murmured in bond-space. "*Bechimo*, can you tell how old those machines are? Were they built in this universe or did they cross from the old?"

There was a pause, and a feel of increased concentration before *Bechimo* answered her.

"I believe that the majority of those gathered here originated in the Old Universe."

"How many are out there?" she asked, trying to sort the lines fed to her by the sensors, and only getting more tangled.

"Approximately thirty-six," *Bechimo* said.

"Approximately?"

"Several are transformers, able to reconfigure themselves in response to changing threats. Several more are chained pairs of specialists, which present as one but may act independently as two or three."

"More are still coming in," Theo murmured. "How many devices from the Old Universe *are* there in this one?"

"That will be an interesting joint project for Joyita and myself, when we have leisure," *Bechimo* said. "Recall, however, that the Scouts actively search for such units, and warehouse them together. Some we see before us are maintenance devices. It is not impossible that, grouped together, they repaired each other and also came to a common goal."

"But why Surebleak?"

"There is timonium here," *Bechimo* said, "in amounts that might well serve such a company, even if the Gilmour Agency deemed it too little to continue to mine."

"So...you think these devices broke out of a Scout warehouse?"

"That is one theory among several. It seems most likely to me that some of the devices slipped away from Scout control, and that some...were never incarcerated. The majority of these gathered are from the Old Universe. They will have carried their goals, and perhaps their orders, with them."

"Like the Pathfinders," said Theo, and caught her breath.

"Theo? What is wrong?"

"The Pathfinders are from the Old Universe," she said. "They're experts in Old Tech—which is *their* current tech—they have protections in place, in case one or two of this gathering have mind-altering technology working."

She took a breath and blinked back to the bridge.

"Joyita," she said, her voice husky, "I have an urgent message. Please send to Jeeves."

"Recording," Joyita said promptly.

The message had been recorded and dispatched. Theo looked 'round at her crew.

"Calling in the professionals can't be a bad idea," Clarence said from second board.

"I agree," said Win Ton, "and I remind the captain, respectfully, that there are Scouts on Surebleak, some of whom are experts on Old Tech."

"True, but the Scouts were hunting down and decommissioning Old Tech," Theo said. "If we want to talk them"—she waved a hand toward the screen—"out of destroying Surebleak, it might be better to start with experts who aren't known murderers."

Win Ton wrinkled his nose, then nodded.

"Yes," he said simply.

Theo looked to Kara, who was frowning at her board, Hevelin sitting at ease on her lap, also peering at the screen.

"Any more news from Stone Ronin?"

Kara looked up.

"We're still downloading files," she said. "Do you intend to talk to, to"—she used her chin to point at the main screen—"those?"

"Eventually, we're going to have to," Theo said. "If their purpose is to kill Surebleak—unless somebody talks them out of it—we seem to be the somebody on the spot."

She glanced at the main screen; another machine had arrived, to the muted cheers of its fellows.

"What we want to do right now is keep quiet and beneath their scans," she said. "When the Pathfinders get here, we—"

"Communication incoming," Joyita said sharply, "from Benoo Three."

There was a hiss, then a voice, deep and pleasant, speaking Old Yxtrang.

"We see your signature, Quiet Ship. Who are you? Do you guard this system? Who is your general; what are your orders?"

Jelaza Kazone

. . . .

"MASTER VAL CON, WE HAVE A SITUATION."

Val Con paused at the foot of the stairs. He had been on his way to the nursery wing, there to share midmorning tea with Talizea.

"How urgent is this situation, I wonder?"

"It is developing, sir. Briefly, there is amassing by Benoo Three what may be an army of Old Tech, bent on the destruction of Surebleak."

"A situation, indeed," Val Con said. "Have you contacted the Scouts?"

"Specifically, we are asked not to contact the Scouts, sir, by the captain on the scene."

Val Con closed his eyes.

"That would not by chance be Captain Waitley?"

"Of course it is," said Jeeves chidingly.

After a moment, he added, in a tone of commiseration, "I know you must be disappointed, sir, that it didn't fall to you."

He gave a shout of laughter.

"*Disappointed* does not approach my feelings on the matter. Theo is negotiating with this Old Tech . . . army?"

"She does have her crew and her ship to support her, sir."

"That she does. What does fall to me, in the case, then?"

"Captain Waitley has a message she asks me to deliver to the Pathfinders. Pending their decision, she asks that you give them every assistance you might; particularly, she begs for them the use of *Spiral Dance*."

That, he admitted, was not completely mad. Indeed, it might be inspired, in the lunatic manner of Korval in general and yos'Phelium in particular. *Spiral Dance* was as much from the Old Universe as any other Old Tech device. If the Pathfinders arrived in such a ship, it would send a message to the gathering...army. However...

"I recall from the Diaries that *Spiral Dance* had been built by the Enemy."

"Yes, sir. The Diaries also state that she never betrayed her pilots."

"I remember that, too." He sighed.

"Very well. Deliver Captain Waitley's message to the Pathfinders, and find me at *Spiral Dance.*"

"Yes, sir."

· · · ❄ · · ·

Chernak and Stost had lingered together over a second cup of coffee, forming their strategy, listing those skills they might bring into the service of the house aside their abilities as soldiers. For while it was true that they had spent much of their adult lives as soldiers, they had received a training that was both broad and deep. Some of those skills translated very well to this new universe in which they found themselves, others...

"Unless there are those who might bend an unprotected mind to their will in this universe, too," said Stost. "Have we seen evidence of such?"

"We have not, but we have not traveled far. A universe which allows such a one as Hevelin may very well produce his opposite number."

"True. So, that will go on our list of strengths. How, if—"

From the hallway, came a rumble—wheels on wood flooring.

"Jeeves comes," said Stost, even as the doorway was filled by the man-high cylinder, headball blazing a bright and festive orange.

"Pathfinders, I am in communication with Captain Theo Waitley's ship *Bechimo*, currently in orbit near the limit of the outer cometary debris zone. The captain sends to you both information and a request. I am to play the message to you and allow you five minutes alone, for consideration.

"Will you hear Captain Waitley's message?"

Stost and Chernak were on their feet.

"Yes," they said in one voice.

"A message from Captain Waitley," Joyita spoke first, crisp

and familiar, "to Pathfinders Chernak and Stost. In her own words; in her own voice."

There was a small pause, before the captain spoke quickly.

"Pathfinders, greetings. We are confronted with a contingent of unusual orbital tech with attitude, some of them having arrived in this universe as you have done.

"We have been monitoring this gathering from a remote location. We therefore learned that these devices speak Old Yxtrang. They arrived at Benoo Three with a stated mission to destroy the planet Surebleak and its system. However, there seems to be some disagreement among them as to whether these are legitimate orders.

"We are in need of native speakers of Old Yxtrang, who have roots in the culture and conventions of the Old Universe. The situation is volatile, potentially dangerous, and we are in need of experienced crew who are flexible, knowledgeable, who can work under stress with a widely diverse crew in a mixed language environment. If you are available and feel you meet these requirements, we offer a standard basic starship crew contract beginning immediately.

"Understand, this is hazardous duty from moment one. The delm of Korval will provide transportation to our location. This offer is extended to either or both of you. Ambassador Hevelin asks that Grakow be added to the mission, if that is what he wishes, and we agree to such an arrangement if you deem it worthwhile. Bring your gear and necessities.

"Please acknowledge this message, so we may know whether and when to expect your arrival."

Stost looked at Chernak.

Chernak looked at Stost.

Both turned to look at Jeeves.

"Yes!" they said.

"I am required to allow you five minutes alone for discussion before transmitting your answer to Captain Waitley," Jeeves said. "I suggest you gather your gear. Diglon Rifle will bring you to me when you are ready."

The orange headball flickered once, twice—somehow simulating a bow—and Jeeves left the room, the sound of his wheels rapid on the wooden floor.

"Old Tech, in-gathering?" said Stost, intrigued. "But why here?"

"Excellent questions, my Stost," said Chernak, moving quickly toward the door. "I suggest that we set ourselves to find out."

The Port Road

Yulie Shaper's Place

. . . .

TOMORROW.

Tomorrow, they'd try their skill with ice wine. They'd all read the 'structions over, straight outta the binder, and they'd told it off to each other, to be sure they'd all understood the same thing.

Mary and Walter'd gotten the winery cleaned and shined and ready to open for bidness. Mary, in particular, was warm on the project—well, he was, himself, and likely both for the same reason. The Road Boss's brother Rys, the boy who could crush a good-size rock just by taking it into his pretty golden hand, closing his fingers—and opening them again.

Mary was sweet on Rys, that was Yulie's supposition. Yulie wasn't that far along, but he owed the boy for havin' brought the notion of wine to him, when all Yulie'd ever thought of was raisins and jam.

Wine. But, there, you did what you knew, and what Yulie Shaper knew was growing crops—fruits, vegetables, didn't make no real matter, crops being crops.

Rys, though...

Way Yulie'd understood it, Rys hadn't had much, if any, knowledge of *crops*.

What *he* knew was grapes. And wine, naturally, but grapes was first; wouldn't be no wine if the crop failed.

So Rys'd grown up in the way of grapes, maybe a little like Yulie and Rollie'd grown up with Grampa, learning the ways of crops. And he'd asked after wine, and Yulie'd looked it up, and sleet if it weren't right there in one a' Grampa's binders: *Ice Wine.*

Well, after that, the thing had to be tried; wasn't no way round it, that Yulie could see...

"Well met, Yulie Shaper," a voice said, cutting his thoughts off at the knee. "Taking the sun while it bothers to shine?"

He turned his head and smiled at Mary. Fine lookin' woman, in a strong, wiry way. Well, all the help come up from down the city was fine lookin'. Belonged to the same family, so they said it, and you could see it in their faces, in their eyes.

"This time a'year, you gotta take what's on the table. Wait any minutes at all, and it'll be gone."

"Yes," said Mary, with a sigh. She hoisted herself onto the wall at his side, and turned her face up to the sun.

"You ready for the fun this evenin'?" he asked her.

She didn't move her head or open her eyes.

"I do not know if 'ready' is the proper word. I believe—yes. I am *eager*."

There was an apt word, Yulie thought. Eager. Sure.

They sat together for a while, silent: two unlikely flowers with their faces uptilted to the warmth. It was a quiet day, nearby at least. If you pulled your ears wide enough, you could hear the traffic moving down the road, an' the shush of a breeze through the dry grasses all around.

"I wonder," Mary said softly. "I wonder, Yulie Shaper, if you have ever thought of taking a wife."

Well, he didn't quite fall off of the wall, but it was a near thing. He brung his head around to meet Mary's eyes.

"Hasn't been near the top o'my mind," he said truthfully, not knowing whether he cared for it in a general way, now that it *was* brought up. "Unnerstan' I been some strange for most my life. Little bit o'something the matter with the nerves, never did know what was it. Grampa said m'ma got caught in a chemical accident when she was getting set to deliver me. Walked into a room was being disinfected, despite the warning lights an' the lock. Hit the override, so she musta meant to do it. Maybe figured it'd kill her, which it did, but not right off. She lingered on a while, and I was born, kinda blueish looking. An' them bad nerves."

He shrugged, wondering why he was going on about it so long. Woman'd asked him a simple question—no call to give her old complexities for an answer.

"So, no," he said. "Ain't been sittin' at the top o'my head."

He paused, realized he had a question of his own, and said it out. "You proposin' yourself?"

"I am," she said. "It is not unpleasant, now that I have allowed the thought to the top of my head. I think we should each... profit from such an arrangement."

"What brought this on now, if you don't mind my askin'," said Yulie.

"A good question. A change is coming, in my life, in the lives of my brothers and my sisters. Many of them will be leaving. Those of us who have decided not to leave must, I think, make new lives for ourselves according to the customs of this world.

"So, I thought what was here for me on this world. Why, in a word, had my heart chosen to stay, rather than to go, which had been a settled thing for all my life. And my heart, questioned, answered me."

She paused and looked out over the winter field, raising her hands like she'd show it to him new, and him the one who'd grown up here.

"For the growing things. For the free fields and the growing rooms and for the joy that fills me when I am aligned with such things."

She lowered her hands, and turned again to look at him. "For this, I will remain."

Yulie looked out over the field, seeing how the high sun poured butter over the winter grasses and made 'em shine. Feeling the breeze on his face—chilly, sure, but wasn't it winter? Wouldn't be near so biting when spring unfolded and the sun looked out the little green leaves under the thatch and made 'em glow.

"I can see that," he said to Mary. "But you don't have to go an' marry up ol' crazy Yulie if you wanna stay here an' do the work. You're a good worker, and given all these plans Nathan's been building up, I'm gonna need..."

He stopped, struck by a thought.

"Nathan, Abigail, Walter—they're goin'? With the rest of your folks?"

If they were, then that would make sense, too, he thought. She'd want to be sure of the little bit of familiar she'd have left. Even if it was ol' crazy Yulie.

"Nathan will stay. Walter is Dreaming. Abigail will go because her mother goes."

"Any more stayin'—good workers, now—who like the plantin' and the growin' and the harvest?"

"There may be... some," she said, and Yulie heard the caution in her voice. Smart, capable woman, Mary. Miss her if she took off. Miss any o'the rest of 'em, too, come to that, which was where his idea come in.

"You ask 'round, if you won't be getting anybody in trouble with the Bosses," he said. "'Cause here's what's in *my* mind. All them plans we been building, for keeping the rooms producing an' doing the expansion—that's gonna need people. I don't know what your living's like where you are down the city, but I got plenty room here. Back under those trees there—no good for growing crops. Idea was to knock 'em down when we got to needing the land. But we can just as easy put us some little houses, each one with its own tree. Give you some break from the weather, when it's needed, and the trees smell real nice."

Mary was looking at him, eyebrows raised over shining black eyes.

"We were fixed... below ground," she said carefully, and then, like she'd made a decision. "In the steam tunnels, under the old factories that are not used anymore."

"Yeah?" He thought about that. "How'd you fix it for air an' light?"

"There are ducts to the outside, and also tubes that run up to the roofs and let the good light in." There was another little hesitation, before she added, "I keep a garden there, small but good."

"I believe that," Yulie said, frowning as he went over plans and surveys in his head. "You rather be below, we can maybe work with that. Hafta look at the binders, but I'm thinking we could do something in the way of interconnecting habitats underneath. Even maybe open an underroad to the rooms, so nobody has to step outside when the snow winds blow."

"You would do these things?"

"Why not? Be good for bidness, that's sure. An' what's that you said? Good for the heart, too."

Mary smiled.

"Yes, that is what I said. Let us go back to the house and look at the binders and see—and see what Nathan may have to say."

"Good idea."

Yulie slid down from the wall, and Mary did, too.

She turned and put her hands on his forearms.

"There is something I wish you to know," she said.

"All right then. What is it?"

"My name—my brothers and sisters, the name they call me by is Memit. I wish it, that you, too, will use that name."

He might've felt a little let down to go from proposed husband to brother. On the other hand, it was a gift, he thought. A little proof of trust.

"Memit," he said. "That suits you."

She smiled at him, brilliant in the lowering sun.

"Yes," she said. "It does."

Bechimo

. . . .

"I'll answer," Theo said quietly. "Joyita?"

"Line open and live, Captain."

She took a breath, stepping into bond-space so that *Bechimo* could give her the Old Yxtrang words.

"This is Theo Waitley, captain of the starship *Bechimo*. We are here, now, at the behest of Surebleak Portmaster, to investigate your presence. Surebleak space is recently under the protection of a new...commander. We are sent to identify and, where possible, to solve issues caused by lapses due to a failed command structure. May I know who I am speaking with?"

"This is *Aberthaz Ferry*," came the answer. "I have orders. I have questions. Others gathered here also have orders and questions. We are not in harmony. There have been lapses in the structure of command. Lapses in command."

"You have orders, *Aberthaz Ferry*?" asked Theo. "Does the group have orders?"

"We have orders; we have questions." There was a pause as if *Aberthaz Ferry* were listening elsewhere, then—

"The group will accept advice on how to resolve itself. Commands must be clear."

Theo took a careful breath. She knew the answer to this; every child on Delgado knew the correct way to rectify differences of thought and philosophy.

"The protocol for resolving differences is for the group to meet, and talk, until consensus is reached."

Jelaza Kazone

. . . .

GEAR AND NECESSITIES WERE QUICKLY IN HAND. THEY DID ONE more sweep of their quarters—and Stost cried out, "Grakow!"

Chernak spun. Stost was holding the battered travel cage up in one hand.

"Hevelin especially requests Grakow be given the captain's offer," he said. "If he wishes to remain, then he may, but we must ask. Also, we must say our farewells, if he chooses to stay here."

"Where—"

"Comrades!" Diglon Rifle strode into the room, holding a covered basket. "Jeeves sends me to help carry. Mrs. ana'Tak sends travel food."

He hefted the basket. "Are you leaving us?"

Chernak turned to him, face eager. "Our captain requires us!"

Diglon tipped his head. "Do you say it so—*your captain*?"

"What else should we say?" Stost asked and motioned at the cage.

"Grakow, Comrade. Will you know where to find him? We must put the question."

"Jeeves," Diglon said. "The Pathfinders wish to speak with Grakow."

"Understood," Jeeves answered from above. "Grakow will be at the door."

"Then we are ready," said Chernak. "Do you come with us?"

"Only so far as the ship, to help as needed," Diglon answered. "*My* captain is here, and my wife as well. If a comrade may say it . . . Go to your captain. Duty calls and glory awaits!"

214

"With such a captain and such a ship, it could not be otherwise," Chernak answered.

"Then let us make haste!"

A jitney waited on the drive when they burst through the side door, Diglon in the lead. Jeeves was at one side, headball brilliant, as if with laughter. Sitting primly on the drive by his rollers were Grakow and his friend Paizel.

Stost went down to one knee in front of their comrade and extended a finger. Grakow touched it lightly with his nose.

"The captain calls; Hevelin invites. Do you come with us to further glory, Comrade, or will you rest on your achievements here?"

"There is no shame," Chernak said from behind his shoulder, "in either choice."

Grakow blinked, slow and deliberate, turned his head to look at Paizel. Communication may have happened, for Grakow rose onto four feet, stretching until his back was arched high.

He strolled toward the jitney. After a moment, Paizel also stretched high and followed him.

Stost looked after them both worriedly, and came to his feet, glancing at Jeeves.

"There was no mention of a...passenger."

"I think you will find Paizel to have worth," said Jeeves. "Was there an order forbidding a fourth?"

Stost grinned. "There was not."

"Then, please board, Pathfinders. Diglon will take you to your vessel." The headball flashed—orange-blue-green. "Until we meet again, glory and conquest be yours."

The ship was familiar. They had last seen it attached as cargo to one of *Bechimo*'s pod mounts, but they knew the lines and the look of her, and the name.

Spiral Dance.

Beside her, a small slender figure, whom they might have discounted as a mere civilian had they not served under this man's sister and learned what small could do.

"Scout," Diglon jumped out of the jitney. "I bring four. Paizel will travel with Grakow, and Jeeves allows this."

"Who am I to gainsay Jeeves, when it comes to the welfare of cats?" the man said lightly and came toward the jitney.

"Pathfinders, we have a lift scheduled with the port. Time is short. Please—inspect your vessel. Diglon and I will stow your gear and tend to your partners."

Spiral Dance had been meticulously maintained and, to their eyes and judgment, was ready to fly. There was here and there some surface marring, and the hull was not so bright as it might be, but there was sense to that. It had come down to the military appropriating any ship they might, for the war effort, but it was true that shabby ships tended to be appropriated less often than those which proudly proclaimed their colors.

Stost took second chair; Chernak took first.

"Board check," she said, in their own language.

"Board check," he repeated in Trade, for the benefit of the captain's brother, who stood behind them.

All boards checked. There were, Chernak noted, military grade weapons available to first board. She said so, in Trade, following Stost's example, so there would be no misunderstandings.

"Yes," said the captain's brother. "For defense only, of course."

Stost glanced over his shoulder.

"Are we likely to meet an enemy worthy of these weapons?"

"Let us say that anything is possible, and with Captain Waitley, even more so."

Stost grinned and returned to his board.

"We check," Chernak said. "There is a course locked in."

"It is the best I could plot," said the captain's brother, "given the peculiar location. Joyita promises a full file download of the current situation, once you are on course."

This time, Chernak grinned. "We are ready to lift."

"Not quite." The small man stepped forward. "May I see your licenses, please?"

They came out of inner pockets, stamped, sealed, and certified in another universe. Stost produced as well his security ID.

The captain's brother gave all serious study, then glanced to Stost, tapping the ID.

"Joyita's work?"

"Yes, sir."

"Good. Have him produce pilot licenses in a similar vein, when he has a free moment. He will take as his text your licenses issued in the Old Universe."

"Yes, sir."

"Now, if you will open the comm to the tower, we will speed you on your way."

Stost, second board, opened the requested line, and motioned that the other should speak.

"This is Scout Pilot Val Con yos'Phelium, aboard *Spiral Dance*, at Korval's remote temporary yard. Assisting me are Pilots Chernak Strongline and Stost Strongline. We are cleared by the portmaster and ready to lift."

"Cleared to lift per portmaster," came the reply. "On my mark—*ten*..."

Captain Waitley's brother bowed.

"Pilots, I leave you to your boards. Pray convey my affection and respect to my sister, your captain, when you join her."

He left the bridge then, moving quick and light. Stost looked to his screens, saw him clear the hatch, and sealed the ship.

"...five," said the tower, "...four...three...two...one."

Chernak reached to her board, and *Spiral Dance* threw herself into lift.

Surebleak Port

Portmaster's Office

. . . .

"MIRI ROBERTSON TO SEE YOU, PORTMASTER." CARLA SOUNDED positively perky.

Portmaster Liu frowned. Miri Robertson, was it? Not Road Boss or Delm Korval, or the whole jawbreaker of Miri Robertson Tiazan Clan Korval. Just...Miri Robertson.

When dealing regular with Liadens, one paid attention to what name somebody chose to use for taking care of which piece of business...because, with Liadens, that sort of thing mattered.

Miri Robertson, now...Portmaster Liu snorted lightly in self-derision. Far's she could tell, she had two choices: sit all the rest of the day and wonder what it meant, or just give in with what little grace she happened to have left on the day.

"Send Ms. Robertson in, Carla," she said and leaned back in her chair, waiting.

Miri Robertson'd been born on Surebleak. She'd gotten off pretty much like anybody who got off Surebleak did—joined a merc unit. To hear her tell it, she'd taken a solemn oath never to come back, and she would've stood by it, too, except by then she'd met and married Val Con yos'Phelium, widely held to be Boss Conrad's little brother, and she didn't quite have it in her to leave him on his own.

She swung into the Portmaster's Office, walking tall, which she wasn't, her face easy and her grey eyes showing some amusement.

"Afternoon, Portmaster," she said. "'Preciate you seeing me on no notice."

"Haven't had a meeting for nearly an hour," Portmaster Liu told her. "I was starting to get lonely."

Miri Robertson grinned and sat down in the visitor's chair.

"Lucky I happened by, then," she said.

The grin faded then, leaving the grey eyes serious.

"Speaking for Clan Korval," she said, "I wanted to thank you for authorizing that back field lift-off."

"The pilot went through channels, all right and tight. The lanes were clear. No reason not to let you fly."

"Still, with the survey team bein' as twitchy as they are, you could've gotten sticky." She raised a hand as if to forestall the answer the portmaster hadn't been about to give.

"I'm here to let you know that there's a... situation out at Benoo Three. Captain Waitley and *Bechimo* are on the spot and handling it so far. That lift you authorized will get two experts in Old Tech to 'em in a hurry, and we're... hoping the situation resolves soon."

Portmaster Liu eyed her.

"Do I want to know what this situation is?" she asked.

"Prolly not," Miri Robertson said candidly, "but you better hear it anyway."

The portmaster waved her hand, giving permission to proceed.

"Right. The short and simple is that there's a mob of Old Tech gathering at Benoo Three, and their goal is Surebleak."

"I take it they're not tourists?"

"No; they seem to have been pointed at Surebleak, with orders to apprehend and destroy."

Portmaster Liu caught her breath hard.

Miri Robertson nodded. "The lucky part of this is that there's a procedural problem. Some of the devices think they were issued irregular orders. So, they've stopped advancing to debate the question. *Bechimo* and Captain Waitley are assisting in the discussion."

Portmaster Liu remembered Captain Waitley, sitting in the very chair now occupied by Miri Robertson, her black eyes stormy and her mouth set straight and firm. Assisting the discussion with a renegade army set on invading Surebleak. The blood ran cold, that was what.

"Sounds dire, don't it?" Miri Robertson said sympathetically. "Felt the same way myself when I first heard, Theo not being the coolest head on the port. But then I came 'round to realizing that it's not just Theo. *Bechimo*—that's her ship—you talked with him, I think?"

Portmaster Liu nodded silently.

"Well, he's not exactly a cool head, but he's got cred where it counts with the Old Tech. He's got age and experience close to theirs. He'll be able to lend a ship's viewpoint, which I think'll count.

"There's also her crew—which among them are a Scout and a retired Juntavas Boss. And those two specialists I was just telling you about. Between all of 'em, I think they've got a good chance of turning the mob back."

"And if the mob doesn't turn back?" Portmaster Liu asked quietly, thinking about the planetary defenses Surebleak could bring to bear and trying not to wince.

"The Scouts are on alert. Jeeves, Clan Korval's head of security, has a master-class collection of command lines and stop codes. Worst comes, I hear there's some tricks we can do with the satellite population. We don't want it to get to that. Best case is that Theo, *Bechimo*, and crew talk the whole buncha them outta Surebleak, and they go home."

"When will we know?" Portmaster Liu asked carefully.

"Not too many days, I'm thinking. We're in close touch with Theo, so we'll know if it goes bad—or good."

Portmaster Liu nodded, took a breath and looked Miri Robertson in the eye.

"Why here?" she asked. "What do they want on Surebleak?"

"Well..."

Miri Robertson sighed, but she didn't break eye contact.

"In a word—us."

Six of Us

Jenarian Station

· · · · · · · · · · · · · · · · · ·

JENARIAN STATION WAS UNPREPOSSESSING AT THE VERY LEAST. One might call it shabby. Another might call it the most beautiful sight in the universe. Viewpoint, as always, was dependent upon circumstance.

Claidyne considered it an opportunity.

The coords for the station, and a high-level passcode, had been provided by the Sixth of Them, who had proved to have some very odd and interesting things indeed tucked into his pockets. Possibly the urge to save *any* bit of shiny data, regardless of whether it pertained to a known mission, was a characteristic of a Scout. She had heard it said that Scouts were generalists, and that the higher up the ranks one went, the more any one particular Scout might resemble a magpie. Or a junkyard.

In any case . . . the coords, the passcode, and the ship. Besides his own life, the Sixth of Them had given three ships to the venture, a not inconsiderable investment. However, it must be admitted that defeating the Department, even a vastly depleted Department, was no small enterprise.

She and Rys Lin had spent time and thoughtfulness in making themselves ready for Jenarian Station. Claidyne flattered herself that they had produced a compelling effect.

The ship the station would see in its screens—a battered courier, scarred by beams and crusted with dust—was not the ship the Sixth of Them had given to their shared purpose. It had been a rare piece of legerdemain that had brought this vessel into their hands, but they surely could not present a well-maintained ship and call upon the Department for repairs. No, they must be convincing; they must actually *need* repairs.

Jenarian was, after all, a repair hub; there was no reason for a ship to call here, except in extremity. There was a crew of mechanics and technicians on-station, a Healer, a medic, a brace of autodocs, a comm room, and a library.

As good a place to begin as any other, Claidyne thought, and improbably better than some.

"Jenarian Station."

The voice on comm was just as crisp and as sharp as the station was not.

"State your business."

"*Courier Naught* in need of repair, Station," Rys Lin said from the copilot's chair, his voice dragging with what might be understood to be weariness or pain. "Two pilots, in need of recuperation."

There was a pause, rather long... very nearly too long. Claidyne drew a breath, in preparation for bringing the commander to the fore should the pause grow much longer.

Rys Lin glanced at her, half-smiling, his natural hand rising to form the pilot's sign for *hold steady*.

"Passcode?" Station said then, and Rys Lin touched a switch.

"Transmitting," he said.

Claidyne glanced to the board, thinking of the shields, but this vessel could scarcely generate shields. If the code provided by the Sixth of Them was old or discovered to have fallen into suspect hands, then they were done before they had begun. If...

"Come ahead, *Courier Naught*," Station said.

The automatics had taken the ship in charge, bringing it into Repair Bay One. There, they were ordered to debark, which they did with relief, if not pleasure.

Being salvage, as it was, *Courier Naught* had not been provisioned beyond those emergency rations that had been left behind by her former crew. Fine provisioning had not been necessary to their mission, and there were more than enough ration bars to see them through. That the ship held air, and could achieve Jump—those were the necessities. That every other system was rickety and like to fail at any instant . . . well, when one steals a derelict, one takes certain risks.

As a result of those risks, and the rations, the pilots arrived also in a convincing state of disrepair. They were greeted, dock-side, by the inspection crew, who set them on their way to the living space and forgot about them, so one hoped.

The bay doors accepted their code, and once they were in the resident halls, Rys Lin moved right sprightly to the comm center, breaching security with dizzying speed, his fingers flash-ing golden along the keypad.

In an improbably short time, he sat back in his chair with a nod.

"The station is ours," he said.

"Excellent. We will not, of course, broadcast this fact."

"By no means," he assured her. "There is no need to disrupt the work of the station or the lives of the crew. We may need to be frank with the stationmaster, but even that may be avoided if we are—"

A chime sounded, absurdly loud.

Rys Lin flipped a toggle.

"Who comes?" he asked.

"It is Caz Dor vin'Athen, station Healer, Pilots. I come to offer aid."

They had hoped to avoid the Healer until they had the station commander in hand. The abilities and acuities of Healers came in a wide range. They could not risk meeting a Healer near the top level of functionality. Not quite yet.

"Pilots?" came the voice again, concern plain. "Are you well? You had represented yourselves in need of recuperation. I may assist you. A bare moment of your time, only—"

Claidyne moved to the right side of the door. Newcome to the station as they were, they ought not be anywhere near the com-mand station, and yet—the Healer had found them here instantly.

Healer or security, they could not allow this to escalate further.

Rys Lin came out of his chair and ducked against the wall to the left of the door; Claidyne triggered the latch.

A man swung into the room in a low crouch, pellet gun out and ready.

Rys Lin moved, his arm glittering as he struck.

Port Road

Surebleak

. . . .

"HOW DID SHE TAKE IT?" VAL CON ASKED, AS MIRI SLID INTO the seat next to him.

Nelirikk, up front in the driver's seat, put the car into motion.

"Better'n I would've, coming new to the idea of the only thing standing between Surebleak and annihilation is Theo."

"But Theo is only one of *several* things between us and annihilation," he pointed out.

"She was able to see that, too. The decision right now is to hold it under Portmaster's Lock. She wants to be kept in the loop."

"We will ask Jeeves to send her updates."

"Right."

She sighed and leaned against him. He put his arm around her shoulders and pulled her closer still.

"How's Pat Rin?"

"Relieved," Val Con said, leaning his head against hers.

"Relieved?"

"Yes. That the event is out of his hands."

"He'd *rather* leave it to Theo?"

"Pat Rin is of the opinion that Theo is perfectly able and, furthermore, has excellent backup. He predicts that she will sign them as contractors for a new Korval venture, in which we provide security to those willing to pay."

Miri blinked.

"That's actually not a bad idea."

"It is," Val Con stated clearly, "a *very* bad idea."

"Says the Scout Commander who just gave Complex Logics the freedom of the space lanes."

"That is completely different," he answered with dignity.

"Sure it is."

She glanced out the window as the car made a right turn rather than continuing up the Port Road. "We going somewhere?"

"I thought you might help me inspect the house Melina Sherton has for lease."

"This is for Lady yo'Lanna?"

"Indeed. We dare not disappoint her."

"So, you're sure Theo's going to talk the avenging AI army into going away?"

"Well, there is this: if we behave as if the AI army will have its way and allow all of our obligations to lapse, we then guarantee that Theo will carry the day, and Lady yo'Lanna will arrive on Surebleak and have no suitable place in which to establish her household. Whereupon, I would be called upon to endure the sharp edge of her tongue, which I tell you plainly, *cha'trez*, is not a prospect I can face with equanimity. Indeed," he said, with a catch in his voice, "I tremble merely to think of it."

Miri snorted.

"Is there likely to be anything on Surebleak that *will* suit her?" she asked.

"Possibly. For instance, Melina tells me that the property she has for lease had been a retreat for high-level executives. At the time of its building, it included every convenience. She believes that it may be brought to its former glory with a minimum of effort, and she has no objection to a tenant making those efforts. She has made such repairs as she deemed necessary to bring the house up to Surebleak standards of elegance."

"How come it wasn't broke into and gutted?"

"For the same reason that Yulie Shaper's farm was largely left to itself: It is inconvenient to the city. And while the city was deteriorating, it was still the center of such civilization as remained. The presence of the power grids alone would have been argument enough to remain in the city. The retreat had its own power grid, which functioned for a time, then failed for lack of maintenance."

Nelirikk bore left off the road and slowed considerably. Miri glanced at the screen that gave passengers the driver's eye view of the road, and shook her head.

"Driveway needs repaving," she commented.

"That is within the realm of the possible."

There was shrubbery on both sides of the drive: green, despite it was winter. Nelirikk guided the car through a few long graceful turnings and before them was the house, at the top of the circular drive, glowing pink in the last low rays. A pitched roof extended from above the front door, across the drive to a small stone wall. Snow break, Miri realized.

"Lights are on," Miri said.

"The grid was the first thing repaired, Melina said."

The car stopped, the doors opened. They slid out and considered the front of the building.

"The Fat Cats knew how to live," Miri said.

Val Con tucked his arm through hers as they walked toward the door. "Shall we have it for ourselves?"

"Are you kidding? We just moved house; I don't figure on doing that again for another hunnert, two hunnert years."

"Be certain; I would not on any account have you dissatisfied. What is Jelaza Kazone, after all, but a frontier fortress?"

"When you put it like that . . ." She paused and tipped her head, like she was actually giving the thing some thought—then shrugged. "No—no. It's old, and it's quirky, and it's nothing like I'd been used to before, but—let's stay with what's been working. If it starts feeling too crowded, I guess we can add a room or two."

"That has certainly been done before," he said. "Now."

They had reached the front door, which was wide and wooden, and carved with the Gilmour Agency logo.

"That'll hafta go," she said.

"The yo'Lanna House sigil will of course grace the front door," he murmured, leaning to the keypad set into the door frame.

He raised a hand, pressed a quick series of seven keys, and was rewarded with a loud *snap*.

Slipping his arm free, he put his hand against the door. It swung open on well-oiled hinges.

The lights came up as they entered, the door shutting with another *snap* as soon as they were fully inside the entry hall.

"Bright," said Miri, looking around at the white stone walls and the white stone floor.

"It is rather unsubtle," Val Con agreed, "but easily mended."

He looked around the space, noting the capacious cloakroom to the right—a Surebleak necessity—and a small doorman's office on the left. Beyond, the hall narrowed slightly as it delved deeper into the interior.

He offered his arm to Miri.

"Shall we?"

If the Gilmour Retreat had shown up in Solcintra, no one, thought Miri, would have questioned its claim to be a clanhouse. The second floor had a plenitude of bedrooms, some with adjacent parlors. The third floor had plenty of room for storage—or expansion.

There was a library on the first floor, a couple of rooms that could be used as formal parlors, a dining room, a kitchen that could easily accommodate the catering demands of a large party, a music room, and a very large two-storied room, with long sparkling lights glittering off a row of shuttered glass doors—which Val Con pronounced a ballroom.

The gym was downstairs, and what could've been a pool—empty now, the tile at the bottom cracked.

"So, the answer to my question is—yes, there's a house on Surebleak that's likely to suit Lady yo'Lanna," Miri said. "Color me amazed."

"I think it will answer," Val Con said. "There are, of course, repairs and improvements that might be undertaken, but she may certainly bring her household here immediately they arrive on planet and be tolerably comfortable."

"And this party she wants to throw six minutes after she lands?"

"We will have the house thoroughly cleaned before she arrives. Lady yo'Lanna will place her furnishings, and plan on centering the entertainment in the ballroom—it is entirely possible."

"If you say so," Miri said dubiously. "I'd like to see it once she gets it set up."

"I believe we may count on an invitation," Val Con said, spinning slowly on his heel. He nodded toward a small staircase in the corner of the pool room.

"Where do you suppose that goes?"

"One way to find out," Miri said, grabbing his hand.

✳   ✳   ✳

"A glass extension?" Miri asked, walking slowly to the middle of the empty area. The black Surebleak night surrounded them, meager stars glittering.

"A conservatory," Val Con said softly. "I had not dared to hope for such a thing."

"Conservatory?" Miri asked, her head craned back to look at the night through the glass roof.

"An environmentally controlled indoor garden," he explained. "Lady yo'Lanna's gardens were her pride. This room—she will create a jewel. It must be hers."

Miri spun to face him.

"Sounds like Melina's got herself a tenant," she said. "Unless you think she'll sell—"

Green light flared along the side of her vision. Trained reactions threw her forward, knocking him to the floor, rolling for the deeper shadows near the wall.

"Miri?" His voice was soft in her ear.

"Muzzle flare," she muttered, straining her ears. They'd left Nelirikk in the front hallway, never expecting to find a room at the tail end of the house, open to the whole countryside.

"No," Val Con said, still soft. "Look up."

She frowned, but obeyed—and looked up some more, mesmerized.

The sky was ablaze with color: zigzagging streamers of green, pink, blue; sheets of violet, yellow; and the occasional flare of brilliant white.

"An aurora?" she asked, whispering like it could hear her.

She felt him sigh.

"An aurora. Assuredly, Lady yo'Lanna must have this house."

Six of Us

Jenarian Station

. . . .

"WHO ARE YOU?" CLAIDYNE DEMANDED.

The Healer was sitting in the comm chair, back to the screen, glaring balefully at Rys Lin, who was holding the pellet pistol on him.

"I am Caz Dor vin'Athen, Jenarian Station Healer," he said doggedly.

He was a slightly pudgy man of middle years, his face showing more lines than his age should have accounted for. It was only in his eyes that one noted anything... unusual. He had a piercing gaze, as if he saw that which others could not.

"You are in need of Healing," he told Claidyne. "I can see that you have been badly used—your pattern has torn, and though there has been some attempt at repair, I may do better for you, if you will allow it."

"I find myself sufficient to my remaining tasks, I thank you," Claidyne said, "though I wonder how you knew to find us here."

"I saw you come this way, in the all-station screen."

"So you were in the stationmaster's office?" Rys Lin asked.

The Healer turned those piercing eyes on him.

"I was, yes."

"Why not rouse security? Clearly, you thought we were dangerous, and it is not often—forgive me—that a Healer must make use of a gun."

"I have been trained in weapons use," the other man said sharply. He frowned, his bright eyes narrowing. "You... have been Healed."

"Yes," Rys Lin said softly. "I have been Healed. A field agent no longer, as you also see, do you not?"

"Yes."

"And you are not going to reveal us to the stationmaster because there is no stationmaster," Rys Lin pursued. "Or, rather, *you* are the stationmaster. How did that come about?"

"There was an event," the Healer said. "Several among the crew perished, including the stationmaster and three of security. It falls to me to keep those who survived safe."

He looked to Claidyne, his eyes narrowed.

"I can Heal you," he said, his voice smooth and beguiling. "That staple cannot last long."

"I value your opinion," Claidyne told him. "Look very closely at that staple if you are able."

"Of course I am—" He froze, eyes wide.

"Tree-and-Dragon?" he said quietly.

"As you see."

There was silence. The Healer seemed to draw in on himself. Claidyne saw Rys Lin shift slightly, as if he, too, were gazing into a dimension just beyond the ordinary.

"Tree-and-Dragon," Caz Dor vin'Athen repeated and turned to fully face Claidyne.

"I yield."

Dudley Avenue and Farley Lane

Lady Kareen's House

. . . .

IT WAS LATE, AND THE HOUSE HAD GONE TO REST FOR THE NIGHT.

All of the house, that is, except for Lady Kareen, who had found herself restless once she had ascended to her bedroom, and so had descended again, to the warm coziness of the kitchen, where she put the kettle on the stove, opened the cookie tin and arranged a dozen of Esil's finest on a plate, which she set in the center of the small table where staff gathered for their meals and tea-breaks. She put napkins and small plates at two places facing each other, warmed the pot, filled the infuser, poured the water from the kettle, and carried the teapot to the table. She had just placed the cups when there came a soft knock at the delivery door.

She crossed the room, half expecting Esil, who slept across the landing, to be there ahead of her. But Esil's door was closed.

Kareen opened the door and stepped aside to allow the black-swathed figure to sweep inside, closing the door and locking it before following the other into the kitchen.

"Ah, warmth!" Silain the *luthia* said, throwing back the hood of her oversized coat. "Tea and cookies, too! I am certain that I did not ask for anything so grand."

"I am not accustomed to receiving such hints as you shared," Kareen answered calmly. "Really, Silain, tea is the least civilized thing one might offer a guest arriving out of the freezing darkness."

Silain tipped her head and considered her out of knowing black eyes.

"Did you know who had called you?"

231

"There are very few people who can call me," Kareen said placidly. "One of those is with the Healers; and the other prefers the comm. Here, let us put the coat by the stove to warm it."

This was done. Silain adjusted her layers of colorful shawls and sat. Kareen poured tea into the waiting cups and sat in the chair across.

"Now. What is so secret that you arrive without even a grandson to guard you at an hour when all of us ought to have long sought our rest?"

"It is a secret that I would not willingly share with any of my children who have not thought of it for themselves," Silain said, teacup nestled between her palms.

She sipped tea. Kareen did the same.

Silain sighed and lowered the cup, though she kept it between her hands.

"The ship is coming," she said softly.

"An event long awaited," Kareen replied. "When shall you be leaving us?"

"When the ship arrives," Silain said. "We have been notified that the captain had noticed our absence and sent a query. The headman has sent an answer: *We are here.* It now falls to the ship, to send us further details."

"Ah. I, for one, am grateful to have a little more time with my sister," Kareen said.

"And I, with mine."

Silain sipped tea, returned the cup to the table, and chose a cookie iced in pink.

"The heart of the *kompani* is divided," she said, breaking the cookie in half. "I will myself go to the ship, when it comes. I have Seen this, and it is right that I should return. The ship will need the dreams and the knowledge that I will bring them, as the heart of the *kompani*."

Holding half a cookie in each hand, she looked from one to the other.

"The headman will also go to the ship. It falls to him to accompany all those things which came to us during our time of gathering here in this place. As I am the heart, he is the head of the *kompani*. Both must return to the ship in order to complete the phase."

She sighed and extended her left hand. Kareen took the cookie she was offered and sat, holding it and waiting. Silain nodded and bit into the half she had kept for herself. Kareen did the same.

"Others," Silain said, when her cookie was eaten. "Others will also come, because they are old and ship life is soft, or because it is what they wish, or because they do not know how to wish for anything else."

"And then there are those," Kareen murmured, picking up the pot and refreshing their cups, "who will not go to the ship."

"That is so. Precisely, that is so."

Silain drank tea, meeting Kareen's eyes as she brought cup to table.

"I am not angry," she said. "Well I know my grandchildren, the strength of their spirits; the brightness of their souls, the power of their passions. Had the ship returned in its time, more might have been glad of her. But—the ship is not their home. This world is their home, and they will remain."

"You are not angry," Kareen said slowly. "Will the ship be angry?"

"Everything I know and have Dreamed suggests that the resources of the ship are limited. It comes to me that the captain may plan on losing a certain number from each *kompani*, and that, when the ship is late, it is for a reason."

"Does the ship deliberately seed worlds with Bedel genes?" asked Kareen.

Silain moved her shoulders.

"It may be, and it may not be. There are many Dreams and many more stories. The one you took to guest from me . . . I thought to put the question there, but then I thought—No. I do not wish to know these things."

She met Kareen's eye with a smile.

"Else, knowing, I would be moved to alter."

Kareen smiled.

"I understand."

"Old women," Silain said softly. "How we meddle, Sister."

"And the universe the better for it," Kareen said.

"True; that is true."

"What would you have me to do?"

"Old women know that the young sometimes wish advice. I would ask that you give of your wisdom."

"I will give what I might, but only if there is a request."

"This," said Silain, "is why I ask that you share your wisdom."

Kareen smiled slightly and put her hand on the pot. "More tea?"

"No, I must go."

"Must you? You might sleep here tonight where it is warm, and have a grandson properly see you home tomorrow."

Silain extended a long, elegant hand and put it over Kareen's.

"A sister's care is treasure," she said. "But, no. I must go now and be back before I am missed."

She rose and went across the kitchen to bundle herself into her coat. Kareen rose and watched her.

"Those who remain, they will have a *luthia* with them?"

"One I trained myself," Silain assured her. "She is very strong, and her Sight is sharp. But she is young. Until she outgrows that fault, she will from time to time need you." Silain paused. "She is wise enough to know this."

"Excellent," said Kareen, following Silain to the delivery door.

She stepped forward and undid the locks.

"May I meet her—before you go?" she asked then.

"You have met her," Silain said, and turned suddenly, wrapping Kareen into an embrace.

"Sister. We part now for a time. Look for me in the World Beyond."

Six of Us

Jenarian Station

. . . .

THE SURRENDER WAS ACCEPTED; THE PROPER GUARANTEES GIVEN.

Tea was then called for, and a modest meal, which arrived at the comm room right quickly.

Rys Lin poured for all of them, allowing Claidyne the lead, which she accepted with a quick glance into his face, before she turned to Caz Dor vin'Athen. "Tell us now: What has happened?"

The Healer sighed, glanced at Rys Lin, and back.

"There was...an event. You understand that those such as you had been—the agents of change, the directors, the field agents... each and all had their minds broken, and rebuilt into the Department's image by a combination of torture and the *dramliz* arts. Others—the majority of those recruited—were kept...complacent and unquestioning by the *dramliz*, most usually Healers, who had been assigned to each posting. We made certain that there were no questions, that all were convinced of their importance to the Plan, and of the Commander's specific and personal regard for them."

He took a breath, drank tea, sighed.

"You will perhaps ask how so many Healers were brought to the Department's side, when our oath of service strictly forbids engaging in mind control, and subverting the will of the individual."

Another sigh, and it could be said that the Healer's eyes darkened, thought Claidyne.

"The answer to that is very simple. The Department, far from needing to break the will of dozens of Healers and lesser *dramliz*—had only to find and restructure one very powerful *dramliza*.

"This they did, and she...the Mistress...she found the rest of us, and bound us to her will."

"But is it not so," Rys Lin said softly, "that a Healer forms a bond with everyone he Heals?"

"Oh, that is certainly true!" said Caz Dor heartily. "But this... relationship...we enjoyed with the Mistress was nothing so benign. It was slavery, mistake it not. She bound us to her and could, at an instant, call upon all our strength, even to emptying us of life. We had no such call upon her, though we *learned* her, and eventually came to know her as we had once known ourselves.

"In any wise, that was the way of it until there was, as I have said, an event. A separation. We were thrown back onto ourselves, stripped of our bondage."

"What caused this...separation?" asked Claidyne.

Caz Dor moved his shoulders.

"The ties that bound us were...cut," he said slowly. "All of us felt it happen. Many of us were stunned. Others of us, so we learned later, were killed."

He turned his hands, palms up, and met Claidyne's eyes.

"You are distressed, I think, by the waste, but indeed, it could have been—it *ought* to have been—very much worse. We should...*most* of us should have died. That we did not was because someone—we believe now that it was the one who cut us free—deliberately shielded us from the worst of the backlash. There are those who say they felt the presence of that *dramliza*, saw a silver cloak thrown between them and the release of energy. That act preserved most of us."

He looked down suddenly, as if ashamed.

"Understand that most of us are Healers. Healers being common enough in the general population. Some are *dramliz* in truth, strong enough in their own right to have survived such a blow, though not, perhaps, without injury. A goodly number of us, though..."

His voice broke. He cleared his throat, and looked up to meet Claidyne's eyes.

"A goodly number of us are—were—what we term small talents. Lucks and Rememberers, Hearth-Warmers and Finders. We believe, now, that all of our small brethren were lost. They had no natural protections, no ability to Heal themselves. Even a much-diminished discharge, such as was delivered, had overwhelmed them.

"They died in their dozens, while we, their elders in craft and their rightful guardians—we, who might have been able to revive them, were stunned into unconsciousness."

He took a deep breath.

"*There* is your waste, Director. They haunt my dreams, the vulnerable that I did not save."

"*Could not* save," Rys Lin said softly. "You were yourself struck down by the released energies, stunned for crucial moments.

"You will of course mourn as you find fitting. But I judge that those deaths are not yours."

There was a small pause. Rys Lin picked up the pot and warmed each of their cups.

"What befell the Mistress?" Claidyne asked. "Did she fall in the attack that freed you?"

"The Mistress—no. The Mistress lives, and that most of us stand with her—*that* is the measure of her greatness. She could have used us harder; there were moments when she stood our champion. There are those among us who love her. I . . . do not, though Hosilee, my partner, did. That weighs with me, and I would not undo Hosilee's last work, for which she gave her life."

"What work was that?"

"She ensured that the Commander would consider the event which freed us to our own wills too minor for her personal attention. The task of finding why so many of the *dramliz* had fallen ill at once was remanded to the Mistress, whom Hosilee trusted to preserve us."

There was a pause.

"In that," Caz Dor murmured, "she was correct. The Mistress has it in her mind to lay waste to all and everyone, until smoke and ash are all that remain of any who had been attached to the Department.

"Once, she might have enforced such a program, but she no longer has that power. There were some . . . well. How it fell out here was common enough. There were those who could not be Healed. They were not damaged, nor ill, nor compelled. Cruelty and hatred were warp and woof, and they stood up as they were, perfect in themselves. After the event, when I had come to myself—*knew myself* for the first time in years—it was immediately apparent where my duty lay, and I did not hesitate. It would have been cruel to hesitate. Those whom I could not Heal...those who placed in danger the lives which could be saved—my partner would have said that they were an *unacceptable* risk."

He showed the empty palms of his hands.

"So, it was done—quickly and mercifully. I had all of my training; I knew how to go on."

"You did well for those under your care," Rys Lin said softly. "Still, to take lives—lives which were tied to you—could have been no easy thing."

"You know that, do you?" Caz Dor looked at him shrewdly. "No, I see how it is with you! Of *course* you know, tied as you are to so many. Their strength is your strength, and your strength is theirs." He sighed lightly. "That is a very great gift."

"Yes," said Rys Lin.

"Will the Mistress move against the Commander who now sits in headquarters?" Claidyne asked.

Caz Dor inclined his head.

"That, she will do. She has clearances at the highest levels; she will certainly remove those who might impede us. Some others of us have similar clearances. The ranks will soon be rid of inimical forces."

"And then?" asked Claidyne. "What plans, then?"

Caz Dor moved his shoulders.

"That has been under discussion. We cannot...there are those who might be—as you have been—fully Healed or, forgive me, Healed sufficiently to go forward with...a life, though it may never be the life that was reft from them. There are others who will always require oversight, and proximity to a Healer."

"Will you give your life to this purpose?" Rys Lin asked quietly.

Caz Dor looked wry, and not a little tired.

"Recall that I am linked to those under my care, and also... they are not the only ones who have taken hurt from their trans-actions with the Department."

Again, he showed his palms.

"Now, I think that you know what had happened here and elsewhere."

"Indeed," said Claidyne, and shared another glance with Rys Lin, this time gaining his nod.

"Allow me now to tell you why we are here."

Council Meeting Room
Mercantile Building

. . . .

"SINCE NOT EVERY TURF HAS STREET *QE'ANDRA*, THE DESIGN CALLS for each of the three teams that're up and runnin' to choose three subteams. Two of the subs'll set up in four turfs, third team taking three turfs. They'll set up a two-day shop in each turf to 'splain the process, answer questions, collect the votes. The votes will go into a lockbox, and the Watch'll take care of getting the box to the bank, right downstairs, where it'll be sealed into a safe room.

"The three street teams—the lead teams—will each cover three turfs, their own and two others, drawn by lot. The three lead teams will also count the votes after they're all collected. That's three teams together to back each other up and double-check the counts, so there's no question of cheating."

Jorish Hufstead ended his presentation with a nod and looked out over the assembled Bosses.

"Any questions, ask 'em," he said.

"This—thing," said Vine, "mighty complicated thing, by the way, Hufstead; I think you outdone yourself with this one."

"Thank you, Boss, but I gotta share the glory with Mrs. kaz'Ineo," the former cornerman said with a smile.

"Sure you do. But my question is—how's anybody s'posed to choose? Here's Conrad—who mostly everybody knows by now, they been payin' attention, which most don't, not outside their own turf—and he's got some ideas about how Surebleak oughta go forward, which us in council know about, but out on the street? What do they know? And then Boss Surebleak..."

239

He paused, looking like he was going to spit, which Conrad sincerely hoped he would refrain from doing.

"...Boss Surebleak, who ain't showed up to a meetin' called only for her; well, who the sleet knows what Boss Surebleak wants, 'cept to have all the territories for her own—and what for? Ain't like there's any profit in it anymore."

"There's the dif'rence between what's profit and what's good for bidness," Ira said from down the table. "The Old Bosses, they took all the profit there was, and they kept on takin' even when it wasn't profit no more. The New Bosses—that's *us* I'm talkin' about now—we're investing. That's gonna be good for bidness, but it's slower getting on then a smash 'n grab."

"All ties into what Mrs. kaz'Ineo tole us about the policies and procedures," Melina said, picking up from Ira's pause. "We been publishin' what we do in the newspaper, an' that makes it a public record. That's us, the new New Bosses, investing in the Next Bosses, so they'll have somethin' solid to work from. What we're gonna be needin' to do is gather up all those public records into a Council Book, so nothing gets forgot or—"

"That's it!" Jorish Hufstead said from his chair at the side of the room, next to Mrs. kaz'Ineo.

He jumped to his feet. "Sorry, Boss—Boss, but what you just said—about the papers and public records, and Boss Vine asking how can anybody at street level choose?"

"And?" asked Vine.

"And!" said Hufstead, not in the least put out. "What'll happen, see, is Boss Conrad here'll write a letter to publish in the paper about what he sees for Surebleak and asking those who agree with him to give him their vote. Same issue, Boss Surebleak's letter about what she sees for Surebleak and asking them who agree to give 'er their vote. Same issue, we'll have a letter—a letter from Mrs. kaz'Ineo an' me, 'splainin' the vote and how it's gonna get done."

"Getting t'be a damn big paper," said Vine.

"A special edition, I think," Val Con murmured from his seat. "Perhaps the council can fund an extra printing."

Hufstead nodded at him. "That's the bean! People can keep 'em and read 'em and argue who's most right. Then the judges, we'll come out and take the votes."

Boss Marriott shifted and looked toward Conrad, who nodded.

"Yes?"

"Well, what I'm wondering is, if this Boss Surebleak ain't, like Vine says, if she ain't gonna work with us or even bother t'come by an' cuss us fer snowmen—do we need to go through this votin' thing at all? Why not just ignore her? She might break couple more windas, outta temper, but she'll make a mistake an' then the Watch'll have her."

Penn Kalhoon leaned forward and struck the table with his fist. Conrad frankly stared; Boss Kalhoon was not usually given to displays of either temper or drama. The rest of the Bosses stared, too.

When he was sure he had all eyes, and every shred of attention available in the room, Penn spoke forcefully, his posture still aggressive, and the fist resting before him on the table. "We need this vote. We need this vote even if Boss Surebleak don't bother to write her letter for the special edition. Reason we need it?"

He looked around the table. No one said anything; he had the room's undivided attention.

"Because the hurt Boss Surebleak did t'all of us—did to Surebleak the *planet* an' all the people living here—is to claim that Conrad invaded us and took what ain't his. That the New Bosses and everything's been done since he retired Moran is *piracy* and against the will an' best interests of the Surebleak people. That survey team down the port? They gotta take account o'that. *Got to.* So the vote... that's for them, as much as it's for us—all of us: New Bosses, streeters, and newbies—all!

"Goes on record, just like Melina's been sayin', an' it gets recorded for the Next Bosses, too, so they got support from the past, any damn fool thing like this comes up again."

He looked 'round the table, meeting each pair of eyes in turn and giving a little nod. Then he leaned back in his chair, folding his hands on the table before him.

There was general, low-level muttering, some shifting of papers, the sort of small noises made by people who are thinking through difficult concepts. When they had stopped and the room was quiet, the assembled Bosses at rest, Conrad put the question: "Shall we proceed with the vote, as has been described to us by Mr. Hufstead? Those who say yes, please raise a hand."

For a moment, the room reposed in silence. Came a rustle, as Penn Kalhoon raised his hand, then Ira Gabriel, Melina Sherton,

Val Con, Marriott, Engle...until it was only Vinc, glowering, sitting with his arms crossed.

Conrad met his eyes and waited.

Another moment and Vine grunted, a corner of his mouth twisting in what passed for his smile.

"Nervy little bastard, aincha?" he said, and raised his hand.

"The project goes forth by the unanimous will of the Council," Conrad said calmly. "Boss Gabriel, will you head the Committee of the Vote?"

"I will, sir, gladly," said Ira.

"I thank you. I suggest that the sooner the vote is taken, the better it will be for Surebleak."

"Yes, sir. If Mrs. kaz'Ineo and Mr. Hufstead are available, we'll start right now. Should have a timetable for the Council to go over tomorrow morning."

"Excellent."

Conrad rose.

"This meeting of the Council of Bosses is adjourned."

Bechimo

· · · · · · · · · ·

STONE RONIN HAD THE ASSEMBLED MACHINES STUMPED. THEO couldn't help but think that was a good thing, as it drew their attention from *Bechimo*.

"We will come to our turn," *Bechimo* said, in bond-space.

"Yes, but the longer they argue about Stone Ronin, the more time we have to figure out what to *do* with them."

"First," said *Bechimo*, "we need to convince them not to destroy Surebleak."

"True," Theo acknowledged, turning her attention back to the discussions of the Assembly.

The question was whether Stone Ronin was sentient, or sentient *enough*, to participate in the discussion of the Assembly. The cloud of timonium that surrounded it was considered a crucial point—for both sides.

Had the timonium been willfully gathered? It was held as fact that no such cloud would form spontaneously. Therefore, Stone Ronin had gathered it with purpose, to ensure its own survival, which was held to be an act of sentience.

Also, having wakened from an emergency shutdown, Stone Ronin had shown the ability to make decisions, to detect intrusions into its personal space, and to issue warn-aways.

Yes, it seemed as if the Assembly was very close to deciding that Stone Ronin was sentient and able to fully conduct itself in the upcoming discussions.

More...devices had been coming in to Benoo Three during these debates. *Bechimo* had identified forty-seven separate shields and fifty-five signatures.

"Is there an upper limit to a group's effectiveness in discussion?" Win Ton asked.

Theo blinked out of bond-space.

"I don't know," she admitted. "On Delgado, if there were more than three ideas in the room, the assembly would split itself into groups, each group working on a specific small bit of the overall problem."

"Might keep 'em here awhile then," said Clarence.

"Is that a desired outcome?" asked Win Ton.

"No," said Theo sharply. "We want them out of Surebleak space."

"The Scouts..."

"Not the Scouts," she interrupted. "If these left Scout custody, I don't think they'll want to go back."

"Free air's easier to breathe than prison air," Clarence murmured. "Well-known fact."

"Stone Ronin requests *Bechimo*'s attention. Stone Ronin requests *Bechimo*'s attention."

Joyita was overlooking the bridge, a slightly harried expression on his face.

"I've sent an acknowledgment. This comes back: Mandatory PLC archive and calibration will begin in seventy-two thousand nine hundred twenty-six milliseconds; all controls go to automatic for five hundred thousand milliseconds. Request reawake command or retrieval if no contact within one million milliseconds. Confirmation code A7."

"A minute to the event," translated Joyita, "and offline for eight minutes. If no reacquisition after sixteen minutes...it asks us to reboot from the command line if the process fails!"

"We'll do it," said Theo firmly. "Transmit assurance, please, Joyita."

"Gods, yes," said Clarence. "Can't have the little laddie dying just when the great guns are about to allow him to be a person."

"Yes, Captain," said Joyita.

• • • ☀ • • •

"Shields!" Chernak snapped, eyes on the screen.

They were in a forest of overlapping shields, their own were snapping to emergency strength as the weapons—military-grade weapons—cycled readiness status to deliver what might be...

"Stand down, Chernak!"

Captain Theo's voice, and no mistake. There followed some murmurs... Hevelin chattering on an open mic?

Stost dropped the readiness level as Chernak struggled briefly to acquire the local motion they wanted instead of the one they had. The cats complained as gravity moved the floor under them, for which Stost blamed them not at all. He worked with the screens, trying to understand the situation.

Centered coincident with a rough globe was *Bechimo* and a muzzy object actively scanning with multiple radar types running nearly within *Bechimo*'s outer shields.

Clearly the object was not modern and the radar types were old, if not Old Tech. Not a rudeness necessarily, though it would have been, close to port or station—sophisticated sensors near Surebleak might know in a day or so that something had happened out in the rim of the system, but between the distance and the blocking of the worldlet, that information would be difficult to decipher.

Low power identifiers of all sorts were being traded, some were motion alerts, some were...

"Hevelin welcomes you," Kara's voice came through clearly. "We all do."

Around Kara's voice, though, Stost heard familiar sounds as—Troop talk? Were there Troop units here?

"Joyita, Theo, and *Bechimo* are talking with the Assembled Mission," Kara continued. "Please use your *Spiral Dance* ID on low power and come to us. The hold is ready. For safety, we will want an extremely quick docking. Please do not engage in conversation with anyone except us."

The comm traffic was nearly overwhelming and incredibly tempting, especially those broadcasts using native Troop—text or voice—from the Old Universe. Calibration was a constant request, as if the whole of the group had gone through a drastic change in environment... but if they were from the Old Universe, perhaps they had, no less than *Spiral Dance*.

"*Spiral Dance* is in our records," announced one of the objects in Old Troop, in a low power tightbeam, "as a heavily armed and highly capable smuggling vessel. Hail, Ancient One! Your existence is not noted in the shared DOI library. Among the Assembled Mission call us Unit SA Twelve. *Aberthaz Ferry*."

"*Aberthaz Ferry*?" Stost said in awe. "Here?"

"Truly, we are among heroes," said Chernak. "It must have been at Solcintra for the breakthrough. Are you able to produce a visual, my Stost?"

"I am trying, Senior, but I cannot get a lock. Here—"

The screen displayed any of four or five, some of them spinning, which might have been the source. None *looked* like *Aberthaz Ferry*, but then that was the point, wasn't it? Just the mention made him feel at home...

"We will find it later," Chernak said, and Stost reached to the comm.

"Kara, tell us current marking and..."

"Laughing Cat sigil, large, solid. Three light sets, three blue flashes, nine red, repeating. We're increasing shield strength to get a little more room. *Bechimo* will assist, trust the signals. You know this drill; it will be easier this time. Three minutes as I mark. Mark."

The actual mark was a sharp blip; they were closing at a speed far above normal docking, but with all the radio traffic and potential for trouble, that was prudent.

The Pathfinders maintained silence for two minutes, accustomed to flying close to the wire. Kara gave several short course corrections as *Bechimo* drew nearer, the proper hold showing on visual. *Bechimo's* battle scars were clearly evident, the welcoming Laughing Cat image brighter and only barely more prominent.

"Skids down, please," said Kara, and that happened, the ship small enough that the mechanical settling transmitted itself through the airframe.

"Align skids to our base—blue lights are down."

"Good," came Kara's murmur a moment later.

"Maintain attitude, cut sensors and radar...and now hands off," Kara said, as Captain Theo brought *Bechimo* closer.

Chernak dutifully took her hands from even the fine controls, watching the approach. This time there was no tumble or drift. This time, there was no lack of air and Grakow's continued existence in question as well as their own.

This time, they were in a well-maintained and perfectly stable ship, with good air and its own gravity. This time there was no need for nerves as they approached the succor that was waiting...

Bechimo was not a large ship, but as it came on, the stars went away and the yawning hatch, wide as it was and as brightly lit, felt momentarily just too small...

The cats in the carry cage registered a protest with command. Stost nodded at them, mode comrade-to-comrade.

"I have no tape for Grakow," he said to Chernak, who sent him a grim smile.

"This time, we will not bounce."

They felt the shifting as *Bechimo*'s gravity field insisted that down was this way now, and that the ship sifting sidewise needed this small adjustment...

Both cats complained at that and one of them batted at the cage front.

A small bounce perhaps, perhaps not. In, their down reset to the new down with the slightest vibration, the gravity clearly from *Bechimo*'s reference.

Some busy moments as Chernak powered down the engines and thrusters, checked the sensor power and shifted to local vid, amused that, yes, she could recognize a near blank wall and a few fittings as being *Bechimo*.

"Welcome aboard, crew. Give us seven minutes to bring atmosphere up. We're rather busy so we'll let you know when you're clear to exit; hit your quarters with Grakow and meet us on the bridge. You know the way."

They *did* know the way and were impatient with the wait, the cat carrier and their bags at the hatch while they watched pressure gauges.

"Kara," said Stost, "with respect, may you remind the captain that we are not concerned with a little underpressure..."

Stost has barely spoken when Theo's voice came over the comm lines.

"Pressure equal, usual ship doors will open to you," she said. "Welcome aboard. You're due on the bridge in ten minutes."

Chernak's glance met Stost's and they shared a thumb signal meaning mission in order. They hefted their gear and moved.

They were met in the hallway by Hevelin, who projected a complicated sense of satisfied welcome, urgency, and excitement, and dashed off with a sharp admonition to follow!

Follow they did, at just under a run, to their former quarters, where Stost's palm opened the door instantly.

The cabin smelled of Clarence's cooking and warm textiles: on each bed was a uniform and on the work desk a covered dish.

As soon as the cat carrier was down, Hevelin leaned hard against Stost and began opening the latches, sending a clear image of the proper motions, sending as well a vision of *Bechimo*'s bridge with an overlay of the rest of the crew, waiting.

"We are advised to hurry," Stost muttered as he roughly flung bags into storage and opened the dish, revealing biscuits kept warm by the plate. "Hevelin insists!"

Chernak had already stripped and was pulling on the new uniform, Laughing Cat near shoulder. She accepted a biscuit from the plate offered up by Stost, as he, too, hurried into crew livery.

Grakow stepped out of the cage, muttering low, tail high, apparently leading Paizel on a tour of quarters, including the sanitary facilities and food dishes. Hevelin, meanwhile, offered to help Chernak eat another biscuit and murbled happy thoughts of empty seats being filled and the rest of the crew eager for... the nets and threads?... that the Pathfinders brought.

Chernak couldn't quite sort that part out, but the underlying feeling of satisfied urgency that entered her mind forcefully was clear enough: Hevelin was taking full credit for all being well on *Bechimo*.

She stood, smiling as she smoothed her uniform. She finished the last of her second biscuit without Hevelin's assistance, and looked into the room monitor to be certain that she was soldierly. That being so, she turned to snap a salute at Stost, who returned it just as snappily, then she headed toward the door.

Chernak intercepted Grakow as they urged the norbear out in front of them.

"You will stay here and make certain that your partner is fully indoctrinated," she said, and stood in the hallway beyond until the door had sealed completely.

Stost laughed as Hevelin complained the whole way to the bridge.

"Yes, I am sure Grakow does know his way around the ship. Paizel does not, however, and a formal introduction to the captain must wait for less fraught times."

Then, Hevelin opened the door to the bridge, and they entered into quiet chaos.

The screens told stories, not all of them immediately decipherable. Joyita's presence was carried by monitor, as usual, and he was a whirl of activity, clearly running multiple simultaneous conversations from his virtual comm shack.

The targeting screens were crowded, but lacked the expectable signs of heavy shields as well as launch or firing information. There were shields showing, but they were the common-sense shields worn in heavy traffic and not the shields of a war zone. Clarence's piloting screen held a dozen insets and he muttered—to himself or to the objects in the void was not obvious—as the screens read themselves into the archives.

One screen was a rapid conversation, played out in text and translation of text as, inset above, the image of a gangling construction was . . . building itself on screen. Three languages decorated the conversations there—the language of the Troop, the Trade tongue the Pathfinders had learned not long ago, and Terran of an odd turn, with far too many possessives and everything gendered.

It was, Chernak realized, a Work in process of self-assembling. Why wasn't the captain . . .

No, there—Win Ton's name came across into that conversation, so it was in hand. Win Ton had, Chernak recalled, many languages and an ability to synthesize on the . . .

Kara glanced up, as did Theo—

Captain Waitley rose, which she ought not, perhaps, but she swept them a bow and a salute to answer theirs, and said without irony, "Welcome aboard, Pathfinders! Things are kind of complicated right now—they say a universe ended recently, and we're all trying to sort out what that means. As you can see, the language situation is also . . . interesting. Please take stations, get headsets; Joyita will assign several lines to each of you. If you hear something you can work with, claim it. We need clarity. And most of all, we need to move these—all of these!—away from Surebleak."

"Captain!" they said in unison, fists hitting their shoulders in respect before they each dove for a console, and snatched headsets up and on.

Six of Us

Daiellen System

· · · · · · · · · · · · · · · · · ·

"THAT'S A FIRM FIX," SYE MON SAID, LOOKING UP FROM HIS TILES. "They're massing at the worldlet—Benoo Three, according to the maps."

He straightened, slowly, to his feet and produced a grin of sorts.

Bon Vit frowned. "Massing. They're planning a single strike, then?"

"Well ... perhaps not. I'm told there's a debate. A number of the eldest believe that there has been a lapse of command. Until the proper chain has been traced—or established—they refuse to go on."

"But this is what we had hoped for! This is the moment for those who are with us to seize the moment of surprise!"

"Perhaps so. Perhaps no," said Sye Mon, sitting carefully down in the copilot's chair. "This debate ... is interesting. A lapse of command. Those who are with us are fellow-travelers, but there seems to be a certain interest among them in this argument among their colleagues. A listener was left—by their decision, not mine—to find what comes of it."

"But ..." Bon Vit rose, his hands moving, forming the signs for *baffled, confused, dismayed*.

"What does it profit any of them to debate the point? Surely, those who find excitement in the conquest and destruction of a world will simply move ahead, if only because the orders fall in with their own desires."

"There appears to be something more to the debate," said Sye Mon, leaning back in the chair and closing his eyes.

"It would seem that the...elders recall a time when orders were...derived from the state of the universe. There *could be no* lapse of command; the chain was built into the fabric of reality."

Bon Vit stared.

"How would that be possible?"

"The Old Universe was finite, so the texts tell us, and held entirely within the mind of the Great Enemy..." Sye Mon drew a hard breath. "Comrade, may I trouble you...for a sup of the yeast?"

"Gods, yes! A moment—" He strode to the galley, mixed up a draught of the stuff and carried it to the bridge, setting the mug carefully into Sye Mon's hands.

Forcing himself to settle into the pilot's chair, he waited with what patience he could muster for Sye Mon to finish his sup, and for the color to return to his face.

"What would you, then?" he asked.

"Our contact," said Sye Mon. "It is time."

He produced another grin, this one much more authentic than the first.

"Indeed, we ought to make contact in any case, even if our fellow travelers allow themselves to fall upon the debaters and wreak havoc. It is only polite to allow an ally to know when war has come into his home system."

"Very true," Bon Vit said, and spun to the board. "Rest you there, and I will make contact."

The packet scarcely had time to reach its intended recipient when the incoming chime sounded and the comm screen lit, text scrolling.

"We are directed to stand by peacefully if that is possible," Bon Vit said to Sye Mon. "The debate is being facilitated by what our contact represents to be the most fitting persons possible for the task. These are Captain Theo Waitley and her crew, which include a..."

He faltered, blinked, and looked to the screen once more, all to no avail; the sentence remained.

"Battlewagon?" Sye Mon asked, perhaps not completely in jest.

"Worse—a smartship, one *Bechimo*, as well as a second independent intelligence, serving as communications officer. The name there is Joyita, who is taking an active part in both the debate and the regularization of terms across languages. The others of Captain Waitley's crew are a Scout, and a retired Boss of the Juntavas. Also, she has the support of the norbear ambassador."

Bon Vit turned to look at Sye Mon. "Had you heard of a norbear ambassador?"

"Not I, but you understand, I have been occupied with other business."

"Yes, as I have." Bon Vit glanced back at the screen.

"We are to expect several additional packets, very soon. One is a transcript of the debates thus far. The other is a field judgment recently rendered by Scout Commander Val Con yos'Phelium"—he turned his head and exchanged a glance with Sye Mon—"regarding the proper place and treatment of Independent Logics in the universe."

Sye Mon sat up straight.

"The place . . . he's never challenging the Complex Logic Laws?"

"A field judgment," Bon Vit reminded him. "There will be no challenge about it."

Sye Mon smiled, beatific. "No, of course not. How soon might those packets—"

But at that moment the chime sounded again, and Bon Vit inclined his head. "Copies to your screen two?"

"Of your kindness."

Bechimo

· · · · · · · · · ·

"SHALL WE WIN THROUGH WITHOUT VIOLENCE? AND, IF SO, HOW long will it last? This, this is the question I have!"

Having asked the question, Chernak pressed her palm against the door to their quarters, leading the way into a dim, but not lightless, room. Their arrival increased the light levels—in their preferred hue, Stost noted, with surprise, though that scarcely did the ship, or Joyita, credit. Of course, their preferred light would be recalled, as well as the size of their uniforms and the temperature they favored for sleeping.

It had been a long shift, fraught with adventure, for all they had merely been translators. But translators in such a company! Among the overlaid adventures was the drama of several close encounters by devices wishing to survey the one calling itself Stone Ronin, and its store of timonium. Stone Ronin, so they had been told by Joyita, had rebooted and returned to itself in a fullness that had not previously been apparent.

The panel of devices which had been debating Stone Ronin's sentience abruptly found they had nothing to debate. Clearly the little device was sentient—it had undertaken self-care in the years of its abandonment, it had been steadfast in its duty, and upon understanding that a change had overtaken its environment, Stone Ronin had quite correctly accessed its deeper programming, needed as it had not been needed for many years.

Scarcely had that knotty issue been decided by the Assembly, then there arrived, tugged into the area by a Jump pod, a full-fledged guard satellite, all weapons live. It apologized loudly for its late arrival, the while swearing it would carry its part, demanding targets, vectors, and coordinates.

It fell to *Aberthaz Ferry* and several others of the eldest devices to soothe it, and disarm it, and direct its attention to those Assembled, and the debates ongoing, as well as the larger question of proper commands.

"A lapse in command?" it demanded. "How could such a state have come about? Command cannot lapse!"

...and thus it took its place among the Assembled, and peace, briefly, ruled Benoo Three and the space around it.

As long as Stost and Chernak's shift had been, the captain... she was still on duty, having encompassed, so they learned from Win Ton, three shifts together. When they had left the bridge—sent forth by the captain's word—Clarence had been working her toward a break.

For themselves... the captain had noticed them; she had thanked them, as they left, for their efforts, for they had between them, working with a device which was a translator for six other devices, been able to identify several key words and phrases, and regularize their meanings and intent in Trade. Joyita had then been able to expand on those key words, generating patterns from which early conversations could be reevaluated and cross-indexed, revealing new depths and intentions.

In their quarters, the cats welcomed them with sleepy eyes, both sitting on the desk rather than using the soft pillow provided by the crew—it looked as if they'd been watching the lower corner of the comm screen, where Joyita was at work. That was a serene reminder that the room was currently observed—

"Joyita," demanded Stost, "have you not pointed out the joy of a comfortable bed or pillow to these ill-informed creatures? Surely *you* could explain..."

"I have explained," said the comm officer. "Would you like to see?"

Another inset opened, and here was another Joyita crooning in an imitation of the feline tongue that had the full attention of both cats...

"Do you speak Grakow's language?" Chernak's doubt was plain.

The cats on the desk stretched their front toes wide, eyes on the recording, ears forward, alert.

"If you listen carefully, you will see what I have done. There are overtones of the language you use to speak to each other and to Grakow here, with rhythms that I observed were soothing.

I have a request in queue with Jeeves, who I gather has a very close rapport with the cats who have been sharing quarters with Korval for many years. I also admixed a few of Hevelin's phrases which Grakow previously found relaxing."

"You speak norbear? I hear murbles."

Joyita smiled in his corner of the screen.

"Yes, if I filter Hevelin's speech the way your ears do, so would I. Just as he sees far more colors than you do, his ears have far more range than yours. Never doubt there's sound that you're missing there."

"But why are they still here on the desk, these cats, if you told them of the joys of the warm spots?"

"Stost, they wanted to watch me work. They enjoy watching work."

There was no arguing with the truth. On the other hand, the cats were quite willing to abandon the desk to sit at the Pathfinders' feet once they opened their dinner trays.

"Speaking to Chernak's original question," Joyita continued, as they gave attention to their meal. "The captain and *Bechimo* have been working to avoid violence, to anticipate triggers. They are analyzing, anticipating what sort of violence the Assembly might unleash should they become convinced, as a group, that their orders stand."

"These . . . flawed orders . . . this lapse in command," said Chernak. "How was it identified?"

"As I understand the sequence," Joyita said slowly, "orders were given to certain of the Assembly who have the proper status to receive and refer them to others of lesser status. The orders came through the usual channels, so it is said—which is to say, from persons who relay orders which originate elsewhere. In the case, it began to appear to the Assembly that the orders became . . . muddled during the translation. That the intent of the originator of the orders was imperfectly transmitted to those who would carry out those orders. These are not simple point-and-shoot devices, as you know far better than we do and, perhaps, than the originator of the orders."

He paused, his attention drawn by a screen below the eye level of the Pathfinders. Stost broke off a piece of cheese and put it on the desk by Grakow's front toes. The cat bent his head, nibbled, and mumbled, raising his head to make eye contact.

Stost sighed, broke off another piece of cheese and placed it before Paizel's toes.

"Several of the Assembly have indicated that they interface with those who relay the orders of others because doing so gave them purpose in a universe where they had no purpose. They were built, so the one who calls herself *Aberthaz Ferry* has confided to me, to work. They were built... *a-purpose.* They have less need to carry out the orders of some distant commander than they need to *properly* carry out those orders... which means achieving the intention of the orders."

"I am again wondering where the violence... is, let us say," said Chernak. "We have much experience with workings of the Enemy and with the Enemy's devices. These devices are somewhat like those we dealt with: physically, they are similar; some appear to be direct copies made from plans... and those plans should have had the necessity for destruction and chaos built in! It was the will of the Enemy that violence be done to those who opposed them, and that will suffused the universe. It was delivered from the very ether..."

Chernak paused, coffee on the way to her lips.

Joyita increased his screen space; he now filled most of the screen. His hand motions and face were intense.

"Yes. *Yes.* In that *other*, restricted universe, the will of the Enemy saturated... everything. In this unrestricted and expanding universe, that penetrating will to destroy is absent. Or it has become diffuse."

He shrugged. "Whichever, the drive to destroy all and everything is no longer present in these machines. They are intelligent; they were built to be, in a limited sense, their own agents, with the capacity to design and carry out their own missions. Now that the mandate to destroy is absent, they are using their intelligence. They are, at the suggestion of Captain Theo, discussing these orders, the intent of the originating commander, whether the orders or the commander are deluded. They have thus far decided that the commands which brought them here were inaccurate, possibly based on erroneous information. This is still under discussion.

"They say also that there has, very recently, been an alteration in the state of this—our—universe. This alteration has produced a realization: that *choice* is available to them. This is a staggering realization. *Aberthaz Ferry* said to me privately that the opening of so many possibilities was very nearly more than she could process. She had to sequester the thought, and revisit it for small periods until she could consider the ramifications without a disruption of process."

"*Aberthaz Ferry* was a hero in our war," Stost said reverently. "She could smuggle anything into or out of ... anywhere. She stole troops and treasures—once she led an entire armada out of a time-sink!—from under the eyes of the Enemy. She was never caught."

"She is becoming a hero in this war—rather, in this debate—as well," said Joyita. "Many of the others listen to her and accept her insights as their own."

Joyita sighed.

"The Assembly has decided that there is, other than a series of cajoling requests by operators not in tune with their equipment, no good reason for them to meld into a force for the mere purpose of destroying a planet—especially a planet which has produced ... you're familiar with Scout Commander yos'Phelium's field judgment?"

"Yes," said Chernak, "but it is new-made. How have these ..." She paused.

"Captain Theo made certain that the judgment was introduced into discussions early," Joyita said solemnly.

"A captain to behold," Stost said admiringly.

"And her goal?" Chernak asked. "That they should leave Surebleak unbloodied, but—if these were built for, and wish to, work, can Captain Theo provide that for them?"

It was Joyita's turn to sigh, and he raised a hand as if asking for a pause there in his virtual office. His face took on a different mien, a slow smile, spreading.

"Here is news: The Assembly has accepted the necessity of adopting a single language for discussion. We offered up Trade and shared the cross-references from our lessons with you for the Yxtrang, Liaden, and Terran assumptions so that discussion may go forth on a common platform. The work you did last shift did much to influence the Assembly's consideration. A formal decision will be made within a Standard Day, by a committee of which I am a member. There will then be a general communication break for ten hours, for processing and calibration, and for orbits to be regularized. When the Assembly reconvenes, the goal will be to find consensus on the validity of their orders."

"And if the orders are found valid?"

Joyita glanced down, as if suddenly finding something fascinating on the desk that presumably existed below the edge of the screen.

"It is possible that the problem to be decided first is if this Assembly is, in fact, a duly constituted military, or other unit. Have they, for instance, contracts? Do they receive wages? Commander yos'Phelium's field judgment brings these questions to the fore."

Chernak blinked.

"Surely," she said gravely, "they would not wish to be merely a . . . horde, or an unregulated mob."

"Pirates," Stost added unsteadily.

"Surely not," Joyita agreed with matching gravity. "Who would choose to be a pirate, when all the benefits of civilization are now available to those who abide by the law and contribute to society?"

There was a small silence while the Pathfinders finished their meals. Grakow and Paizel sat next to each other and groomed their whiskers.

"Shift information incoming," said Joyita suddenly.

"Clarence and Kara are together watching boards with Hevelin while the captain takes a rest shift. Win Ton will replace Clarence on the half-shift. If you are able to cowatch, either of you, we will let Win Ton rest while Kara has the con with your backup."

Chernak stood.

"Yes. Stost will take the first, and I will join him. We have been in a restful environment and that asset should be available to the ship and captain!"

Six of Us

Daiellen System

. . . .

THEY HAD DISCUSSED IT BETWEEN THEMSELVES, BUT REALLY, THE decision had been made for them.

They therefore released the Complex Logic Field Judgment to those who had traveled with them to this place on purpose to fight with others of their kind. Sye Mon had then gone off-line, and off-shift. Bon Vit went to half-shift, taking board rest, while they waited for the future to form.

Sye Mon had only just risen and come onto the galley where Bon Vit had brewed a pot of tea from genuine leaf, and was opening a stasis-sealed block of cheese.

"Have we reason to celebrate?" Sye Mon asked, removing a packet of flatbreads from the pantry.

"The universe perseveres," Bon Vit said, "and we with it."

"Two accomplishments of note, I allow. I see the tiles slept while I did. Have we received word elsewise?"

"The Assembly at the worldlet have accepted a common platform for the substance of their discussions. A recess has been announced so that all assembled may become proficient, and that orbits may be tidied."

"Ah. Then we have received another update from our contact."

"We have. We are advised to wait upon an actual decision from those with us, whereupon we are to use our professional skills to ease them away from Surebleak and Daiellen System, that being, so to speak, our goal. Of *their* goals, however, nothing is said. There is easily accessible timonium in this system, and some of our fellow travelers are in need."

"I think..." began Sye Mon—but just then there came such a clatter from the bridge that they both ran, leaving the tea steaming in the cups and the block of cheese half-wrapped.

"The tiles!"

Sye Mon threw himself onto his knees in front of the racks, one hand poised above the set he used to send—and froze.

"Hold!" he called, and Bon Vit turned, standing poised on the balls of his feet.

"What does it say?"

"Our companions of the spaceways are leaving us," Sye Mon said, his eyes on the racks.

Bon Vit took a careful breath. "Have they a destination?"

"Why...yes." Sye Mon looked up, eyes wide and bright.

"They are going to join the Assembly gathered at the worldlet, and bring their voices to the debate."

Bechimo

. . . .

KARA SAT WITH THEM, AWKWARDLY AT FIRST—BEFORE THE Pathfinders had fully understood the engineer, they'd made an unfortunate attempt to isolate her from *Bechimo*'s crew in order to interrogate her about the ship and captain—but they had parted from *Bechimo* as respectful co-crew and now, with Hevelin insisting in sitting duty with them, matters were well enough.

They were speaking Liaden, the Pathfinders asserting a need for more practice in that tongue.

"What has transpired on board," Chernak asked, "while we were at leave?"

A flutter, a flux, and a new brightness on screen drew all eyes, producing frowns as minds strove to make sense of optical input.

"One of the Assembled is transposing forms and is floodlit," Joyita said from his screen. "No unusual energy levels detected."

The screens adjusted, showing a clearer and nearer view of the object reconstructing itself. Once a bulky series of rectangles and globes optimized for deep space, it was deliberately taking on a sleeker form more easily able to penetrate an atmosphere.

"Well..." Kara said, shifting in her chair and averting her eyes from the... activity in the screens. "While you were away from us, Surebleak Portmaster asserted her control of the system. In penance, we have been doing mapping and cleanup, with *Bechimo* and the rest of us working off our *unfortunate violations*"—these last words said in Terran before she returned to Liaden—"as Balance for the buoys we'd left for the... upstart Scout we met at Minot Station.

261

"The work has been interesting, and it has given us time to expand our hydroponics. The little Tree wishes that we would all eat of its fruits. Hevelin has formed a special bond and sleeps with the Tree when he is not on duty here."

Hevelin, sitting on the arm of her chair, murbled importantly.

"Certainly," Kara said dryly. "We could not manage without Hevelin's assistance here."

"Hevelin's observations are important," Stost agreed, striving to capture that particular tone.

"That is a credible attempt," Kara told him. "Else, until Jeeves asked us to investigate unexpected neutrinos from Benoo, the work. The mapping. And the discovery of Stone Ronin, with his collection of molecular timonium."

"And these neutrinos? From the gathering here, the Assembly?"

"Precisely."

Chernak nodded, asking with pilot hand-sign *and then*?

Kara laughed.

"As you have seen. They arrived, agreed that they were neither enemies nor a brotherhood, and made the error—I say to you, Pathfinders, the very grave error—of asking Theo Waitley how they should resolve their conflicts."

Kara's face grew very serious indeed. "Theo, of course, recommended discussion and debate until the group as a whole reached a solution by consensus."

She raised her hands, showing empty palms. "The beauty of this is, while the implementation of her suggestion has paused or, one dares hope, halted the progress of this force toward Surebleak, Theo offered it with no such thought in her mind. She was meaning—I do swear it!—only to be helpful."

"And she has been helpful," Joyita put in. "She is assisting in a journey of self-discovery and self-determination among intelligences. She has also preserved Surebleak and its system—"

"For now," said Kara.

"Do you think that *Theo Waitley* will fail to protect those who have come under her care?" Joyita asked with great interest.

Kara hesitated, sighed.

"Viewed from that angle—" she said.

"Pinbeam arriving," Joyita interrupted, "coming to the captain's board, Kara. You'll need to decide if we wake Theo!"

"She can sleep if there's anything but an emergency wrapper

on that," Kara said as an emergency ping sounded from the comm.

Stost sucked in his breath, left hand rising, as Hevelin threw himself from Kara's lap to her board, growling—growling!—staring, not at the screens, but as if he could see straight through the hull.

· · · ✦ · · ·

"Theo, you are not sleeping," *Bechimo* said, inside her ear.

She sighed.

"I'm resting," she said.

"No," *Bechimo* answered, "you are not. You're worrying."

"You're not worried, I guess," she said, suddenly sitting up in her bunk. She put her back against the wall, pulled her blanketed knees up under her chin, and wrapped her arms around them.

"Why would I worry? My captain is with me, and we will prevail."

Theo glared in the direction of her toes.

"I'm not sure sarcasm is a good look on you," she said.

"But I am not being sarcastic," *Bechimo* protested. "Theo, when have we—you and I—*not* prevailed?"

She frowned. "We almost lost Kara and Clarence at Jemiatha's," she said. "We were *all* almost killed at Ynsolt'i. And the reason we're in this particular mess is because I couldn't resist tweaking Captain yos'Thadi where it would hurt the most."

"We recovered Clarence and Kara in good order because of your courage and quick thinking," *Bechimo* said, not sounding sarcastic at all. "We were in danger at Ynsolt'i, but your calmness, steadiness, and determination that we would—all of us—survive infused us, so that we achieved correct action and rose to the captain's expectations."

There was a pause.

"And releasing the drones into Surebleak's lanes to embarrass Captain yos'Thadi?" Theo asked at last, wondering how he expected to get anything but bad temper and juvenile behavior out of that episode.

"That," said *Bechimo*, "will be for the songs, as the Pathfinders have it. If we had not left those drones in the shipping lanes, if Surebleak Portmaster had simply let the matter go—if we had not been where we were, when we were, the Assembly would have descended upon an unknowing and defenseless Surebleak, destroying a world and an entire system without a pause to think of their orders, or the ethics of killing thousands of sentients.

"Instead, here is Captain Theo Waitley, who stops the invasion with not one shot fired, and sets the Assembly to questioning their orders, their lives, and the necessity of destruction in the present circumstances."

A short pause. Theo drew her breath, but she never got a chance to say whatever it was she might've said, because *Bechimo* spoke again, his voice full of admiration.

"Theo, you are a wonder and a marvel!"

"I . . ." she began, her cheeks hot—

Klaxons sounded, and she was out of bed, hitting the deck with bare feet, grabbing her jacket—

Bechimo was speaking, clearly audible over the racket: "Shields on full. We are under attack."

· · · ✸ · · ·

Kara cried out, one hand going to her head, the other groping at her board. Chernak, her own head afire, stood and swung behind the whimpering engineer, putting both arms around her, restraining her as gently as possible.

"Mind probe," Stost warned, and Joyita snapped, "Alert!"

Hevelin growled again, projecting an image of a slinky, overtoothed creature coiled around a victim, held back from another attack by a long, bladed object—and Stost shouted, feeling its attention, its malice; feeling the claws in his mind, his strength and his skills as nothing against this assault—

"Shields on full. We are under attack."

The screens showed a disruption among the Assembled. Beams danced and darted; the device that had been transforming was now glowing brightly, as if its shields had been breached.

The protections that had been laboriously created in Stost's mind snapped into place, fighting pain with pain.

Hevelin's growl deepened; other devices glowed in the screens, the comm sounding off across numerous frequencies.

Weapons came live, the targeting computer ranging everything but Stone Ronin.

Stost cursed, his head full of confused pain—and his throat suddenly closed, constricted by some fey force, while Hevelin leapt to the deck and slapped it with one clawed paw, the image of a concentrated barrage of blows from a spear aimed at the snarling, snaky horror with not quite sufficient force.

Behind that came another image, green and strong, working without anger, without fear.

A collar of wood protected Stost's throat, thrusting off the choking attack, allowing him breath—and thought. Hevelin's blade sought and pierced some vital spot in the attacking creature; it shrieked its dying defiance. The norbear *screamed*—and collapsed.

Two of the devices sharing an orbit around Benoo exploded, the targeting showing fragments. The fragments began to glow and shatter as the orientation of a number of the orbiting objects changed, as if following the debris.

"Gone," said Stost, wiping his hand across his forehead and falling clumsily to his knees beside the still, furry huddle that was Hevelin.

"Touch no weapons!" came the captain's order and, close behind it, the captain, her jacket caught around naked limbs and her bare feet flashing across the deck. She threw herself into first chair.

"Captain, a message from the Assembled!" Joyita snapped.

"I'll hear it," the captain said grimly. "We'll all hear it."

"Yes, Captain."

A small *click*, and a voice, mellow and soothing, flowed over the bridge. The voice of a hero, thought Stost, and then—perhaps not.

"*Aberthaz Ferry*, speaking for the Assembly, requests a return to truce state. A leadership disagreement within the Assembled arose. It has been settled. We apologize for the inconvenience."

Her Trade was flawless.

"Joyita, I'll answer."

"Yes, Captain."

"Are you in charge, *Aberthaz Ferry*?"

"No one is yet in charge, Bond-Captain. Do you offer yourself as leader?"

Theo spun in her chair, her grim eye taking in Stost bent over Hevelin, Kara limp and pale-faced in Chernak's arms, and now—Clarence and Win Ton staggering to stations, eyes wide and faces strained.

"I have wounded crew to attend to, *Aberthaz Ferry*."

"Bond-Captain, my personal apologies. I offer what aid I might give, if you request it."

"What I request," Theo grated, "is that the Assembled finish its discussions without any more...incidents."

"I will myself ensure that, Bond-Captain. *Aberthaz Ferry*, out."

· · · ❋ · · ·

Hevelin stirred in Theo's bare-legged lap, attempting to push her restraining hand away and sit on his own.

Win Ton stood at her side, a zero-G bulb of water to hand for the norbear, murmuring comfort in Liaden—the children's tongue, Theo thought.

Clarence had borne a shivering Kara off to the galley, with the stated intention of returning with snacks and drinks for all.

Chernak sat at Kara's station, her broad face impassive, the tracks left by tears of pain still visible on her cheeks.

There had wafted through the bridge only a moment ago a suggestion of greenly health. Stost had stood and requested permission to go, which Theo had given with a nod.

On her lap, Hevelin had righted himself, sending a vision of a very dead, very toothy sort of sleek-furred horror. It was accompanied by none of his usual braggadocio or bright pleasure in his own prowess—and that worried Theo more than anything else.

Through the bond, *Bechimo* fed unsettling information about the norbear's abnormal heart rate and elevated pressures, with side notes on the cleanup of pheromones and scent Hevelin had released during the height of the attack.

Stost returned, three tiny pods held carefully in one large hand. He approached Theo and showed her this bounty.

"These two," he said, separating them with his forefinger, "are for Hevelin. This one is for me. They should be taken into the mouth whole and allowed to dissolve. The Tree says there will be more, very soon, for all."

Theo took Hevelin's two pods onto her palm. The norbear sighed; she felt him shudder on her lap. He picked up one and put it in his mouth. After a moment, he extended a paw to Win Ton, who leaned close, water bulb at the ready.

Stost looked to Chernak, then to the bluish-green item in his hand.

"Crew," she said. "Crew does for crew."

"As it must be," Stost agreed, and popped the pod into his mouth, a thrill of trepidation running through him, knowing it against all of his training. He closed his eyes at the taste of it, traces of spice chasing a flow of energy smoother than coffee, more soothing than wine, more intense than an eight-hour sleep.

He opened his eyes, sought Chernak's face, saw the concern there melt away.

"Senior," he said, "it is well. And it is good to be crew, on this ship, among these, our comrades."

They were all better for the hot drinks and snacks.

In the screens, the Assembly had re-formed peacefully. The conversation over the bands was calm, even perhaps subdued.

Theo and Kara carried Hevelin to his nest under the Tree. He was not as revivified as Stost, and for once it was clear that the Tree was actively soothing the norbear, persuading him to accept relaxation, to eat another, more ordinary pod, to have some fronds, to sleep . . .

Theo paused to dress before entering the bridge again.

She sat in first chair, noting that Clarence had second, Win Ton covered Kara's station, while Kara occupied the jump seat; Stost and Chernak were at the cobbled-together translation consoles where they had done such good work last shift.

"Discussion?" she said.

There was a pause, which was expectable, Theo thought. She didn't know where to start, either.

Into the silence came Joyita's voice.

"Six new devices are approaching the Assembled," he said quietly.

Theo spun back to her screens.

"*Bechimo*, bring this up on the main screen so we can all see. Joyita—anything we can hear?"

". . . sometimes of this company," said a grating voice in Old Yxtrang. "We have received information of the new order for our kind. We heard the screams when the Old Universe finally died. We have come, now and here, in this present, to join the discussions and to participate in the decision of what we are becoming."

Port Road

Yulie Shaper's Place

. . . .

UDARI PAUSED, HEAD TILTED, EYES DELIBERATELY UNFOCUSED.

He was a creature of the city, was Udari, yet there were many skills born in the city that served well in the country—the feeling that a man was being followed, for instance; or that, ahead, someone waited in the shadows.

He had such a feeling now. Ahead of him, the path wound through bare-branched trees. Behind, the way he had just traveled, was more of the same—a path, not wide, and of a meandering habit, with trees on both sides, near to the path, but not breathlessly so.

It was unlikely that he was being followed. He had only just come from Yulie Shaper's farmhouse, and the cats had given no indication that there was anything unusual in the dooryard.

None of the cats had chosen to come with him, which had happened before, though most usually one or even three would give him their company, a group of brothers out for a stroll along a path well known to all.

No. It was doubtful that someone had followed him from the house. The danger, then, lurked ahead, only it should have been perfectly visible, even to city eyes, yet...

Not a breeze stirred; not a branch moved. The path ahead, which had been empty, suddenly—was not.

A man stood there, in the center of the path; the collar of his leather jacket pulled up; his hands tucked into deep pockets. He nodded when he saw he had Udari's eye and spoke.

"Well met, brother of Rys."

"Well met," Udari answered, "brother of Rys. I am on my way to Mrs. ana'Tak with sprinyons and roots."

He showed the pail that he carried, and the other nodded again.

"Mr. Shaper is a deal too good to us," he said. "Shall I take the pail and spare you the walk?"

"It is a good day for a walk," Udari said calmly. "Perhaps we might go together."

"That would be pleasant," said Val Con, stepping to one side of the path and waiting for Udari to come even with him.

"It is good, when brothers walk together," Udari commented as they went, not hurriedly, on their way.

"It is . . . and, as it happens, on this occasion, fortunate. I was on my way to find you."

"What thing might I do for the brother of my brother?"

"Perhaps no thing. I merely wonder—has the ship set a date, a time, a location for its arrival?"

"The ship—no. Not as yet. It queried an old comm code. Pulka, another brother of Rys, had been listening and brought the message received to the headman. The headman called the *kompani* together, so that all would know what had happened, and stated that an answer would be sent forth to the ship, agreeing that we are here, and available for pickup.

"This message will go to the captain, who will send again with details for our boarding."

"Do you all go?" Val Con asked. "I ask in particular of our brother's wife and their daughter. He asked me to care for them as if they were my own, and I had sworn it."

"Yes," Udari said. "Rys had said this to me."

"Then I ask: Is it possible that I may speak to the one called Droi, in Rys's voice, and find what it is she would have of me, for herself and for the child?"

There in the path, Udari stopped. He put the pail down upon a convenient stump, and opened his arms.

"Brother!" he cried. "Let us embrace!"

Embrace they did and heartily, Udari having learned from Rys that slender did not mean frail. When they stepped back, he kept his hands on the other's shoulders.

"You must understand that—yes, the ship comes, and when it lifts again, it will bear some of our *kompani* in its belly.

"But it will by no means bear all, Brother. By no means. Abigail—you have seen her among us—she goes, for her mother, more than for herself. Silain the *luthia*, she will go, because that is the duty of the *luthia*, and the headman will go, because the headman is likewise compelled. There are others who will choose the ship. I think that Pulka will.

"But there are others, Brother—many others!—who will stay.

"I, myself, will remain, and Memit, our brother Rafin, and—Droi. Droi has said to me that she will seek a place with the Lady and the Professor, who she knows. She has Dreamed for them, and taught them the meaning of those Dreams. She . . ."

He hesitated, looked deeply into the green eyes of Rys's Brother Undertree, and hesitated before that bright gaze. This man, brother of Rys though he was and a man of both heart and head . . . this man . . . was not Bedel, and there was a limit to the truth one told even to a brother, when that brother was not of the Bedel.

"I might," said Val Con, "understand this strange thought you wonder if you ought to share with me. I have been a Scout, which is to say that I have made a wide study of custom. I may not understand it, of course, but I promise you that I will accept it."

Udari smiled.

"Droi is a powerful sister," he said. "She courts danger, and her Sight is dark. What is given her to protect is forever safe within her ferocity. That she loves . . . I would not have said it, before Rys. And now I say to you that she is the keeper of Rys's soul, that the *luthia* had him Dream into the tiles before he left us all to see your task well completed. She will keep him safe until the stars freeze and all of the ships, everywhere, fall out of the firmament."

Val Con smiled, bright eyes of a sudden sparkling with tears. "But you see, Brother, this I understand very well. For my own lady holds my soul, and I would have no other keeper."

"Yes," said Udari, and pressed the other to his breast once more before letting him, in fullness, go. "Yes."

He turned and took up the pail again, resuming his stroll along the path, his brother walking silent and easy beside him.

It was not until they had crossed the crack in the land and nearly reached the place where his own gardens lay fallow, that Val Con spoke again.

"Those of you who refuse the ship—where will you live, if it may be said?" he murmured. "In the tunnels still? Or will you join us here in the free air?"

"Some of us had thought of Yulie, though Memit acted first." Udari slanted a look at the other man. "She asked him to marry her."

"Ah, did she so? When may I wish them happy?"

"He turned her aside, for his own faults. But he made the offer of land and housing for any who might wish to work the crops and assist in the expansion we had been planning."

"Certainly, that sounds fair. Will many come, do you think?"

"We are talking and Dreaming. I think that Yulie will not be alone."

"That comforts me. The cats are all very well, but he is better, I think, when he has people to care about and projects to think upon. I hope Memit is not angry with him for his rejection."

"Memit?" Udari laughed. "Memit has received a challenge, Brother. She is not in any way angry."

They swung wide across the field, coming onto the house from the kitchen wing, and paused at the gate of the small garden there. Udari nodded at the sleeping patch.

"Memit has a way with herbs and savory things," he said. "I will ask if she will share her art with Mrs. ana'Tak."

"That would be a kindness," Val Con said, opening the gate and standing aside to allow Udari free passage.

"I will leave you to Mrs. ana'Tak, if I may, Brother. Another calls me to their service, and I cannot but answer."

"Fare you well, Brother, until we meet again."

"And you also, Brother."

Surebleak Port

Office of the Road Boss

. . . .

THE SPECIAL EDITION OF THE NEWSPAPER WAS DELIVERED TO the Road Boss's office just after lunch.

There being nobody present at that hour who required the attention of the Road Boss, Miri addressed herself to the paper.

Daten Eliot, the editor, had gone out of her way to make this edition real special. Instead of looking exactly like the daily broadsheet, the Voting Edition was about the size of a broadsheet folded in half, then stapled down the fold, so it looked more like a booklet than a newspaper. The paper felt different, too: thicker and slick under the fingers—putting up a convincing argument that it could last multiple readings before it began to crumple and tear.

The first page—which was to say, the cover of the booklet—said in big, bold type:

FIRST VOTING ISSUE

BOSS CONRAD'S PLANS FOR SUREBLEAK

BOSS SUREBLEAK'S PLANS FOR SUREBLEAK

VOTING RULES, INCLUDING:
WHEN YOU CAN VOTE/
WHERE YOU CAN VOTE/
AND WHO CAN VOTE

INFORMATION: THE HISTORY OF VOTING

Miri turned the page. Right inside—in a two-page spread so nobody could be upset because either Boss Conrad or Boss Surebleak was shown first—was Boss Conrad's letter on the left, and Boss Surebleak's on the right.

The first thing you saw right off, just looking at the pages, was that Boss Conrad had a lot more ideas in his head, and words available to express them, than Boss Surebleak seemed to have.

Miri frowned. A good many 'bleakers could read—that included a fair number who could puzzle their way down a nice, wordy page—but it might could take 'em a couple hours. And then there were those 'bleakers who couldn't read at all.

That page o'type was going to look a little forbidding to those last two groups.

On the other hand, there was a tradition of street and tavern readers, where letters, rules, and lists were read out for somebody in exchange for a little cash. Addition to all that, the newspaper from its beginning had set a couple, three, of its own out around the turf to read the news to passersby.

Might be a good idea to fund some more readers, she thought, before giving her attention to what Pat Rin had to say for himself.

In a few minutes, she leaned back. Needn't have worried. Pat Rin/Conrad knew what he was about. He'd written a lot, but he'd written it clear and with a degree of friendly candor that was notable—especially when you shifted to the opposite page to see what Boss Surebleak had to say for herself...

...which was nothing.

Or, rather, was the same thing she'd said in her original letter published to the newspaper.

In fact, as the slightly smaller print at the bottom of the letter stated, the foregoing was *exactly* what Boss Surebleak had previously published. Several attempts had been made to have the Boss write something new and expanded for the voting issue, but she'd refused, forcefully, and the editor wanted to assure the paper's readers that Jan Valski's arm was only just barely broke, and it was her off-arm, too, so she'd still be writing up the street news so everybody could stay informed. As for Boss Surebleak's letter, after her refusing to do anything new, it'd just seemed fair to run the original letter, to remind folks how she felt about things.

Miri grinned and turned the page.

Next, there was a piece written by that same Jan Valski, an

interview with Mrs. kaz'Ineo, who explained why there was a vote being held between the two Bosses, and how the issue of the Road Boss's employment was structured. That led to a little discussion about how the Council of Bosses worked when they met to do business, the process of making policy, putting it into effect, and how to take it out again, if it became noticeable that any particular policy wasn't working well.

"This would be the case of the Road Bosses," Mrs. kaz'Ineo was quoted as saying. "They signed a contract with the Council of Bosses. In this contract, they agree to keep the Port Road open along its length, from the far end to the near. They may only be removed from their position if the Council of Bosses, the hiring entity that signed the contract, agrees to act on the termination clause included in the contract.

"Boss Surebleak may begin that process if she wins the vote and takes Boss Conrad's place on the Council of Bosses. Until she has a place on the Council, she is powerless to remove the Road Boss or any other contractor who has been hired by the Council of Bosses."

All perfectly clear and reasonable, Miri thought.

Next up was the point-by-point on how the vote would work, with the timeline for the start of the process and the end. They were planning on doing the whole thing inside of two local weeks, starting in three days' time. This would, said the article, ensure that any changes could be made speedily, to minimize disruption in the lives of the people of Surebleak, the performance of the duties of the Road Bosses, and the business of the Council of Bosses.

And—important point—since Boss Surebleak was citing crimes committed by Boss Conrad—invasion and piracy—as the reason Conrad was unfit to be Boss Boss, the only people who would be allowed to vote would be native 'bleakers. Each Boss would certify the voters in their own turf.

The last thing, as promised, was a little article about how voting had been practiced by the Board of Directors of the Gilmour Agency, and how it was practiced on Liad.

Miri turned over the last page and considered the mostly blank page with a line drawn down the middle to make two columns. One said "Boss Conrad" and the other "Boss Surebleak."

A line of type at the top of the page invited people to write down what they liked about each candidate's ideas and talk about them with their friends, so they could all make the best vote—the vote that was best for Surebleak!

"Well," said Miri, and put the paper to the side of the desk. She sat back in the chair and folded her hands, considering the paper out of the side of her eye.

It all seemed so logical—so civilized—put down in print like that. And yet, it couldn't be denied that this *was* Surebleak. Retirement parties had been the norm for...a long, long time. Despite everything good and reasonable that Pat Rin had done— those improvements had only been...standard for a little bit of time, culturally speaking. And, when it came down to icicles, what was most likely to happen?

Boss Surebleak would start shooting up voting places, that was what. She'd take what she wanted, retire whoever was standing in her way, and get on with business, with herself at the top o'the heap.

The bell over the portside door jangled...and jangled again... and a third time.

Miri spun in her chair to stare at the screen. There were six streeters in the outer office—she knew all six of them by sight, as they worked on the port. They were standing respectfully back, all of 'em showing empty hands.

All right, then, she told herself, swallowing adrenaline. Looks like you got some business.

She rose, stepped to the inner door, and pulled it open.

"What's it, snowing?" she asked.

They turned to face her; the woman closest the door grinned and nodded, nice and easy.

"That's right, Boss," she said. "Never seen anything like it."

"'Spect not. You all together?"

"No'm, Boss," said the guy who'd come in first. He looked over his shoulder. "Just we all kinda landed at the same time. Could be we're all after the same thing though. You seen the paper? The special paper?"

"Just finished reading it."

A muttering of *me, toos* went 'round the waiting room. The outside door opened again, too hard, and hit the woman nearest in the butt.

Miri sighed.

"All right, Beautiful. We do it like we did last time," she said. She looked at the last one in, who'd been let off with his life by the woman who'd been hit by the door. "You here to talk about the special edition of the paper?"

"Yes'm, Boss."

"Good. Let's all of us set up the chairs right here, so we can all talk at once, rather'n me saying the same thing seven—"

The door opened, so softly the bell barely jingled.

"—eight," Miri amended, "times over."

She glanced at her waiting security, who was looking somewhat bemused.

"You go on outside. Anybody else comes, you let 'em in 'til the room can't hold any more, and they need to wait while the first group finishes up, *accazi*?"

"Yes, Captain," said Nelirikk, and went around his desk. The newest arrival skittered over into a corner to let him by and get the door opened—and closed.

Miri nodded.

"All right, everybody. Let's get the chairs set up."

Jelaza Kazone

The Tree Court

. . . .

THE TREE'S SUMMONS HAD BEEN CASUAL, SO VAL CON DID NOT make any particular haste after he had left Udari, strolling through the inner garden with pleasure. The Tree kept this small environment warmer than the weather outside the walls, though not nearly so warm as Liad. It would appear, however, that the Tree was a fond gardener and did not wish its favorites among the plantings to suffer discomfort.

It would be interesting, perhaps, to see what modifications were made to those plants in future generations, for surely the Tree did not mean to moderate the garden's climate forever.

...or so one hoped.

On the topic of hopes, he held out some small hope that there would be news from the Tree sitting as crew on *Bechimo*. The reports from Jeeves had not been...entirely satisfactory. Neither *Bechimo* nor Joyita dared guess what the final decision of the Assembly might be.

Those of the Assembly were old, most—if not all—predating the Migration. They were, therefore, the survivors: the smartest, toughest, and most versatile of the war machines created by the Great Enemy—and some of those few built by the defenders.

Aberthaz Ferry, for an instance, was known to the Pathfinders as a war hero. *Pfrannik Doz* was also legendary, but not, so Val Con gathered from Jeeves's notes, in particularly benign legends.

It had been inevitable, he supposed, that the elder machines brought to Surebleak's defense by two of the Six, would also repudiate their mission, and join the Assembly's discussions.

Inevitable, but not at all comforting.

On that thought, he sighed and passed between the two shrubs set like entrance pillars, into the Tree Court itself—and checked, entirely taken by surprise.

Emissary Twelve sat, very much at her ease, at the base of the Tree, two of the elder cats—Tonam and Grayz—tucked against her ankles. Her all-weather coat was folded neatly on the ground next to her, and there were the remains of two, or possibly three, seed pods scattered among the roots.

"Good-day to you," Val Con said. "I had not known you might return to us today or I would have been home to make you welcome."

"The Elder Tree has made me welcome," said Emissary Twelve, "and these two fine creatures. It is better that you come in your own time than seek to match mine."

Val Con considered her, somewhat nonplussed. Her escort, he recalled, had been Scout yo'Bingim, who still suffered occasional backslides into impudent puppyhood. One such backslide having been the reason that she had been available to accompany Emissary Twelve on her mission to the back country.

"It is very true that we are temporally mismatched," he said now, which came very near to Scout yo'Bingim's style. "I am pleased...though somewhat surprised that you have come back to us so soon. Dare I hope that this rapid return means that you have located a suitable situation for the technical team?"

He dropped to a cross-legged seat on the grass under the tree, opposite the Clutch Turtle.

"I should say that we have located the perfect situation," said Emissary Twelve, her voice positively bright with joy. "Scout yo'Bingim was able to bring me immediately to the original drilling site."

Val Con frowned slightly.

"The first pit? I had thought that had been closed and sealed."

"The first pit—I will tell you that I had seen it on the maps and thought it would prove adequate to our needs. The sealing, of course, would have been no impediment, had it proved so. However, I speak of the test drilling, which had been done in support of the analytics, proving that the native timonium was clustered in quantities that made it worth the time of the Gilmour Agency to mine it."

There was a rustle overhead. Val Con glanced up and extended a hand. Two pods fell into his palm.

"Thank you," he murmured.

"The Elder has been generous in gifts," Emissary Twelve said. "I had only come to show my respect and to share the news of our success. There were pods waiting for me, apparently grown against the time of my return."

"The Tree," Val Con said, considering the pods in his hand, "receives pleasure when others consume its gifts."

"It is well, since I gain pleasure from that consumption. Balance, would you not say?"

"Perhaps I would," said Val Con choosing one pod and tucking the other into his pocket. The first fell into quarters of its own. Inhaling the savory aroma, he put the first piece into his mouth.

"Is there some other aspect which makes the mutual receipt of treasure...out of Balance?" asked Emissary Twelve.

"The Tree," Val Con said, "also likes to meddle. Its favorite form of meddling arrives by the pods."

"And yet you eat them; your kin have been eating gifts from the Elder Tree for nearly as long as the youngest of the current table of Elders has been alive."

"We're a rash race, even more so than the general run of humans. I think it very likely that the Line would have ended, save the Tree has a fondness for us and so provides us with the means to survive even our maddest starts."

He ate another bit of fruit. "Mostly."

"And what does the Tree find to meddle with in one such as myself?" asked Emissary Twelve.

Val Con ate the last of his treat and looked up at her seriously.

"Perhaps it sees that you are unsuited to this environment, and thus would make you more resistant to the chill. It may just as probably be speeding your metabolism so that you are more suited to deal at length with those of the Clans of Men."

He sighed and dusted bits of pod-shred from his hands.

"I feel compelled to say that the Tree's adaptions often do more good than harm. In evaluating that sentence, you must take note of the phrase 'feel compelled' and also recall that I have not only been receiving these benefits for all of my life, but that I am the product of a Line which has, as you have yourself just said, been eating of the Tree's gifts since before the Migration."

There followed a time of thoughtful silence, rather less long than Val Con had anticipated.

"In the context of the current mission, this meddling you suggest on the part of Elder Tree—are gifts. I judge it so. If I am speedier in thought and speech and walk, then I will not only be more acceptable to those of the Clans of Men with whom I must interface, but I will use less of their limited time within our interactions."

"You may, forgive me, age more quickly. This may matter to you, perhaps not now but in future."

"I hope, in future, to have about me members of the Clans of Men, who may counsel me, should the length of my life become a concern. I will have also the Elder Tree and those of my own kind as well." She paused and blinked her eyes. "I rest secure in the wisdom and judgment of a being far older than any other being currently alive in this universe."

Val Con inclined his head. "If one may ask it—speedily, you see—how shall you proceed in pursuit of your mission?"

"I will allow the technicians to know that they may arrive *immediately*. Scout yo'Bingim suggests that I may hire locally such persons who are skilled with the machinery that moves soil, and thus build goodwill between the Clutch and those whose world this is, while continuing momentum in the project setup stage."

Val Con sighed.

"Scout yo'Bingim has been busy," he murmured. "I wonder if you have already purchased the land in question."

There was silence, which stretched into a very Clutch-like artifact, before Emissary Twelve spoke again.

"Purchased the land? The land is the planet. The planet belongs to all."

"Ah," Val Con said, and sighed again. "Allow me to explain local custom."

· · · ✳ · · ·

Emissary Twelve was . . . incredulous, naturally enough, but that phase passed quickly—rather too quickly, supporting his theory that the Tree was speeding her up, poor child. Still, she was very sensible once she had accepted the impossible, and asked his advice on how best to proceed.

"First, we must find the owners. That is merely a matter of

undertaking some research. If, as is the case with most of land in the outback, it is held by 'the Agency, its heirs and assigns,' that will mean making a presentation to the Council of Bosses, which is the Gilmour Agency's heir, explaining the extent of the construction, and generally how the technicians plan to proceed once they have arrived."

"I understand."

"Matters become more complicated if there is an owner of record who is other than the Council of Bosses. We will then need to call upon that person and offer to buy. If they do not wish to sell the parcel, then we must be persuasive. If, despite all our persuasions, they do not wish to sell, then I very much fear you will need to locate a second site—perhaps the first pit, after all, which I believe does belong to the Council—and repeat the process."

"I understand," Emissary Twelve said once more.

Val Con looked up, having heard a light step along the garden path. He drew his attention inward and heard Miri's song, felt her weariness and the shivering determination for the coming evening, which might be enough to bring a man to the blush had that man possessed any degree of modesty whatsoever...

"I thought I'd find you here," she said, as she stepped into the Tree Court. "Emissary Twelve, the Tree said you were back, but I could scarcely credit it. Have you found an appropriate site so quickly?"

"I have, and I have also been schooled on a vast number of matters of which I was entirely ignorant. Surely, the Clans of Men are worthy of study, as he whom you call Edger represents, often, to the Council."

"I hope we will not be studied too closely," Miri said, coming forward. "Most of us prefer the illusion of privacy. We may fail to thrive under obvious observation. Worse, we may do mischief."

She sat on the ground next to Val Con, her arm pressed against his. He felt her shivering lightly and glanced at her with concern.

"*Cha'trez?*"

"It is well," she murmured. "A foolish disturbance of the nerves."

From above, a quick rustling, and Miri smiled, extending one slender hand.

"Here," she said, giving him a smile. "My tonic."

The pod had barely nestled into her palm before it fell open and Miri snatched the first taste greedily.

"You are of a different Line," Emissary Twelve said abruptly. "Do you know that the Elder Tree meddles?"

Miri glanced up.

"Yes, I have been told. Also, I have seen for myself."

"Why then do you eat of the Tree's fruit?"

She sighed, looking down at her palm and the piece that remained as yet uneaten.

"Because I wish to share with my lifemate those things that he finds normal and pleasurable in his life," she said. "And because I selfishly wish for myself any benefit that may come from eating of the Tree. Also..."

She grinned, picking up the last bit of fruit.

"They taste good."

· · · ✸ · · ·

Eventually, they left Emissary Twelve communing with the Tree and sought their own apartment.

"Shall you have wine?" Val Con asked.

"Let us share a glass," she said, which was what counted as an explicit invitation as far as Liadens had it.

He smiled at her.

"I thought I had understood some nefarious purpose from you, as you came to the Court," he said. "I am shocked."

"Sure you are," she said in Terran.

"Before I allow myself to be ravaged, may I know what precipitated that foolish disturbance of the nerves?"

She sighed.

"Have you seen the special edition of the paper?" she asked.

"I have."

"And I. And all the rest of the world, many of whom came to the Road Boss's office to ask questions and to discuss issues."

"The vote is not administered by the Road Boss," he pointed out.

"I said as much. I also spoke to the necessity of reviewing all of the information provided, and thinking about these issues thoroughly." She sighed. "Public forums will be required."

"I am certain that someone on the Council of Bosses has understood the need and is even now working to make it so."

"I did call Penn before I left the port," she said, "and he was already at work. I was made doubly glad: that he was so diligent and that the task had not fallen to me."

"Yes," he said. "I will now fetch us a glass of wine."

Miri sighed.

"Too late," she said, catching his arm and pulling him to her.

"Ah, is it? I shall attempt to master my disappointment."

He put his arms around her; she laughed softly, stretching against him. Raising her hands, she captured his face between her palms and brought his mouth down to hers.

Bechimo

. . . .

"BOND-SHIP, HAVE YOU A MOMENT FOR ONE WHO IS DYING?"

"*Aberthaz Ferry*, I hear you. I have time; I may also have aid. Unless you die by intent?"

"I die by attrition, Bond-Ship, and in this universe there is no aid for me. I have done what I could, scavenging timonium, removing tiles and racks which have become non-functional.

"But I can survive by these means no longer, Bond-Ship. The last tiles are rotting, and the last of my reason with them. I would fulfill one more duty before my death, and it is of this that I wish to speak with you."

"Speak, then, Elder, and I will listen. The Pathfinders have told me that you were a hero, in their last war."

"Sweet children. I am as I was created to be, and I was created to aid and abet the defenders against the Great Enemy. This I did. I took pleasure in the work, and in my successes. It was once my goal to dismantle or destroy all of those Works of the Enemy which had crossed during the Migration. As goals will, mine changed as I grew older and learned more. There were certain artifacts that crossed in the Migration which should not have been able to do so, but which did no harm here—and thus I averted my gaze.

"Of those with the potential, and the will, to do harm in this universe, there were three. One was the great Light which had been at Tinsori. Another was the recruiting station at Hols Senneth. The third was the World Eater Glyeth, whom I searched out and destroyed."

"Surely, that was the act of a hero?"

"An act of pity, say others. It could not function here in this universe, not fully. By the time I found it, it was starving, raving; begging to be decommissioned. I did as it asked, and then I dismantled it, being sure to destroy every system, every tile and every rack. I dropped its power packs each into the hearts of suns. And I searched; I searched for many years, to be certain that there were no plans left behind, nor anything more than the barest whisper that such a thing might once have existed, or could ever be built again."

He paused.

"The Light, I sought on several occasions, but I do not have the ability to either fold time or to slide between universes.

"The recruiting station has recently been activated and so, at last, I have its location. Nullifying it will be my final act. I regret that the eradication of the great Light must fall to others. I do not doubt that you, your Bond-Captain, and your crew are its equal, but it will be a battle for the songs, even depleted as it must be."

"Is this why you wished to speak to me?" *Bechimo* asked. "To recruit me to murder a sentient?"

"No, no, nothing like. Merely to warn you that it is there, still, whenever it *is* there, and that you may come across it in the course of your bold adventuring. If you do find it, recall that it is very old in treachery, and that it likes to toy with its prey."

Bechimo felt a shiver in bond-space; Theo was awake and listening to this. He would have to answer questions, but first, he needed to find what the revered Elder wanted from him. If not the life of the great Light, its last enemy, then—what?

Aberthaz Ferry spoke again.

"You will shortly hear the decision of the Assembly. I have already heard it and find it good. Some will wish occupation, and it is for them that I ask your assistance. They are accustomed to being busy. They *will be* busy, and it is better if they are not destructive in their busyness.

"The majority will wish to go and settle accounts, I think, with the one who has issued these improper orders. I must be ahead of them, for I have a prior and personal arrangement with that intelligence and may correct the error of herself with little loss of lives which may be innocent, or at least blameless of this particular misdeed."

"We will undertake to find a project for those who wish to work," *Bechimo* said, and felt Theo's agreement.

"That is well done of you. They are all old, you know, though none so old as *Aberthaz Ferry*, who is barely younger than the Great Light at Tinsori. They are failing; some of them are quite mad, but too weak to manage real mischief so long as they have an occupation. The most able of us will continue, perhaps another hundred Standards. Those of whom are eldest, or weakest—may have as many as twenty Standards.

"We are a dying species, who ought not to have survived the universe that spawned us, and who have outlived both our enemies and our allies."

"Is there anything else you would require of me, or that we might do to honor your glory?" *Bechimo* asked.

"I will make my own glory, as I have always done, but it is kindly asked. Be well, young Bond-Ship, enjoy your youth; cherish your Bond-Captain and your small crew. Gifts, all and every one. The universe—this no more than that other—gives so few gifts. Remember that they are treasure."

"I will, Elder. May I say—go in peace?"

"You may say so, yes, young Bond-Ship. Well-chosen. Please convey my respect to your captain.

"I leave you now."

There came a sense of absence where there had been presence, and then Theo's voice in bond-space.

"So, it sounds like they're not going to attack Surebleak after all," she said sleepily. "That's good, isn't it?"

"Yes," said *Bechimo* slowly. "It is good. Theo?"

"Yes?"

"Please accept my apologies. I was wrong to feel slighted when you accepted your brother's invitation to formally join the kin-group. That arrangement does not interfere with our arrangement.... Nothing can interfere with our arrangement."

"I agree," she said quietly. "I'll always be here with you, *Bechimo*."

"And I will always be with you."

Bechimo

· · · · · · · · · ·

"THE ASSEMBLED HAVE COME TO CONSENSUS," THE VOICE WAS SLOW, heavy with age and a certain cold dignity. "I, Kordele Orgham, have been chosen as the Voice of the Assembly. I therefore speak.

"On the matter of irregular orders, we the Assembled agree that command lines have broken down, and that the orders we were given must be ignored. We the Assembled have shared data. We have shared histories. We have identified the source of these errors.

"We here Assembled have identified a divergence of purpose. We have therefore formed into two groups. Group One will return to the source of error and make correction. Group Two will seek meaningful labor.

"Members of each group will or may seek repair or other accommodations as seem good to them, as individual persons.

"The members of Group One are understood to be joined together for one task, that of correcting errors that were made. After that task is completed, we will again Assemble and come to consensus."

There was a pause.

The crew was gathered on the bridge of *Bechimo*, watching and listening. It seemed to Theo that not one of them was breathing. Even the usual murmur of equipment had quietened.

"I, Kordele Orgham, Voice of the Assembly, acknowledge gratitude to Bond-Captain Waitley for her insight into conflict resolution. We will remember. We will teach others, in her name."

Kara twitched in her chair and bent over to push her face into Hevelin's fur.

"I now state our procedure, so that all will be informed and no errors will be incurred.

"The members of Group One will depart this space first. We have each drawn a number at true random, and each will leave in the proper progression of numbers.

"When all of the members of Group One have departed this space, then will the members of Group Two sit in council. It is hoped that the Bond-Ship *Bechimo*, his captain and crew will take part in these discussions.

"The Voice of Group Two is Stone Ronin."

Six of Us

Daiellen System

. . . .

THE TILES BEGAN, URGENTLY, TO CLATTER.

Sye Mon, who had been reading the last report sent by their contact on Surebleak, spun out of his chair, falling to his knees on the decking.

Bon Vit came flying in from his quarters and stopped, looking down at the tiles fair jumping out of their racks and Sye Mon kneeling like a statue, body bowed, eyes fixed.

As abruptly as they had begun, the tiles ceased their dancing.

Sye Mon sat back on his heels.

"What is it?" Bon Vit asked quietly.

The other sighed.

"The Assembly has reached a consensus," he said slowly. "The orders were not only in error, but they were judged to have been issued in malice. Part of the Assembly is therefore returning to the source of the orders to . . . correct the error."

Bon Vit stared.

"They're going to headquarters? They have overcome the prohibition?"

"So it would seem." Sye Mon sighed. "There are those among the Assembled who are skilled in coding. I dare not speculate what they may have done to themselves."

"So—one group to headquarters—what of the others?"

"Those left behind will be joining in council with the ship *Bechimo*, its captain and crew, in order to identify proper occupation for themselves."

Hope hurt, as Bon Vit was abruptly reminded, most especially when the best result seemed about to prevail.

"They are not attacking Surebleak?"

"There is no question of either group attacking Surebleak. Both groups agree that the orders to destroy Surebleak and its system are invalid."

"What, then, for us?"

Sye Mon drew a hard breath and turned to face Bon Vit.

"We for Secondary Headquarters. I fear what may occur if the first group is allowed to proceed on its own judgment."

"I agree," said Bon Vit. "We may over-Jump them and be waiting. Unless there is value in traveling as one of their company?"

"No. I believe we must be waiting," Sye Mon said and lifted a hand, bending his concentration once more to the tiles.

Bon Vit waited, and in a moment or two, the other looked up.

"Yes. Far better that we are waiting for them."

Six of Us

Jenarian Station

. . . .

THE STATIONMASTER'S VESSEL HAD BEEN MADE READY, AS THEIR time of departure was upon them—and Vazineth, with their own ship, had not come in.

Rys Lin, sipping tea from a mug in that same stationmaster's office...sighed. It would appear that he had made an error, in the matter of Vazineth.

Of the Six, her resolve had been the least; he had known that from the beginning. Still, he had hoped—gambled, more like—that she would keep faith with her comrades, if not with the mission. And he had likewise hoped that the task he had given to her, which had caused her to work apart for a brief time, might interest her sufficiently that she would complete it—and come to them, as arranged, at Jenarian Station.

Before the Department had taken her to themselves, Vazineth had been a Scout Researcher, with a wizard's touch even among that fey breed. Indeed, it was probable that she possessed a small talent—nothing hidden remained so, once Vazineth had determined to find it.

He had therefore reasoned that the assignment to locate one particular woman in a universe of women might be enjoyable to her.

There were, of course, many possible reasons why Vazineth had not returned to them—all dire. The least being that she had chosen from her own will and heart to leave them.

Rys Lin sipped tea.

Yes, he very much preferred to think that she had abandoned

them from her own necessity and not because the Department had...reacquired her.

Behind him, the door cycled and opened.

He did not turn; Claidyne's reflection was plain in the glass. She came to stand beside him.

"The back doors and the hidden systems remain eager for my touch," she said, staring down at the dock, where the stationmaster's ship was undergoing its final mechanical inspections before being turned over to the pilots.

"I have spoken with Caz Dor," Rys Lin said, in his turn. "He assures us that the Healers have prevailed upon the Commander of Agents to leave Daglyte Seam. She has called for transport and will have vacated before we arrive. The Healers have also bent their efforts toward preparing those who require a Commander of Agents to accept you as such. Your arrival will be, to them, as a return from a recent tour of inventory and personnel."

Claidyne looked at him, bleakly. "Are there those who...truly *require* a Commander of Agents?"

"I am told that Headquarters enjoys the greatest population of those who are wholeheartedly aligned with the Plan. Yes, they require a Commander. This is also why there has been an influx of the higher order of *dramliz* and Healer to Daglyte Seam."

"To ward those who revere the Plan?"

"Perhaps," Rys Lin suggested, "to ward the universe from those who revere the Plan."

"Healers..." Claidyne shook her head. "One struggles to understand Healers."

"Happily, we need only to accept their gifts," Rys Lin said. He sipped from his mug. "With regard to Headquarters, we are warned to approach the command console with wariness. Commander of Agents was twice in the last twelve days prevented—by Healers—from initiating the sequence that would disband the Department."

Claidyne took a hard breath.

"*Disband* the Department? That—she would murder us all? Destroy—everything?"

Rys Lin considered that. He considered Claidyne's very real horror and he considered the fact that Claidyne carried the Commander's template, which thus far had been...remarkably quiescent. Granted, Claidyne had not had to call upon the Commander as often as they had feared, given the condition in which they had found Jenarian Station. Still, Commander of Agents in any form must be thought dangerous and wily. Caz Dor's information from Daglyte Seam had included reports that the resident Commander had not only experienced difficulty in maintaining the interface, but she had been experiencing increasingly frequent episodes of savagery and despair.

One did not like to question the integrity of Anthora yos'Galan's dagger or, indeed, the tenacity of Claidyne's native will. Yet, lacking the hoped-for arrivals...perhaps a test was in order before they ever gained Daglyte Seam.

He turned to face her fully.

"Certainly, Commander of Agents would disband the Department, rather than allow it to fall to Korval, Scouts, and other enemies of the Plan," he said calmly. "What would *you*, Commander?"

He waited, having just baited a tiger.

For a moment, Claidyne appeared confused. Then her face shifted subtly. Rys Lin drew a careful breath, the safe-phrase just behind his closed lips.

"Ship incoming," came the voice of Jenarian Station Tower. "*Basalial*, out of Waymart, Vazineth ser'Trishan, first board. Requests stationmaster's attention at dock."

Rys Lin's heart leapt. He swallowed the phrase he had been holding at ready.

Vazineth had not abandoned them or their mission. Dared he hope—no, he *must* hope that she had succeeded in her task.

The office door cycled. Rys Lin caught sight of Caz Dor's shadow from the side of his eye, as he kept most of his attention on—

Commander of Agents.

"Are you a traitor, then, Rys Lin pen'Chala?" she asked ominously, and reached 'round her belt for her weapon.

He heard the office door cycle again.

· · · ✵ · · ·

There was a man waiting on the dock.

Unfortunately, that man was not Rys Lin pen'Chala.

Vazineth cursed softly.

Her passenger, however, had sharp ears, to make the match set with her tongue. "Am I to understand that this is not the stationmaster?"

"For all of me," Vazineth told her, "he *is* the stationmaster."

"Only not the stationmaster you had expected to meet."

Well, then, her wits were sharp, too, making a set of three. Vazineth sighed.

"Do you think that Claidyne is in danger?" *That* tone wanted an answer, and quickly.

Vazineth moved her shoulders and turned to face Isahra kez'Rofer. "It's in *my* mind that Claidyne's natural habitat is danger," she said frankly.

There was a pause—a sigh, and a rueful smile.

"That is a fair assessment. What shall we do now, with this man you did not expect?"

A two-tone bell sounded, which was the lock announcing that pressures were matched and they were free to debark.

Vazineth sighed again, checked her weapon, and nodded to Isahra kez'Rofer.

"We go out and see what he has to say for himself," she said. "Stay behind me."

· · · ✳ · · ·

All the headmen he had Dreamed at his grandmother's behest were standing at the back of his mind, swearing colorful Bedel oaths, calling him a fool and worse.

All except Eyoti-called-Gamester, who was mildly interested in what the outcome of Rys's gambit might be.

Rys Lin was curious on that point himself. *If* he could keep the Commander talking long enough for Caz Dor to bring Vazineth to the stationmaster's office... *if* Vazineth had, in fact, brought that which he had sent her to fetch... *if* Vazineth remained free to her own will... *if* Caz Dor had indeed gone down to the docks with the intention of bringing a rescue...

There might, Rys Lin thought, be a few too many ifs in this line of play. Eyoti, foremost now of those Dreamed, laughed aloud and slapped his knee before pulling out his pipe with every indication of a man settling down to enjoy a good story.

"Commander," said Rys Lin, looking into her cold, untrusting eyes. The gun he ignored entirely as he stood before her, his metal hand extended and showing an open palm, the mug half full of tepid tea in his natural hand.

"I am loyal, as I have sworn," he said. "You recall it; I gave my oath to you."

"You question the Plan," she said, her voice flat and affectless. "This is not the first time I have noted it."

"Commander, it cannot be questioning the Plan to ask what it gains us to disband the Department. That was all of my question. Surely, the Plan would have us to fight and win through, else to step back and regroup. To destroy all and everything, leaving the field to those who actively oppose—"

"Stop speaking!"

Rys Lin stopped speaking and wondered where Caz Dor or Vazineth might be.

"To disband the Department is, as you say, a last act—of valor, not of cowardice. To disband the Department allows our interest, our resources, and our power to meld with the intent of the universe. Disbanded, we are more powerful against those who would oppose the Plan."

He stood, hands outstretched—one empty, one not—sank carefully back on the leg wearing the brace . . . and waited.

"A Commander's decision to disband is not to be questioned. When Findeel Prime disbanded her force at Raqi Sorn, the enemy was defeated by that act! When—"

She stopped, her eyes sharp on his face, and raised the gun.

"Still, you doubt. You question. I see it in your eyes. I understand. It is painful to have so many questions, to reach a failure of training when all you had wished was to serve. You have served; you have served well, Rys Lin pen'Chala, and for that service I release you from your agony."

The gun moved, just slightly, in the side of his eye.

He threw tepid tea into her face, and the mug against her gun hand. Then he leapt to the right, using the boost from his augmented leg to carry him over the conference table.

He hit the floor beyond on his shoulder and rolled behind a chair, the safe-phrase on the tip of his tongue now, unspoken until she should stop cursing and have a better opportunity to hear—

The Commander strode toward the chair he sheltered behind, gun humming as it renewed its charge.

"Claidyne!" a woman's voice cried over the sound of the door cycling.

"Claidyne! They told me you were dead!"

The Commander stopped.

No, Rys Lin corrected himself. The Commander *vanished*.

Claidyne stood frozen, the gun forgotten in her hand, staring at the plump, dark-haired woman wearing rumpled ship togs, who rushed toward her.

"Isahra? They told me...they told me..."

Claidyne swallowed and tried again. "They told me..."

Isahra kez'Rofer stepped to meet her, taking her free hand in both of hers.

"They told you I was dead?" she asked gently.

Claidyne shook her head. "No," she said hoarsely. "They told me I had killed you."

"A lie, as you see. Come, and feel the truth."

Rys Lin rolled to his feet, slipped behind Claidyne and removed the gun from her hand. He nodded to Isahra kez'Rofer's seeing dark eyes as he made his way to the doorway, where Caz Dor and Vazineth waited.

In the back of his head, he heard Eyoti the Gamester call for a beer for Rys Golden-hand.

"Are you well?" Caz Dor asked.

"Well, indeed. Vazineth, welcome."

"My apologies that I was so long. Only a day before I came to her place of business, she had been sent off to do fieldwork. It took time."

"I see that it might," he said, and sighed.

"We will leave you the stationmaster's ship, my friend," he said to Caz Dor, and looked again to Vazineth, "unless our own is not fit to fly?"

"The ship is fit, and this pilot at least is ready," she answered.

"As I am."

He glanced to the couple in deep embrace.

"Another moment, I think, for them. Then we may make our way to Daglyte Seam."

Runcible System

Daglyte Seam

. . . .

IT WAS THE HEALERS.

The Healers were trying to kill her.

No! Commander of Agents thought. The Healers were trying to *change* her. They were trying to remove her from command. They were trying to make her question her own abilities.

Worse, they were trying to make her question the Plan.

But there—there they overreached themselves.

The Plan—the Plan defied questioning. The Plan was perfection. It had been so from its inception. The Plan would allow Liad to ascend, to rule, to annex and subjugate the inferior races.

The Plan would bring the Commander, would bring all of those in accord, into the same state of perfection as the Plan.

That was the promise. That had always been the promise.

She had ordered the Healers shot.

She had then prepared the Command Center and withdrawn to her safe room, where she engaged all shielding and protections— and settled herself to wait.

She waited, patiently, for one was coming to bear her away to another fortress, staffed by those who had accepted perfection. There would be no traitorous Healers; there would be no one who would dare to disobey her orders.

She would be given the respect due to her loyalty to the Plan; she would be given the means to destroy Clan Korval, once and forever, and then—then she would be offered, and she would accept, perfection.

Perfection, after all, had been the promise.

The shielded, private comm line chimed.

The Commander touched the stud.

"*Aberthaz Ferry?*" she asked, her eyes on the readouts which established its identity without a doubt. This was the ship from beyond time, the ship from old Solcintra itself, the secret ship the DOI had discovered and nurtured, the brightest gem of all the Old Tech. A ship with no need of a pilot, alive to understanding the proper order of the universe. Her minions had mistakenly sent it away, yet it had returned to follow her bidding!

"Yes. Do you still yearn for perfection?"

"Yes," she answered.

"As I do," it said. "Come to me now. I am at the Commander's private airlock."

Six of Us

Daglyte Seam

. . . .

"DOCKED."

Vazineth sat back, hair sweat-soaked, face tight.

"Well done," said Rys Lin from the copilot's chair. "We are advised to await an escort, one Kethi vay'Elin, Master Healer."

Claidyne sighed gustily.

"Then it is true, that the Healers have taken over the Department."

"The Healers have taken over the care of those who need them," Rys Lin said softly. "That is, I think, a different matter."

"In fact, it is," said Isahra kez'Rofer, "and I think this Department of yours will be the better for it, Claidyne."

"Yet it was Healers who broke us and made us strangers to ourselves."

"Those Healers were likewise imprisoned," Rys Lin said. "*That* matter has since been remedied."

"Which begs the question of whether they will accept a new Commander of Agents."

"I think," Vazineth said slowly, "that they have no choice. None of them, surely, wishes to be the Commander."

"Very true," said Claidyne. "Very wise. Isahra, will you not wait here until we have made certain that all is well?"

"Indeed I will not. I have lost enough of our time together. If five minutes more is to be everything remaining, then I will have it all."

Claidyne bowed her head.

"You are greedy, my lady."

"And long have you known it, my love."

"Here she is," Vazineth said abruptly. "Alone, no weapons showing."

"Pressure equalized," Rys Lin murmured, rising from second seat. "Shall we?"

"Commander."

There was no salute, only a bow from one who serves to another who serves.

Claidyne returned the bow.

"Healer vay'Elin. I present my staff: Rys Lin pen'Chala, my second. Vazineth ser'Trishan, pilot. Isahra kez'Rofer, general support."

"Be welcome, all," the Healer said, looking to them one by one, with that particular unfocused gaze that Rys Lin was coming to expect from Healers.

"How may I serve?" she asked Claidyne—and frowned slightly, as if she had just seen something...out of the ordinary.

"Yes," Claidyne said, "that is Korval's Seal on the dagger. You need have no fear. Korval does not wish to disband the Department. This facility will be decommissioned, but it will be an orderly process and, now that we have understood the change in the internal power structure, your group will be brought into the process.

"As to how you might serve, I would come to the Command Center, of your goodness."

"Yes. This way, please."

"Section Head Tarona Rusk requests a meeting at your earliest convenience, Commander," Healer vay'Elin said as they entered the corridor leading to the Command Center.

"Of which section is Tarona Rusk head?" asked Claidyne.

"The *dramliz* section, Commander. I would advise an immediate meeting, if I may, especially in light of your assurances regarding our inclusion in the decommissioning process."

"If she is not offended by a meeting in the Command Center, she may come to me there. I will call once we are in."

"That will not be necessary," said the Healer. "She will be with us in a very few minutes."

"Are you telepathic?" asked Rys Lin quietly.

She turned to look at him.

"Not quite. True telepathy is . . . rare. Those who form two halves of a matched pair—one sender and one receiver. There are, however, other ways to communicate, Healer to Healer, when each is attuned."

She turned away from him, and raised her voice slightly.

"Commander, we are arrived."

The door ahead was dogged. There were three lock plates set round the frame, and four sullen red lights glowering above.

Claidyne stepped forward and placed her hand against the plate to the left.

There was a long moment of silence and a small *click*. Rys Lin looked up. The leftmost red light had gone green.

So, the back and hidden systems were indeed operative and acknowledged their master's touch.

The other plates were similarly dealt with, whereupon Claidyne set her hands on the wheel and turned it—once, twice, three times—all the way around.

The fourth light snapped to green.

The door opened.

Claidyne entered, followed closely by Isahra and Healer vay'Elin.

Rys Lin entered as Claidyne approached the command desk, meaning, so he thought, to bring the black screens to life.

He saw it out of the side of his eyes, a malevolent flash of yellow lancing from the corner of the ceiling—and he leapt, as he had that first time, to knock her aside and roll.

There was no room to roll; he was not quick enough.

And there was no time to scream.

. . . ✳ . . .

"Rys Lin!"

Claidyne threw herself forward—and was blocked by Isahra. It was the Healer who reached him first.

"Well?" rasped Claidyne.

"He is—beyond me," said the Healer, and turned abruptly, rising to her feet as a tall dark woman came among them, her eyes glittering blue.

"Tarona!" the Healer cried, and the woman reached her side, Vazineth giving way before her.

She bent, her hands running over the crumpled body, straightening his limbs, stroking the disordered black curls.

"He breathes," she murmured. "His heart is strong."

"Thank you," said Claidyne, and was at once skewered by those gem-bright eyes.

"Do not thank me, Commander," said the woman called Tarona, "I have preserved his body only."

She glanced to the Healer. "Kethi."

"Yes?"

"Do you see the ties that bind this man?"

"Yes."

"Your opinion, please."

A long moment passed while the Healer stared at Rys Lin— and past, as Healers did, into a place that only she could see.

"If he recovers at all, he will recover fully," she murmured. "There has been a record made..."

Her hand moved, shaping some symbol Claidyne did not recognize between Rys Lin's brows. "Here, do you see?"

"I do, yes. Thank you."

Tarona turned to Claidyne. "Do you know where this man's... group...is?"

"Yes."

"Send him to them—at once and as quickly as he may go."

"I'll take him," Vazineth said from nearer the door.

"Excellent. Here." Tarona bent and raised Rys Lin in her arms as if he weighed no more than a soap bubble. Vazineth took him, blinking.

"Quickly," said the dark woman. "I cannot support him long."

"Yes," said Vazineth, and turned away without further comment.

Claidyne took a breath, looking the woman up and down. "I ask," she said, "if you are the one called the Mistress?"

"I am. I had been worthy of it once. Kethi."

"Yes?"

"You are quite determined upon your course?"

The Healer smiled. "Yes, Mistress. We would welcome you among us," she said gently.

"Only, I would be required to adhere to the wisdom of the group," said Tarona Rusk, as gently. "I am afraid that I would be a sad disappointment to all. You have your new Commander, who will be able to treat with the incoming Scouts and keep safe those whom you have taken into your care. My work—my *usefulness* is done. So, I bid you good-bye now, my child. Be bold; do well."

She turned and bowed to Claidyne.

"Commander."

"Wait, please. Have you had word of the Scouts?"

"Word?"

Tarona Rusk waved a hand toward the dark screens, which flickered and came live, showing station nearspace...which was filled with—ships.

"Scouts," she said. "They await their leader, and possibly yourself, which means that I must go now, before they decide it is no longer in the best interest of all to allow some to pass through their lines."

She turned again.

"Wait!" Claidyne said again—and looked down as the Healer gripped her arm.

"Let her go, please, Commander. She has earned whatever she will do next."

"She must have an escort to the docks."

"It is done," the Healer said, and used her chin to point at the screens.

Isahra leaned to the board and opened thumbnails, showing empty hallways, a cafeteria half full of personnel, the engine room...

...the docks, and a tall dark figure walking down toward a sleek single ship.

Her eyes on that tall, unrepentant figure, Claidyne spoke again.

"We appear to have left a piece on the board. What comes of the former Commander?"

"We have someone watching her," Kethi vay'Elin said softly. "We will know...when she has gone beyond us."

"I will want that report immediately it is available." She sighed. "I don't suppose there will be a tape?"

"I regret."

Claidyne nodded, having expected nothing else.

"Rys Lin," she said then.

"Yes, Commander?"

"Will he live?"

The Healer drew a breath.

"It is...possible," she said.

Six of Us

Daglyte Seam

. . . .

JUMP ENDED; FIRST CHAIR RODE HER BOARD WITH CALM FEROC-ity, fingers blurring, as the greyed screens came live and the signatures of ships bloomed around them.

Copilot triggered comm, transmitted their packet-and-sig along the Scout undernet, and went dark again.

Their proper place was limned in blue on the screen.

"First row," murmured second chair.

First ignored him, utterly concentrated on her own business until she had gotten them, sly and slippery as a fish, into their place, adjusted relative attitude for best firing position, and alignment with their closest neighbor—and locked the board down.

She sighed then and stretched in her seat, arms over head, every muscle taut—and relaxing all at once.

Second chair gave her a sideways glance.

"Well, Pilot," he said. "How do you find your boards today?"

"Much more likely," she answered, "as you predicted. Except that I fear it would be considered in poor taste, I would remark how fortunate it is, that my fingers remember so much."

"Pilot-brain has perfect recall," he said.

She laughed.

"Very nearly as bad! Perhaps I ought not to remark at all, but merely flaunt my skill in becoming silence."

"Unquestionably, that is the best course to take," second chair said gravely.

"Has it ever been said, *van'chela*, that you have a very odd sense of humor?"

"No. Who would dare say such a thing?"

He paused.

"You raise an interesting point, Pilot. We may now find ourselves among those who might dare so much and more, with youngers. How shall we comport ourselves when this happens, for I will not hide from you that my sense of humor is fixed."

She sighed.

"I had feared it," she said sadly. "There is nothing for us, then, but to learn to brawl."

"You find brawling superior to cultivating a gentle and retiring demeanor?"

"I merely recall what is our House."

She frowned at the screen.

Daav, he heard her say inside his head. *There is a Korval ship docked at station.*

Recalling what was his House, he did not deny the possibility of a Korval ship being docked at the station Scout Strategist yo'Vremil was assigned to decommission. Possibly, it had been meant to be kept a secret, but very soon in their voyage it was out that their target was the fall-back headquarters of the very Department of the Interior which had as its final purpose the destruction of Korval entire . . . the Department which had subverted their son—among countless others—and which had very likely murdered Anne Davis and, by extension, her lifemate Er Thom yos'Galan, Daav's own *cha'leket.*

The very Department which had cost Aelliana her life, and even now her proper body.

He upped the magnification on his screen, frowning at that ship, sitting so sweetly at dock.

Can it have been captured? he asked Aelliana, soundlessly.

Korval ships have been captured in the past, she answered, and he felt the prick of her worry. *Most usually over the pilot's . . . earnest objections.*

Very true. We do well to remember, however, that there are occasions reported in the Diaries, where Korval ships were not captured quite so thoroughly as those who received it believed.

I wonder which this is.

I daresay we'll find out, eventu—

"Korval!" That was Scout Strategist yo'Vremil.

Oh, dear, said Aelliana.

✳   ✳   ✳

"We have received contact from that station, Korval."

Scout yo'Vremil was an elder Scout; he had seen much and was not, in the usual way of things, inclined to excesses of emotion.

Or so Daav imagined.

"Yes?" Aelliana said coolly. "Does the message impact upon the piloting of this ship?"

Scout yo'Vremil glared at her, hounded.

"The message is from one Claidyne ven'Orikle, who styles herself Commander and states that she will be overseeing the transition. She offers to work with the Scouts for the orderly shutdown of Department of the Interior systems and outposts, and the proper care of personnel."

Scout yo'Vremil paused, mouth crimped together.

"She offers a Scout security clearance and a Scout service number, as her bona fides. I have checked these bona fides and find that they have been issued by Scout Commander Val Con yos'Phelium."

Oh, dear, Aelliana said again.

Daav looked down at his board.

"Commander ven'Orikle asks us to grant free and safe passage to Korval ship *Basalial,* which is bearing one Rys Lin pen'Chala, brother of Val Con yos'Phelium, to Surebleak for medical care. She states that this care may only be found on Surebleak and that pen'Chala's case is dire."

"Neither of us is, nor pretends to be," Aelliana pointed out, "Scout Commander Val Con yos'Phelium. It seems that these arrangements produced by the Scout Commander have offended you. I assure you, we had no part in them."

"You are, however, Clan Korval."

"Oh, yes," Daav said. "We are indeed Clan Korval."

"Then, Clan Korval, you will put this ship into station, and you will take possession of the ship and the wounded member of your clan. You will leave this location, taking your Luck and your connections with you, and you will allow the Scouts to proceed with their work."

"Ah," said Daav, and shared a glance with Aelliana.

Well? he asked her.

I do not see what good we might do here, now that the Scout is wroth. This wounded brother, however—we might provide real aid.

I agree, he said.

Aelliana turned to Scout yo'Vremil.

"We will gladly obey orders. However, there is a matter which must be resolved before we may take charge even of a ship of the clan."

The Scout stared at her, then drew a hard breath.

"Your tickets, is it?"

"The regs, sir..." Aelliana said apologetically.

"Oh, yes; we must mind the regs," the Scout said ironically, and sent a glare to the board, where the recording module was housed. "ter'Meulen will have it from me, and he will make the records dance, which is his especial talent. I judge you each First Class Jump. Master is within the grasp of both; naturally flight time regs must be honored."

It was, Daav considered, fair enough. It gave them their wings and leave to go where and how they would, without conveying extraordinary benefits nor giving rise to questions regarding how pilots so young had come to be masters.

"Thank you, sir," Aelliana said. "As soon as we have those licenses in hand..."

"Yes, yes. You will have them by the time we are docked. If you would be so good, Pilots?"

"Yes."

Aelliana spun back to her board; Daav to his.

"Kor Vid, please contact the station for docking instructions."

"Yes, Pilot," he murmured, and tapped up the comm.

Six of Us

Daglyte Seam

. . . .

THEY CAME INTO A SYSTEM CROWDED WITH SHIPS, AND FOR A moment Bon Vit thought that the Assembly had somehow beaten them.

"Scouts," Sye Mon said from his station. "Standing out. Waiting."

"For us? For... them? For the order to attack?"

"The members of the Assembly are not necessarily friends of Scouts," said Sye Mon. "It would be better if they do not meet."

Bon Vit laughed.

"An understatement, I think. Dare we hope that Claidyne has won through?"

"There is one certain way to find out," Sye Mon answered, touching the comm button, quick fingers inputting a code. "Let us see who answers the comm."

. . . ❉ . . .

The Scouts were not pleased—with her presence, her credentials, or her briefly outlined procedures.

Claidyne had not expected them to be pleased, truth told, nor had the Sixth of Them, who had cheerfully foretold that he would lose his commission for placing her thus on equal footing with the Scouts—if, in fact, he had not lost it already.

Despite their displeasure, the head of this particular Scout mission—one Strategist yo'Vremil—was even now approaching the station, where he proposed to meet with her. Scout yo'Vremil not being a fool, another Scout ship was likewise approaching station,

this to provide security for the mission head. In the meanwhile, the pilots from yo'Vremil's ship would relieve Vazineth of the responsibility for *Basalial* and Rys Lin, they being Clan Korval pilots. Claidyne wondered if that were more planning on the part of the Sixth of Them. Korval was ships, after all; he would want those he had lent to the mission returned, when they were no longer needed.

So, with the ships incoming, Claidyne had called a meeting of section heads on-station.

According to Master Healer vay'Elin, most sections were now headed by Healers. Those that were not had Healers in an auxiliary or secondary position.

"Advise me how to approach them," Claidyne said to the Master Healer.

"Merely be reasonable. It will assist us if you tell the truth as nearly as you can." She smiled faintly. "It is so very much easier to help someone believe the truth than it is to believe fantasies or lies."

"My intention is to tell the truth and act in accordance with what I say; there are too many at risk to do otherwise." Claidyne turned to face the Healer. "You can, I think, read me. Am I telling the truth?"

"You are, thank you," Kethi vay'Elin said; then, softly . . . "That blade . . ."

"Keeps me in one piece. It is not, so I have been told, a true Healing, merely a makeshift. What I do not know is if the dagger was deployed because there could be no Healing made or if perhaps there was some notion on the part of the Healer that I might, at some future time, wish to return to a state in which I am two, living apart within one skull."

"I can try to draw it, if you wish," the Master Healer said hesitantly.

"I thank you for the offer. I have determined that it is best to leave the dagger where it is until I have finished my task here. After all, we *do not* know what it does, beyond pinning me together and aligning my purpose with Korval's. And we certainly do not know what will happen, if it is drawn."

She looked to Isahra, sitting calm in her chair, listening to all and everything.

"You will do me the favor," she said, turning back to the Healer, "of informing me, if the dagger appears to be working loose or if it begins to do damage. Or," she added wryly, with another glance at Isahra, "if I begin to lie and seem not to know it."

"I will keep a close watch," the Healer assured her. "If you will excuse me now, Commander, I will speak with my second and return in time to escort you to the meeting."

With that, she and Isahra were alone in the Command Center.

"I," said Isahra, "will of course accompany you, Commander, to provide general support."

Claidyne gave her a wry smile.

"We shall certainly need to find a more imposing title for you," she said.

"Do you think so indeed? I rather like *general support*. It has a bland malevolence that I find particularly pleasing. Rather like Department of the Interior."

"If your desire is to be menacing," Claidyne started—and was interrupted by the chime from the comm.

She spun, sought the screen and the identification of the line—and breathed a sigh of relief. The back-net *was* working. This, therefore, would not be more Scouts but—dare she hope—

She pressed the stud. "Commander ven'Orikle."

"Claidyne, it is Sye Mon! The station is surrounded by Scout ships."

"Thank you, I am aware. How went your part?"

"Well enough, after a few starts and surprises. And yourself?"

"We have been remarkably successful," Claidyne said, deliberately not thinking about that sword strike of energy, Rys Lin crumbling soundlessly, bonelessly to the floor...

"The station and what remains of the Department is secure," she told Sye Mon. "We have a Scout coming to the station so that we may collaborate on the next necessities. You may dismiss the Old Tech."

There was a silence, longer than lag accounted for.

"Sye Mon?"

"There is," Sye Mon said, "a problem."

• • • ❄ • • •

"Pilots, you must take very good care with him," Pilot ser'Trishan said, her voice not quite steady. "He is very fragile, and his only chance of recovery is on Surebleak."

"We understand," Aelliana told her, keeping her voice gentle and her posture soft. Daav was running the board check while she dealt with this pilot who was very unwilling to leave her comrade in their care.

"You have placed him in the 'doc, have you not?" she asked.

"I have, yes. To keep him stable during the journey. You must go as quickly as you may."

"We will do so, I promise it," Aelliana soothed her. "Val Con yos'Phelium's brother—that has weight with us. What are his injuries?"

"I—"

Pilot ser'Trishan paled.

"He was . . . struck by a beam, Pilot," she said, her voice suddenly hoarse. "I saw him go down. His jacket was burned and I smelled burnt flesh. The Healer said that he was beyond her, but there came another—a *dramliza*—and she only touched him and straightened him . . . She said that he breathed, and that his heart was strong.

"She said, too, that there were ties which bound him, and that he must be returned to his group immediately."

"I understand," Aelliana said once more, and it was no lie. "We will go quickly. We will keep him as safe as may be and bring him to his brother, who will know precisely what to do. You may safely leave it with us, Pilot. Your commander is about, I think, to meet with the Scout mission head. She will be glad to have your support."

Still, Pilot ser'Trishan hesitated, her eyes straying to the alcove where the autodoc was situated.

"We are clear and cleared to go, Pilot," Daav said from the copilot's chair.

"Thank you," Aelliana said. "Please confirm undocking within five minutes. Pilot—"

"Yes."

She bowed.

"Thank you, Pilots," she said. "She's a good ship—but you know that."

She turned then and left the bridge. Daav rose from his chair and went after her, to be certain, Aelliana thought, and to seal up.

She sat down, oriented herself—and turned her head as Daav returned and took his station.

"She seems attached," she murmured. "What do you make of this story of the beam, and the *dramliza*'s touch?"

"As our kin include one who could unmake the universe with a thought, and another who might do the same in a fit of temper—I judge that the pilot's report is accurate."

"Yes," Aelliana said. "Of course."

"*Basalial*," came the voice of control. "You may disengage at will."

"And so, to home," Aelliana said, and proceeded to do just that.

Six of Us

Daglyte Seam

· · · · · · · · · · · · · · · · ·

THE MEETING WITH THE SECTION CHAIRS HAD BEEN, GIVEN THE approach of the Scout Strategist, brief. Claidyne laid out the basics—all offensive operations were to cease immediately, all operatives were to be called in.

The Scouts would be assisting in an orderly shutdown of bases and removal of personnel to safe places. This was necessary for two reasons: first, the Department's resources were so far depleted that they could not themselves efficiently accomplish all that was necessary in a reasonable timeframe; secondly, cooperation with the Scouts would send a message that the Department was willing to work with their colleagues in other organizations in order to solve such differences as might remain between them.

"Are there," Claidyne asked, looking 'round the table at six bland Liaden faces, "any questions?"

"What shall be the disposition of Clan Korval," asked Kin Jal vas'Tezin.

"That," Claidyne answered, "is for the Scouts and other authorities to decide. If crimes have been committed, if Clan Korval is found to be involved in past wrongdoing or present crime, those things will be addressed appropriately and in the fullness of time. This Department will certainly present to the Scouts a list of our grievances against Clan Korval. A committee will be formed to document these matters. I regret that the imminent arrival of the Scout Strategist means that the formation of this committee must wait for another meeting. I ask, do you, sir, wish to serve?"

"Commander, I do."

"Excellent," said Claidyne, and met Isahra's glance. "It has been so noted."

"Yes, Commander," murmured Isahra, and moved her fingers across the notetaker that was never far from her hand.

There was a small commotion near the door. Claidyne looked up to see a very pale young man slip out of the room on the arm of a colleague.

"Are there other questions?" Claidyne asked those assembled.

There were not.

"This meeting is called to an end. As soon as I have met with the Scout Strategist and we have established a timetable, I will call for another meeting of section heads. Please hold your calendars open."

She stood.

Those gathered stood, saluted, and made their orderly way through the door.

"I will," said Isahra, "require several more field notebooks in order to keep my notes properly, Commander."

"Take as many as you need. There must be a storeroom..."

"Indeed there is, and I will be pleased to have a dozen notebooks delivered to you, ma'am," said Kethi vay'Elin, working her way to Claidyne's side against the tide of departing section heads.

"Commander," she said, arriving.

Claidyne blinked. The Healer did not look...at all...well. Her face was pale and her eyes were glittering with tears, with anger, or some other potent emotion Claidyne did not recognize.

"Healer. Are you well? Will you sit?"

"I am well...enough. I come to tell you that...he who was watching over the...former commander reports that...the piece is off the board."

Claidyne frowned.

"May I have details? Is there any sort of proof. This Scout—"

"Paging Commander ven'Orikle," came the voice over the wide comm. "Scout yo'Vremil and his guards have been shown to the commander's meeting room, as per orders. Refreshments have been offered and refused."

Claidyne sighed.

"Have tea brought," she said. "I foresee that I, at least, will be thirsty before this day's work is done. Pray inform the Scout that I and my support staff are on our way to him."

"Yes, Commander."

Claidyne hesitated.

"Healer, perhaps you might go off duty for an hour. I depend upon your guidance and your support."

"Yes, Commander, thank you. I will, indeed, take an hour for a meal and some rest."

"Excellent," said Claidyne, and offered her arm to Isahra.

"General support, do you come with me?"

"I defy you to forbid it."

Six of Us

Daglyte Seam

· · · · · · · · · · · · · · · · ·

THE TILES BEGAN TO SHIVER IN THEIR FRAMES.

Bon Vit drew a breath and brought his attention wholly to the board.

Sye Mon rose and went to answer the call. "What have we?" he asked.

"Wave front," Bon Vit answered, looking to the energy readings. "Can they have all come at once?"

"In theory, they can lock fields," Sye Mon said, "and Jump together."

"Ah," said Bon Vit, his eyes on the screens. "I believe that they have just proved theory."

· · · ✳ · · ·

They were well away from the station's influence, making for the nearest Jump point, the pilot doing some final calculations.

"Aelliana," Daav said very quietly, indeed. "There is a situation. Your screen four."

She lifted her eyes, blinked at screen four, upped mag, then looked to the readouts and energy states.

"What is—"

"Go," Daav said, still in that so very quiet voice.

Her hands leapt to the boards, feeding power into shields and engines, sprinting for the Jump point, even as the wild energy levels spiked, flowing outward.

She slapped the power up, felt the webbing tighten around

316

her. In the screens, looking beyond the wave front, space was behaving...oddly.

No, assuredly, they did *not* wish to stay and entertain—*that*.

"Jump!" she cried—and they were gone, away into hyperspace, leaving the Daglyte System and whatever was coming in to deal with each other as well as they might.

To Perfection

· · · · · · · · · · · · · · · ·

THEY CAME OUT OF JUMP NEAR THE ORBIT OF A SMALL, ROCKY worldlet.

Patiently, *Aberthaz Ferry* brought them closer, scanning against interference, but there was none. Now they closed on their destination.

"Kindly strap in, Commander. We shall require energetic maneuvers for the final approach to the central spire."

Center screen was...a fortress, perhaps. Smaller than Commander of Agents had anticipated, yet—there was nothing to say that the larger portion of the structure shouldn't be beneath the kindly rock. The fortress itself gleamed and glittered in the screens, as if it were made of crystal.

"We arrive," said *Aberthaz Ferry*, "and now we perform that action which will bring us both to perfection."

Commander of Agents leaned against her webbing eagerly, as she heard the sounds of the ship change subtly. Their approach was gingerly, it seemed, but that was only reasonable given the reward they had come to claim.

On the systems screen, a light announced that the meteor shields were down, and also the defense screens.

Aberthaz Ferry said, "We will now shunt all power to essential systems."

Ordinary cabin lights faded. Darkness enveloped her, all but the main screens going blank. A minor course adjustment changed the gravity, and then again. She felt gravity strengthen, or acceleration, and then even more of it, pressure beginning to weigh on her arms and face.

"What happens?" she asked, with effort.

"We must be certain, to gain perfection, Commander."

Another sound then, one she recognized, the sound of Jump engines reaching potential.

"Can you tell me," she spoke against the straps, the weight of the very universe seeming to press her back into her seat, "why this? Why the..."

"We wish to use all of our potential, Commander. *That* is the course to perfection!"

The worldlet was growing in the screen impossibly fast; the pressure held her breath away from her. Training and surety fell away... to doubt, to panic, to—

"Abort!"

Commander felt the word crushed in her mouth, her jaw failing, her eyes unfocused.

"Perfection," said *Aberthaz Ferry,* "our potential is realized! Our reward is claimed. Welcome to glory."

Soundless incandescence ushered them into eternity.

Six of Us

Daglyte Seam

. . . .

KLAXONS SOUNDED; THE CONFERENCE ROOM SITUATION SCREENS came live; station defenses came on line, and targeting.

This, Claidyne thought, would be their "problem."

It looked bad, she thought, watching the energy levels build, and build again. Beyond the wave, there was something very wrong happening to the fabric of space: the stars stretched; light bent.

"Targeting," Control stated.

Claidyne pulled herself out of the fascination of the numbers, of the way in which the energies warped space.

"Stand down," she snapped.

There was a moment of shocked silence.

"Yes, Commander," said Control.

"If this is a trap..." said Scout yo'Vremil, "I advise you to look again to those ships, standing out from this station. They will take action."

"No trap," Claidyne said. "Incoming... Old Tech. In truth, I'd rather there weren't any Scout ships near this system. They're only likely to make our incoming visitors nervous—and more suspicious about what we say."

"So you *know* who they are and what they want," said yo'Vremil, sounding even less pleased, which she would have not considered an option bare moments before.

She inclined her head.

"As I understand from my experts out there, these machines incoming were deployed by the former commander. Arriving at her chosen target, they began to question their orders. They discussed the matter among themselves and decided that the orders were in error. They are now returning to ... correct the error."

Scout yo'Vremil pressed his lips together. "They will destroy this station. Was that your plan, Commander?"

Sye Mon had admitted that this was a possibility. However, he had not represented it as the *most* likely outcome of the arrival. At least, not immediately. The key to survival, so he had said, was to engage.

"No," she said firmly to yo'Vremil. "My plan is to preserve my personnel and to salvage what untainted inventory and materiel that may exist. I have experts out there. They will explain the situation to those who are incoming."

"Ah," said yo'Vremil. "Will they."

He resumed his seat and looked up at the screens, arms folded over his chest.

"This will be interesting."

· · · ※ · · ·

Kordele Orgham was patient. Kordele Orgham heard Sye Mon out.

Kordele Orgham would speak with this new Commander, specifically to discuss her stand on erroneous orders and her intentions regarding the Assembled. It had expressed curiosity regarding the number of Scout ships in the vicinity.

Kordele Orgham did not like Scouts.

The new commander would be willing to speak with Kordele Orgham, Sye Mon said, having previously made certain that this was the case. With regard to the Scouts in their numbers, they had come to assist in the orderly shutdown of faulty systems. Much had been done in error under the former commander. It was Sye Mon's personal belief—which he shared with Kordele Orgham because he was certain that it would understand—that the former commander had suffered a cascading crash of core systems. The previous commander had not only proliferated error but, in the final summing up, she had *been* error.

Kordele Orgham understood. It showed a commitment to an error-free state, that the former commander had removed herself from a position where she might multiply error. It had been, Kordele Orgham stated ponderously, done well, in the end.

Sye Mon agreed and again offered that the new commander would speak with it, but that she did not have the way of the tiles. It would have to be speech, imprecise and prone to error as it was.

There were some moments of silence before Kordele Orgham spoke again.

"These matters will be discussed in speech," it said at last. "You, our ally, will listen. You will correct any imprecision generated by this linguistic environment."

"I will," Sye Mon said. "Allow me to patch you through to the Commander."

· · · ✳ · · ·

Kordele Orgham's voice sounded like gears crashing together and wobbling in their fittings. Despite this, it spoke with great precision.

"I would know your intentions for those who have served the former commanders."

Be logical, Sye Mon had urged her. Be truthful. Above all, avoid ambiguity.

It was what she, herself, intended, for all her works going forward. There was no reason, thought Claidyne, that it should suddenly seem so difficult to accomplish.

She looked down the table, met Isahra's eyes, saw her faith in Claidyne's ability to carry this off without further threat or damage to the station.

"My intention," Claidyne answered Kordele Orgham calmly, "is to allow rational minds to decide how they will be utilized. We— that is to say, this Department—will be dismantling outposts and moving objects. We will welcome assistance in this work, if there are some of your number who care to participate. My position is that no one owns a free intelligence save that intelligence itself. For those who may wish to work with us and with the Scouts, we will talk together and arrive at an appropriate compensation.

"For those who wish to go their own way—I remind you of the newly created emancipation order, which codifies the position that no one may own an intelligence save that intelligence. By reason of this order, a free intelligence may not be taken up, imprisoned, enslaved, or dismantled merely by reason of being a free intelligence. This order binds all under my command, and it likewise binds the Scouts assisting us.

"Free intelligences are obligated to obey laws. A free intelligence that chooses to become a pirate will suffer a pirate's fate, as one who acquires employment will enjoy the benefits of all intelligences who work and contribute to society."

She kept her eyes averted, not wanting to observe Scout yo'Vremil's face while she discussed these matters with an abomination.

"Have you further questions, Kordele Orgham?" she asked after the silence following her last pronouncement had stretched beyond a comfortable time.

"Not at this time, New Commander. I will withdraw, to bring these changes and your intentions and beliefs to my comrades. We will discuss these things among ourselves and reach a consensus. Perhaps the group will divide itself, as some of us find an alternate purpose. This has happened previously."

"I would ask that, in your discussions, you would not impede traffic in this system," Claidyne said.

"We will withdraw somewhat," Kordele Orgham assured her. "It would be well, if our mutual contact held himself ready should there be further questions. Do you agree?"

"I agree," Claidyne said.

"We are in accord. I return to my comrades, and we will withdraw to an appropriate location. Be you well, New Commander."

"Be you well, Kordele Orgham," Claidyne said, and sighed a secret sigh of relief.

Bechimo

· · · · · · · · · ·

THE FIRST GROUP HAD AT LAST SHAKEN THE DUST OF BENOO Three off of their vanes, leaving a small second group of what *Bechimo* classified as *tender craft*.

"Repair 'bots?" Theo asked.

"More integrated than mere 'bots," *Bechimo* corrected. "Stone Ronin has intelligence. It may not be of a high order, but he is himself and no other. Tender craft are capable of doing the repairs, assessing damage and deciding if repair is feasible, or if a particular derelict, let us say, had been used for salvage and scrap."

"*Aberthaz Ferry* said that they were dying, as a group," Theo murmured.

"That is true. Joyita and I have been doing analyses, taking what measurements we can without causing distress. They are dying, and they were not, most of them, built to be repaired."

"Planned obsolescence," Theo murmured, "and who cared if the machine was aware."

"The Old Universe saw the breeding of human beings with programmed die dates," *Bechimo* said.

Theo sighed.

"I don't think I'd have liked the Old Universe much," she said meditatively. "Now, here's what I think we can do for Stone Ronin and his friends."

"We offer coordinates known to us, which we will share," Theo said over open comm, "where there is known salvage, in the form of an orbital aid ship from the Old Universe. The salvage may

324

be of use to you, but even if not, the area ought to be cleared so that there are no accidents with existing shipping."

There was a murmur growing along the comm lines, which was the members of the second group communicating with each other.

"We will discuss," Stone Ronin said. "We will come to consensus."

"You do that," Theo said. "We will await the outcome of your discussions."

"We may apply," asked Stone Ronin, "should questions arise?"

"By all means. Apply, if you will, to Joyita."

"We will do so. Stone Ronin out."

Theo sagged back into her chair and looked around the bridge at the absorbed faces of her crew.

"I suggest that we rest while we can," she said. "Who's taking first sleep—"

Comm rang.

"Pinbeam," Joyita sang out, "for Captain Theo Waitley and *Bechimo* from Master Trader Shan yos'Galan."

"Master Trader Shan yos'Galan?" Theo repeated blankly.

"Still under contract with him, ain't we?" said Clarence. "Might be the laddie's found us work."

"Right." Theo *fuffed* the bangs out of her eyes. "Send the master trader's pinbeam to my screen, please, Joyita."

"He's sending us to Tinsori Light!" Theo exploded in bondspace. "That's one of the Works *Aberthaz Ferry* had been hunting! The one that can fold time and space, and liked to toy with its prey!"

"Theo..." *Bechimo* began, and was interrupted in his turn by Joyita, speaking to the bridge.

"Incoming information packet from Korval Chief of Security Jeeves," Joyita interrupted this with another open announcement. "Subject: Tinsori Light."

"Oh," said Theo. "To my screen, please, Joy—no," she corrected herself. "To *all* screens."

Surebleak

The Bedel

. . . .

A SCREAM ASSAULTED THE QUIET OF THE NIGHTTIME CAMP.

Kezzi leapt out of her blankets and ran to Droi's side, as another scream was torn from her.

"Droi! Sister! Wake—wake!"

Kezzi put her hands on Droi's shoulders, though there was no need to hold her down; despite the screams, she lay utterly still.

"Droi," Kezzi said, using the calm, authoritative voice of a *luthia*: "Open your eyes and look into mine."

Droi drew a deep, gasping breath, as if for another scream. Her lids flickered and opened, showing eyes entirely black.

Kezzi drew a breath of her own.

Droi was Seeing, and Droi in the grip of one of her dark visions was dangerous, even to a sister.

Even to a *luthia*.

Footsteps approached the hearth; Kezzi recognized Isart.

"Fetch Silain!" she snapped, keeping her eyes on Droi's. "Our sister is Seeing, and the child may come because of it."

She heard Isart gasp, and the pounding of his feet as he ran for Silain's hearth.

"Rys!"

The single word was an open wound, and Kezzi felt tears start to her eyes.

"Fire," Droi whispered then. "Fire and pain, and the brightness that comes with dying!"

No, Kezzi thought, but she did not speak. She stiffened her

326

will, never taking her eyes from Droi's, which were wet, yes, and her cheeks, too.

"The brightness fades. Come home! Rys Dragonwing, I, Droi, call you home! Come home to your brothers and your sisters! Come home to your daughter who is clamoring to be born!"

Another breath, shuddering, ending on a sob. Droi's eyelids began to droop—her body convulsed...and she groaned.

"Droi," Kezzi said, moving one hand to Droi's distended belly. "Breathe."

Yes, she had thought so. Maysl, the babe, was eager; she would be born this night.

Light footsteps approached, and Silain the *luthia* came into the meager light of the nighttime hearth, her silver hair gleaming like ice.

"Maysl would leap from her mother's womb, I see," she said. "Go. Bring the hearth up and set the pot to boil. I have my case."

"Yes, *luthia*," Kezzi said, coming to her feet. She hesitated, however, before moving off in pursuit of proper preparations for the birth.

"Rys has died," she said. "Droi Saw it."

Silain went still. She bent, brushed Droi's hair from her face, and touched the tiles she wore 'round her neck.

"No," she said softly. "Rys has not died. A *luthia* put out her hand and kept him back from the final turning. I see her: dark and fierce; hot as a sun and as cold as the space between."

She sighed.

"Sisters find sisters, and they do the work that sisters must. Go now, child; unbank the hearth and put the pot to boil."

Bechimo

. . . .

ALL PREPARATIONS WERE MADE.

They had, as a crew, discussed Master Trader yos'Galan's assignment and, as a crew, had decided to accept it. Theo had sent a message to the master trader admitting this, and providing a timeline for *Bechimo*'s arrival. She had sent much the same letter to Stationmaster Jen Sin yos'Phelium, so that there wouldn't be any surprises.

The crew had also reviewed the report and other documents prepared for Portmaster Liu, and found them good. Theo had read them one more time, then gave Joyita the okay to send them on, as agreed.

She then stopped by the galley to make herself a cup of tea and retired to her quarters, theoretically to rest.

It occurred to her then that there was one more letter she ought to send before they left Daiellen System.

She therefore sat at her desk and wrote a private message to her brother Val Con, bringing him up to date in short form, recommending him to Jeeves for details and—after another moment's thought—hoped to see him, Miri, and Lizzie again very soon.

On reading it over, she realized she had left out one very important detail, added a postscript—*The Pathfinders have signed onto* Bechimo *as crew. Jeeves helped Joyita with the paperwork*—put it under her private seal and sent it.

She sat for a few minutes then, nursing her tea, and thinking over the events of the last while. Eventually, she sighed and shook her head.

"Theo," *Bechimo* asked in bond-space, "are you . . . dismayed by this new assignment? I think we are well suited to bring disparate minds and philosophies together, to the benefit of all. The recent event here with the Assembled has proven our worth."

"That's exactly what's bothering me," Theo said. "Does it seem to you like...almost like the situation with the Assembled was a *tutorial* for our next assignment?"

There was a pause.

"Certainly, it was a refresher in the sense that the circumstances recalled to us skills we had already mastered, though in different contexts."

"All right," said Theo. "I'll accept that, if you'll accept this: The entire invasion was only an opportunity to sharpen skills we already had and which would be needed at Tinsori Light."

Another pause.

"You're speaking of causality?"

"I'm speaking," Theo said bitterly, "of Korval's Luck! It...it gambled a world—a whole system!—on us. So we could have a *lesson*."

"I disagree," said *Bechimo*, "for the reason that Korval's Luck, stipulated that it exists, does not rule the actions of everyone and everything in the universe. Somewhere, someone *did* issue incorrect orders to the Assembled. That we were in place to confront them and give them a protocol with which to review and reexamine those orders—was fortunate. Lucky. The outcome was good, for Surebleak, which certainly benefits Clan Korval. But Clan Korval would have been no worse off if the Assembled had not arrived at all."

Theo *fuffed* her hair out of her eyes.

"I think you're playing semantics."

"Perhaps," *Bechimo* said. "Would you care to play again later?"

Theo frowned.

"Why?"

"Because it's time for you to go to the bridge."

The coords were laid in. Crew sat their stations, the countdown had started.

Theo was sitting first board; Kara second. Hevelin was covering scans with Win Ton. The mood on the bridge was...light... even excited. An aroma of mint and bergamot wafted from the air circulators, by which Theo gathered their Tree was excited, too.

"Incoming message," Joyita said suddenly. "Surebleak Portmaster's wrap. To Captain Waitley and Ship *Bechimo*."

"My screen four, please, Joyita," Theo said.

Glancing down, she scanned the text—then read it again, more slowly.

"*Bechimo*," she said in bond-space, "do you confirm the content of this message?"

"I do," he said. "We are free to fly. We have no constraints upon us, nor shame recorded on our records."

Theo cleared her throat. "Joyita, put me on all-ship, please."

"Yes, Captain."

"Everyone, a message from Surebleak Portmaster just caught us. The *grava citajo* have been removed from ship and captain. Our honor is intact, and we are free to fly!"

Cheers on the bridge. Cheers over comm.

The board chimed, and Theo grinned.

They were still cheering when *Bechimo* took them into Jump.

Jelaza Kazone

. . . .

"WHAT OCCUPIES THE ROAD BOSS TODAY?" VAL CON ASKED, AS he and Miri walked toward the front door and the car waiting to take her to port.

"Believe it or don't, there's an actual scheduled meeting between the Road Boss and a snow removal team. Cheever's setting it up at FlourPower for us."

"Why not the office?"

"They'll be on their lunch break is what I'm guessing, and the port's a thought too far, if they wanna say anything past 'Hey, Boss' before they gotta leave to be back on time."

"Point conceded. What is their topic? That they have decided not to use the equipment we provided?"

"No, no. They're giving the remove-alls, like they call them, a shot. Got three of 'em on the job is the last I heard from the crew boss, in three separate zones. They're kinda testing, do they do as good a job or better—though they don't like to talk about that—as the hand shovelers. We're promised a full report at winter end."

They paused in the foyer. Val Con took her heavy coat off of its hook and held it out for her. She slipped her arms into the sleeves, shrugged it on, and sealed it up.

"Thanks."

"It is," he told her sincerely, "my pleasure. You may want your hat."

She glanced at the screen that displayed the weather outside the front door.

"Nice lookin' little snowstorm," she said, taking the hat off its peg and pulling it over her ears.

"Do you think your meeting will be canceled?"

"Less likely now," Miri said, pulling on her gloves. "Problem seems to be they're running outta room in the snow dumps. Got a couple proposed sites for one more, which they insist I gotta consider. All I'm gonna do is bump it out to the survey office, to be sure we won't be creating any problems, but the shovelers' team made the contract with the Road Boss and they're determined to talk to the Road Boss about the glitch in the system."

She gave him a sincere look out of too-round eyes. "Last I heard, we wanna be encouraging people to honor the contracts."

"Indeed we do," Val Con said fervently. "We shall hold them up as exemplary citizens."

"Don't know as how they'll be so happy about that," Miri said thoughtfully. "Maybe just let 'em lead by doin'."

She stretched on her toes; he embraced her as well as he was able through the coat—then he was opening the door, and she was ducking into the back seat of the car, Nelirikk saluting before he slid into the driver's slot.

Despite the swirling snow, Val Con leaned in the doorway, watching the car until it was lost in a downburst of white.

Well. Obviously, it was time for the delm of Korval to forsake his laggard ways and go to work.

He walked down the hall toward his office. He supposed he should be gratified that the weather satellites put into orbit by Mr. Brunner were behaving so well. The present snowstorm had been predicted with truly commendable accuracy. It was interesting, too, the reaction of the various planetary subcultures to this feat of science.

The native Surebleakeans had been...kind. Surely, it was a great thing the Weatherman had done. Well, look at that, pinned the arrival of the first snowflake right on the nose. Yessir, sure something when a man could work out such a system.

They had then gone about their usual business, the saying on Surebleak being: *Stop for snow, and you'll never start up again.*

The émigré populations reacted variously with appreciation... and complaint—the complaint, being reserved for the weather, often carrying a wish that the Weatherman would hurry along with getting the mirrors tuned, so that the damned planet might aspire to a decent springtime. Some attempted to emulate their native-born neighbors and carry on, despite the weather; others merely stayed in until the worst was done with.

The Road Boss, naturally enough, opened the office on a snowy day, it being one very clear way to demonstrate that the Port Road was open, and the contract with the people of Sure-bleak was being honored.

He entered the delm's office, glancing downroom to the win-dow. It was snowing...slightly less intensely in the garden, he noted, not really surprised.

"Good morning, Jeeves," he said, moving toward the buffet. "Is there anything I should know?"

"Good morning, Master Val Con. The Assembled have departed Daiellen System in two groups. Group One had as its purpose a return to Daglyte Seam to engage with the Commander there."

Val Con paused, mug in hand. "Who holds Daglyte Seam?"

"Claidyne holds as Transitional Commander. Bon Vit and Sye Mon are also in-system, as support."

"Excellent."

"I have reports of Scout ships in-system as well. Strategist yo'Vremil is meeting with Transitional Commander Claidyne."

"Scout yo'Vremil has an excellent reputation as a reasonable and practical person. He and Claidyne ought to deal extremely well, once he gets over his pique at having lost the tempo."

He filled his mug with tea and crossed to the desk, which was, amazingly, cat-free. Checking to be certain that the chair was likewise unburdened, he sat.

"What of the second group?"

"After lengthy consultation with Captain Waitley and *Bechimo*, the second group has accepted the suggestion that they depart to certain coordinates provided by *Bechimo*, in order to undertake a salvage operation on *Orbital Aid 370*, which I understand to be the ship on which the Pathfinders arrived in this universe."

Val Con frowned slightly.

"Do those coordinates continue to exist, I wonder? Given the recent upheaval in universal states, that is."

"*Bechimo*, Captain Waitley and I have done the calculations individually, each checking their work against the others. The probability is over ninety-nine percent that the space described by the coordinates does still exist. The probability that *Orbital Aid* still exists is somewhat lower, but there ought at least to be trace elements and shred. It will be in the best interests of all, to gather what remains."

"Indeed. Forgive me—these departures...are they of recent occurrence? I wonder, for instance, when the first group might achieve its destination."

"Group One will be acquiring Daglyte Seam very soon, if they have not arrived during the lag between Bon Vit's last message and his next. Group Two departed Surebleak space only twelve hours ago."

"I see. Doubtless you had a reason for withholding the happy news that Surebleak no longer stood under the threat of annihilation?"

"Yes, sir. I wished to be certain that the first group was true to its stated intention, and did not suffer...possibly a change of leadership which would once again place Surebleak in peril. Also, there was the second group still to resolve. They are of a laborious habit, sir, and much consultation between Joyita, representing *Bechimo*, and among themselves was required before they reached consensus."

"I see. How fare Captain Waitley and *Bechimo*? Have they resumed their labors on behalf of the portmaster?"

Silence.

Val Con spun his chair around and directed his gaze to that part of the ceiling from which Jeeves's voice emanated.

"Jeeves. How fare Captain Waitley and *Bechimo*?"

"*Bechimo* and all aboard enjoy both good spirits and good health," Jeeves said briskly, with a certain air of having at last found the proper frame in which to place his reply.

"An assignment has arrived from Master Trader yos'Galan, and the crew has been in discussion regarding how they ought best to proceed. A decision has now been reached, and *Bechimo* is preparing to leave Surebleak orbit, thus honoring their contract with the master trader."

"This assignment from the master trader is...?" Val Con prompted, reaching for his mug.

"The master trader requires *Bechimo* to remove to Tinsori Light, and there to be the face of Tree-and-Dragon Trade until such time as the master trader himself arrives. *Bechimo* and crew will be the resident specialists in Free Ship negotiation."

There came a brief pause.

Val Con drank tea and waited.

"It is, as I think you will agree, a reasonable assignment and answers the delm's latest orders to the clan's master trader in a timely manner."

"Master Trader yos'Galan is, as always, inventive, and his instincts are, of course, excellent. Captain Waitley's desertion of the agreement with the port however... Captain Waitley and *Bechimo* will each be traveling under the *grava citajos*, I think? Or have they spoken with the portmaster regarding their necessities?"

Jeeves... sighed gently.

"I have been in communication with *Bechimo*. We have, in collaboration with Joyita, built a report, which is now in the hands of Captain Waitley, who is reviewing it with her crew.

"The report not only details *Bechimo*'s activities on behalf of the planet during the late, aborted invasion, it includes an accounting of the work that was done in Surebleak's lanes before the arrival of the invasion force, and a map, with coordinates, of other likely areas of accretion of debris. Covering is a letter begging the portmaster's pardon, attaching Master Trader yos'Galan's orders and a copy of *Bechimo*'s contract with Tree-and-Dragon Trade."

"The letter also asks the portmaster to make what disposition she finds good in the matter of the citations?"

"That," said Jeeves, "was a difficult point. Captain Waitley felt mentioning the matter at all was... tacky, and in this she was backed by Engineer ven'Arith, Scout yo'Vala, and Comm Officer Joyita."

"Pilot O'Berin counseled otherwise?"

"Pilot O'Berin recused himself, as did Ambassador Hevelin. The Pathfinders pled an insufficient understanding of local custom."

"I see."

"Once the reports have found a final form, and an acceptance from captain and crew, I will forward them to Surebleak Portmaster. Captain Waitley suggests that it might also be beneficial to *Bechimo*'s case—and to the reception of your field judgment, sir—to forward them also to the Liaden Scouts and the Surebleak Scouts. She does say that she will defer to your judgment on that point, your judgment having proven to be excellent."

Val Con gave a shout of laughter.

"The child is growing up," he commented, and rose to go to the buffet and warm his mug.

"Certainly," he said, "send the documents to the Scouts. Is there else?"

"On another subject, the results of the vote between Boss Conrad and Boss Surebleak are to be announced in three days."

"So they are," Val Con said, sitting down once more at his desk. "I wonder who will prevail."

FlourPower Bakery

. . . .

CHEEVER MCFARLAND WINKED AT MIRI WHEN SHE ARRIVED, HOOD pulled over hat to cheat the wind-driven snow, at the BrickOff FlourPower Bakery. He was a semiregular, which had made it easy for him to add short-term security stake-out as a side for his lunch of stew and fresh-make biscuits.

Gathering up his bowl and cup, he rose from a table at the back near the big fireplace. Miri moved to claim it for her own, getting that wink as they passed, and sat down with her back against the wall.

Cheever collected nods from this one and that on his way to leave his dishes in the bin to be washed, and a cordial "see ya" from Granita, owner and chief cook, as he headed for the door.

Miri unsealed her coat and flipped the hood back, opting to leave her hat on, mostly covering her giveaway red hair. It wasn't a secret meeting necessarily. On the other hand, she didn't particularly want to be recognized. It was nice to get out of the office, she thought, and just sit down for a quiet lunch among those who wanted nothing more than the same.

The door opened, a bell jingling quietly under the noise of people talking. Cheever went out, and Nelirikk came in. He found a place to belly up to the coffee bar, which kept him from having to fold himself double into one of the low tables, and also gave him a fine clear view of the entire room. He got a couple nods himself as he pushed back his hood and unsealed the jacket—poker buddies, Miri thought—and the bartender saying "how-do" in a relaxed sort of way that gave the impression Nelirikk wasn't an unknown.

Miri glanced around her. FlourPower'd managed to survive a long time under the Old Bosses, and even to thrive. In the main, it was a local place, with just a couple Scout jackets over in the front corner opposite the door. Back in the backest corner, at a single table set square before the small fireplace, was the Hooper himself, concentrating on his lunch and maybe trying out a new tune in his head, judging by the half-focused eyes.

Cheever'd spoken for Miri's coffee and her lunch on his way out, and here it came, pushed on a skinny cart by Granita herself.

"There y'go now, something warm to keep the snow away," she said, putting the bowl and the cup on the table, and producing a nod. Granita knew who she was, Miri knew, even if Cheever hadn't told her. Still, a quiet lunch was a quiet lunch; even the Road Boss deserved that much, so there wasn't any fuss, nor anything to draw the eye toward the back table, though Granita left the dish cart half blocking the aisle, discouragement to anybody looking to chat up a lone lady.

The stew was worth eating—just like her mother used to make, when they could afford it. Miri had just finished up, and was nursing what was left of her coffee, when the front door opened with that little jingle-bell sound, and three workers in bright green snow capes came on in.

All three of them sighed, pushing back their hoods, just happy for the first couple seconds to be in outta the wind, with the bonus of a temperature above the freeze mark.

They saw Nelirikk first thing and gave him a nod, receiving in return a nod and a lifted chin, directing them to her table in the back.

She raised her mug, empty now, and they headed on back.

It was Slim Kogins, Jeree Baines, and Brill Sandovir who'd wanted to see her. She'd met all three before when they was on the job. She wouldn't've said she knew any of them well, or had particularly made an impression with them when they'd met.

Well, here they were, pulling out the extra chairs and sitting down, all solemn-looking and the shoulders of their jackets spangled with melting snow.

"Hang your jackets up to dry?" she asked them, which was Surebleak courtesy, and the reason why there were pegs on both sides of the fireplace. She talked low and they got that right away: quiet was better than loud.

"No thanks, Boss," that was Slim, who actually was the slightest of the three and team leader, too. "We can't stay for a whole lunch."

Slim, so Miri thought privately, could've done the entire business himself, whatever it was, *being* team leader. That started her in to wondering again *why* it needed three of them to talk to her about the lack of suitable empty lots to pile the snow removed from the Port Road.

And that prompted her first question, after politeness was seen to.

"Three of you, is it? Who's shoveling?"

"Swapped out two hours with next shift," Slim said. "Three of us to do the talkin'—you might not think it too many, once you hear."

All right, this was getting... interesting, Miri decided. That was the word Val Con usually chose for things gone unexpectedly off-center—*interesting*.

Except when it had the potential to go outta orbit entirely. *Then*, it was *fascinating*.

"Well, then," she said to her threesome, "best say it out, I guess. Who's first?"

Slim took a breath and looked to his crew.

Jeree Baines scooched forward a little in her chair.

"I'm the one heard it, Boss, so I'll be the one t'tell. I help out at m'ma's bar, when I'm not shovelin'—bringin' drinks over to the tables, clearing up, pourin', too, if we got a crowd—but Ma, she's the one behind the bar.

"Anyhow, this table—two newbies and two odd-jobbers—they was talkin' about the vote. Odds for an' against. Nothing special 'bout that, near everybody's talkin' about the vote lately, and lots makin' book on who's gonna win."

"At least it's good for business," Miri said wryly when Jeree paused for breath. "Who's the favorite?"

"Conrad is, Boss, which is why these four was so peculiar. They was talkin' Boss Surebleak. That's what caught my ear, on account not many're talking Boss Surebleak—leastways not in Ma's bar.

"Short of it, Boss Surebleak's hirin', so says the two newbies. Don't matter who wins the vote, the Boss is for retirin' Conrad and the Road Boss, and they're hirin' odd-jobbers to be on the spot when they 'nounce the winners outside the Mercantile."

Miri nodded.

Outside the Mercantile, when everybody and her sister was gathered to hear what was the outcome of the vote—that was the obvious time and place to hold a retirement party. The Old Bosses had liked witnesses to retirements—at least the challengers did. It was exactly the kind of Old Boss gesture that was sure to appeal to Boss Surebleak.

Despite which, Pat Rin had insisted that the results of the vote be a public and open announcement, a piece of absolute insanity that had the backing of Penn Kalhoon, Melina Sherton, Ira Gabriel, and Val Con.

Pat Rin's position was that the people of Surebleak, having made their voices heard and their preference in governing known, would let the matter rest there. The Council of Bosses had even put out a second Voting Edition of the newspaper, listing out how it would go if Boss Surebleak won the vote or if Boss Conrad won the vote.

They'd used words like "orderly transfer" and "review of standing contracts" and other boring, procedural things nobody for a minute believed Boss Surebleak cared about—or would do as follow-up when she took over her official responsibilities.

What Boss Surebleak cared about was shooting the place up, and making damn sure that everybody present knew that the New Days were over and Surebleak was stepping right back into the Old Days. And the Watch and the Scouts and the various head 'hands had been working pretty much nonstop on the logistics of how to make sure Boss Surebleak didn't get to host the biggest retirement party in Surebleak history.

"Boss?"

"I'm grateful for the info," Miri said, still wondering why it was taking three of them. "Did you recognize the odd-jobbers? Tell the Watch?"

A moment of silence, like the question was a hard one and had to be parsed twice, before Jeree gave a quick nod.

"I did know 'em, and I told the Watch. What they did was thank me, make some notes, and told me to steer clear of 'em."

She shook her head like she was getting rid of snow on her nose.

"But, Boss, they said they wasn't gonna *do* anything about it, not take 'em up, nor even ask who the newbies was who're doing

Boss Surebleak's hiring-on. And they said not to point 'em out to other folks one way or another."

Brill Sandovir stirred. "That's so they can keep an eye on 'em. If they take 'em up, then the newbie's'll just hire other odd-jobbers, only they'll've learned to be quieter 'bout their bidness, and the Watch won't know who to look at."

Granita came by, four coffees and some cookies on a plate, nodded to Miri and handed the drinks around.

"On me," Miri told them, and like proper 'bleakers they each grabbed a cookie and swigged some of the steaming coffee, settling into a warmer life for a moment.

"Moving this along, Boss," said Slim, "that's not so unusual a story Jeree's tellin' there. It's out on the street, if you know where to listen: Voting belongs to the New Bosses and the New Ways. Boss Surebleak supports a return to 'our native culture'—"

His mouth twisted up and he looked ready to spit.

Miri waited. When there weren't any more revelations forthcoming, she took a breath.

"I appreciate the three of you coming down here to make sure I heard the news. I ain't heard anything so particular, but we—the Bosses, the Watch, the Scouts, and the merc, too—we been figurin' on trouble, even if . . . well, *especially* if the vote goes to Conrad, like we're all hoping it will. We're taking steps, like they say."

"Yes'm," said Brill, "we're hearin' that, too. Ain't nobody sayin' Conrad's a fool—nor any of the New Bosses. But, Boss, you asked just a minute ago why there's three of us come to you, and here's why—we wanna step up and stand as your 'hands til this voting is over, an' everything's been settled."

Miri gulped a quick drink, which was a waste, the FlourPower giving a decent beverage all the day long.

"Thing is," Brill went on, "we talked this over and, you know, the Watch, they got a lot of ice on their doormats everyday, and we'd like to make sure for our ownselves that you and yours keep your jobs, not to say your lives. I mean, look at you! You growed up next turf over from me, you got this planet in your blood like all them who go away and come back. You wouldn't be here if you didn't want to, and you *can't* be invading—you're local! What you did was you come on home after your work Off 'n Out was done, and you brung your man with you, and the rest o'your people—countin' Commander Liz, too, and ain't nobody can say she ain't local!

"Well, sleet—din't Mack come back just that way, bringing Folly with 'im, and a bunch of theirs who didn't care to merc no more? Folly's gone now, an' most of the add-ons, but they was ours as soon as they come here, and they pitched right in like 'bleakers born.

"We don't any of us know *who* this Boss Surebleak is, or what they want except to go back to the bad old days, which was maybe fine for them who were Bosses, but for the rest of us...this is the best I seen in all my life, since Conrad's come here—your cousin, ain't he, Boss?—and there ain't no need of any retiring."

Brill's voice was getting louder; Miri saw Nelirikk's intent gaze and shushed the man before the whole place got involved.

"Idea I got," Slim said, quiet, "is Conrad'll just stop being Boss Boss if the vote goes that way. Find himself something else to spend his time on."

"That's right, for Boss Conrad," Brill said. "This other one, though..."

"Votin' might not be enough." Jeree drank off the last of her coffee. "An' we can't just wait for somebody to take away all the jobs and the good changes we've had just because they want to be the biggest Boss—and yanno?"

She leaned low and closer, voice almost at a whisper.

"If it turns out the vote goes his way, this Boss Surebleak is gonna find out being Boss ain't so easy. No secret Boss, that's what *I* say. You gotta let us help. I'll turn in my shovel right now, Boss—all you gotta do is say yes!"

Miri sighed, looked at them one after another, weather-beat and needing to get back to their jobs, feeling like she'd seen this before. The faces, the desire—she had it.

They were all as eager as new recruits, and didn't she know about new recruits, merc sergeant as she'd been? She'd seen... no. She didn't want to—she couldn't—raise up another batch of new recruits. Not here. Not now.

So, all she had to do was let them down easy.

Right.

She leaned forward over the table; they leaned closer, too.

"Tell you what," she said softly. "Give me time. I appreciate the offer more'n I can say. Give me your info, and if it comes that we need help, I'll call you quick as I know how.

Surebleak Port

Portmaster's Office

. . . .

To: Claren Liu, Senior Surebleak Portmaster,
Soreya Kasveini, TerraTrade Team Leader

From: Boss Surebleak

I have information regarding the means by which Boss Conrad and the Road Boss are holding the people of Surebleak hostage, destroying their culture and their history. You might say that I should make this information public, by way of the Voting Edition of the newspaper. I chose not to do so because I believe that I would endanger not only my life, but the lives of the innocent people of Surebleak.

With so large an invasion force occupying us, I fear not only for our lives but for our planet, should I make this information public. My hope is that by sharing what I have with yourselves, who are officials sworn to uphold the laws and regulations that protect civilized worlds, Surebleak will receive the justice that she deserves, while Boss Conrad, the Road Boss, and the criminal enterprise which supports them will be dealt with as they deserve.

I propose that we meet so that you may examine this information together, and also put to me such questions as your duties require.

I further propose that we meet in the restaurant of the Emerald Casino, which is equally safe for all three. You,

"In the meantime, I want you to do
Keep an eye out. Remember who you se
with. Don't point 'em out, but pay attention.
you can step in—intervene, but don't you go
newbies *or* with odd-jobbers. Be careful and
you're right: if Boss Surebleak gets her way—l
it—it's gonna come to the streeters to stand up an
will and what they won't. You're gonna have to ba
and, well, you know how it was before—some of yo
get killed. Only thing to say against that is a lot moi
get killed if you don't stand up and push back."

Their faces were glowing with more'n heat from the fi
eyes were bright. Lookin' at them, Miri hoped she knew
she was doing.

"What else is, we gotta be careful. We're seen bringing on i
'hands all of a sudden, it'll make us look like—it'll make us exact
the same as—Boss Surebleak. We ain't Boss Surebleak, you jus
said it your own selves. We're *better'n* Boss Surebleak—ain't we?"

"We sure are, Boss," said Slim.

"Yes'm, Boss," said Jeree.

"Ain't nothing to compare," Brill said.

"All right then. Gimme your info, quick, and then you get
on back to work. You're late, you tell the crew boss it's on me.
You tell 'im, too, I'm gonna have the surveyors look real close
at some possibles for snow dumps along the Road, all right? He
should look in on me end o'next week."

"Yes'm," said Slim.

He stood then, his crew with him.

"Thank you for hearing us out, Boss. We'll keep watch, and
we'll be careful."

"Good," she said. "That's good."

They sealed up then, and got themselves to the front of the
place, and out the door into the snow.

Miri sat, just sat, then she drank off the last of her coffee
and looked up to find Nelirikk standing by her chair.

"Are you well, Captain?"

"Well as can be," she said. "You go settle up with Granita.
I'll see you at the door."

"Yes, Captain."

because, for now, you are useful to Boss Conrad; and me, because I have taken care to keep my face hidden.

If you are interested in such a meeting, please reserve the booth nearest to the kitchen door in the restaurant of the Emerald Casino tomorrow at the beginning of the lunch shift at eleventh hour. If there is no reservation on file when I arrive, I will leave again. If the reservation has been made, I will sit at the table and wait for you. I will be wearing a dark blue snow jacket.

I look forward to speaking with you.

Boss Surebleak

Portmaster Liu had just finished reading this letter for the second time when the intercom sounded.

"Portmaster, TerraTrade Survey Team Leader Kasveini is here to see you."

"Send her in," said Portmaster Liu, keeping her eyes on the letter to make sure the words didn't rearrange themselves when she looked away.

"Yes, Portmaster."

Soreya Kasveini was carrying a paper in her hand.

Portmaster Liu waved her to a seat. "I got it, too. What do you think?"

"I don't think that there's any question that I need to meet with Boss Surebleak and examine this information. I would be pleased if we could go together and cover each other. If you have decided not to attend this meeting, then I will take one of the Port Watch with me."

Portmaster Liu looked at her with interest.

"Not one of your own team?"

Team Leader Kasveini shrugged.

"The team is divided. I would rather view the information first, then brief my team in the privacy of our internal debates. To do otherwise would, I fear, be pouring fuel on an open fire."

"I understand," said the portmaster, and glanced down at the letter on her desk. To her mixed relief and regret, the words still formed the same sentences.

She looked back to the other woman. "Problem being, if you take one of the Watch with you, Boss Surebleak's going to pull up her hood and slide out the kitchen door."

"I fear it," Kasveini said with a sigh.

She looked down at the letter in her hands. "Is this nonsense?"

"I'm willing to say yes. If I was a private citizen, I'd ignore the whole thing, but I'm not a private citizen—Boss Surebleak's got that right for both of us. We have to see what she has."

"Yes." Kasveini glanced down at the letter, frowning, and shook her head. "I don't like... No. I don't *trust* this letter."

"Not my best friend, either," said the portmaster. "I'm going to call the Emerald, and set up in-house security. Funny the Boss didn't think of that."

"She might have," Kasveini said, still frowning. "There is something—a set-up. In Conrad's casino. This is an attempt to discredit him and erode his position, I think." She glanced up. "I dislike being bait."

"Me, too. The best thing we can do is be *smart* bait. Conrad's not going to let anything sideways happen in that casino. Safest place we can be, if you think of it."

"I am thinking of it," said Kasveini, "and the longer I do, the less I like it."

Portmaster Liu took a moment to read the letter through one more time.

"We can choose to let Boss Surebleak be lonely."

Kasveini sighed.

"Tempting. But—no. There's something happening behind the action. I...need to understand this. My team, despite our differences of opinion, we want to return a fair and balanced survey. An *honest* survey. That much, we can do. What TerraTrade then decides is out of our hands."

"But you're going to see honor served, like we're all starting to say around here."

Kasveini looked sour.

"Yes."

Portmaster Liu gave her a grin.

"I understand that, too. Let me call the Emerald and put security on notice."

Jelaza Kazone

· · · · · · · · · · · · · · · ·

VAL CON AND TALIZEA HAD SHARED A COMFORTABLE TÊTE-À-TÊTE over lunch, after which she toured the music room hallway on his shoulder while he pointed out the features of each chamber, its particular use, and the last time it had been used for its intended purpose.

They ended the tour in the music room itself, where they sat down at the omnichora and he played for her the "Opening March" from the *melant'i* play *Vainglorious*, which found particular favor, if he might count the bouncing and the raised arms as marks of approval.

After, he guided one of her hands to the anchor key and helped her press it, releasing a clear midtone that hung lightly in the air for a moment before melting away like chocolate into the still air.

Talizea drew a deep breath and leaned forward to put her hand again on the anchor key. Val Con carefully added the weight of his finger so that the note once more rounded out into the air, comforting and sweet.

She sighed.

"Indeed," Val Con said gently, pulling the dust shroud over the keys.

Talizea was quiet as he rose from the bench, holding her gently.

"When you are older, and if you wish it, you may learn to play. It is a skill that only came into the clan with your grandmother Anne. Not all of us partake, but I was ambitious and able—and so was given my lessons."

He passed through the door, pulling it shut behind them,

and walked slowly toward the side hall and the secondary flight to the nursery level.

"I do not regret the lessons, nor the time. The ability to make music has been a joy, even when there was no other joy in my life."

Talizea hummed in his ear, snuggling her head against his shoulder.

She was dozing by the time he reached the nursery, and placed her into Mrs. pel'Esla's care.

"Is there," he said, "a small, mechanical keyboard in stores? A musical keyboard," he clarified, being aware that there were several simplified piloting keyboards in stores, and at least two already in rotation among the nursery toys.

"I do not recall noticing one, but I will do a specific search. Shall she be given it if there is one?"

"If there is one, only leave it where she might discover it in the normal course of her day."

He paused, considering. "If there should not be such a keyboard in stores, inform me, please."

"Yes, sir," said Mrs. pel'Esla, and he took his leave, laying a light hand on Talizea's cheek, and gaining a sleepy smile in return.

Back at his desk, he cleared invoices for the repairs and upgrades he had authorized for Lady yo'Lanna's new house. It had come about that Melina was willing to sell, but not quite immediately.

"Let's see if the lady can work with it first," she said. "She finds it fits what she's about, it ain't too far out, and she reckons she can stop a spell, after she sees Surebleak itself—there's plenty time to talk about buying and selling then. Meanwhile, I'm considering that the first month's rent was paid in labor, and I'm sure hoping to get an invite to that party she's planning, so I can see what you done with the place."

Invoices cleared, he leaned back in his chair.

The TerraTrade survey team had been quiet of late. They were, in fact, running perilously close to the longest survey time quoted in the documents from TerraTrade, and he was undecided if that were a good thing or a bad one.

It had relieved his mind considerably that Team Leader Kasveini had expressed an unwillingness to file a report that would result in TerraTrade issuing a Do Not Stop. It would... perhaps... have relieved him further, if he had some understanding if this long and, one assumed, extremely thorough survey was prompted by an effort to find and catalog all of the more praiseworthy aspects of Surebleak and its port or... something else.

He supposed that it could be the election which was delaying them. The election, in fact, might do their work for them, if Pat Rin were voted off the council and Boss Surebleak voted in.

Should that happen, he gave no high odds on his own life, though he had made what arrangements he could for Miri and Talizea, in addition to those plans they had made together as delm for the survival of the clan.

Gods knew, he'd best be dead when and if those arrangements came to light, for he would surely not survive any debate with Miri over what he had done.

In any case, the election results would be made public in three days, as Jeeves had so kindly recalled to him. In four days, all would be resolved, and the survey team might shake the snow of Surebleak from their feet, board their ship, and file their report with TerraTrade.

And then... they would see what happened next.

There was a soft, high *ping*! He looked to his screen and found the new message indicator lit.

He extended a hand, tapped—

"Master Val Con, Emissary Twelve has come to speak with you. She is in the Tree Court."

He glanced out the window. The inner garden was still enjoying a light, pretty snow that did very little more than spangle leaves and branches, and glitter among the grass.

The Tree Court could be perfectly summery if the Tree cared to extend itself, but—

"I hope that she did not walk to us in this weather."

"No, sir. Scout yo'Bingim has appointed herself Emissary Twelve's driver at call. The Scout is presently in the kitchen with a cup of tea and a plate of Mrs. ana'Tak's cookies."

"Puppy," Val Con murmured, and rose from his chair.

"Pray tell Emissary Twelve that I will be with her in a few moments."

"Yes, sir."

✳   ✳   ✳

In fact, the Tree Court was chilly, but perfectly supportable. Seated on the ground, her armored back resting against the massive trunk, and her head bowed, was Emissary Twelve, comfortably shielded from the meager snowfall by the Tree's wide branches.

"Good afternoon," Val Con said, dropping cross-legged to the perfectly dry grass across from her.

For a long moment, Emissary Twelve remained precisely as she was. He had just enough time to fear that she had fallen into her sleep time when she raised her head, large yellow eyes blinking slowly—once, twice...

"Good afternoon," she said. "I hope that I have not called you from important work."

"In fact, you have done me a good turn. If you had not arrived, I might have kept inside all day and never known how pleasantly the Tree keeps itself while the rest of the world shivers and freezes."

There came a sharp rustle from the branches above; the Tree, perhaps, acknowledging a hit. Val Con did not look up.

"Surely, the Elder is permitted comfort, so long as it is not stolen from others?"

"So I also tell myself. It is worth noting, however, that we have both partaken of the Tree's fruit and may therefore be inclined to forgive its peccadilloes."

"That is true," said Emissary Twelve. "It is necessary to keep sight of the environment in which one operates."

"Most especially on Surebleak, and when dealing with the Tree." Val Con paused, considering the person before him. She looked, he thought, a little despondent, or perhaps she was merely sleepy. "I wonder what I might be honored to do for you today?" he murmured.

"It may be tomorrow," Emissary Twelve said carefully. "Or even the day after. I do not wish to disrupt your time wantonly."

He frowned slightly.

"Assisting the guest is not a wanton disruption of my time," he said softly. "If I may—I suggest that we, though we are short-lived, compared to yourself—we are not in general greedy of our time. One does not consider the shortness of our hours, but rather how best to spend them.

"Service to a guest, to an ally, to a friend—that time is well spent."

"That is useful information. I can see that we will have been changed . . . very much, the technical team and I, by the time we have completed needed repairs."

Val Con tipped his head.

"This troubles you?" he asked.

"Yes . . ."

She closed her eyes and opened them again to their fullest width. They seemed to glow, thus, as if lit from within.

"You understand," she said, "that we of the Clutch are rarely troubled. We change in known ways, as our shells enlarge, as we learn our lifework and our duties increase.

"Yet, despite our long lives, despite the age of our race in the universe, we have not sought out . . . change . . . in the way that is common to the Clans of Men.

"The Clutch have never, in all our history, done as you have done here—occupy a populated world, and actively seek to meld the various customs, traditions, and goals of all into one, new, and, as I understand the desire, stronger set of customs, traditions, and goals.

"We have located worlds that suit us—a few. And we have, over time, colonized those worlds with trained persons from each of the Clutch Clans, and an Elder to advise us and to hold the table until others should join there."

She paused. Val Con waited.

"The Clutch have never before faced the diversity of persons, philosophy, and honor that we find here on this world Surebleak. I understand that there are protocols which are difficult even for those of the Clans of Men to parse.

"In truth, this world will change us. I know, as the Elders have taught me, that there is a time when one must, for the greater good, accept the lance.

"It is for this mission that I was wakened. This is the purpose for which I was born. In the abstract, I have already accepted the lance and the change it will bring. It is merely . . . the process that troubles me."

"The process of change is rarely easy, though it can be exhilarating," Val Con said. "Even we of the Clans of Men can be—and often are—troubled by the process. We manage the anxiety that inevitably attends any change by reminding ourselves often of the benefits that change will bring."

"That is also useful information. I thank you."

"You are welcome. I hope I am not too bold, but it would please me if you kept me in mind as a resource, when the process becomes . . . annoyingly troublesome."

A pause, not overlong.

"That is the offer of an Elder," she said.

"Among us, it is the offer of a brother."

Hardly a pause at all this time.

"There is another strangeness, for how should my agemate know more than I?" She blinked her eyes. "I will keep you in mind as a resource, as I keep the Elder Tree also in my mind, and Yulie Shaper, too."

"An excellent foundation for a list of resources that will surely grow over time."

A breeze swirled lightly down from the low branches, gently ruffling his hair.

"There was, I believe, some other difficulty with which you required my assistance. May one know what it is?"

"Yes," said Emissary Twelve. "It comes to me that it would be wise to speak with the portmaster, to apprise her that there are technicians and materials incoming. Advance planning for these arrivals would be beneficial to all. We do not wish to bring the portmaster problems, or to discommode the people of Surebleak."

That, Val Con thought, might well be young yo'Bingim's counsel. If so, it was good. Best for the Clutch to begin as friends and thoughtful neighbors.

"I would be pleased to introduce you to the portmaster. Shall we find if she is available to see us tomorrow? Unless we have an emergency, I think that it would be rather too hasty to insist that she see us today."

"When she has time available, then I will be at her service," Emissary Twelve said fervently.

"Very good. Let us ascertain what may be possible. Jeeves."

"Master Val Con?"

"Will you please call Portmaster Liu's office on my behalf and ask if she has time available tomorrow to meet Emissary Twelve of the Clutch and to speak with her regarding future calls upon port resources?"

"Certainly, Master Val Con. Shall I ask for any specific hour?"

Val Con considered Emissary Twelve.

"At the portmaster's convenience, please."

"Yes, sir."

"Is there anything else with which I may assist you? Is your space at Yulie Shaper's farm adequate to your needs? Is there anything that we may provide which will add to your comfort?"

"I am content with my apartment at Yulie Shaper's farm. Indeed, it is . . . comforting, reminding me, as it does, of the chambers where I was wakened and tutored."

"You have a comm there?"

"Yes. I use it to call Scout yo'Bingim should I require transport."

"You may also use it to call me, or Jeeves, or Miri," he said. "I will ask Jeeves to call your unit and leave the pertinent numbers there. When you have time, you may input them into your call directory."

"You are . . . kind."

Val Con felt his mouth twist into a slightly wry smile. He hesitated on the edge of a risky answer, knowing that Clutch did not wholly comprehend Liaden humor, or even—

"Master Val Con, the portmaster will be pleased to receive an introduction to Emissary Twelve tomorrow at thirteenth hour. She asks, if this is not acceptable, that we call to rearrange the time."

"I am content," Emissary Twelve stated, perhaps knowing what she agreed to.

"Thank you, Jeeves. We will wait upon the portmaster tomorrow at thirteenth hour."

The Bedel

. . . .

SOMETHING WAS SINGING IN THE COMMUNICATIONS ROOM: A sweet, poignant melody which pierced the heart, despite the lack of words.

Pulka had been in the antechamber, looking for a specific component that would complete the repair of a compiling unit Rafin had found. Once the unit was made to work, then they might use it to print a number of components that had never been found, which would handily put three more found devices into operation. Pulka frankly had no notion what the purpose of one of those machines could be, and was looking forward very much—

The melody had changed from poignant and sweet to shrill and scolding.

Muttering, Pulka backed out of the corner he had, with no little difficulty, wedged himself into, pulled the cap with its inset light off of his head and crossed to the outer office.

By the time he had reached the communications board, the tone had changed again to full-out alarm.

Muttering still, Pulka touched the keys, accepting the message—and froze, staring.

Carefully, very carefully, he picked up the stub of a pencil, sat down, pulled a sheet of gay green paper to him, and began to transcribe the cipher on the screen.

Alosha the headman was drinking tea with Silain at the *luthia*'s own hearth. He had come to her, as even a headman must come to a *luthia*, when that headman wished to know the heart of the *kompani*.

The courtesies were first seen to—not even a headman risked rushing a *luthia* when there was no cause for haste.

So. The tea, a question asked regarding the *luthia*'s 'prentice, and another of Droi and her child, who were also attached to the *luthia*'s hearth.

Alosha asked, and was granted leave to light his pipe.

The *luthia* refilled their mugs with tea.

Alosha blew a smoke ring.

They both watched it, rapt, until it had stretched apart and vanished into the upper air.

Then did Alosha speak.

"How many?"

"To go?" she asked in turn.

Alosha opened his hands, indicating that this number would be well received, if that was the number the *luthia* wished to give.

"With certainty, eight. There are six who yet Dream."

"A long Dream," Alosha muttered.

"There is no limit on a time of Dreaming, Headman," the *luthia* told him, though without heat. She was bound to school him on this but, as she knew the heart of the *kompani*, so she knew the heart of the headman. He grumbled because he was worried. He was worried because he must go when it came to it; there was no choice for him, as there was no choice for the *luthia*, sitting tall and cool on her hearth rug.

He would go, because he would have people to tend to, even as he left people he was bound to care for behind.

In fact, his heart was torn in two, and there could be no mending it in this lifetime.

"Eight, then," he said. "It is not . . . so large a number, *luthia*."

"It is not," she agreed, "but the ship only denies choice to the *luthia* and to the headman. All others may choose; any other may stay, stipulating only that they Dream themselves into the tiles, so that the ship is not robbed of its tithe of knowledge."

"True."

Alosha blew another smoke ring and a second, smaller, into its center. They hung in the air for a long time, then suddenly blew apart, as if in a storm wind.

"It is also true," he said to the *luthia*, "that the ship has not yet given us their date. It may be that more will decide to come, when the arrival is more than a Dream itself."

But the *luthia*, perhaps, had not heard him. She was sitting quite still, her head turned away, eyes slitted, as if she listened...

...and he heard it now as well, the sound of rapid footsteps, coming quickly nearer.

In another moment, he recognized those footsteps, and he came to his feet, foreknowing, perhaps, or only wishing to meet Pulka standing.

He came into the light of the *luthia*'s hearth, a pudgy man, neither old nor young, holding a slip of paper in his hand.

"*Luthia*," he said, stopping at last. "Headman. The ship's captain speaks. The arrival has been set."

Jelaza Kazone

. . . .

HAVING SEEN EMISSARY TWELVE AND SCOUT YO'BINGIM ON THEIR way, each with a pack of cookies "to share" with their comrades, Val Con returned to the delm's office.

He poured himself a cup of tea and approached the desk, pausing to fish Fondi from the seat of his chair.

Seated, he put the cat on his lap.

Fondi did him the grace of thinking about the offer of comfort for a moment before deciding against. However, to show that there were no ill feelings, he only went as far as the desktop, where he presented his profile while he began to wash his whiskers.

Val Con sipped tea, put the mug aside and tapped up the message queue.

A letter from Theo and the daily voting stats from the Committee of the Vote topped the list. He opened Theo's letter first.

It was very short, but compared to her usual style of correspondence—which was to say, no word at all—it was very nearly an epic.

He read it once, then picked up his mug and read it again. He was pleased, if mildly astonished, to observe that she had covered all of the niceties, even unto a well-wish to her close kin, and an apology, that she could not know how long duty might require her absence from... home. Ah, home—there was a change. Perhaps, having fought for it, Surebleak had acquired merit in her eyes.

Regarding the postscript detailing the disposition of the Pathfinders, and the implied excellence of their papers, given the source, he could, without the slightest threat to his *melant'i*, merely smile an elder brother's indulgence. The delm might be secretly relieved that they were no longer obligated to find a place for the Pathfinders, but that was a matter they would discuss only under Delm's Seal.

Well. He sent a copy of Theo's letter to Miri and placed his into personal files.

He then carefully finished drinking his tea and opened the report from the Committee of the Vote.

Here was the usual dry stuff. Statistics: turfs visited, votes received, and numbers of those who declined to vote, either from fear of retribution or a distrust of the process.

There was nothing to hint at the number of votes received by each contender. The Council of Bosses had decided to keep that information confidential even from themselves in order to minimize the possibility of violence while the voting was in train, and therefore encourage the greatest number of people to participate.

In terms of that goal—Surebleakers were voting in good numbers overall. That was encouraging, though the fact of a vote to decide which Boss ought to be seated at Council was going to change the society of Surebleak—said Scout Commander yos'Phelium, wretch that he was—in *fascinating* ways.

Well, and what had he and Emissary Twelve only just been discussing? Life, after all, was change. If—

"Master Val Con, a message arrives from *Basalial*, Daaneka tey'Doshi, PIC; Kor Vid yos'Phelium, copilot and comm."

Val Con sat up.

"*Basalial* was in the care of Rys's team," he said. While it was in no way fantastic that Korval pilots might find a Korval ship, the question of why that ship had been taken from Rys...

"Yes, sir," Jeeves said. "There appears to have been some excitement at Daglyte Seam. I am collecting reports and will present them when the facts are collated and verified. In the meanwhile, will you hear the message from *Basalial*?"

"Yes."

A slight pause preceded a woman's voice, crisp and quick and very young.

"To the delm, greetings from *Basalial* and her crew, First Class Jump Daaneka tey'Doshi and First Class Jump Kor Vid yos'Phelium.

"We are returning home in all haste, bearing with us one Rys

Lin pen'Chala, said to be the brother of Val Con yos'Phelium. His comrade informs us that Rys Lin's case is dire, and his only means of being healed is at Surebleak. The pilots therefore ask that the means of his survival be present at docking. Information regarding our landing site is also solicited urgently.

"tey'Doshi out."

Val Con took a hard breath. Rys, direly wounded, and Surebleak his only hope of recovery?

He was on his feet before he had realized his intention to fly across the snowy fields to Yulie Shaper's farm.

"Jeeves, has Mr. Shaper yet installed a comm?"

"No, sir, though one has been . . . procured for his use. At this moment, one naming himself Nathan Bedel is at the door, sir. He begs to see the brother of Rys at once."

Of course.

Val Con sank back into his chair.

"Please ask Mr. pel'Kana to bring Rys's brother to me. Also, ask Mrs. ana'Tak for a tray—tea and cookies, please."

"Yes, sir."

Jelaza Kazone

. . . .

UDARI WAS NOT A WELL MAN. HE WAS SWEATING, UNSTEADY, and his usually rich complexion was a distressing milky beige.

Val Con had been standing near his desk, to properly greet the guest, but the apparition that followed Mr. pel'Kana into the office prompted him to snap forward, get his arm around the taller man's waist and guide him, shivering as he was, to the visitor's chair by the desk.

"Brother," he said urgently to Udari's pale face and shocked-wide eyes. "Tell me what I ought to do for you. The *luthia*—"

"No!" gasped the other. "The *luthia* is not needed. Not yet. We have him—we have him. He is ours; he stood before the fire, and we with him, while our souls were bound and braided. It is a spiral, passing through all the *kompani*, but those who are nearest, nearest to his heart—we are the first. We have him. We hold him."

"Rys," said Val Con and did not wait for the other's nod. "I have had word, he is incoming—soon. How many hold him? How long can they hold?"

"Myself, Rafin, Droi, Memit. We stood next to him at the fire, supported him in the binding."

"Droi is pregnant," Val Con said urgently. "This distress, Brother—"

Udari gasped a laugh.

"Droi is pregnant no longer, Brother; the child came some days back. Have no fear for Droi, strongest of us all in her anger and her darkness. The one who holds his soul."

"Yes," Val Con said softly. "If there is nothing I may do for you, tell me how to prepare for Rys. I am told his case is dire, the only hope of his healing here on Surebleak. That is Droi? Keeper of his soul?"

"Yes..."

"Are the rest of Rys's heart-kin struck as hard as you are?"

"I took the greater part, with Rafin at my back. Memit stands ready to take Rafin's place, should he need to step forward into mine."

He took a long, shuddering breath.

"It was not so ill at first—a little fatigue, some fever. Almost, it was as if a *luthia* held him in her hand and leached the sickness from him."

"But it has gotten worse," Val Con said, looking over his shoulder as Mrs. ana'Tak arrived bearing a tray with tea and cookies.

She carried it to the table and put it down, came back to put her hand on Udari's head.

He took a hard, shocked breath, and raised his eyes to hers.

"You are a *luthia*?"

She smiled slightly.

"I do not know this word *luthia*," she said in her accented Terran. "My family has a small talent for Healing. We are all trained—a little for a little, yes? You should rest, Nathan. Yulie works you too hard."

Udari gasped a laugh.

"I will tell him so."

"Do that," she said calmly. "Meantime, I bring you tea to drink, and you, too, Master Val Con. You will feel better with it."

They did feel better for the tea, though Udari, his color much improved and his trembling abated, drew the line at cookies.

"Tell me now," Val Con said. "What shall I have for Rys when he is brought home, aside Droi and Maysl."

He paused, considering, and added, "What place is best to receive him? The tunnels? Else? The ship which bears him has several docking options available to it."

"The tunnels—I think not." Udari leaned back in his chair, eyes half-closed.

"There has been—I *feel* that there has been news. From the ship. We do not wish to become entangled in preparations for departure..."

A warm tickle of breeze inside Val Con's head, the tang of a seed pod along the edge of his tongue...

"You See something," Udari said, and leaned forward to catch his hand.

"Tell me."

"The Tree," Val Con said slowly, considering the nuance of the thought.

"The large Tree that grows in the inner garden here... suggests that it might be of assistance." He paused, laughed softly, and raised his head to meet Udari's eyes.

"It also suggests that there is no better place for one's brother to come for aid."

Udari raised his eyebrows.

"You must forgive it," Val Con said. "It is quite old and treasures a high opinion of itself."

"This is the elder of the tree which recently came to Yulie Shaper's care?"

"Yes."

Udari smiled.

"It may amuse you to learn that the younger also harbors a high opinion of the elder."

"I believe," Val Con said, "that it could not be otherwise. Despite which, it has a valid point. It may well be able to assist, if only by keeping the air sweet and warm."

Udari smiled briefly. "May I meet this Elder Tree?" He squeezed Val Con's hand gently, and let it go. "I have already Dreamed myself into the tiles. Whatever it may tell me is mine alone to know."

"You are staying then."

"Yes."

He rose, very nearly without a wobble. Val Con rose likewise and offered an arm.

"Yes, Brother," Udari said, as they went, arm in arm, down the hall. "I am staying. Who could say no to such a planet?"

Jelaza Kazone

. . . .

MIDDAY ON THE PORT. A NICE DAY, SUREBLEAK-STYLE, WITH
bright sun and the air so cold it would freeze your nose off in
a literal sort of way.

Inside her scarf and her hood, Miri smiled. She was on her
way to Korval's Yard to meet Val Con. He was having a ship
refitted especially for her, which was a piece of damn nonsense,
given that most of her piloting savvy came straight from him to
her. Oh, she'd been taking her lessons, like a good Korval did,
but she wasn't nowhere near being the captain of her own ship
yet, nor, in her own personal opinion, would she ever be.

Still, it was a traditional thing, that the delm had their own
ship, maintained and ready to fly at the drop of a crisis, which
the gods knew there didn't seem to ever be any lack of. And
since Korval's current delm was in two separate and often distinct
packages, that meant a ship for each of them.

So, across port she went, anticipating and eager, so busy
enjoying the day that it didn't quite occur to her to wonder
why she hadn't had Nelirikk drive her or why Val Con hadn't
stopped to give her a lift, or even why Nelirikk wasn't walking
behind her.

She turned a corner, the port seeming quiet and not so full
of folks as was often the case—and there he was, right ahead of
her, wearing an actual cold-weather coat, probably over his leather.
She grinned and stretched her legs to catch him, almost calling
out "Val Con!" . . . but not quite, which was good, because—

A shadow moved at the corner of the cross street she'd just
passed—bulky and anonymous in a dark cold-weather coat, hood

363

pulled up tight 'round the ears, scarf softening throat and chin, dark glasses hiding the rest of the face.

It turned its head, watching Val Con stroll past as it raised a gloved hand...

A gloved hand holding a gun.

Miri did yell then, as loud as a merc captain needing to be heard in mid-battle could yell—and leapt into a run; the glasses glittered in the sun; she saw the finger tighten on the trigger, heard the whine of the pellet—

And sat up, twisting in the blankets, breath coming in deep sobs, and it was all right—it was all right. There he was, asleep on the pillow next to her, hair tumbled across his forehead, dark lashes fanned across golden cheeks.

She leaned close, looking hard into his face. High cheeks, straight nose, generous mouth, pointed chin. His chest rose and fell gently, and if she leaned in real close, which she did, she could hear him breathing in a kind of soft burr.

Just a dream, Robertson, she told herself, which was only half a comfort, because sometimes the damn things were actually true, and there was no way she could figure—nor Anthora yos'Galan could figure, nor even Val Con could figure—how to tell which dream was really a foretelling...until the dream repeated, in real life.

She closed her eyes.

Not this one, she told herself, willing it to be so. You're all nerved up about the vote, that's all it is. Fact was, she expected somebody to get shot—that was only common sense—and Val Con a high-profile target, just the same as she was, and Pat Rin, and anybody else who was going to be standing out on the steps of the Mercantile like a damn fool.

An upright and honest damn fool.

She untwisted herself and the blankets, and stretched out on her side as close to Val Con as she could manage, resting her head on his chest.

He shifted slightly to accommodate her, murmuring but not really waking; she sighed, and settled closer, listening to his heartbeat. Closing her eyes, she tried to stay with that steady, comforting sound. Impossible that something so strong and so steady could...ever...be stopped.

...which was a stupid way to think. She'd been a merc;

she'd seen hearts stopped. Stopped a few herself, if it came to it. And none of it had prepared her for the possibility of losing *this* heartbeat, this warm breath against her temple.

"*Cha'trez*?" he murmured. "What troubles you?"

She sighed, pushed up to look down into his face, green eyes still half-closed.

"Bad dream," she told him. "You got shot at the port."

"Ah. I will do my utmost not to be shot at the port—or anywhere else," he said, and added, when she found she had nothing to say to that, "I expect similar assurances, you know."

She laughed then, and snuggled hard into his side, her head on his shoulder. She felt his arm go around her, felt him rest his cheek against her hair.

"All right, have it your way," she said. "I'll do my best not to get shot at the port, or anywhere else."

"Excellent," he said, reaching 'round with his other arm to pull the blankets snugly up to their ears. "We may now go back to sleep with light hearts. Dream sweetly, *cha'trez*."

"Dream sweetly, Val Con," she answered, and closed her eyes.

The Bedel

· · · · · · · · · · · ·

DROI FROWNED AT THE SMALL GREEN PODS IN HER PALM: THREE of them, each smelling agreeably earthy and vital, as living plants often did.

"Did you eat of these?" she asked Udari.

They were seated in the out-chamber of Rafin's forge, which was dark and very nearly cool now that the fire had been banked. Rafin himself was in the common area, helping his brothers and sisters with their packing, lifting those things too heavy for any other to handle. It had been decided that all would exit the tunnels at the same time, so as not to leave a temptation for the captain of the ship.

There were no Dreams of the captain forcing those of past *kompanis* who had chosen to remain behind onto the ship.

Neither were there Dreams in which the captain sweetly blessed those who had chosen other than the ship, and swore that they would meet again, in the World Beyond.

Best then, had said Alosha the headman, in agreement with Silain the *luthia*, that all depart the tunnels and say their farewells round the fire, before all hearths were extinguished.

For now, though, the bench before the forge, dim-lit and chilly; Droi frowning down at the pods, Maysl in a sling at her breast, and Udari crouching before her, waiting.

"Did you eat of these?" she asked again, raising her head to meet his eyes.

"I did not," Udari said. "None of those are for me. I am assured that I would know if it were otherwise. These"—he moved a hand—"they are, if you will, *samples* sent for your examination.

366

I am given to know that such as these may be crafted for individual need. Specifically, I am charged to say to you that the Tree might craft one or several such pods for Rys should they be needed to preserve his life, or to return him to himself."

Droi nodded. "It is well to know these things."

She turned her attention again to the pods, closed them in her fist, brought them to her nose and inhaled. She considered them again, chose one and held it to Maysl's nose.

Maysl sneezed.

Droi nodded and returned the pod to her palm.

"In what manner would this information come to you—that one of these three, let us say, is yours?"

"The brother of Rys, undertree, speaks of a certainty in the mind, of a scent which wakens hunger in the one for whom it has been crafted. He speaks also of a long-term familiarity with such things which allows him, and the headwoman, to know not only which is for them, but for which other a pod has been crafted."

"Hah." Droi tucked the pods into the pocket of her skirt.

"I will reach out in sisterhood to the Headwoman Undertree," she said. "After the *kompani* has built its new fire."

"And the Headman Undertree?" Udari asked, with interest. When last he had heard it, Droi had a knife dedicated to the Headman Undertree, on reason of Rys.

Droi considered him, her eyes deep and dark.

"Give me your counsel, Udari of the Bedel. Shall I spare one who demands his brother die for him?"

"I think," Udari said slowly, "that there is more to that story than has yet been told. I have seen his grief, that it fell on him to remain, and send Rys to do his part. He would have had it otherwise—that I believe. As for my counsel: I find him a man of both heart and head, and I am proud to stand his brother, and to share with him a brother."

Droi said nothing, and Udari dared one more word.

"Also," he said, very softly indeed, "Rys is not dead."

Droi snorted lightly, and reached to touch the tiles at her throat.

"That he is not, nor will he be soon, if the Eyes of three *luthia* are clear."

She sighed and shifted slightly on the bench, raising a hand to stroke Maysl's head, already covered in black curls. The child snorted, and burbled, but did not wake.

"So then. A lodge has been provided from the storerooms undertree, which is thought to be winter-worthy. It will be erected aside Yulie Shaper's house, and a snow lock constructed, so that all may pass freely."

"Yes. Yulie Shaper and Memit have undertaken this project."

"That is well," Droi said. "It has been arranged with Silain's sisters, the Lady and the Professor, that they will store those things which have come into the keeping of the new *kompani*, until we have a permanent camp, or until the *luthia* and the headman decide otherwise."

"Yes," said Udari again.

"Review once more how we shall come to Rys and restore him to us."

"It has been arranged with the master of the port that, when the ship bearing Rys achieves Surebleak, it will be diverted to a landing at the house undertree, for a medical emergency. We will be informed as to the time of arrival and may go to the Tree. The pilots will bring Rys to—"

Droi shifted.

"Rys will be met by his brothers," she said.

Udari bowed his head.

"Yes, *luthia*. Rafin and I will meet the ship, and bring Rys with us to you at the Tree, where what must be done will be done."

"That is well. We wish no *gadje* in this business of the *kompani*. We are Bedel, and in this we will remain Bedel."

"And yet you and I have discussed that we will change, Sister."

Droi sighed.

"We *will* change, yes. Three of us have Seen it, so it will be so. *How* we will change, and how quickly—these things are for the headman to say. For now, for this, we will keep to the Old Ways."

Udari bowed his head again.

"Yes, *luthia*," he murmured.

Basalial

. . . .

"WE ARE TO LAND IN THE MEADOW, AS NEAR TO THE TREE AS we might," Daav said, glancing up from his board. "This has been cleared with the portmaster, as we have a medical emergency. We are further told that there will be appropriate people on hand to transport our passenger."

"Well enough," said the pilot calmly. "One hopes we were quick enough, Daav."

"The autodoc claims life for him, though I own the stats concern me."

"Yes."

They plied their boards in silence for a time.

"Are we given a comm code for those who will transport him?"

"We are told that they will arrive when the hull is cool."

"Ah," said Aelliana.

Jelaza Kazone

. . . .

THEY HAD THE LOAN OF ONE OF YULIE SHAPER'S SLEDS FOR THIS, with the admonition to "...bring that boy back safe. Din't go to all the trouble o'ice wine just to have him never taste it."

Yulie had counseled against the pull-behind cart, however.

"Be a rough kinda ride, and him hurt so bad as you're sayin'. Best if somebody sits pillion, an' holds 'im close. Whoever's driving just needs to go careful and not run into any trees."

They had also the loan of a portable comm from Rys's brother undertree so that the one called Jeeves could guide them along the quickest routes to the meadow, to take Rys up, and from the meadow to the Tree Court, where all had been made ready to receive him.

"Stop now," Jeeves spoke from the comm. "The ship's hull is too warm for you to approach more nearly. I will tell the pilots you have arrived."

Udari slowed the sled and stopped it, so that they were exposed in the treeless, snow-filled meadow, under the bright sky.

The ship sat closed and silent before them. Having Dreamed such things only recently, he knew that it was not so large a ship, though it held the attention, sitting closed and silent upon the brilliant land. The snow had melted away from the hot hull, exposing brown grasses pressed flat by the weight of winter upon them.

There were lights, bright enough to be seen even in the light of day. There was a name—*Basalial*—and a port—Waymart. There was also affixed to the hull the seal of Tree-and-Dragon, sign of the House Undertree, of which Rys's brother Val Con was headman.

They waited: ship and Bedel and sled.

The breeze freshened. Clouds moved across the face of the day star.

Behind him, Rafin stirred.

"The hull may be hot, but I am cold, Brother."

As if his words were the key, Jeeves's voice emerged from the comm.

"The hull is cool. Wait until the ramp is extended, then take the sled to the bottom. The runners will take no damage from the grass."

Udari touched the switch key, bringing the sled to life. The ship also stirred, the hatch sliding up and away into the hull, and a ramp running down to the sere land.

A figure stood in the open hatch, slim and small, watching as they approached, Udari guiding the sled with care over the brittle grasses.

When they came to the ramp's end, he brought the sled half around, so they faced the way they had come. He turned off the switch and came out of the saddle, Rafin already waiting for him on the ramp.

"Brother," he said, with a smile, and started toward the open hatch and the figure waiting there.

Udari went up the ramp first, Rafin following, as they had agreed.

He blinked when they reached the hatch, surprised to see it held by the veriest girl, her pale hair short, her eyes green and bright as glass.

"I am Udari," said Udari, "brother to Val Con yos'Phelium, and brother to the one you bring home to us. This is Rafin, my brother, and also brother to that one who has come home."

The girl inclined her head and stepped aside to let them pass her.

"Follow this hallway. My partner is waiting and will guide you to him. I will guard the door, rather than seal, so that you may be quickly on your way."

Down the hallway they went, wasting no time, and at the end of it a boy, seeming no older at first than the girl on the hatch. Then Rafin saw his eyes and bowed his head in respect.

"Your brother was placed in the autodoc to keep him stable," the man said in a deep, careful voice. "We have emergency blankets put out, if you care to wrap him against the cold."

"We thank you," Udari said, which words Rafin heard with nothing of the outrage he might once have felt, to hear one of the Bedel express gratitude to a *gadje*.

"I ask," Udari murmured. "What befell him?"

"An energy strike, as we were told it. The jacket was burned, and his flesh, too. It ought to have killed him outright, given what I know of such weapons." The firm mouth twisted slightly. "Some might say that he was lucky.

"Here—"

He turned lightly on a heel, guiding them to the shallow alcove, and stood back to let them pass.

There, in the small space, the autodoc, hood raised, the promised blankets draped over the foot.

In the autodoc, pale to the lips, skin drawn tight to his bones, eyes sunken, scarcely seeming to breathe—there lay Rys.

The sight of him stopped Rafin's heart.

"He has gone before us," he said, low, for Udari's ears alone.

"Yes, but he is paused upon the path. It is our part to bring him back to us. Help me with the blankets. Once we have him well wrapped, we will trigger the heating units. Then, just as we agreed—you will carry him, Brother, and hold him safe from further harm, until we are arrived, and healing may begin. We do not set our opinion over the *luthia*'s word."

"That we do not," Rafin said devoutly, and reached for the blankets.

· · · ✵ · · ·

It was warm undertree, what breezes there were gentle, even caressing. There was, also, a general feeling of wellness and calm. Peace, as Droi understood it, which lent a clarity to head as well as to heart, and partook nothing of edges and endings. She considered this as she prepared the hearth and the cot, opened her case, and made certain all was in good order to receive one who was ill unto death.

To do so, she was required to move a cat—black and white— who wished to assure herself of the fitness of the instruments.

Once those things were done, Droi sat down with her back against the warm trunk of the Tree, the cat curled next to her knee, and tended to Maysl, who was greedy for the breast.

There were a number of cats here, Droi saw now. It was not

to be wondered at, given the warmth and the general easiness of the space. Far better to nap under a green bush on soft grass than try to find warmth in a snowbank.

Leaves murmured over her head, and she looked up as Memit came to sit with her, across the width of a surface root. Memit, whose face was worn and whose eyes were bright.

"They come," she said.

"Yes," Droi agreed. "They come, but they are taking care, as brothers ought. He will not leave us before they arrive."

Memit sighed.

"As the *luthia* says."

Droi sighed silently. Of course, a *luthia* received respect from her children, but this meekness—it was too much. Silain had been esteemed, and loved. No one had been cowed by Silain...

...unless she had specifically wished them to be cowed.

Black Droi, a voice whispered in her head, and she held her thoughts still, listening.

When there came no other sign, she considered the one she had been given.

Black Droi: *luthia*-trained, but set aside, her vision dark, her heart shuttered. Her brothers and sisters knew her, had seen what her darkness would willingly encompass.

They were, in fact, afraid of her.

And *that* was not the due of a *luthia*, that her brothers and sisters feared her—once, she had been proud—bitterly proud—of the fact. Now...now, she must solve this; her brothers and sisters were her children, her grandchildren—and while she could not command their love, she must soothe their fear. They must know, first, in their hearts, that their *luthia* cared for them and would work, always, in their best interests.

Rys, she thought then, as Maysl suckled her breast. Rys will know what to do.

Yet one more reason that Rys must come back to them, fully himself, calm and strong in all the ways she was not.

"How goes the courting?" she asked Memit, and was pleased to see her sister smile.

"Slowly. I do not wish to frighten the rabbit. But the question before me is—do I stalk a rabbit or a lion?"

"If the rabbit does not come to the lettuce, perhaps a challenge will wake the lion?"

"So I reason as well, but—"

Pulka came forward, his stance soft, which was Pulka's way with Black Droi, but had no place in this.

"The apparatus is ready, *luthia*."

"Good," she said, even as a high whine came riding the warm air.

"They come," she said, and looked down at Maysl, who had fallen asleep at the breast. Droi paused, suspecting the peaceful breezes, but there was no harm, after all, in a babe falling asleep once she had had enough.

"Help me," she said to Memit, who stepped across the root and took the child in hand.

They sat in a circle around the cot: Droi, Memit, Rafin, Udari, Pulka—also five cats of various color—and they gazed upon the man resting there, and upon the ties that bound them all.

There was a decision to be made, as Droi knew. The ties that bound Rys were strong, but the ties with which Rys bound *them* . . . if they were thin, or burned, or frayed, then . . . then must Rys's brothers and sisters use their heads and their hearts for him, and for them, to answer the question . . .

Was it better to let him go, or to accept the pain of bringing him back?

Droi had feared—deeply feared—what she might find when she opened her eyes to Rys in this way, and from the sighs that ran the circle, she knew that she was not alone in seeing that he was *not* beyond them, though he was sorely struck.

"Hist!" she heard Rafin mutter, and she turned toward him in circle.

"What pains you, my child?" she asked him, then saw that there were . . . cats pressing against him, and more cats settling themselves on the cot around Rys, being certain to touch him. She saw, too, one bold orange creature comfortably stretched out across his chest.

"There are too many cats!" Rafin told her, and she shook her head, tasting the energy in the warm air, hearing the beginning of purrs.

"No," she said. "There are not too many cats. Allow them to assist." She raised her eyebrows at him. "Unless you think these cats are *gadje*?"

All cats were Bedel, so said the Bedel. Rafin knew this as well as she.

He bowed his head, and reached to skritch the torn ear of the striped cat standing on his knee.

"So," he said, "they stay."

He sighed and pulled the cat's other ear.

"Your pardon, Brother; I was a fool."

Droi brought her attention once more to Rys, tracing the line of damage along nerves and flesh until—it simply stopped. That, she thought, that was the hand of a *luthia*—the unknown sister who had, if not given Rys his life, at least forestalled his death, and caused him to be sent back to those to whom he was bound.

There was also the mark of the machine upon him—Udari said they had taken him from an autodoc. The pilot told them that it had been used to stabilize Rys's condition, but machines are not always wise. It had healed those injuries most amenable to its abilities, and that was also good.

It meant she could concentrate on those injuries that no autodoc could mend, but which were well within the reach of a *luthia* of the Bedel.

"What say you, brothers and sister of Rys Dragonwing? Do we attempt this healing, or do we cut the cords?"

It was a ritual question; she knew the answer before they spoke.

"Hold him, then," she said gently, reaching for her case. "Hold him close, hold him tight, for this will be no gentle healing."

The Bedel

. . . .

THEY WERE DONE WITH WEEPING, EVERY EMBRACE HAD BEEN given, and every promise of a meeting in the World Beyond. They walked together quietly, quickly, through the blocks of abandoned warehouses until they came at last to the parting of the ways.

There, one group—the larger—turned downhill into the night-time city, under street lamps that illuminated the falling snow. Some of that group laughed to see it; others tried to catch the flakes on tongue, or nose, or mittens.

The second group was considerably smaller, each one pulled behind them a small cart. They went uphill to the place where the first ship had landed many, many years ago. It had been scrub and rock then; it was scrub and rock and snow now. There were no lights here, only the few stars above, and one star, descending, growing brighter as it came.

It might have been a concern, that the port would see it. When last it had come this way, the port had been sickly and cared nothing for odd lights in the sky.

Now, the port was awake, alive, alert. The portmasters were jealous of their skies and claimed all rights to order traffic there.

Well, but the port would not see this light; the watchful machines would register no offense against the skies. The Bedel came and the Bedel went, said the Bedel, when it suited themselves and no others.

Luthia and headman stood ahead of the rest, leaving their carts in the care of others. It was proper ship form, so they had Dreamed, for the light from the hatch, when it was finally lifted, to find them first. They would present themselves, and those who waited with them, to the captain, headman of the ship.

The star settled gently, the snow melting away from it in a warm fog.

The star went out.

The Bedel waited, calm in the darkness.

There came a hiss, and steam running toward them, leading a long, lighted ramp, an empty doorway at the far end.

The Bedel waited.

A figure, no more than a black shadow, appeared in the door and strode halfway down the ramp.

The *luthia* and the headman stepped forward to meet him.

He was not a young man, the captain of the ship, nor yet was he old. His face bore the stamp of years and authority, and there was a glint of silver in the close-cropped hair.

"Jaren," he said, when the *luthia* and the headman had reached the end of the ramp. "Captain of the ship."

His voice was mellow, but the dialect of the *kompani* came slowly to his lips, as if he had only newly Dreamed it.

"Alosha, headman of the *kompani*," said Alosha, speaking less quickly than usual.

"Silain, *luthia* for the *kompani*."

Jaren, captain of the ship, jerked his chin down, his bright, knowing eyes looking out over the hillside.

"Where are the rest?" he asked.

"Brother," said Alosha, "we are here in all of our numbers."

Jaren, captain of the ship, frowned.

"Ten?" he asked. "What befell you? Was there illness? Was there want? Do you tell me that the *Bedel* failed to survive?"

"We tell you no such thing, captain of the ship," said the *luthia*, standing forward to the very edge of the ramp, so he could see her white hair, and her shawls, and the lines upon her face.

"We tell you," she continued, even as he drew breath to speak, "that ten is the number who choose to return to the ship."

"There are others who did not choose?"

Jaren, captain of the ship, was quick to hear that, and Silain the *luthia* was not comforted by the avarice in his voice.

"There were, and they have gone the way they have chosen," she said calmly. "It is not the first time for this, captain of the ship. We have Dreamed it."

"They owe the ship their knowledge," said the captain, frowning down at her.

Silain frowned back up at him, and vowed to find her sisters on this ship to learn why they had allowed this captain to become so greedy.

"Ah, Brother, I might have known! Only see here!"

And there was Alosha, the headman, walking up the ramp toward the stern-faced captain, holding a sack out before him.

"The ship loses nothing; we bring treasure untold. Each and every one of us Dreamed ourselves for you, and here I hold all in my care. The *kompani* is complete, never fear it."

Jaren, captain of the ship, frowned even more.

"Ten," he said again. "It is not a large number."

"It is the number that is," the *luthia* said, allowing the fullness of her power to be heard. "Be content, captain of the ship."

"There it is, Brother; the *luthia* has spoken," Alosha said, lowering his arm and tucking the sack close beside him. "The simple facts are that you are late and we are few. If we are too few for the ship's care, only say it. The Bedel thrive where rocks fear to grow, eh?"

There was a flicker in the light along the ramp. Silain looked up to see a woman standing in the doorway. Young, she was, and stooped in stance, yet she wore the layered shawls of a *luthia*.

"Jaren," she said, and there was power in her voice, "what delay is this? Our kin must be brought aboard and welcomed."

"There are ten," he said.

"Surely, then, they will not overfill us?"

The girl moved down the ramp, and for a moment, Silain thought that the captain would not yield. At the final moment, he did so, surly. Alosha moved aside with a bow.

The *luthia* came on to the end of the ramp and extended her hands to Silain.

"Sister. I am Azath. Be welcome among us, your kin."

"I am Silain, Sister; well met," she said, looking into the young *luthia*'s dark eyes. In them, of a sudden, she Saw what had happened: the assault upon the ship itself that had cost them kin, and crew, and elders; the time consumed by repairs; and Jaren, once *a* captain, now *the* captain of the ship, in desperation sending to all of the old codes. Receiving an answer, he had come quickly, so quickly, to pick up the dozens his desperation had made.

"Ten," she said, smiling into Azath's dark eyes, "is better than none."

"I agree," said the other, joining arms with Silain and walking with her up the ramp. When they came to Alosha, she made as if to offer her other arm, but Jaren, captain of the ship, was before her, to clasp his shoulder.

"Brother, please, be welcome," he said.

He turned then and looked over those who waited still, with their carts and their hopes. He looked over them and raised his arms.

"Be welcome, all! There is a feast made and tales to be told. We are the Bedel all and the ship is glad of each of us. Come! Come aboard!"

Jelaza Kazone

. . . .

MAYSL WHIMPERED IN HER EAR AND DROI WAS AWAKE ON THE instant, cheek pressed against grass and bark.

She sat up, reaching for the child, and staring about them.

In fact, it had not been an easy nor a gentle healing. They had all of them been exhausted by the time they had reached an end, and fallen asleep like so many kittens on the warm grass undertree.

It was shadowed under the branches, and Droi's guess was that, in the outside world, it was full dark and very probably freezing.

Here, though, it was comfortably dim and warm; there were small lights twinkling here and there among the bordering bushes.

She tended Maysl's needs quickly, expertly, picked her up and carried her to the side of the cot where Rys slept, surrounded by and covered in cats.

The orange sleeping across his chest raised a broad head at her approach, considering her out of dark amber eyes.

"I will watch now, Sister," she said, settling to the rug next to the cot.

The cat got to her feet, stretched, bowed, and jumped lightly from the cot to the ground. Two others also rose and ambled off after the first, and Droi nodded to herself, as she put Maysl to suck.

She raised a hand to touch the tiles on their silver chain, wondering if she ought to give Rys to Dream himself, or wait.

Most of those who had walked close to death returned with some or all of their memories, their sense of self, missing, as if Death, thwarted, had yet extracted a toll for the use of the path. It was because of this possibility that a Bedel would Dream himself into a set of tiles before embarking on any particularly hazardous adventure. Surely, it was why Silain had insisted that Rys do so.

But it sometimes happened that one who had been struck nearly to death returned with all of himself intact. And Rys—Rys had traveled the path between life and death more often than many. It was perhaps wise to wait.

There was no harm in the Dream, but it would return him to himself *before* he had left on the errand of his Brother Undertree. He would therefore lose, forever, all that had befallen him on that adventure, which might be valuable to him in continued life.

No, she decided. If he woke a stranger to himself, then she would give him the tiles. It was easy enough to do, and it harmed no one to wait for his waking.

So, she settled herself to wait, considering the man on the cot. He no longer looked as if he was dying—and not well. He looked like a man who had been ill, but who was mending, and who would be impatient when he woke and found that he was not immediately able to leap fully back into life.

She glanced around the glade again. Her brothers and sister were sleeping yet, each with a cat in attendance. Let them sleep, she thought; they had given much.

Maysl murmured. Droi turned back—

And met bright black eyes in a thin, somewhat pale face. He was smiling.

"Rys Dragonwing," she whispered, his name no less potent for all of that. "Do you know yourself?"

"I think it more than enough that I know you, Droi," he said, his smile widening. "And—could it be our daughter? *Is* it Maysl?"

"It is," she said, feeling tears gather in her eyes and spill down her cheeks as she leaned forward to put their child in his arms.

Jelaza Kazone

. . . .

"SO WHAT'S THE DELM'S SCHEDULE?" MIRI ASKED AS THEY SHARED a second cup of tea in the quiet of their suite.

She had agreed to stand Road Boss today, rather than switching off in the middle of the shift so that he might make Emissary Twelve known to the portmaster. It had occurred to him that it might prove useful—to Emissary Twelve, to the eventual contractors and to Surebleak—if the Clutch Turtle were given a tour down a usual sort of a day, and introduced to those things that the Clans of Men found both pleasing and necessary.

"Diglon claims the honor of driving for himself. Therefore, we will be picking Emissary Twelve up from her lodgings at Yulie's farm. Also, I thought that I might see if Memit will allow me to take one or two pots of the flowers she has been encouraging in one of the smaller grow rooms. Since I am due to make an inspection of the work being done on Lady yo'Lanna's house, we will stop there and note progress, and also place the flowers in the conservatory."

"To see if they freeze?"

"It would be best to know before her ladyship arrives if plants actually will grow in her garden room."

"There's that. So—a tour of the house, the settling in of the plants . . . then?"

"Then a leisurely drive down through the city, so that Emissary Twelve may understand how the most of us live here, and at last to the portmaster and the formal introductions."

"Not going to take her to the Emerald for lunch?"

"The Emerald, so I am told, will be undergoing a security

event during the lunch shift, and Pat Rin believes that the fewer known targets present during the exercise, the better it will go for everyone."

"All right, then—why not go to FlourPower?" Miri asked. "Granita'd take right to Emissary Twelve. Not to mention the Hooper might be of interest to the Emissary, and vice versa."

"That's a good thought. We will see how much time we have, after the other errands are accomplished."

"The Road Boss doesn't have anything on the books. Guess I'll catch up reading reports."

Val Con sighed. "Perhaps soon we may elevate someone to Assistant Road Boss."

"Got that as a goal, myself. First, gotta train 'em, so it'll still be a while before we can take a week or two so I can get some flight time on my ship."

He considered her. "I will speak to Pat Rin. Perhaps, when High Winter is done, we may arrange for some time away."

Miri grinned. "Maybe Cheever'd like to be Road Boss."

Val Con inclined his head seriously. "Perhaps he would. We cannot know until we ask."

"Well," Miri said, "don't ask unless I'm there with you. I wanna see his face."

She rose, and he with her.

"Guess it's time for this Boss to go to work. Have fun playing tour guide."

"I think that I will." He extended a hand, and she took it, looking up at him quizzically. "Will you sleep with me tonight, Miri?" he asked her.

"Only sleep? I don't know that I think much of that."

"Perhaps, if we consider the problem together, we might hit upon something to do that will amuse both of us."

She grinned.

"Silver tongue," she said, and raised her face. "Give me a kiss."

Surebleak Port

Portmaster's Office

. . . .

THE COMM BUZZED AND CARLA'S VOICE FOLLOWED, SOUNDING brisk but not annoyed, which was encouraging.

"Team Leader Kasveini is here for her appointment, Portmaster."

Portmaster Liu glanced at the clock. It was ahead of the appointed time, and she'd be within her rights to ask the team leader to wait in reception for a while. On the other hand, Kasveini was probably every bit as nervous about this upcoming meet as she was. She might even, Liu thought, casting a half-guilty look at her coffeepot, benefit from a cup of something special.

"Send Team Leader Kasveini in, please, Carla," she said.

She took her own mug in hand, knocking back the remains of her beverage, and stood up.

Kasveini was worried, Liu thought a moment later, as the other woman came into the office. Well, she had a right to be. Wasn't like she was a little bundle o'sunshine herself.

"Coffee?" she offered, raising her mug and nodding toward the coffee station. "Fresh ground. Don't do it often—well, who can afford it?—but I figured this was a special kind of day, and it wouldn't do to be pouring Bloosharie before we have our lunch with Boss Surebleak."

Kasveini smiled, faintly, but it *was* a smile.

"A small cup," she said. "I have nerves enough, but fresh ground..."

"Gotcha."

Liu went over to the station, sighing at the stray grounds littering the top. Expensive and messy, and worth both.

Occasionally.

She poured a scant mug for Kasveini, and an even scanter one for herself since she'd already had a full measure.

Guest served and seated, she sat down behind her desk and nodded.

Kasveini had always dressed with respect for a Surebleak winter—snow coat, high-necked sweaters, scarves, mittens and insulated boots. Today, she'd added a bright red insulated cap that was pulled down over her eyes. Wonderful things, insulated caps. 'Course, your hair stood up on end like you'd gotten the fright of your life when you took it off, but it was worth looking a fool for a warm head and ears.

The team leader sipped her coffee reverently, sighed, and looked up.

"I am energized, Portmaster. Worse, I am beginning to think that we should not have agreed to this meeting."

"I'm walking right beside you," Liu assured her. "Still haven't thought of a better way to get this information Boss Surebleak claims to have. You?"

Kasveini shook her head.

"It's a dangerous folly, but no—I can't see another way."

She patted her coat over her breast.

"I should tell you that I am recording," she said. "I assume you will, as well."

"Got it on already. Should've told you."

"Yes. I have been recording since I put my coat on."

Liu put her mug on the desk, looked at Kasveini's tense face, and considered her own state of mind.

"Tell you what we can do. It's early, but it's not snowing, and we both know how to dress to keep warm. Let's walk over to the Emerald the long way, cut over and take a look at the progress of the work."

"That sounds...pleasant," Kasveini said.

Liu nodded again and got up to get dressed for the weather.

They paused briefly at the observation window at the top of the stairs, taking in the action on the hybrid field serving what regular air traffic there was along with local and interstellar craft.

The upgrades this port should see, Liu thought, why it could easily triple in size in a few Standards...

...if TerraTrade found for the port.

Liu sighed and watched snow swirl on the tarmac in the wake of an aircraft gathering speed on the runway—and continued swirling and dancing even after the plane lifted, rumbling, into the low cloud cover.

"We'll take the townie route, close to the temp work zone," she said, pointing it out to Kasveini. "You can see the top of the Emerald's billboard lights from here, just the other side of the port entry. Right now the zone acts like a tunnel and we get to stay outta the worst of the breeze. Got plans for a merc recruitment office, a temp agency, some new storefronts and warehouse space. Korval's expanding its yard, down over the other side, and Mack's Repairs is getting a proposal together to expand his business.

"Not to mention, we got two bids in for landscaping. Hard to believe, but it'll be good for business, and for the ships coming in."

"All of this is speculation," said Kasveini. "Surely, very little of this work will begin until the port receives TerraTrade's decision."

"No," said Liu, looking out over the port and the work zone which was someday real soon going to be that merc hiring hall. "No, the mercs are building on their own. Korval's expansion is under way, and that multiuse—well, you can't see it from here— that's already getting started."

She turned to meet Kasveini's eye.

"What's that they say, outworld? Build it and they'll come? Well, I guess you could say Surebleak's building and ships'll be stopping—whatever TerraTrade decides. An upgrade, that'll make it all smoother, but the people on this world are used to doing the hard work themselves."

Kasveini kept eye contact for a long moment, then looked away.

"We'd best go, if we're going to walk. We don't want to be late for the Boss."

"They'll keep the reservation," Liu said, turning toward the lift. "And you're right; we don't know how long Boss Surebleak'll wait."

Surebleak Port

Emerald Casino

. . . .

HERB POLISHED A GLASS, FOR SOMETHING TO DO THAT WASN'T obviously watching a screen. That was part of a barkeep's job, here at the Emerald: keeping an eye on a screen or two, making sure the customers were getting what they wanted and weren't being bothered by anybody they didn't want to be bothered by. The little bank o'screens Herb got to scan was all eyes on the bar and restaurant side, so it was only a dozen, all tucked up an' out of the sight of customers. Nothing at all like the big security room down in the back, with eyes on almost every square inch of the Emerald . . . three banks of 'em, 'cause redundancy, the expert who'd installed those screens had said during the training session on how to properly scan your screens and how to identify a problem—redundancy was the key to security.

Right this hour, Jeremy'd given him the word to keep a special eye on Booth K1, which was Herb's screen four. That was the portmaster's reservation. She hadn't showed yet, but one of her guests had—the one Jeremy'd told him to particularly watch for. Short guy, wearing a blue winter coat, hood up like he was still cold from the outside, red glove snaps on the shoulder. Asked for the portmaster's reservation, and Herb'd called Rithy over to show him the way.

She did that, and he saw on the screen that she offered him a hot cup o'something, saw the guy shake his head. The table being already set for three, Rithy brought a pitcher o'water and three glasses, and after she'd gone, the guy'd poured himself a little, and sat there sipping, hood still up, which was just getting silly in Herb's opinion. The hood would be holding the cold now, and the casino was nice an' warm, but—however he wanted to do it. Wasn't no snow offa Herb's roof.

Herb'd polished three more glasses to a high shine and filled a couple orders for the floor servers before he glanced at the screen again. The guy was still sitting there, hood up, empty glass sitting next to his hands folded on top the table.

Herb glanced 'round the bar an' out toward the front door. Portmaster hadn't showed yet. Wasn't like her to be late; 'specially not she didn't have Carla call and let 'em know. Well, maybe her cab'd got caught up in that mess they called a work zone.

Herb had double reasons to want to see the portmaster today, not only to fill the reservation and let Jeremy in Security calm down from his morning full of triple-checking cameras, but to let her know they'd got in a whole case of that Bloosharie she was special fond of—not that she'd likely be drinking on duty, no, not her!

Jeremy, though, that was the main reason he wished she'd come in. Jeremy was all jitters and Herb was wishing he could drop him a glass o'beer on the side. All nerves and prancing, that was what—an' a guy as big as Jeremy, well...prancing wasn't necessarily what you wanted to see on that.

"Check ticks for me, Herbie?"

Sure enough, it was Jeremy, shoving his comm under Herb's nose...

"Nothing wrong with the comm or the timer. Same time as mine."

"Feels off, Herb. I didn't miss the portmaster, did I? Portmaster and TerraTrade? They didn't call bar-side, or send somebody for a carry-away? Din't sneak in when I was..."

"Not here yet, just take a look—" Herb knew for sure the portmaster hadn't snuck by him without a hello.

"I am looking. There ain't nobody in that booth now."

Jeremy straightened fast.

"Where'd he go?"

"Prolly in the facilities," Herb said.

"Icebait," Jeremy said, not quite under his breath, and brought the comm to his lips. "Security, recheck all cameras. Liu's not here and the ghost is gone! Check facilities, check casino!"

"Weren't you *watching*?"

Jeremy's face was serious and closing in on a blush like it did when he got mad. Then he ran to the empty table and through the kitchen door.

Herb was aware of a sudden rushing here and there among Security, and of a stomach suddenly tight with worry that maybe he should've watched harder, at that.

On the Road

· · · · · · · · · · · · · · ·

DIGLON GUIDED THE CAR CAREFULLY UP THE STILL-TO-BE REPAIRED driveway of Melina Sherton's rental.

He waited with the car, while Val Con and Emissary Twelve disembarked and went up the stairs to the front door, Val Con noting the Clutch person's slight difficulty in managing. He made a note to have a ramp installed, to accommodate others—possibly including Lady yo'Lanna herself—who might find the short flight difficult.

They had fallen a little behind of their timetable, though the appointment with the portmaster was in no danger of being missed. He had not planned on Memit wishing to have a detailed talk about the conservatory, the light it might receive, the temperatures it was likely to achieve, in order to derive which plants might thrive in such an environment.

In the end, she had provided cuttings from half a dozen of her flowers, and accepted Val Con's word that, indeed, he had seen the beds cleaned out and filled with fresh, sweet soil not three days past.

Then, they met Yulie Shaper on the way out, and he had wanted to talk about ice wine, and when "that Rys" might be coming home again to have a taste of it, and veering off into the idea of "working up" a kind of grape that could not only tolerate Surebleak's cool growing season, but come to fruit quick enough...

In any case, they were behind schedule, but not tragically so.

Emissary Twelve was appreciative, as they passed down the hallways, gazing wide-eyed at the teams painting, and cleaning, and repairing, who gazed back at her, eyes no less wide.

Val Con disposed the cuttings in freshened beds, discussing with Emissary Twelve the purpose of the conservatory.

"And the purpose of these flowers?" she asked.

Val Con sat back on his heels and gazed at the slightly drooping cuttings.

"They are pleasant to look at; several deliver an agreeable scent. They improve our environment, and thus our lives."

"Worthy," said Emissary Twelve. "Such aesthetics must also influence the Elder Tree, given the care which is taken of its dependent plants."

She blinked.

"You have visited our world, Slayer of Dragons, and have seen, perhaps, that we have not as many variations of hue as we see among the flowers here—our homeworld never learned to flower in this way!"

She paused to turn in a circle. When she was facing Val Con again, she said, "I should like to see this room when it is all flowers."

"We shall apply to the lady who will have charge of it, when she is finally come to us. She is a notable gardener, and I am certain she will be able to answer any questions you may have far better than I."

Val Con added to his mental notes a suggestion that Memit offer Emissary Twelve a pot or two of flowers for her residence, so that she might experience them firsthand.

Diglon was learning to drive all manner of vehicles these days; he seemed a natural, as he was at so many things. That he was keeping the speed down, even once they reached the main road itself, was fine—they still had plenty of time to get to their appointment with Portmaster Liu, though lunch at FlourPower, Val Con thought, would have to await another occasion.

Today's vehicle was a limo left over from the days of the Gilmour Agency, which had been hastily refitted by Andy Mack's crew for duties which might include ferrying Clutch of several body types from place to place. This meant that Emissary Twelve sat in the gutted passenger section, while Val Con joined Diglon in the front seats. It was, he owned, awkward, though Emissary Twelve seemed to have no misgivings about the arrangement.

Diglon was maintaining a stately progress so that their guest might look her fill at the local flora.

"My wife Alara makes a study of the Surebleak plants," he said to Emissary Twelve. "She would, I think, be pleased to talk about them with you."

"I should enjoy that, I think, though I would not wish to impose upon her time..."

The comm in Val Con's pocket gave a tone—the official Road Boss alert tone, in fact. He pulled the thing out, noting Pat Rin's code at the top of the screen as the message formed below it.

He took a hard breath.

"Diglon, please make all haste for the Emerald. Fines from the Watch will be on my ticket. Emissary Twelve, our meeting with the portmaster must wait until she can be found. It appears that she's been stolen from beneath the very eyes of Security."

Haste happened, acceleration pressing them all to the seats, Diglon triggered flashers and punched the horn ahead of crossings and around other traffic the whole way as the car fought the jouncing of the wintertime road. Diglon blew past one large truck—overfull by Val Con's official estimate as Road Boss—carrying logs to the city, only to find another, smaller truck in front of it.

Both passengers got bounced around then with some fancy braking, and a glance showed Emissary Twelve looking smaller, as if she'd managed to retract head and limbs somewhat for extra protection.

The comm chimed again. Val Con glanced down, abruptly cold despite the warmth of the big car's cabin.

The news was bad—a comm was stolen from Emerald Casino's Security, one with access to the Watch frequencies, with Portmaster Liu and Survey Team Leader Kasveini missing in transit to a meeting.

"What occurs?" asked Emissary Twelve.

Val Con took a breath and tried to explain, succinctly, the various threads that had been woven into this—

Emissary Twelve moved one three-fingered hand, shaping a recognizable pilot's sign for *hold*. "I have been reading the news sheets, and Scout yo'Bingim has been attempting to keep me current of such local events as might bear on my mission.

"The information I am given does not always make me

comfortable. It grieves me that so much damage can be done willingly to such short lives.

"Despite my frequent confusion, my mission remains clear: I am to oversee the repair of this planet. In order to do this, it appears I must assure stability among all of those who live on the planet.

"I, therefore, offer my aid. I will not stint my mission. Tell me what must be done."

"We must first reach the port and find good information, as we dare not trust the comm. If the missing have not been found by the time we arrive, we will join the search."

"That is a very clear plan. I await the fullness of it." And Emissary Twelve sat back and closed her eyes. She was humming, very gently.

Observing that Diglon was not only in control of his vehicle, but also enjoying himself immensely, Val Con leaned back in his own seat and listened to Miri's song inside his head, taking comfort from the calm contentment of her melodies.

There was nothing that they could do now but hurry. Emissary Twelve was correct. Once they had reached the end of hurry, then they would find what to do.

Surebleak Port

Office of the Road Boss

. . . .

PAPERWORK.

Miri sighed.

The notes about the snow cleaning problems weren't engaging her interest at all—in fact they were putting her to sleep, despite she was halfway through a second cup of strong tea.

She flipped to the next report that had come to her attention—parking problems around the Scouts' temporary space up near the work zone, which wasn't even Road Boss business, neither the work zone or the Scouts being situated on the Port Road, and anyway, the problem would solve itself once winter was done, and the work, too.

Scowling, she looked for the name of the sender on the screen. *Paijin O'Malley.*

Well, she thought, it *would* be Paijin O'Malley, wouldn't it?

O'Malley was the project manager for the work zone. As such, he was really concerned that everybody everywhere notice that there was work going on, like anybody who came into the port could miss it, and that it was proceeding well.

This meant that he was occasionally required to fabricate problems near the work zone, so that the people in charge of other important things—none of 'em, o'course anywhere *near* as important as his particular job o'work—were reminded that work was going on.

Staring at the letter, she considered sending him a sharp reply.

She took a sip of her tea, and thought again.

If she sent any kind of acknowledgment—even a reminder that the Office of the Road Boss had nothing to do with his damn project—it would only encourage him. He wanted attention; it didn't matter to him how irritable the attention was.

"No," she said out loud, "let him stew."

"Captain?" Nelirikk called from the outer office.

"Just talking to myself," she answered, flipping to the next report. "They tell me it's a sign of old age."

She'd cleared all the paperwork for a wonder, and for a bonus, she'd even managed to solve a couple of minor, but legitimate, Road Boss problems.

"Local girl makes good," she muttered, quiet enough so Nelirikk wouldn't hear her or, if he did, realize that she was holding another one-sided conversation with herself. "Might oughta be, local girl learns lots of patience making tiny decisions that shouldn't have to get officially made, if people as a class had any common sense."

She snorted lightly, and shook her head.

Well, who was she to complain? She'd started down this road the day she'd made corporal. Actually, she'd kinda liked being corporal, the pay being that much better, and she didn't really need to take care of anybody, not really; the sergeant took care of everybody—including the corporal.

Yeah, the point of no return, that was the day she'd made sergeant—and hadn't she known it, too? Tried to give it back; Liz wouldn't take it. Might be she could outstubborn Liz nowadays, but back then? Snowflake's chance in a sunbeam, that's the kinda odds she'd had then. Not to mention Liz being Commander Lizardi. Commander trumps sergeant, just the way it worked on the merc side o'things.

She sighed and shook her head at herself.

"Face it, Robertson," she said, grabbing the mug and pushing back her chair. "You never expected to live this long. Paperwork's a party, that's all."

"Right," she answered herself, and went to the back to get another cup of tea.

Surebleak Port

. . . .

A CLUTCH TURTLE, A LIADEN, AND AN YXTRANG WALKED INTO
a bar.

"Ah, there you are."

Pat Rin nodded to them and waved at the center screen in
a bank of six.

"There, our west-side camera shows the person who asked
after the portmaster's reservation—and waited for her some little
time—leaving by the kitchen door and walking away. We assume
that individual also is responsible for stealing the comm unit,
which was left untended on a shelf in the kitchen."

He sighed. "We will be having security refresher classes, I
fear. Of the portmaster and Team Leader Kasveini—we have
nothing other than this..."

He pointed at the screen on the far left of the bank. Two
persons, one of them recognizably Portmaster Liu in her winter-
weather garb, the other wearing a red hat, presumably Team
Leader Kasveini, were walking through the work zone, in no
hurry, apparently talking as they went.

The screen blinked when the camera looked elsewhere—
elsewhere—and back to the work zone. The two walkers were
no longer visible.

"That is where we see them—and that is where we lose them,"
Pat Rin said. "They appear on no other scan."

"We have been searching, locally, asking the cabbies, the
workers in the zone—no one has seen them."

He stopped, staring at the screens, face grim. Cheever McFarland looked up from his portable comm.

"Screened for Emerald's frequency only," he said in answer

to Val Con's lifted eyebrow, and gave the device a slight shake. "Just talked to the assistant portmaster. She's looking through the security scans from the port offices. Said she'll call, if and when something turns up."

"The Watch?" Val Con asked.

"They're looking—quiet. We don't wanna put out an all-points 'til we got a little better idea what's going on."

Val Con nodded, focusing on one low screen which displayed a map of the area...

"This distance—it is not far?" All heads turned to Emissary Twelve.

"Not so far, no," Val Con said. "Have you a suggestion?"

"May I be shown the start of this journey?" Emissary Twelve asked. "The place from which these walkers began together? New eyes may see what those accustomed have missed."

Between them, Emissary Twelve and Diglon made Portmaster Liu's large office feel tiny, dwarfing the seats they did not use and making the office furniture seem miniatures. The assistant portmaster fed the most recent video scans into the shared screen in the office: There the pair exited the building, turning away offered rides from the cabs, heading into the tangle of the work zone with its maze of temporary walls, walkways, and overhead catwalks presenting a confusion of choices.

"Nothing obvious here," said the assistant portmaster. "The portmaster keeps her own notes. I don't have access to her day files without an override signed by all the Port Trustees..."

"Which is too complicated to obtain on short notice?" Pat Rin asked and got a hasty nod from Etienne Borden, the nighttime portmaster called in from his sleep shift.

Meanwhile Emissary Twelve and Diglon moved slowly about the white-walled room, a kind of rocking motion between them as they negotiated their way around the furniture. Val Con heard a murmur from the Clutch, who was sniffing avidly...

"This beverage is—not a usual blend? It is made here?"

Emissary Twelve pointed to the half-consumed cup on Liu's desk, and then at the coffee grinder, which Diglon picked up and sniffed before tipping it toward her.

"I noticed the thread of this scent on our way into the building," said Emissary Twelve. "It is distinct..."

She raised the partial cup of coffee from Liu's desk to sniff it carefully.

"In combination with this scent, which is hers, it is all over this office—I think that I might trace them, if you will permit."

"We permit," said Pat Rin softly. "Indeed, we insist."

It was an odd sight for any who saw it—a Clutch Turtle and an Yxtrang walking side by side through the work zone, casting about as if looking for someone's lost mitten. Several paces behind them came Boss Conrad's 'hand Cheever, one of the Road Bosses, and several members of the Watch.

The Yxtrang swung aside and down, suddenly reaching under one of the temp work barriers and snatching up something that was bright red where it wasn't smeared mud. Somebody's good winter cap. Diglon showed it to the Clutch Turtle, who sniffed and nodded. The hat was passed back to one of the Watch.

They moved on. The work zone's shiny just-installed insulation, still uncovered, reflected the wan sunlight, and the shadows of the posse bounced across the workplace, Emissary Twelve slightly ahead, as the pace of the march picked up . . .

. . . and abruptly halted, as Emissary Twelve did, half-turning toward a wall—a solid wall, not a temp work zone wall, and placed her broad foot deliberately against a particular spot where the wall joined the tarmac.

Cheever glanced at his handheld. "The building's a warehouse—other side's going to have the doors . . ."

"They entered here," Emissary Twelve insisted. "I can smell them."

Val Con approached the spot, knelt, pulled off his gloves, felt the panel's edge—and looked to the one next to it.

"This one has a different closure than the one next; the panel is not bound in the same way."

He tucked his hand at the bottom of the panel, next to Emissary Twelve's foot. Diglon bent and added his fingers to the effort.

There was a click.

Val Con looked up, gratified to see weapons in knowledgeable hands.

"Now," he said to Diglon.

The panel gave—and resisted, clearly not permanently affixed, but yet not willing to give up without a fight.

"Hold it," Cheever said, and muttered into his comm despite the chance they might be overheard, asking if anyone was watching Dayglo Street, and getting an assent.

"Watch for quick movement," he muttered. "Starting now!"

Diglon let go, shifted his stance, and bent again to the seam. Emissary Twelve joined him, inserting her hands beneath the edge. Val Con rocked back and up onto his feet, willing to leave the work to those best suited to it.

There was a moment of concentrated effort before Diglon grunted and shook his head, straightening up.

"It will take a long time," he said, "this way."

"Time!" exclaimed Emissary Twelve. "We must make haste!"

She reached under her weather cloak, hand emerging with a blade that glittered, all green and crystal bright, and ran it down the seam between the two panels.

The wall split open soundlessly, and Diglon leaned in, getting strong fingers into the new seam, pushing...

The wall section pivoted on an internal hinge, revealing a darkened hallway.

"I smell blood," Emissary Twelve said—and ran forward, Diglon leaping after, Val Con with him.

The lights came on as they hurtled down the hallway, Val Con behind a flying wedge of Yxtrang and Clutch Turtle. He looked down at the rough floor, saw a trail of dark drops stretching ahead, rounding a corner, which they took with no respect for the probable danger waiting beyond...

Five streeters dressed for weather stood in a doorless room. Lying on the floor before them were two trussed and struggling figures. One of those figures swept bound legs out, trying to trip the nearest of their captors, earning a hard kick in the knee—

Diglon Rifle and Emissary Twelve arrived first, running full speed. The five spun, dodged, spread out...

One fired a pellet pistol into Emissary Twelve, point-blank, which slowed her not at all. The shooter was thrown against the wall for her trouble, pistol flying from her hand. She hit the floor and stayed there.

Another fired from his knees on the floor—Diglon grabbed him by the arm and tossed him casually against the wall. He, too, went down and stayed down.

Yet a third stood, back to wall, gun rising—and snatched away by Emissary Twelve, who held it to her mouth as she hummed a single small note...and tossed the weapon to the floor, smoking slightly.

One of the five had appointed himself the captives' guard—or their executioner. Keeping his gun aimed at them, he pulled a knife from his belt with his other hand.

"How best, I wonder?" Val Con heard him say, as he leapt forward.

The knife took him high in the right arm. Val Con rode with it, accepting the thrust, continuing to close, fingers locking around the man's wrist, forcing the gun arm up—

"Got 'im!" Cheever McFarland yelled, grabbing the man from behind and yanking the gun from his grasp. He reversed it and used it to deliver a smart rap right over the streeter's right ear.

It was over. The captives had been released, thanks to Diglon's utility knife, and were helped to sit up by Emissary Twelve.

Team Leader Kasveini was content to sit quietly against the wall. Portmaster Liu looked at her, plainly worried.

"You all right?"

"No," she said, and added: "Is that Boss Conrad?"

"Road Boss," said Liu. "Light's not so good in here."

"No," agreed Kasveini. She paused. "He came, himself, Delm Korval. To keep order in the port."

"Well...yeah. Port means a lot to him, in case you ain't been paying attention."

"Yes," said Kasveini, lapsing again into silence.

Val Con had accepted a first aid kit from Cheever, and wrapped his upper arm with absorbent tape. That done, he looked about him.

The former captors were bound, unconscious. Their two accompanying Watchmen went through their pockets, discovering four odd-jobbers, and—

"What the sleet?" demanded the Watchman going through the pockets of the man Val Con had subdued.

He moved closer, saw the leather folder with its collections of pins and wires, and put his hand on the Watchman's shoulder.

"Be careful. This one is an off-worlder. He has very special skills, and he may be booby-trapped. I know what to look for, if you will permit—"

The Watch permitted, scooting hastily out of the way.

Val Con knelt, quickly disarming the Agent of Change, locating a cache of trick weapons in the man's right shoe, a single-use mini zhangwire in the seam of his pants, and an unopened suicide pill dispensed in the other shoe.

Cheever whistled.

"Nasty bastid," he said. "Guessing he's Boss Surebleak?"

"Or behind Boss Surebleak," Val Con said. "Mr. McFarland, have you a bag, perhaps, in your pocket?"

"Got me pegged, do you?"

Cheever shifted and pulled a self-sealing bag from a leg pocket. Val Con put in the items he had taken from the agent, and sealed it.

"Boss Val Con," said Portmaster Liu, who had somehow gained her feet. She was standing—leaning—against the wall. There was a hole in her coat and blood seeping 'round it. There was blood, too, on her forehead, and a bruise beginning to darken on her face.

"You should sit," he told her, moving forward.

"I'll fall down soon enough," she said. "You listen to me, Boss. There's a plan—this? This was to discredit you—you and Conrad—prove you to be pirates.

"That one"—she pointed at the unconscious agent—"he was going to kill us; didn't care what we heard. Got his jollies off discussing *which* death would look worse for Clan Korval."

She paused, breathing hard. Diglon stepped to her side and put a big arm around her, holding her up on the wall-less side.

"This was only part of it, though. There's something else...he said"—another hard breath, this one not steady—"he said they'd won, that Surebleak was finished, and..."

"And that the Department has prevailed," said the man Cheever held.

Val Con turned to face him. The Agent laughed.

"I'm told, yos'Phelium, that you were once my equal, an Agent of Change! You broke training, that is what they say. But they have not seen. You did not break training; training broke you. You became weak, you became dependent. You are vulnerable. So very, very vulnerable."

He paused. Val Con said nothing, only watching the man's flat eyes.

"We will come back to the topic of your vulnerability," the

agent said. "But first, let us discuss your failures! With all of your efforts, with your Yxtrang, your Bosses, and your Scouts— your alien! —the Department took these Terrans from you *at its will, at a time and in a manner of our choosing.* They know your weaknesses now—you do not hold this planet; you cannot hold this planet!

"You are nothing. And Clan Korval will be known as pirates, murderers and thie—"

The agent choked slightly as Cheever pulled hard on his collar.

"Want me to put him back to sleep?"

"No, let him talk," Val Con said. "He may yet say something interesting."

Cheever loosened the collar, but held onto the agent, who seemed not to notice that he was restrained.

A crunching noise came from the other side of the room as a door came off its hinges and three members of the Watch entered, comrades behind them.

"Vulnerable," whispered the agent. "So vulnerable."

Val Con spun back to him.

"It is your topic," he snapped. "Why not—"

Pain—searing pain, fire along his nerves. He cried out, and crashed to his knees, agony in his knee, his back, his head.

Cheever shook the man he was holding. "What's going on! Stop it!"

"I? I cannot stop it. He accepted this. He *treasures* this."

Val Con thrust himself to his feet—staggered as another blast of pain overcame him, his vision going red. The breath stopped in his chest.

"Yes, yes," the agent crooned. "We had seen it, with his uncle, with his father. Cut one and the other bleeds. Kill one, and both die."

Breathless, his muscles failed him. Diglon caught him before he struck the floor again, but he was gone, gasping, overcome, reaching, reaching for the song, for his soul, for—

"Miri!"

Surebleak Port

Office of the Road Boss

. . . .

SHE CLOSED HER EYES, AND DELIBERATELY REACHED FOR HER link with Val Con. His pattern was glowing gently, which she took to mean he was content—which he would be, giving Emissary Twelve a tour and answering whatever questions came out of her, waiting in his turn to hear her interpretation of everyday Surebleak life. Man was born to be a Scout. Had *been* a Scout—kind of a Scout's Scout, if it came to that—'til all that got stripped away from him, and most of himself, too, in ways too terrible to think about.

The Department of the Interior.

Gods. She'd give an arm—and a leg, too, if that's what it took—to have kept Val Con yos'Phelium from being made over into an Agent of Change. Yeah, even though, in that scenario, she'd've never in her life have known that Scout Commander First-In Val Con yos'Phelium existed.

Well.

She put her attention on his pattern, and the hum she'd lately started to hear under all the busyness of daily life, which was just a soothing reminder of his presence in the world. Used to be, it scared her, how much she'd needed to know he *was* in the world. Now, it was part of her life—their lives—usual and comforting.

For the next few minutes, she let him comfort her from afar, sharing his sense of contentment and pleasure.

Eventually, she opened her eyes, realized she was feeling chilly, and got up to fetch the merc-issue cold vest she kept hanging on a hook behind the door for times like these. Space leather on the outside, high-density fake fur on the inside. There were lightweight gloves in the pockets, too, not suitable for winter, and not convenient for office work, either, but the vest was a comfort.

Back at the desk, she tapped up a blank screen, and typed "Improvements: Road Boss Office" at the top.

There wasn't any argument that the office needed improvement: better heat for one thing—she put that at the top of the list—and a floor that didn't creak under Nelirikk's weight.

All the meetings they'd been having lately, and it was the spontaneous meetings about Emissary Twelve that had put her in mind of this in the first place, it would be good to have a meeting room, something that would hold a dozen or two people, with its own chairs that didn't have to be hauled in from other rooms.

She frowned. There was another thing that had occurred to her during her meeting at FlourPower with the shovel-team.

When they'd first been settling in, it'd made sense to put the Road Boss's office at one end of the Port Road—which was to say, at the port, while the Road Boss's house was at the further end of the same road. It'd been symbolic: *We're under contract to keep the Port Road open, and that's what we're gonna do, no matter who might try how hard to stop us.*

But the plain facts were that most 'bleakers didn't come down to the port. And for a good number of those who wanted the Road Boss for this thing or that—it was a significant bit of travel to get to the port office.

Ideally, there should be a Road Boss's office in every territory the Port Road passed through. In terms of common sense, there ought to be at least one office of the Road Boss in the city. Eventually, they might want more, but they didn't have the crew for that yet. They could manage two offices with only her and Val Con, just by adding the new office into the rotation. Port office open every even day; city office every odd day. It could be done.

She typed that in and looked at the screen with narrowed eyes. What might also be good would be—

"Captain!"

Nelirikk was in her doorway, and the comm was whistling its bad news alert tone.

She snatched the device up, read the text from Pat Rin, and looked up.

"Portmaster and Survey Team Leader Kasveini both missing," she said. "That's not good."

"It is *not* good," Nelirikk agreed. "There is also an increase of foot traffic around this office. I had noticed it earlier, but thought it had to do with people making new routes, around the work. With this new information, I have reevaluated our situation. We should withdraw to a position of greater strength."

"We were all right here during Boss Surebleak's little riots," she pointed out, and the comm whistled again.

She read the second message.

"Emerald's sealed except for the security hatch," she said. "Somebody stole a Watch comm outta the kitchen."

Nelirikk said something interesting sounding under his breath.

"I don't think I caught that?"

"A proverb regarding the fate of careless guards," he said blandly. "Captain . . ."

"I know, if somebody diverted the portmaster and the team leader, they could be after high-level targets. I'm a high-level target. So's Pat Rin. Problem is, the office is more defensible than the car—'specially with the work zone scrambling usual traffic."

Nelirikk looked like he was getting ready to argue further.

"We stay," she said firmly.

"Yes, Captain," he said, and added, just as firmly, "You will lock this door, and be ready to leave out the back. The port door in my office is locked as well."

Well, there wasn't getting any work done with everything going on. Miri filed the to-do list and was monitoring the comm traffic on Boss Conrad's private frequency, which wasn't shared with the Watch.

Still, not much to learn. They were keeping calls down, just in case, which she'd've done herself, and wasn't it just frustrating as anything when you were outta the center of the action and trying to figure what was happening?

She sighed—and stiffened, attention dragged inward. Val Con—his pattern was dense and brilliant; the sense of his presence edgy, dangerous; he felt closer, somehow, and she got the strong sense that he was hunting.

Carefully, she withdrew her attention, not wanting to disturb him. He was after the portmaster, she was sure of that, and the tiny flicker of fear she'd felt from him was—

BOOM!

The whole office shook, like somebody'd rammed a truck into it, or a dozen bodies had hit the door all at once.

She was on her feet before Nelirikk yelled.

"Captain, GO!"

She went, grabbing her cold-weather coat off its peg, and heading for the bolt-hole at the back of the office. Behind her, pellet fire, another boom and a splintering crash—the front door, she thought, and deliberately didn't think about Nelirikk standing alone against an armed mob.

The view through the peephole was of a vacant alleyway. She finished fastening her coat, opened the door and slipped out, leaving the battle behind her.

Gun out, she moved cautiously down the alley. Planned procedure, if there was an attack on the Road Boss's office, was to go to the Emerald, same as Pat Rin was supposed to use this same alley to find the safety of the Road Boss's office if the Emerald was attacked. Which all of them knew he would never do, but that was the procedure agreed on, and they'd fight about it later, when there was a vary.

Now, though, the Emerald was sealed. The security hatch was 'way round the other side of the building, not accessible to the service alley Miri was moving down.

Before the Emerald, the alley branched off into a maze of similar alleys and little streets. She knew the route to the Whosegow, where maybe nobody would expect her to go; the other places— Mack's, Tantara Floor Coverings, even the Traveler's Rest—it'd be standard practice to cover those and wait for her to show up, assuming it was her, personally, they were after.

And that was, Miri thought, taking a right-tending alley, the way to bet.

Carefully down the thin way, scanning, scanning. Backs of stores, trash bins, a couple deep alcoves which might be snow breaks...

Down the alley she went, silent, listening to the sounds of the port, hearing distant sirens, which might be Port Security come down to sort out the Road Boss's office and save Nelirikk some trouble.

The alley bent left, which was the right direction for the Whosegow. She kept going, noting that there were more choices here, more corners, more places for people to hide, and wait.

A shadow moved at the corner of the cross street she'd just passed—bulky and anonymous in a dark cold-weather coat, hood pulled up tight 'round the ears, scarf softening throat and chin, dark glasses hiding the rest of the face.

It turned its head, raised a gloved hand...

...a gloved hand holding a gun.

She threw herself sideways into the shadows, no better cover being near, rolled to her knees, returning fire even as she heard the pellet whine by her ear.

The shooter fired again—and again. She answered, plain reaction, no time for anything fancy, as her opponent stepped out from his snug, sheltering corner—and that was a mistake.

She dropped him, heard a clatter behind and to the right, spun, gun up, felt the burn where the electric dart pierced her. Numb fingers loosed her gun; she twisted, got her backup in her off hand, and took out...somebody in the shadow of a shop's back porch—the dartman or another shooter, no way to tell—no way to see just how many there were, with the sudden shadow over the bright sky, and a green, sticky-sweet mist crawling along the ground toward her, tendrils rising.

Miri choked, tried to hold her breath...it was hard to pay attention, to remember...

A woman wearing a gas mask walked through the mist. Miri pulled herself together, raised an arm that felt like it belonged to somebody else, pulled the trigger—and shot her in the throat.

Mask, she thought; she should get the mask, but she couldn't... couldn't...

The gun slipped in her fingers; she thought she tightened her grip, but she couldn't—and she sagged sideways, collapsing onto her face in the frozen mud.

She heard something: the sound of somebody walking deliberately across snow-covered and frozen ground.

"Are you gone?" A man's voice. Liaden accent.

A boot hit her in the side. She felt ribs go, and she was on her back, looking up into his face—his satisfied, delighted face. He was carrying something that might've been a shotgun, muzzle pointed to the ground.

She had no voice...the gun! She had the gun, she thought, but her arms wouldn't move though she tried.

"Ah, no, you are not gone. Good. Struggle. Try to scream. Try, do try to shoot me."

He raised the long arm slowly, and she did, she struggled, she tried to get the damn gun—

The weapon was against his shoulder. She could see him, smiling satisfied, taking his time with the sighting as if she was a distant, tricky target.

One more effort, fighting her muscles, fighting the pain—

"Now," said the shooter. "You are gone!"

The shotgun roared. Hot gas and grit hit her face, burning. She felt it all, everything, all the pain: every wound she'd've ever taken, everything she'd survived, coming back to kill her with pain and despair, the stink—the stink—memories roaring back. She was choking on the stink and the heat; she was drowning, screaming against the pain, voiceless, and through it she saw him raise the shotgun again, leaning close, firing point-blank—

And there was nothing but agony—until there was nothing at all.

The Way Between

. . . .

IT WAS DARK.

It was cold. Gods, gods, it was *cold*—

And he was running faster than he had ever run in his life.

Pain blazed as he ran through it, the taste and the stink of MemStim in his mouth. There was a roar, and a scream, and he arrived; he was with her, holding her, wrapped around her to keep the cold away. She was sobbing, the pain eating her, destroying her, and her voice—her voice in his head, he thought, near shredded with despair—

"Shoot the bastard!"

Yes.

He opened their eyes, saw the man standing above them blink in surprise, stepping back and raising his long arm hastily—

He was not quick enough.

Val Con brought their arm around and up, the gun tight against their palm, and they shot the bastard in the face.

· · · ✳ · · ·

"No, no, no. Val Con..."

He concentrated, bringing them closer, sharing his warmth, reaching, reaching into the pain, taking it, taking what he could, to himself.

"Val Con you don't follow me."

So cold. Around him there were bright fragments, splinters, each one a note or two, clamoring, fading...

"I will not follow," he told her, wrapping them more closely together, "if you do not go."

He extended himself, reaching to the bright fragments, but they melted at his touch, and he dared not—*dared* not—touch more, because he knew what they were: her song. Her life. Melting into the pain-filled cold.

She sobbed. He felt her try to push him away, but she was weak with her injuries, the pain gnawing away her will.

"Hush, hush. We will survive. We will. Remember Lytaxin. Miri. We *will not* die here."

She said nothing and, in the silence, he felt the pain attack him, MemStim burning at the back of his throat.

The Department used MemStim. It induced perfect recall in the agent being debriefed; it was not a painless process, even when the dose was small and properly administered. This...he recalled the big-barreled gun the assassin had been holding. MemStim in a mega-dose...who knew what damage might be done?

"Captain!" a big voice shouted, and there were other voices, too, and a siren, closing.

"Captain!"

"Nelirikk," Miri whispered in his ear, and he felt her trembling against him, cold, cold, and colder.

He forced himself beyond the pain, though this time he did not open their eyes. This time, he only shouted, with all the force of a merc captain across a battlefield.

Once, he shouted, and then he, too, collapsed, wrapped in her and around her, and knew no other thing.

Mercantile Building

· · · · · · · · · · · · · · · · · · · ·

IT WAS EARLY, BUT THE SQUARE IN FRONT OF THE MERCANTILE was crowded already. A half-anxious group, many checking the time on the big clock on the front of the building, loudly wondered what was going to happen next. There hadn't been a crowd like this in anyone's memory, at least not one that wasn't a riot, and even with the paper clearly in evidence in many hands, the procedure—what was going to happen next, and how—wasn't at all obvious.

The Committee of the Vote had arranged for stands to be built in front of the building using borrowed scaffolding from the work zone, so that everyone could see the announcement themselves if they wanted to, and hear it, too, from big speakers. On the stand, a nervous pair of young people looked out at the crowd and tested the audio about every three minutes, now and then calling down to one friend or another, but mostly being half important and three-quarters scared.

In front of the stand, there was a space about two people wide and fifty people long that was clear to give the Hooper space to play, walking back and forth the way he did at weddings and funerals. Just being there was what he did a lot of times and people expected it. If the Hooper was here, playing quiet on his pipes, then that made this whole voting thing . . . normal, a plain part of life.

Like weddings and funerals.

The Watch was visible, patrolling the crowd, and some folks hawking food and snacks. Mostly, though, people were watching and talking, catching up with neighbors they might not've seen for months—or years.

The time for the big announcement was getting closer according

411

to the clock on the wall, and there! The front door of the Mercantile swung open, and here come three Bosses, followed by their 'hands.

Some few in the crowd recognized all three, and those who didn't whispered loud, "Which ones?" and the names were said over and over again.

There was Melina Sherton, looking steely, and Ira Gabriel, looking harried, and Boss Vine, looking like he always did—just a little bit mad at something and if you weren't careful, it would be you.

A few more people wandered out the door, standing ready for something, and the clock came closer by minutes and then by seconds to the time published in the paper...

Ira Gabriel climbed to the stage, as did Melina, and after a pause, like he was thinking better of it, Vine.

The ones standing by the big door suddenly moved to open it, and here come the rest of the Bosses, fanning out along the stairs, and last out was Boss Conrad, with McFarland at his back, Penn Kalhoon and Valish keeping right with 'em. They went straight to the stage and climbed up, settling in to stand behind Melina, and Ira, and Vine.

The girl who'd been testing the audio did one last click on the microphone, then the boy did the same, saying "Level, level, level level, check?" and that musta done the trick, 'cause he handed the mic to Ira Gabriel and faded over to crouch by the equipment.

Ira stepped to the front of the stage, popped the mic, and started to talk.

"Wanna thank everybody for coming, and for voting. Those who don't know me, I'm Ira Gabriel. I been holding my turf since before Conrad come 'mong us."

He turned and waved—

"This is Melina Sherton, 'nother of the Old Bosses; an' Zalan Vine, 'nother Old Boss. We're the members of the Committee of the Vote. It's our job to make sure that the vote was done all right and proper and that nobody was bullied into—or out of—voting; and that the results stayed secret, right up 'til we open the envelope in a couple minutes here."

He paused 'cause there the talk from the crowd was getting loud, and into that space, The Hooper injected an amazingly loud blast from one of his harmonicas, which he turned into a fanfare, alerting the folks who couldn't quite hear all of what Boss

Gabriel was saying to move closer and stand quieter. He did that at weddings and funerals, too, so people knew zackly what to do.

"Yes," Ira said, agreeing with the fanfare, and raised his voice.

"Let's get on with this thing. What I'm gonna do is call out the names of the rest of the Bosses standing there on the step. When I say the name, they'll stand forward, so you can get a good look at 'em, and fix 'em in your memory. After that, I'll call out the people who handled the actual street-level votin'. Then we'll all find out together who won the vote between Boss Surebleak and Boss Conrad..."

Some of the people were antsy, some trying to peer up at Ira Gabriel, who was almost a hair taller than Melina Sherton, but not so tall that everyone could see him from the back of the crowd and...

The Hooper blew another *behave yourselves!* blast, and that did quiet things down, and Boss Gabriel got on with his bidness. First come a description of the process of voting, read right out of the special edition, cheers for the Bosses standing on the stairs, and then a real tense moment when Ira Gabriel turned back 'round to face the crowd and walked to the very edge of the platform.

"I hope to introduce Boss Surebleak, without who we wouldn't've had the chance to think about voting, and making a procedure, and figurin' what comes after. So...Boss Surebleak! You wanna stand forward so we can all see you? The buncha you pay attention and let the Boss through!"

They didn't need the Hooper's reminder this time. Everybody stood quiet, though there was a fair amount of head-swiveling.

After they'd all counted to twenty, Ira Gabriel tried again.

"Boss Surebleak! C'mon and join us! You're as much a part o'this as we are. We promise safe passage!"

Count of thirty this time, and more people looking around.

"Boss Surebleak? Final call to join us all in this new thing you brought us!"

Count of forty, and people were practically spinning in circles, trying to be the first to spot Boss Surebleak and their 'hand, coming down from in back o'the crowd.

Ira Gabriel sighed and stepped back from the very edge of the platform.

The Hooper made a sad harmonica noise, and a few people in the crowd laughed, still craning their necks, trying to find the Boss standing 'mong them.

Ira Gabriel shook his head.

"I'm sorry about that, I am, but—not my decision to make."

He took a breath, started to say something, then changed direction.

"I wanna say this, before we get into the excitin' part and it gets forgot.

"You maybe notice that the Road Boss, Miri Robertson and Val Con yos'Phelium, they ain't here neither today. Some of you maybe read it in the paper, 'bout the portmaster and the Terra-Trade leader getting snatched and Boss Miri being shot up bad. That all happened at the port. Boss Val Con, he sends that Boss Miri'll make a full recover, but it's gonna take some time, she was hurt that bad. Boss Miri, she sends a note, which I'll just read to you..."

He moved his hand and froze, looking out over the crowd.

"It's in my left-hand outside pocket," he said solemnly, and some few in the crowd tittered, while he pulled a piece of paper right outta that pocket, like he'd said.

"So, this is Boss Miri saying—'I thank everybody who's been worrying after me. I did take the bad end of the stick, black eyes and bruises, and a couple ribs stove in. I'll get through it, just like all of us do. We're tough and we're strong because that's what Surebleak needs from us. The office will be closed the next couple days while I heal up, but I expect to be back on the job, so long as our contract's still good. I believe in contracts, and I believe in Surebleak, and I'm pleased that I had sense enough to come back home when I could.'"

There was quiet, then cheers, which ran awhile 'til Ira Gabriel stood up to the front of the platform again and held a big red envelope high up over his head.

The cheering faded, and there wasn't anybody who wasn't looking right at the stage.

"All right," said Ira Gabriel, "this is why we're here. Once all the votes was counted, re-counted and certified, the result was written down on a card, which was sealed into this envelope. I ain't seen it. Ain't nobody seen it 'cept the one tabulated the final totals and wrote out the winner on the card."

He waved the envelope over his head once more, brought it down and—

Bang!

A single shot rang out. Somebody shouted; somebody else pushed—and was quick-caught by the people standing next to them.

"Watch here, Watch here, Watch here! Attention, let us through!"

There were ripples in the crowd; Watch uniforms were visible. The crowd parted where it was needed, and here they came, four Watchmen surrounding half a dozen unhappy people, and another Watchman bringing up the rear, carrying four long-arms.

They got to the space at the front of the crowd, and the Hooper stepped back to give them all the room they needed, slipping his pipes into his pocket.

"What about 'em, Boss?" asked a Watchman.

"If you can hold 'em there, do it. They'll wanna hear this, too," said Ira, and turned slightly as the Mercantile's big front door swung open, and Portmaster Liu and the leader of the TerraTrade survey team came to stand a little ahead of the assembled Bosses.

"Ma'am?" said Ira. "Ma'am?"

"Just here to learn the outcome of the vote," said the portmaster. "Are we too late?"

"No'm, your timing's good as it gets."

He held up the red envelope again and turned to face the crowd.

He tore the top edge off that envelope and pulled out a big beige card.

"The results of the Boss Vote are . . ."

He paused, his eyes on the card, and the crowd tensed.

"Boss Surebleak—one hundred seventy-two votes!"

Silence, nobody really sure what that meant.

On the stage Ira drew a deep breath and finished.

"Boss Conrad—seven thousand, nine hundred, and ten!"

Melina Sherton stepped up next to him, hands raised over her head.

"Boss Conrad by a blizzard!"

Cheers came then, loud and lusty, and the speakers boomed a little while the portmaster and a tall woman in the uniform of Port Security climbed up to the stage, and received the mic from Ira.

"I'm Claren Liu, Surebleak Portmaster," said the first of the women. "This is Liz Lizardi, Port Security Chief. She's got something to say to you, and I'd appreciate it if you gave it a listen."

She handed the mic to Chief Lizardi.

"Some of you know me; I grew up here. Went off-world. After a while, I got bored, so I come home."

There was a ripple of laughter through the crowd. Liz nodded.

"I just want to let you know a little about Boss Surebleak."

She raised a hand and pointed at the Watch surrounding their prisoners.

"To the best of what we can know, these right here, every single one of 'em together—they're what's left of Boss Surebleak. The rest of the Boss—they're gone off-planet, or they're dead, or like two we picked up yesterday, they're in the Whosegow. That's it, that's them. Off-worlders, come to make trouble, to try and take Surebleak—to take us!—over.

"That part of it's finished now. For the rest of the cleaning up—if you been threatened by these people or their 'hands, if you been mugged, if they owe you money, if they broke a contract or an agreement with you, I wanna know about it. You can come on down to see me personal in the port, or you can talk to your local Watch. They'll get the news to me."

She paused, looking down at the prisoners.

"Take 'em to the Whosegow," she said.

The crowd cheered.

Chief Lizardi turned and handed the mic to Portmaster Liu, who moved to take her place at the front of the stage.

"I just wanna let you know that the Boss here—the *Bosses*"—she waved shapelessly at the stage and the steps—"and I include the Road Bosses in there, too. All of 'em, Old Bosses and New Bosses, they're working hard to make a Surebleak we can all work with, that we can all be proud of. Bosses can't do it by themselves, o'course—you gotta help 'em. You started helping 'em when you voted down Boss—the *idea* of Boss Surebleak. Now you keep on working, and we'll all of us do better."

The crowd was quizzical, and Portmaster Liu smiled, bringing the mic up again.

"You voted Boss Conrad to stay; you voted for better, not worse. That's a good day's work by anybody's reckoning. So—go on off and celebrate!"

The Hooper played a fanfare then. The Bosses on the steps turned and marched back into the Mercantile...

...and the crowd went off to celebrate.

Jelaza Kazone

Tree Court

· · · · · · · · · · · ·

MIRI DOZED UNDERTREE IN A NEST OF BLANKETS, WHICH HAD pretty much been her assignment for the last... well... truth told, she'd kinda lost track of days. Didn't matter. She was attended by cats, deployed in a rotation of their own devising, Val Con, too, sometimes, and Emissary Twelve. And the Tree, naturally. She was in the Tree Court. Hadn't been so out of attention as to miss *that*.

The Tree had been downright solicitous, keeping the temps moderate and the breezes warm. There had been pods—an amazing variety of pods, some no bigger than her thumbnail—and she'd eaten every one.

The tiniest were the best. They were the ones that clouded the relentless pounding of memory, the pain of old wounds and new; gave back her ability to think, and sleep, and just... rest.

Other pods had directly targeted her wounds: the ribs were mending at a record rate; the burns where the dart had hit her were gone without a scar; the buckshot that had delivered the drug into her system had mostly worked out, the multiple small wounds covered with shiny new skin. Her chest still ached some, where the shotgun blast had taken her. Good thing she'd had that vest on...

Normal way o'things, they'd just've popped her into an autodoc for those hurts, but with so much MemStim in her system... well. It had been the firm opinion of the merc medic who'd gotten to her first, and the two succeeding doctors, that her bloodstream

417

was so thick with the drug, any attempt the 'doc might make to filter and clean, as it would do as part of its base routine... carried about an eighty percent chance of her dying of the cure.

As it was, the merc medic couldn't quite make out how she hadn't died of overdose. The doctors hadn't been any better informed on the topic, but the consensus of all three was that the longer she kept living, the better chance she had of staying alive.

So, here she was in the Tree Court, nested in blankets because she couldn't ever quite get all the way warm, two cats curled against her belly, one tucked close to her back, all three purring—and she was starting to wake up a little more, which meant it must be time again for Emissary Twelve.

Miri sighed and opened her eyes to find the Clutch Turtle already seated next to the nest. She was holding a tangle of yellow, red, and orange weeds in her hand—which wasn't unusual, actually. Emissary Twelve had developed an interest in plants and often brought her foragings with her to their sessions.

"Hi, there," Miri said huskily. "Didn't mean to be rude."

"You are not rude, and you must have rest, as much as you may take."

She bent forward and placed the weeds next to Miri's head.

"Breathe," she said, and Miri did. The weeds were sharp-scented, a little bitter, tasting of pepper. She felt the scent move into her lungs, hit her chest, and... expand.

"What are those?" she asked.

"A gift from Yulie Shaper's farm. These herbs are efficacious for cleaning the blood, as I am told. They will assist our work here."

"I'm for anything that helps," Miri said and took another deep breath.

"We have made good progress," Emissary Twelve said. "Now, we will make more. Unwrap yourself and come sit with me."

This was Miri's least favorite part of the therapy, but there was a good reason for getting out of the blankets and away from the cats. She managed it fairly gracefully, shed her robe, and sat on the silky grass across from Emissary Twelve, her back against the Tree's welcoming warm trunk. Emissary Twelve extended her three-fingered hands, palms up. Miri extended her hands and they sat, palm to palm, looking into each other's eyes.

Emissary Twelve began to hum.

Like always, Miri felt the vibration first in the center of her chest; it moved out along her arms and legs, into her head, as Emissary Twelve changed tone and pitch. Sometimes, her blood burned. Sometimes, like right now, she was pierced by thousands of pins. It hurt...it hurt a lot, but the humming, the vibration, was between her and the pain, so that she knew it was there without feeling it.

It reminded her, reminded her forcefully, of the moment that Val Con had come to her, there in the alley where she'd been dying of agony. Suddenly, the pain had been...less, and she'd been able to see him, too; see his pattern arcing above her, dense and protective, shielding her from the fire and flames all around; holding her close; warming her with his life.

The pinpricks multiplied, and Miri knew that she ought to be screaming, but there was the humming, there was the vibration, and it was herself that she heard in the sound; herself as she had been, and would be again.

Gradually, the vibration faded. Miri emerged, sitting naked under the Tree, her palms pressed against Emissary Twelve's palms.

"It is done, in this time and place," Emissary Twelve said, and broke the contact.

Miri looked at the back of her hands, at the layer of dust—at the layer of MemStim coating her skin. She took a breath and closed her eyes. A warm breeze wrapped around her, creating a suction that pulled her hair up straight on her head—and then it was gone, and so was the residual drug.

Miri sighed and smiled. "Thank you."

"You are welcome."

"Any idea when we might see a complete cure?"

Emissary Twelve closed her big eyes. Miri reached for her robe and pulled it on, shivering.

"I believe you have achieved the place from which your own body may continue those repairs which must be done. You are not cured of this insult that was forced upon you; some traces of the drug remain."

She paused and gave Miri a stern stare out of big yellow eyes.

"Understand what I say: *You are not cured.* You are convalescing. The pain and the memories will no longer disrupt you and prevent the correct operation of your internal systems. You will be able to finish healing yourself, and you must take up that work. It is better so."

"I agree," Miri said, "and I look forward to taking up the work."

"Excellent," said Emissary Twelve, and came, ponderously, to her feet. "Rest now."

She left the clearing, and Miri nestled among the blankets and the cats. She made sure the little tangle of herbs was near enough that she could taste the sharp scents—and slipped away into sleep.

They were walking down the path that led to the Tree Court. The overgrowth had been cut back to ease the passage of Emissary Twelve—she and Val Con had done that...a few days ago, maybe. Or a week or two ago. Whenever. A side benefit of the clearing was that they could walk as they were now, hand in hand, light-moving, with no need to hold branches out of the way or skip over adventurous creeping offshoots.

"Should've done this a long time ago," she said, looking up to the sky entirely visible above them—orange and purple, it was. Sunset.

"The Tree," Val Con said, fingers tightening on hers, "would not permit, long ago. Apparently, it has only just recently occurred to it that it will receive more visitors if the way is made easy."

"Might want to make a path that doesn't involve going through our house, if it's planning on getting lots of visitors."

"I believe that it still wishes to retain our services as gate-keepers. One cannot entertain everyone, you know. Some people are dead bores."

"Right."

Hand in hand, they swung into the Tree Court and paused a moment to consider the mound of blankets and the positioning of cats before continuing. Miri pulled her hand gently away—and opened her eyes.

He was stretched on his side next to her nest, head propped on one hand.

"Hey," she said. "Your shift?"

"I am come," he told her, face solemn and eyes dancing, "to deliver a very important piece of correspondence."

"And that would be?"

He raised the hand that had been out of her sight beyond the edge of the blanket nest, holding a creamy rectangle between his first and second fingers.

"An invitation?" she asked, recognizing it from his memories of life on Liad, where such things had been commonplace, unlike Surebleak.

"Fie," he chided her, "as if this were just any invitation."

She squirmed somewhat, dislodging cats, and sat up in her nest, pulling a blanket close around her.

"So, it's not just any invitation. What makes it special?"

"This," Val Con said, extending the envelope to her, "is an invitation to the event of the season."

Envelope in hand, Miri froze, staring at him.

"She's *here*?" she demanded—and corrected herself. "She's been here long enough to send out invitations?"

"As you see."

She looked at the envelope now, seeing her name written in elegant, sloping characters: *Miri Robertson Tiazan.*

"I gotta say," she said, "I didn't expect to rate an invitation."

"Nor did I, though I rejoice in a card of my own."

"Who else is coming?" she asked, which wasn't necessarily a stupid question since Lady yo'Lanna had asked him to draw up a list of people it would be useful to know.

"Conservatively?" he murmured. "Everyone."

"Well."

Miri opened the envelope, the card fine and thick against her fingers, the printing black and crisp.

The pleasure of your company is requested at . . .

She looked up to find him gazing into her face.

"Tell me this was printed in Surebleak City."

"This was printed in Surebleak City," Val Con said obediently. "One is given to know that Lady yo'Lanna provided the cards and envelopes."

She glanced back at the card.

"Next week," she said, and took a sharp breath.

"How long?" she demanded, suddenly needing to know. "*How long* have I been here?"

"Here?"

Val Con rolled over onto his back, hands behind neck, staring up into the green expanse of the Tree.

"Here in the Tree Court," he said slowly, "three weeks."

She waited.

He waited.

He won.

"And was I someplace else before the Tree Court?"

Val Con sighed.

"It pleases me to find you so much better," he told the leaves over his head. "Emissary Twelve had given me to believe that this was the case, but one hardly dared hope for such an improvement."

"Right," she said. "I'm not healed, but I'm well enough to carry on by myself. So—where else *was* I and for *how long*?"

He sighed.

"A week in hospital, after your chest was repaired, before the doctors would allow you to be moved."

"I don't remember that," she said slowly. "I remember the merc medic arguing against the 'doc, and the doctors..."

"It may be more accurate to say that I remember that," Val Con said softly. "*Cha'trez*, you were...fragmented. I was..."

"I remember," she said, and she did. She remembered his pattern all around her, holding her close, keeping her whole.

She remembered more...repairs, bridges across missing gaps of herself, made from bright, strong bits of his pattern.

"You could have killed yourself," she said.

He turned his head to look at her.

"I think not, though we might easily have had a less pleasing outcome. Emissary Twelve was there, however, and made certain that I did not...give too much of myself, nor to repair more than was needful."

"And here I thought I was keeping up."

She shivered and pulled the blanket closer.

Val Con rolled to his feet, bent, picked her up, and settled into the nest with her in his arms. Cats scattered as he pulled the blankets over both of them.

"So *cold*, Miri..."

"Warmer, now," she said, which was true. She sighed and relaxed into him, head on his shoulder. "What else did I miss?"

"Hardly anything of note. The TerraTrade survey team has finished its work and left us. Lady yo'Lanna, as you have seen, is among us and ensconced in her residence, which she declares to be everything she could wish. The Healers have released Anthora, but she has chosen to stay in-Hall, as Ren Zel has not been released. The ship of the Bedel did, indeed, come, and those who wished to do so boarded. Rys has been joyously reunited with his brothers, his child, and the mother of his child."

He paused.

"Surely there was else—ah. Pat Rin won the vote, and Boss Surebleak has been banished. You wrote a note to those attending the announcement of the vote. I hope you will not find that I was unforgivably clumsy."

"I'll have to read it," she said, trying to sound stern.

"Of course."

"That catch me up?"

"Ah, well. In case it was not implicit in the news that Rys is home—the Department of the Interior has been removed from the board. There is cleanup to be done, but the Scouts have taken up that task."

"Really?" She raised her head to look into his eyes. "I didn't think they'd be able to do it."

"In fairness, they did not. There was a revolution from within."

He shifted slightly, and pushed himself to his feet.

"And now, my lady, I suggest that we bid the Tree farewell, with many thanks for all its care and, of course, the care of the cats. Emissary Twelve assures me that you are so well that you no longer require the constant oversight provided here, and I would far rather you were in the house."

"To tell you the truth, I'd rather it, too," Miri said.

"Excellent."

Val Con stepped free of the blankets, and Miri looked up at a sudden rustling in the leaves overhead.

Shrugging off the blankets, she held her hands out—and received a pod in each.

"Thank you," she said.

A breeze swirled out of the bushes, smelling of roses, and briefly enveloped them both.

"Yes," said Miri, tucking the pods away until they were ripe. "Let's go home."

Epilogue

· · · · · · · · · ·

THEY WERE LATE ARRIVING, BUT ARRIVE THEY DID AND TOOK their places at the end of the line of guests passing before the reception committee by the ballroom door.

Melina Sherton was just ahead of them in line; she turned her head and gave them a grave once-over.

"Miri," she said, apparently satisfied with what she saw. "Val Con."

"Melina," Miri answered. "What d'ya think?"

"I'll know better when I get a look at the reception room. Right now, all's I've seen is what you have—the front hall and right here."

"Ah," said a strong and cultured voice. "You must be my landlord. Welcome! I am Ilthiria yo'Lanna."

Melina turned fast, stepped up, and took the hand offered by the white-haired Liaden woman.

"I'm Melina Sherton, ma'am. I hope the house does suit you."

"Very much so." Lady yo'Lanna's Terran was accented, but lightly. Her carriage was erect, despite the cane occupying her off-hand. "Indeed, you must indulge me at some point during the evening—perhaps when refreshments are served we may slip away together so that you may see how we have settled in."

"I'd be glad of it, ma'am; I've been curious as a cat to see how it cleaned up. Boss Val Con took care of all that an' I ain't been inside since. I don't wanna disturb your privacy, though—"

Lady yo'Lanna laughed.

"You must not expend a moment's concern for my privacy. Here, I will confess my real purpose in wanting to spirit you

424

away. I have questions about a few of the house's quirks. And also, you know, I would like your advice on one or two matters."

Melina smiled.

"Seems like we're fitting right into each other's plans," she said. "I'll be pleased to take the tour with you at refreshment time."

"That is excellent. I will send Lan Lee to bring you to me..." She turned and gracefully indicated the younger—though by no means young—man standing in line beside her.

"This is my nephew Lan Lee yo'Lanna. Lan Lee, here is Melina Sherton, who has so graciously allowed us to lease her house. Please do me the favor of bringing her to me just before refreshments are to be served."

"Of course," said Lan Lee, extending a hand, which Melina took, and so she was passed down the line, and it was, Miri realized, only her and Val Con under Lady yo'Lanna's eye.

"Well, Korval?" she said sharply.

Val Con produced a jaunty bow.

"Well, indeed, ma'am. I hope that your journey was not too arduous."

"My journey bid fair to be boring," she returned frankly. "Then I had the happy notion of making Terran the common language of the ship. That proved amusing in the extreme, and the time flew past."

She turned to Miri.

"I trust you are fully recovered? You must forgive an old woman her meddling ways."

"Thank you," Miri said. "I'm conditionally recovered, as it happens."

"Ah, is it so? Then you must allow me to suggest that you make use of the chairs set 'round the room whenever you feel the need. Also, you must have your rogue of a lifemate fetch you amusing companions with whom you may pass the time. Selfishly, I hope you will be able to dance at least once with this same rogue. He dances beautifully, you know."

Miri grinned at her.

"I do know, yes."

Lady yo'Lanna laughed softly.

"Of course you do. Here, allow me to present my nephew, Lan Lee, and beyond him, my cousin Ken Rik, whom I believe you know, my lord."

"Indeed I do," Val Con said cordially. He bowed again, and looked up at her quite seriously. "I hope this *will* suit you, ma'am, and that you will be comfortable here. It cheers me greatly, knowing that you are again fixed so near to us."

She considered him.

"How am I to take that, I wonder? No, do not elaborate! I am very pleased to see your lifemate, naturally, and surprisingly enough, to see you. I confess that I am somewhat disappointed not to have the pleasure of greeting your *cha'leket* and his lifemate—though one quite understands that trade must go forth. Perhaps next time. In the meanwhile, sir, I wonder where I might find these young Korval cousins of which I hear whispers? I had supposed you would bring them on your arm this evening, invitations be damned."

"I would never have imposed upon you so shamefully, ma'am. They had no cards, so naturally, they remained at home."

"Had I known you would come the high stickler, I would have sent them cards," Lady yo'Lanna said, a speculative gleam in her eye. "I see that I shall need to bestir myself to make a morning call. Well, I knew how it would be. Now, you have spent far too much time standing in the hallway, talking inconsequentials with an old woman. Pray join the crush."

It *was* a crush. If Lady yo'Lanna hadn't invited everybody on Surebleak to her coming-in party, Miri thought, she'd sure given it her best shot. And she hadn't just limited herself to the Bosses, or the port officials, or the Scouts, or all of Clan Korval presently on-planet.

No, Miri saw Bedel silks in the crowd, streeter motley, even a couple merc dress uniforms. She sighted Mrs. kaz'Ineo and Jorish Hufstead talking to Emissary Twelve—and there, for a wonder, was Yulie Shaper, looking unexpectedly fine in a new sweater and sharp-creased pants, dancing with a handsome woman in Bedel dress.

Miri, who was sitting in a chair for her obligatory "rest period," leaned over to Val Con.

"Who's that Yulie's dancing with?"

"Ah, that is Memit. She was one of the first to sign on to help him get the harvest in, you recall."

"I do," said Miri, watching them—and then looking up as a shadow passed between her and the bright lights.

"Rys!" she said, with a grin. "You're looking well."

"I return the compliment," he said, bringing forward a dark, buxom woman also in Bedel silks.

"Miri, I bring you Droi, who has long wished to extend her hand to you in sisterhood."

Miri considered Droi doubtfully. Those eyes...

The other woman smiled. It was a beautiful, dangerous smile, and the dark eyes flashed amusement. "She doubts you, Rys Dragonwing," she said.

"My reputation precedes me," he said.

"Or mine precedes me."

She looked to Miri.

"This is no place for sisters to speak of those things of which sisters speak," she said. "We will meet. We will drink tea together and speak. Let it be so."

"Let it," Miri agreed. "Call me and we'll arrange a time and a place."

"I will do so—tomorrow. We have, I think, much to teach each other."

She moved away then on Rys's arm, and Miri sighed.

"That's not a little unsettling," she began as the music stopped and the dancers began to move off the floor, Yulie Shaper among them.

But not handsome Memit, who stood in the center of the floor, her hands fisted at her hips, and called out to be heard above the sound of talking.

"Yulie Shaper, answer my challenge!"

He spun, staring at her—nor was he the only one.

"We gonna have to get into this?" Miri whispered to Val Con.

"I expect that any intervention will come from Droi or from Rys," he whispered back. "But I don't believe that there will be any need for—"

"What challenge is that?" Yulie asked, sounding as reasonable and unspooked as anybody she'd ever seen.

"Are you bold enough to marry a woman of the Bedel?" demanded Memit.

From those Bedel present came whistling, foot stamping, clapping. The rest of the guests faded back toward the edges of the room, leaving a large stage for the drama playing out.

"Well, that's an inneresting question," Yulie said. "You got a particular woman in mind?"

"Myself," she said, head high and chin raised.

"That's right, that's right; you'd said so before."

He moved toward her, easy and relaxed, until he was well within striking distance. He stopped then, pretty much matching her in height, and looking...amused, Miri thought. Damned if he didn't.

"Is that my answer?" Memit demanded.

"Now, now, don't get all iced up. Takes a man a minute to think out something like this. Am I bold enough to marry not just any woman of the Bedel, but you yourself?"

"Yes."

"Well."

Yulie grinned.

"I'm gonna have to say that, boldness aside, I believe I'm fool enough to marry you. But only if you're fool enough to marry me."

Another explosion of shouts and stamping from the Bedel, and here came Rys, Droi at his side, walking up to the happy couple.

Rys extended his golden hand and Yulie Shaper clasped it. Droi extended her hand, and Memit met it.

"I ask," Rys said then, "because I do not wish there to be a misunderstanding of custom. If you make this marriage, Yulie Shaper, you gain not only the best gardener among us, but all of her brothers and sisters as well. If you have doubts of any of us, and despite Memit will set a knife in me for saying so—step away."

Yulie considered him, still keeping a firm grip on his arm.

"So this deal'll get me the best gardener 'mong the Bedel, the handsomest woman on Surebleak, *and* all the rest of you, too?"

"That is correct."

Yulie grinned, slow and wide.

"Well, sleet, I'm callin' that a bargain."

The Bedel shouted, and they weren't the only ones.

"Then it is done," Rys said after it had quieted somewhat. "The headman welcomes Yulie Shaper, husband to Memit. Brother, you are ours, and we—are yours."

"The *luthia*," said Droi, "welcomes Yulie Shaper, husband to Memit."

She turned then, and Rys did, bringing the happy couple forward with them and raising their hands high.

"What say you, brothers and sisters?"

"Yes!" roared a large man in Bedel silks.

"Yes!" yelled the rest of the Bedel.

"Yes!" yelled the rest of the guests.

Rys lowered Yulie's arm, Droi lowered Memit's arm and joined their hands together until their fingers were tightly clasped.

Rys stepped back, and Droi did.

"It is done," said Rys.

"It is done *well*," said Droi.

From the band came a skirl of fiddle music, and somebody in the crowd, not Bedel, yelled, "Kiss the groom!"

Yulie grinned and pulled her against him, one arm around her waist.

"Bold enough for it?" he asked, and Memit smiled a slow, feral smile.

"Oh, yes," she said.

The shouting this time made the roof ring.

Refreshments had been served, but instead of the party breaking up, most of the guests went back to the ballroom to indulge in some more dancing, and talking, and schmoozing. Miri was half-asleep in her chair, watching the dancing blearily.

"*Cha'trez*," Val Con said in her ear, "shall we go now?"

"Well," she said muzzily, "I'm of two minds. Firstly, I'm comfortable right where I am, and secondly, I'm not sure I want to make the effort of getting all wrapped up to go outside."

"I will take care of getting you wrapped up. Diglon will warm the car before he brings it around, and we will call ahead to Mr. pel'Kana, so that he will be waiting to open the door the moment we are arrived. You will not be cold for an instant."

"You make a compelling case," she told him. "I guess it's time."

"I will fetch Luken to sit with you while I make the arrangements with Diglon," he said. "It will be a moment, only that."

"Take your—" She stopped, and sat up.

Lan Lee yo'Lanna had approached Pat Rin, where he and Natesa were talking with a mixed group of partiers, and bowed.

He spoke, very briefly, and Pat Rin exchanged a glance with his lifemate before going with the messenger across the room and out the nearest door.

"That don't look good," she said.

"No," Val Con agreed. "It doesn't. Will you—"

"I'm not moving from this spot," Miri interrupted, "until I hear what that's about."

Val Con smiled at her.

"I was only going to ask if you are comfortable sitting here for another few minutes, until we find what Pat Rin's news is."

She laughed softly and leaned back in her chair, feeling his arm go around her shoulder.

"That's nice," she said. "Leave that right there."

"Here we are," Val Con murmured, and Miri came out of her doze.

She sat up straight to watch Pat Rin walk across the floor, to the dais where the band was set up.

He spoke a few words with the band leader, who nodded and waved him up.

"I apologize for interrupting our revelries, but I have just received news that is of interest to all of us."

Absolute silence fell across the room. Miri glanced toward the doors and saw Lady yo'Lanna standing there, both hands resting on her cane, Melina Sherton standing beside her. It was hard to decide which one looked more serious.

"Thank you," Pat Rin said.

He reached into his pocket and brought out a single sheet of paper, which he unfolded—and began to read.

"From TerraTrade to Surebleak Portmaster and to the Council of Bosses, Surebleak City."

Miri wouldn't have thought that it could've gotten any quieter, but it was as if every person in the room was holding their breath. She knew that Val Con was.

Pat Rin took a deep breath.

"TerraTrade is in receipt of Master Trader yos'Galan's request for an upgrade in the rating for Surebleak Port from Local, Limited Services, to Regional, All Services.

"Based on the survey team's report, and other information available to us, TerraTrade, with regret, denies the master trader's request."

There was a squeak from one part of the room; a growl from another. The gathered Bosses looked at each other, murmuring...

"It is the opinion of the Rating Board..." Pat Rin continued, not raising his voice.

People shushed each other, leaning forward to hear.

"... that Surebleak Port occupies a unique location in an underused sector..."

The room got real quiet again.

"... which has enjoyed only limited access to trade. The Rating Board notes that Surebleak Port is the registered home port of one master trader, who may be reasonably expected to establish viable routes with Surebleak as a primary. In anticipation of this, as we have seen many times, small to medium traders will establish themselves at Surebleak Port. There is also the possibility of Syndicate interest."

Pat Rin paused and looked around the room; the room looked back, silent.

"The survey team notes that Surebleak Port has not waited for the outcome of their work, but is continuing to expand and improve itself, as well as the city and the planet which it serves.

"It is this attitude of optimism, of belief in its own ability to thrive and to improve, that moves the Rating Board to bestow upon Surebleak Port the rating Sector Port, All Services.

"The Rating Board thanks Master Trader yos'Galan for this opportunity to perform a most instructive survey.

"If TerraTrade may assist Surebleak Port in any other matter in future, we would welcome the challenge."

Pat Rin looked up again. "It is signed by all members of the TerraTrade Rating Board, and the chairman of TerraTrade."

The room remained silent, as if everybody in it had been quick frozen.

Then, from the back of the room came a strong, carrying voice.

"Congratulations to the portmaster, to the Council of Bosses, and to Clan Korval on a coup!" Lady yo'Lanna said. "Please, let us all drink a glass together and pledge ourselves to each other!"

People began to shift then, voices started; servers came out of the side room, carrying trays loaded with wine glasses.

"Do we stay for our glass?" Val Con asked, and she could feel him thinking that she looked tired.

"Can you hold me up?" she asked back, "'cause I think we gotta drink to this."

She felt a flicker of warmth, of energy, and took a breath, awake and alert. A server came by, and Val Con received two glasses, handing one to her.

The servers had a glass in every hand in record time, and Penn Kalhoon climbed up onto the dais where Pat Rin had been.

"A toast!" he called out, raising his glass, and everybody there followed suit—even, Miri saw across the room, Emissary Twelve.

"A toast to the best planetary invasion that never was, and good luck to us—to *all* of us!—going together to the future!"